The WARHORSE
1250–1600

ANN HYLAND

SUTTON PUBLISHING

First published in 1998 by
Sutton Publishing Limited · Phoenix Mill
Thrupp · Stroud · Gloucestershire · GL5 2BU

British Library Cataloguing in Publication Data
A catalogue record for this book is available from the British Library

ISBN 0-7509-0746-0

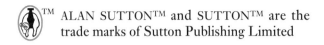
TM ALAN SUTTON™ and SUTTON™ are the
trade marks of Sutton Publishing Limited

Typeset in 11/12pt Ehrhardt.
Typesetting and origination by
Sutton Publishing Limited.
Printed in Great Britain by
Butler & Tanner, Frome, Somerset.

Contents

To my generous friends:
Tootoo Imam – Bihar
Shri Raghuraj Sinh Jhala
HH Mahipendra Singh, Maharana of Danta
HH Darbar Satyajit Khacha, Maharana of Jasdan

Acknowledgements

Once again my thanks go to Professor Michael Prestwich for writing the foreword; to my veterinary surgeon, Russel Lyon, MRCVS for discussion of ancient diseases; to Frank Brudenell for use of his extensive reference library, and for translations from German – invaluable for the section on the Teutonic Knights; to Professor Frank Walbank for hospitality and great help with reference books; to Janet Dixon for reading the draft mss; to Suzanne Watling for looking after my horses and my parrot when I disappear on research trips, especially during my extended trip to India; to Tony and Jane Hales for having Pliny the parrot for that time; and in India to Liz Rembowska for putting me up several times in Delhi between stages of my Indian sojourn. My thanks and deep appreciation to my generous Indian friends who welcomed me into their homes and drove me around much of their beautiful country to studs and farms, some quite inaccessible. In particular my thanks in this respect to Tootoo Imam who was the catalyst for my Indian travels and who made many of the prior arrangements for subsequent visits; to his family for two weeks spent at 'Kehilan'; to Raghuraj Sinh Jhala who took me around Saurashtra, visiting Kathiawari studs, and for the wonderful rides in the Gir National Forest on Tajun; to HH Darbar Satyajit Khacha, Maharana of Jasdan for hospitality and for many of the Indian photographs; to His Holiness Ghanshyamji, Maharaj of Gondal, Raja Bhupat Singh of Jodhpur, and finally to HH Mahipendra Singh, Maharana of Danta for his hospitality, visiting Marwari studs, and for reading the draft of my Indian chapter.

While every effort has been made by the author and publisher to contact copyright holders for illustrations reproduced in this book, we apologise for any omissions and will be happy to rectify them if so advised.

The maps were drawn by Aardvark Illustrations, Nailsworth, Glos.

Foreword

The horse was as much a hero in late medieval warfare as was the knight who rode him. Depictions of knights by artists such as Ucello, Dürer and Leonardo da Vinci glory as much in the horse as in his rider. It is true that the horse did not always dominate in battle; the great English victories of the Hundred Years War were won by archers and men-at-arms who fought on foot. They could not have fought, however, had they not ridden to war. Great armies were heavily dependent on the pack-horses and cart-horses which provided vital logistic support. The *chevauchée*, the mounted raid, was a central element of the military methods of later medieval Europe. The culture of medieval war, chivalry, owed its very name to the horse. To the east, the horse was yet more important. The Mamlūks and above all the Mongols depended on the horse, and it is not surprising that Arabic treatises are far more informative about horses and the training of their riders than anything written in Western Europe. Mongol success demonstrates the extraordinary way in which a horse-based society could conquer and dominate vast swathes of territory. In India, too, the horse was an essential element in military and political success. At the end of the period the horse was a vital element in the Spanish armoury employed in the conquest of the New World, providing armies with mobility and a fighting capability lacked by the native population.

In contrast to the writings of most historians, this book is informed by a deep understanding of horses and how they can be handled. There is a wealth of evidence available relating to horses. For example, the voluminous records of the English government provide details about the royal stud farms, the care given to the horses, their price, their colour, and their diet. The writings of Arab scholars give information on the breed of horses, their training and that of their riders. It requires a special practical expertise to appreciate the full implications of all this information for the interpretation of the past. There are not many who are in a position to try out a Tudor bit on their own horse, as Ann Hyland has done. To modify one of her own phrases, the hoofbeats of the past echo through the pages of this book.

Michael Prestwich

Introduction

The warhorse scene from 1250 to 1600 presents a massive and ever-changing panorama.

Many countries consolidated. Borders changed frequently. In England, France and Scotland, Plantagenet supremacy gave way to the superior military tactics of Continental Europe – France, Spain, the Italian states, Switzerland and Germany. The heyday of the mercenary trooper arrived; he went where gold beckoned. Great equestrian changes occurred in Europe, from the build-up of organized cavalry on somewhat lighter horses under Edward I (reigned 1272–1307), through heavily armoured knights on more solid horses as heavily armoured as their riders, and frequently wasted in chaotic charges, as is illustrated by the irresponsible use of English cavalry at Bannockburn in 1314 and some of the French débâcles of the Hundred Years War (1337–1453), to a reappraisal of cavalry's role and the emergence of lighter, quality horses, which were more efficient, as were the better disciplined cavalry units.

Asiatic and oriental cavalry offered a different picture. In Mamlūk, Ottoman, Indian and Turkic/Mongolian spheres the warhorse was supreme, and contemporary authors gave him much attention. The ideal can be pinpointed more readily – breed preferences were established well before similar selectiveness in Europe. Specific equestrian information is rarer in Europe where the warhorse was a commodity, albeit with colour, markings and price described. Rarely was he an individual, although we may be sure to his rider his abilities and characteristics were crucial as a means of self-preservation. Conversely, in the sixteenth century European treatises on horsemanship and veterinary medicine proliferated centuries after similar Indian, Persian, Turkish and Arabic works.

Much of the European lack can be supplied by knowledge of the sheer physical expenditure involved in getting to and from theatres of conflict, and of how horses perform under stress. This comes from using horses to their full potential in which stress in all departments except the belligerent is present. A study of the psychology of horses and of horse behaviour under herd conditions and in individual confrontations supplies this lack. Hunting and racing illustrate behaviour when under pressure from speed. Conflict sports such as polo indicate a horse's courage and usefulness in a one-to-one situation. Horses fight among themselves, inflicting and receiving serious damage, yet still continue fighting. In warfare there are occasional references to this. Usāmah ibn Munqidh recalled seeing two cavaliers kill one another and fall dead from their horses, which went

Frisian stallion, Bertus, owned by Keith and Corinna Turner, showing compact and elegant conformation. This breed has changed little over the last four centuries. (Photo: author)

on attacking each other.[1] A similar episode, in a medieval European manuscript, clearly shows two knights fighting with swords on foot behind their horses, which are rearing with forefeet locked in battle.[2]

BREED PROVENANCE

In Europe one country stands out – Spain. To her *estancias* and royal farms, buyers flocked from the courts of Europe. Spain sought expansion and was the catalyst in the opening of the Americas where her horses were invaluable, and the forerunner of what is arguably the most diverse of equestrian cultures. Today's Americas boast the greatest variety of breeds and the widest range of uses to which the horse is put.

Spanish military presence in Naples and Sicily left its equine legacy. Elsewhere in an Italy ravaged by French armies a similar infusion occurred as France imported Castilian and Aragonese horses throughout the eleventh to fifteenth centuries, also obtaining warstock from Gascony, Hungary and Syria.[3]

The Emperor Charles V (reigned 1516–56) continued Spanish expansion into the Netherlands, which had its Frisian warhorse, noted by Vegetius and used on

Spanish (Andalusian) horse from the Duke of Newcastle's Méthode de Dresser les Chevaux.
(Photo: John Clark)

the continent and in Britain in Roman times. Like the Andalusian, the Frisian bred true to type. Even with infusions of Spanish blood during the sixteenth-century occupation, it retained its indigenous characteristics, taking the best from both breeds. The Frisian is mentioned in sixteenth- and seventeenth-century works, good comments outweighing critical ones. The main criticism was of its stubbornness, according to Blundeville and Markham, the latter also noting the Frisian's fierce courage and suitability for war. Newcastle esteemed its looks and ability. In the context of the era 'stubborn' may be associated with docility, which would make a courageous horse eminently suitable for war, lacking the volatility of some breeds, or the phlegm of very heavy ones. Generally black, the Frisian was around 15 hh with strong, cobby conformation, but with a deal more elegance and quality. The noted gait was the strong trot coming from powerful quarters. Nowadays, though breed definition is retained, the size has markedly increased, as has that of most breeds due to improved rearing and dietary methods.[4]

Italian stock was of a different stamp, albeit with Spanish influence, but Spain too received drafts of Mantuan horses,[5] and Francis I of France (reigned 1515–47) also benefited from Mantuan and Andalusian horses.[6]

EQUESTRIAN ART

From the fifteenth century onwards we get better portraits of warhorses. These show individual horses, sometimes complete with conformation faults such as curbs, spavins, etc., but generalities still occurred. Illustrations from Blundeville (1593) and the Duke of Newcastle (from the 1650s) show many breeds with little variation, except in bulk when differentiating between heavier Germanic and lighter oriental and European types. The most accurate limners of medieval and Renaissance horses were Pisanello (1395–1455), Albrecht Dürer (1471–1528) and Leonardo da Vinci (1452–1519). Leonardo travelled widely; was employed by the Medici; received a commission from the Sforzas of Milan for a huge equestrian statue of the Condottiere Francesco Sforza; painted the Duchess of Mantua in 1499, and was with Cesare Borgia when he sacked Urbino in 1502. A pupil of Verrocchio, who had modelled the equestrian statue of Bartolomeo Colleoni, Leonardo was also familiar with Donatello's Gattemalata equestrian statue. His notebooks show keen observation. Of the statue in the piazza at Pavia he said the action was 'deserving of praise . . . the trot has almost the quality of a free horse'. A sketch for the Sforza horse has marginal comments: 'Messer Galeazzo's big genet', 'Messer Galeazzo's Sicilian horse', 'measurement of the Sicilian horse, the leg from behind, in front lifted and extended'. Notes made in 1493 show Leonardo's meticulous minutiae of equine conformation: 'Messer Mariolo's morel (black) the Florentine is a big horse with a fine neck and a beautiful head', 'the white stallion belonging to the falconer has fine hindquarters'.[7]

Leonardo's patron Lorenzo de Medici loved good horses. In 1470 he acquired four from Sicily, followed by two from Ferrante, King of Naples. Four years later he purchased horses from Rimini and Perugia; in 1477, when Leonardo entered his service, he purchased Neapolitans and sent his agent to buy horses in Sicily and Tunisia. In 1482 Ferrante sent him a booty horse taken from Turks at the recapture of Otranto, and in the same year the Duke of Urbino sent him a warhorse.[8]

Leonardo was ideally placed at a time when Italy's *condottieri* made great use of cavalry; the ducal houses were renowned for their military bent and their studs, and were closely interwoven by marriage and the diplomatic exchange of gifts.

The Royal Collection at Windsor has many da Vinci cartoons portraying horses in movement; others depict parts of equine anatomy, muscling, proportions, etc. Variant types are shown, but they have general points in common: short coupling, high head carriage, heavily crested, upright necks with pronounced underneck muscling. Most are high on the leg showing much daylight; hooves are deep and not overlarge; limb joints are large, cannons rounded; heads are mostly long and narrow, profiles straight or slightly convex. Bone mass and flesh are similar to a middleweight cob, but with more quality. None is cold-blooded. Even da Vinci's *carectarius* is of warhorse stamp. Most studies show clear Spanish influence, but not the marked definitions of the purebred.

Documents from the medieval and succeeding periods throw light on the horse-world. One is struck by the impressive number of horses that went to the battlefront and, behind the grim war façade, by the logistics in European, oriental, Indian and early American spheres; a huge task tackled according to dynastic dictates. In spite of geographical and cultural differences, there were basic similarities as even when feudalism was waning all spheres still operated a distinctly feudal approach to raising cavalry: the European fief, the Mamlūk *iqta*, the Ottoman *timar*, the Indian *jagir*, the indenture and, at the end of the Tudor period, the Elizabethan demand couched as voluntary proofs of affection for the sovereign.

Leonardo da Vinci's study for the Sforza monument, c. 1488, showing the type of conformation of horses used by the Italian condottieri *of affluent means. (Photo: © Her Majesty the Queen, Royal Collection Enterprises)*

This book shows the warhorse with his abilities and characteristics, influenced by his individual sphere – climate, tactics, perceived utility, etc. With the aid of as much contemporary evidence as possible, and in four geographical sectors, it traces his medieval rise, supremacy and decline, and his re-emergence as the sixteenth century drew to a close. It touches on the new improved methods of riding in Europe introduced by the Italians who had clearly learnt much from oriental influences via Sicily. Curiously the high school airs above the ground, once considered to have their roots in European mounted warfare, are open to question. Some of these airs stem from Roman days; others were embodied in Indian warhorse training in an attempt to combat that other Asian war animal – the elephant.

EQUIPMENT

Saddlery

European saddlery, bitting and horse armour underwent changes. Warsaddles on rigid wooden trees developed from the Norman straight seat with raised bow and cantle to one affording more security with a higher bow protecting the rider's abdomen, later extended down to the knees and incorporating plating, called 'saddle steels', which enabled him to dispense with thigh armour. The cantle developed to encase the hips; some of these later saddles were so confining that falling out was difficult. This brought the danger of being trapped underneath a fallen horse, but had the advantage of giving a heavily armoured knight stability, enabling him to regain his balance after an attacker's blow; the unbalancing effect of his own armour was curtailed.

The weight of armoured man and armoured horse, combined with the pounding gaits of some increasingly heavy horses and the violent movements of a battling knight aboard, necessitated a well-crafted saddle able to withstand stresses. In 1386 the Breton knight de Tournemine instructed his saddler:

> first shall my said horse . . . be saddled with a saddle whose pommel and cantle are of wood, garnished with bound horn and garnished in iron and steel, or in one of these two, and ribbed and glued, the pommel and cantle high in front

Henry V's war saddle. Note the seat raised off the bars, the retaining cantle and the protection to the lower abdomen afforded by the high pommel. (Copyright: Dean and Chapter of Westminster)

and back and open at the sides as they should be, garnished and covered in leather, linen or light silk, studded and garnished with iron, steel or other metal, gilt or tinned.[9]

Indeed law governed manufacture. The 1403 statutes of the Saddlers' Company of Limoges stipulated that the tree's joints be well glued and reinforced by rivets, that it be 'well sinewed above and below' and that 'the underneath should be well covered so that the horse's sweat shall not damage the sinews'. This entailed encasing the tree in shredded ox sinews, gluing them on, allowing the glue to cool, applying a second coat and finishing with a linen covering.[10]

In London's Wallace Collection the late medieval saddles range from highly ornamented state saddles weighing only 7 lb (3.1 kg) to tournament and warhorse saddles weighing from 21 to 33 lb (9.5 to 15 kg). These weights are moderate, considering the structure, and if spread over the horse's back not unduly burdensome. Saddles designed for roping cattle weigh in excess of 33 lb (15 kg).

Some military men still rode with stirrupless pad saddles as Sir Henry Crystede told Froissart after his seven-year Irish captivity. Sir Henry, fighting with the Earl of Ormonde against the Irish in 1394–5, was captured when his horse bolted, but his captivity was not onerous. He married his captor's daughter and spent his captivity teaching the Irish the finer points of English cavalry methods, but he had difficulty in persuading them to change from their stirrupless saddles to English equipment.[11]

BITTING

Bits were snaffles and curbs. Snaffles, usually jointed, are generally milder than curbs, acting on the tongue and bars of the mouth. Many varieties occur; wide mouthpieces spread pressure, being less severe than thin bits. Some have external branches to prevent the bit from being pulled through the mouth. Snaffles entail direct action on the bit ring.

Curbs are harsher and used with indirect reining. Medieval curbs come in a great variety. Some are moderately severe with medium ports; others resemble a jointed pelham and have four reins. Those falling into the severest category were instruments of torture with excessively high ports, some rising to over 5½ inches (13 cm). Port apexes differ but all are punitive when pressed against the palate. Several have a double mouthpiece so metal was in contact with the palate from tushes to molars. Attached to the upper mouthpiece of some was a metal curbstrap; when the reins were activated this clamped into the chin groove, while internal pressures were exerted with the double mouthpiece culminating in the top of the port pressing against the palate as the bit rotated. If roughly used, or with a snatch action, the port without a doubt would have punctured the palate. Extremely long shanks exacerbated severity. To gain partial relief a horse would hold his head in a flexed position, which also allowed more rapid rider contact. Poking his nose with such a bit meant added discomfort. Some curbs had leather straps attached to each side of the bit, meeting centrally over the brow and secured to the browband, adding external pressures as the reins were pulled.

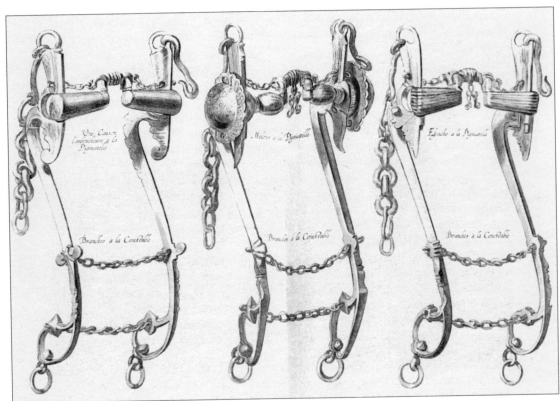

Selection of bits from the Duke of Newcastle's Méthode de Dresser les Chevaux. *Similar bits were in use throughout the sixteenth and seventeenth centuries. (Photo: John Clark)*

However, horses were ridden loose-reined and prior conditioning through pain in the mouth warned the horse what would happen if he fought restraint. Conversely some horses become uncontrollable with too severe a bit. In general, hot-blooded horses have nerve endings closer to the surface than do cold-blooded horses and, also in general, temperaments are hot-blooded/greater sensitivity, cold-blooded/more placid. In the medieval period there were no doubt good, bad, indifferent, and downright cruel riders as there are today, much cruelty being caused through ineptitude or ignorance.

In the sixteenth century the bits became more scientific, and although curbs were still severe, with sometimes inordinately long shanks, there were many that, while looking 'a real mouthful', were quite tolerable, well-designed for use with a well-schooled horse. I was allowed to use a Tudor period bit from the Museum of London. It was 4½ inches (11.5 cm) wide with short cheekpieces both above and below the mouthpiece, which meant curb action was not severe, and poll pressure was limited. The mouthpiece had three barrel-shaped rollers with keys depending from the central roller encouraging the horse to mouth the bit, so keeping his mouth moist – an aid to a good mouth. The thin chain over the movable parts was

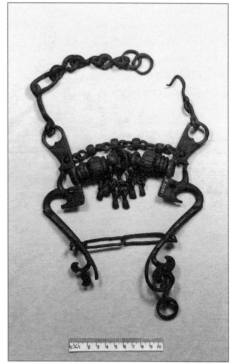

Sixteenth-century curb from the Museum of London Collection, here used on the author's Arabian stallion Nizzolan, who went extremely well in it when ridden on a loose rein with minimal operative contact. (Photos: John Clark)

in contact with the corners and bars of the mouth. Two large links in the mid-section of the lower shanks prevented their flying apart and kept the contact the same both sides, even if reins were of disparate length. Used harshly the thin chain would have been painful; my Arab stallion Nizzolan went extremely well in this bit, but he was on a loose rein, as were the horses shown in Newcastle's work.[12]

HORSE ARMOUR

Only the wealthiest knights could afford complete horse armour. From Edward III's time, plate got increasingly heavier, though given the limited time the destrier was ridden in battle, it was not overburdensome except for some of the German *reiters* in Henry VIII's armies (see below).

On a foray to the Tower of London Armouries I measured two bards from the early Tudor period. One Flemish bard was made for Henry VIII's destrier. After allowing for the horse's shoulder movement and for protective padding to take some of the internal space my conclusions were that although a weight-carrying horse was used, he was of moderate, stocky proportions. I compared the measurements with those of several horses:

a shire of 18 hh
a Suffolk punch of 16.2 hh, but heavier than the shire
a heavyweight hunter of 16 hh

and with two of my own:

Granicus, 16.1 hh, Arabian/Standardbred cross who is well built with good depth to chest, barrel and width across loin area
Katchina, 14.3 hh, stocky, up to weight but not coarse.

This armour would not have fitted Granicus and would not have been excessively large on Katchina. The critical measurements were width across loin from hip to hip, and dock to loin, just behind the cantle area. In the peytral area the crucial measurement was taken around the chest at the upper shoulder, i.e. round the chest from the pommel arch on one side to the pommel arch on the other. In this area Granicus, with his measurements taken skin to tape-measure, was 12 inches (30 cm) bigger than the actual bard figures. Granicus has a good deep body but would by no means be considered stocky.

Such practical tests are important, but an awareness of horses' movement has to be allied to fitting certain elements of armour. Internal padding was vital to avoid chafing and as most campaigns were in summer this absorbed sweat and prevented hot metal from scalding the skin.

Since these measurements were taken, the Royal Armouries, now moved to Leeds, have bought four Lithuanian draught horses which stand 15 to 15.2 hh. They resemble heavyweight hunters. The mare Fleur was used as the model for making statues to display armour from the fifteenth to seventeenth centuries. The original armours fitted perfectly, so apart from an unusually large horse, we can safely say that destriers were of moderate height and robust build.

SHOEING

From the early Norman period onwards, shoeing developed gradually from the narrow-rimmed, wavy-outlined shoe, with 'fiddle-key'-shaped nails that protruded half their length, forcing the horse on to the nails rather than the shoe, to a wider-webbed, firm-outlined, heavier shoe, with nails of square section having 'T'-shaped heads. Sizes increased as saddle and warhorses became larger, especially with the introduction of Low Country horses. This necessitated variety in shoe weights. Nails diversified, allowing for specialist use, such as 'frost nails' for icy conditions. Nail heads no longer protruded so much, allowing hooves closer contact with the ground. Calkins were usually present, either on both heels or on the outer branch only. Regional differences abounded, and a sixteenth-century continental treatise by Caesar Fiaschi shows a great variety of styles for specialist use as the farrier's craft expanded.[13]

PART I

Europe

In the Plantagenet era, under the first three Edwards of England, the horse was exceptionally important and well documented. Later Henry V was to utilize it in whirlwind *chevauchées* in France, striking where least expected. In fourteenth- and fifteenth-century Italy and France the horse was vital to the Italian *condottieri* and the French *écorcheurs* – mercenary bands open to the highest bidder, not averse to changing sides, and the scourge of the countryside.

After the Hundred Years War (1337–1453) English cavalry strength declined and in Tudor times it shrank further, although horses were essential to Scots and English in border warfare.

In eastern Europe and the Balkans the scene against which the warhorse played its part was very diverse. European character prevailed in the cavalry of the Teutonic Knights in Poland, Lithuania, Estonia and Latvia. In Russia there was some Germanic influence, but the Mongol presence had the heavier impact. Poland and Hungary were a meeting-place for Asiatic, Turkish and European traditions. In the Balkans the Ottomans pursued their conquests.

European equestrianism unfolds with the wars of the three Edwards, kings of England from 1272 to 1377.

ONE

England and the Three Edwards

Cavalry played a significant part at the battles of Lewes in 1264 and Evesham in 1265 when England was riven by the barons' wars in the later years of Henry III's reign; in the Welsh wars of his son Edward I; and in the destructive wars with Scotland that occurred during the last decade of Edward I's life, throughout the reign of his son Edward II, and in much of Edward III's reign. Records list numbers of cavalry horses; losses incurred; difficulty of procurement; provenance and price for some of the better imports; and perceived battle-worthiness, which is a better guide to type and substance than the term 'Great Horse' applied to medieval destriers.

Edward I succeeded his father in 1272, while returning from crusade; he reached England in 1274. His reign was notable on several counts. Legislation was overhauled; corruption investigated and largely terminated; taxes were levied to help finance his crusade and military actions.[1] In 1277 he launched his first Welsh war; others followed in 1282–3 and 1294–5. After prolonged aggression between French and Gascons, culminating in Philip IV of France's confiscation of the duchy of Gascony, for which Edward had done homage in 1286 under the 1259 Treaty of Paris, war was waged with France from 1294 to 1298.[2] The Scottish wars began in 1296.

The *Documents relating to Scotland* (Bain, 1884, 1887) show most aspects of equestrian military practice. This needed a huge investment in cash and labour. Horses kept medieval rolling stock on schedule. To gain a balanced picture we need to look at the horse as part of the Plantagenet military machine. Horses of all degrees were used, from droves of *carectarii* hauling supplies, to cavalry horses. The sad *Restauro Equorum* documents listed those that had died in service. The battle of Falkirk (1298) and the Caerlaverock campaign (1300) showed an especially high toll. Add to these the thousands of whose loss no records survive and it is an indictment of usage of animals in war. Reiving by marauding Scots increased losses. Documentation from the reign of Edward II (1307–27) shows his preferences via the types of horses imported. Much information comes from Edward III's reign (1327–77). He spent lavishly, upgrading stock in royal studs, aided by the Brocas family – one member served as his Master of Horse in what became almost a hereditary appointment. Edward III's costs were huge. *The Wardrobe Book of Wm. de Norwell, 1338–40* shows *Restauro Equorum* of £6,632 13s 4d for over 400 horses,[3] plus the expense of hiring retinues with their animals, and the overseas shipping costs. The king sailed for Antwerp in July 1338, but the accounts do not show passage payments for individual retinues and it may be ships were hired directly by him.[4] In January and February 1340, leaders and individuals paid their horses' return passage at half a mark per horse, indenting for repayment. Norwell's accounts show £1,540 6s 8d for 4,621 horses shipped back.[5]

STOCKING THE STUDS AND STABLES

Most information is from royal sources but some documents show other landholders' assets. The Countess of Leicester, wife of Simon de Montfort and Edward I's aunt, had useful papers. In the crucial lead-up to the battle of Evesham, Countess Eleanor's Odiham accounts show that from 25 April to 10 May stabled horses ranged between 30 and 36, not counting foals. Earlier in the year numbers rose from 44 on Sunday 15 March to 172 on Tuesday 17 March and 334 on Thursday 19 March when Earl Simon and his retinue arrived for a two-week stay. This stretched supplies to breaking point, forcing the marshal to buy nine quarters of oats (3,600 lb). That summer Eleanor hastened to Dover Castle, held by her son Henry. Her entourage, including her son Amaury and the men-at-arms of her son Simon, used 84 horses, including carthorses. The mention of foals implies stallions and broodmares. Although stallions would have been stabled, broodmares at grass need not have appeared in spring accounts, but were vital for any baronial establishment's military needs. Only five foals were noted but more could have been born later.

Oat quantities for a nucleus of 31 to 36 horses are noted. Amounts varied, which suggests much activity with more grain for hard-worked horses. This is backed up by references to messengers, which account for number fluctuations. One man called Gobothesti made three trips to the west in May 1265, once to Cardiff and twice to Earl Simon at Hereford,[6] covering over 600 miles (965 km). Considering poor roads and dangers in a country in upheaval it shows the type of horse needed for messengers – fast, fit, well fed. Although the daily half-bushel (25 lb) per warhorse estimated for English garrisons in Scotland[7] is excessive, a galloper used more energy than a warhorse, which worked at full stretch for limited periods.

A lesser stud was that of the late John Wake of Lidell with 39 horses – mares and youngstock – which were appropriated for the king in 1300 by Sir Simon de Lindesey, Keeper of Lidell.[8]

HORSE-DEALING

Horse-dealing formed a major part of national and international fairs and markets.[9] In 1430 the Castilian Pero Tafur described the horse fairs at Cologne, Frankfurt, Geneva, Antwerp and Medina, singling out English hackneys and trotters for praise.[10]

The wardens of the great fairs of Champagne and Brie had a lively correspondence with the Mayor of London in 1299 concerning payment owed by the Florentine horse-dealers Fauberti, currently dealing in England. The Fauberti claimed they had paid the debt, which had been incurred in Bari in 1292 and had followed them around ever since. The mayor 'passed the buck', blaming the war with Scotland, which tied his hands as the king was unavailable to decide the issue.[11]

The livelihood of a peripatetic horse-dealer was often disrupted by export bans. All three Edwards imported from Spain, which periodically banned exports, but exemptions could be bought. Other sources were Navarre, Sicily and Lombardy in the century and a half prior to the Hundred Years War. Stock was largely of Spanish blood but with infusions of oriental blood in horses from Sicily. After 1334 trade in Spanish stock ceased as licences became increasingly difficult to obtain; Spain had allied with France and needed horses for her own *reconquista*.[12]

France also needed warhorses. In 1279 Philip III decreed that any landowner with 200 *livres tournois* (*lt*) per annum was to keep a broodmare and that nobility with sufficient pasture were to keep at least four broodmares, and if possible, six; mares and foals were not to be distrained for fines or debts. A ceiling of 60 *lt* was put on the price for a palfrey; 15–25 *lt* for a rouncy. No merchants were to bring more than 30 warhorses to a fair under pain of forfeiting the surplus to the local lord. In 1282 the exporting of horses from France was banned. Philip imported heavily from Frisia, his agent, Pierre de Condé, at one time paying almost 35,000 *lt* for stock. In May 1282 Maurice de Craon, Edward I's future Lieutenant of Gascony, told Edward that Philip had refused permission for any horses to be sent *from* France. In June Gaston de Béarn told him that Philip refused to allow any horses passage *through* France. Finally Edward appealed direct to Philip for passage of 24 horses that a Florentine merchant had bought on his behalf. This was emphatically refused. Philip reasoned that France lacked horses and after careful consideration he would not permit export, because France must be furnished with horses for her own security.[13] Here there is more than just the ban at issue. Edward had yet to do homage to Philip for Gascony.

In January 1306[7][14] Edward forbade Great Yarmouth and 24 other English ports to export horses, provisions and arms, except to Gascony, as these were needed for the Scottish expedition.[15] In January 1310[11] Edward II banned similar exports from Ireland to Scotland on pain of the 'highest penalties'. Again Scottish war needs were emphasized.[16] Under Edward III it was a felony to export horses to Scotland.[17]

Warhorses were considered potential weapons and no country ever had enough. The bans highlight favoured types – Spanish horses crop up repeatedly. Ireland produced lightweight hobbies used by both sides in the Scottish wars.

A look at the wider picture in the time of the three Edwards reveals the importance of the horse. The wardrobe books and Scottish documents show how dependent Edward I was on all types of equine. His grandson recognized that outcrossing was vital, making heavy use of Spanish horses.

MAJOR STUDS: BREEDING FOR WAR USE

There were three systems for raising horses.

Wild stock ran on moors where an annual round-up culled herds and removed animals for use. This was the method used by Cistercians and other noted ecclesiastic horse-breeders. In 1200 King John ordered his

> Master Forester, Hugh de Neville, and other powerful men to notify all Cistercians to remove their stud horses, pigs and flocks from the royal forests within the week. At the end of this term any found within the forest were to be taken for the king's use.[18]

One boon work from an abbatial tenant was rounding up the abbot's mares and foals on the 'waste'.[19]

Moorland ponies though small by military standards were weight-carriers. The larger, such as the Fell pony, of Frisian ancestry, could have carried a trooper with his warhorse led alongside, and was adequate for lighter cavalry action. Ordinary troopers were allowed three horses on *some* expeditions,[20] though customarily only one would appear in the valuation lists.[21]

A trace of the enclosure system, the second method, remains in the present-day landscape as parks were specifically for keeping deer and equine breeding stock.

In the third system a stallion was introduced to the mare in the covering yard. This method included the travelling stallion although he may have run temporarily with mares when visiting his owner's studs. However, a stallion needed protection. Many novice stallions are severely battered until they learn the appropriate time to approach mares. Destriers, whose more pleasant tasks were stud duties, presumably after proving themselves in war, were unlikely to be put at risk from a mare's heels.

The earliest surviving royal reference to the travelling stallion comes in 1130, in a pipe roll. The king's scutifer received 30*s* for travelling with the king's stallion to Gillingham, Dorset, to cover the royal mares,[22] which implies a stay for the whole covering season.

THE FITZALAN STUDS

Fitzalan manors' accounts from 1313 to 1394 offer important details. In 1313 Edmund Fitzalan, Earl of Arundel, and his squire Richard Coccus led Edmund's destrier Morel Lestrange on circuit. It is strange to find the earl doing this himself but maybe Morel was especially valuable. Also in 1313 William de Wyrecester, two grooms and 12 colts visited Fitzalan studs at Rednal, Ruyton, Shrawardine, Wroxeter, Withyford and Lydley Heys. John Lestrange, sixth Baron Knokyn of Shropshire and Lord of Great Ness, had died in 1311 and his horses were acquired by the Fitzalans who used the same farrier from Ness. He had been Lestrange's stud groom and remembered Morel. In 1314 he treated him and nine other horses for mange.[23] The connection continued. In 1337 Sir Roger Lestrange was steward to Richard, Edmund's heir.[24]

In 1314 the earl refused to accompany Edward II to the relief of Stirling.[25] Maybe he pleaded lack of horses to mount his retinue! It would not be the first or last time such an excuse was given. Ecclesiastics used it. In March 1291[2] the Abbot of Holmcoltron was unable to obey the king's order to mount the Bishop of Bath and Wells, the king's Chancellor, for 'scarcity of horses'.[26] At Croyland and Spalding in April and May 1333 scarcity led the monks to beg off sending transport for victuals to Scotland.[27]

In 1381 Fitzalans still owned large studs, Rednal and Ruyton operating as stallion headquarters where numbers occasionally rose to 4 senior and 15 junior stallions. Other studs were at Bromhurst (Bromwich Park), Maesbury and Upper and Lower Parks at Oswestry where 22 mares and 52 colts and fillies were kept. At Adderley Manor between Oswestry and Ruyton the king kept carthorses and vehicles; costs appear in Fitzalan accounts.[28] This is no surprise. Richard Fitzalan's father was executed by the Mortimer faction, his lands sequestered. Edward III returned them in 1330. In 1338 he appointed Richard co-Regent with the Earl of Huntingdon and Lord Neville when he left for the Continent. Richard figured in administration throughout the 1340s and 1350s, and was close to the king during the 1360s. The Fitzalans were possibly the wealthiest magnates. From 1370 to 1374 Richard loaned the king at least £38,500, most of which was quickly repaid, with interest, while other lenders had to wait.[29] Wealth suggests Fitzalan studs were on a greater scale than those of other magnates. Although analysis of all Fitzalan accounts is incomplete, the details noted show the extent and importance of home breeding under the Edwards.[30]

NUMBERS ON CAMPAIGN

The 1340 accounts for shipping horses to England from Antwerp show the period norm. Each magnate had six horses, knights banneret five, ordinary knights four, men-at-arms three. The Earl of Salisbury had 387 for 117 men; the Bishop of Lincoln 352 for 105; Henry of Lancaster 312 for 94; the Earl of Suffolk 110 for 32. Many knights banneret had sizeable retinues: Henry Ferrers 235 for 70; Reginald Cobham 115 for 36. Simple knights, sometimes with another knight in the retinue, provided small groups: William Stury had 25 horses for himself and seven men-at-arms. Most had only two or three men to provide for.[31] Even so the financial input was considerable. A well-stocked stud with youngsters maturing was necessary to replace mounts lost to death, capture, injury, lameness, bodily lesions, sickness, old age.

MURRAIN

A recurrent note in documents is loss of horses, and other stock, to 'murrain', which may be an umbrella name for unspecified but often fatal diseases. In 1299 accounts for Dumfries Castle, held by the Constable, Sir J. de Dolyn, showed several carthorses dead of murrain.[32] In Edward III's reign it took a constant toll of livestock, particularly sheep. Heacham Manor in Norfolk lost horses in

13 years between the twenty-first and forty-seventh years of Edward III's reign and in 10 years of Richard II's reign.[33] Partly because of persistent murrain north of the Trent, late in his reign Edward III reduced the overall size of royal studs.[34]

THE ROYAL ESTABLISHMENT

Valuable warhorses feature prominently in *Equitia* accounts outlining royal stud policies. The name 'stud' may be traced back to the seventh-century Kentish Chronicles where Stodmarsh on the Great Stour is noted, *stod* meaning a herd or stud of horses.[35]

Edward I's grandfather King John imported 100 stallions of large stature from Flanders, Holland and the banks of the Elbe.[36] These would soon have upgraded domestic warstock.

Master of Horse

From 1206 the chief keeper of King John's horses was Thomas de Landa.[37] He supervised and sometimes personally attended all movements of the royal horses. Between 1257 and 1269 Ellis of Rochester appears as King's Farrier, Sergeant or Keeper of the King's Horses, finally as Marshal of the King's Horses,[38] a title that eventually became Master of Horse.

The Brocas Family

The Brocases arrived in Edward II's reign. Arnald Brocas was killed in the Scottish wars; his sons John, Bernard and Arnald and their relatives Simon and Menauld worked their way up the court appointments ladder. Arnald Brocas was Master of Horse to Edward II's younger brother John of Eltham; John Brocas became Master of Horse to Edward III and Menauld Brocas was Keeper of the King's Horses north of the Trent and second-in-command to John. Their duties included cavalry organization for Edward's French and Scottish wars.[39] John and Menauld appear often in Norwell's accounts, John with nine of his own men-at-arms, one being Menauld. He indented for eight lost horses worth £53 13s 4d, Menauld losing two. John served 483 days with his men, each of whom received 2s per day although John received only 18d per day for 458 days and 3s per day for 25 days.[40] Other Brocas references concern royal horse and equipment purchases and receiving into care 'gift' horses.

STUDS AND THEIR MAINTENANCE

In King John's reign (1199–1216) there was a group of keepers, of whom at least 12 are named. Their movements indicate location of studs and parks. De Landa moved frequently in short-term residence with his charges, or probably on routine inspections, as may be seen from Table 1.1.

Table 1.1 Studs and parks of royal horses, 1211–15

Date	Location	Numbers
1211–12	Yorkshire	not stated
Nov. 1211–Feb. 1212	Northamptonshire	15
Aug. 1212	Worcester	24
Sept. 1213	Yorkshire	7
Winter 1214	Kent	organizing shipments of horses for transport to France
Nov. 1214	Wilton	not stated
Dec. 1214	Tewkesbury, Worcs	not stated
27 Dec. 1214–5 Jan. 1215	Berkshire	9–6 destriers, 1 mule, 2 rouncies
Feb. 1215	Berkshire	13–11 destriers, 2 others
1215	London	5–3 were the king's

Henry III added more locations. In 1217[41] Adam of Guildford was keeper at Tewkesbury; John de Oyse was paid for horses in his care; there was a stud across the Channel at La Rochelle. John had placed many horses with the monks at Beaulieu Abbey in Hampshire (at their cost) for when his son Henry came of age. By Edward's accession in 1272 royal establishments had mushroomed, organization being divided into studs north and south of the Trent, each division controlled by a deputy keeper under whom the stud masters operated individual studs.[42] Edward III had establishments in at least 25 English counties, mostly in East Anglia, the south and south-east, and the Midlands. Some were used more continuously than others.[43]

Expansion demanded new buildings and enclosures. Henry III erected 80 stables at Freemantle in the manor of Kingsclere in the mid-1240s. Edward I gave Freemantle to Payn de Chaworth, a household knight, who was one of his crusading companions and a commander in his first Welsh war.[44] It reverted to Edward in 1286 and thereafter the cost of maintaining the stables and their environs fell on the sheriffs of Hampshire. In 1282–3 200 stables were built at Clipstone, Notts for £104 8s 5d. In 1369 new stabling was erected at Sheen in Surrey by John Stiward for Edward III, and large sums continued to appear in the Sheen accounts under Richard II.[45]

County sheriffs also paid for shoeing, medicines, stable staff's wages, small items of tack – bridles, halters, etc. Purveyors of foodstuffs had the right of pre-emption, issuing tallies for goods taken, redeemable for cash when presented to the sheriff. Abuses were many. Grains and pulses could be bought by the heaped but paid by the razed or stricken measure, the difference sold for the purveyor's pocket. A purveyor could pre-empt an excess and sell the surplus; sheriffs could delay payment; worst of all, false purveyors could issue worthless tallies that left vendors totally out of pocket. The three Edwards made continuous attempts to ensure fair dealing, but abuses were constantly registered.[46]

Stud maintenance was a major item of national expenditure, especially in periods of warfare where needs were heaviest.

MOVEMENTS AND DISPERSALS

As youngstock matured some fillies and mares would have been sent to other studs to avoid inbreeding. Stallions were travelled to avoid their repeatedly covering the same mares. Edward III's studs show stocking levels. At Princes Risborough the keeper, William de Fremelsworth, reported 57 head from 1 March 1334 to 29 September 1336. The 1345 accounts of William le Ferrours, Keeper of the King's Great Horses in the South, showed stock fluctuating from 44 to 72. The 1359 account of Thomas del Bothe, Keeper in the North, listed 50 horses.[47] Among Fremelsworth's 57 were 10 horses, 17 mares (1 had died) and 12 youngstock aged from one to four. Of 9 foals, 1 had died. The 8 foals from 16 mares resident prior to March 1334 is not a good fertility rate. Possibly stud practice was to breed every other year, but the ages of youngstock suggest that is unlikely. Only one foal was a colt. In medieval wars, in the short term, more colts were needed, but a long-term balance was vital. Bothe's account shows the practice of moving horses around. Of the 50 head 22 were resident the previous year; 9 arrived from Edmund Rowe; the remaining 19 varied in age from two to three and a half years, and came from Burstwick, Plumptonsland and Knaresborough, and from John Rose. Mortality was high, 5 dying. Bothe's stud may have been a base for youngstock as no foals or mares are shown, only horses, unless Bothe was not as meticulous as Fremelsworth who lists mature horses by sex.

Periodically horses went for war use. In 1292 Edward I issued a writ of aid for Richard Foun who toured the king's studs to select colts, halter and break them.[48] In 1338 Fremelsworth was told to hand over four destriers to Menauld Brocas for shipment to the king overseas. Other movements included horses sent inland to guard against loss to (possible) French invasion. Colts and stallions were brought south of the Trent. Many mature stallions were taken to Westminster; Fremelsworth was to take delivery of all colts over two years of age. Feeble mares, horses and youngstock were culled. In the 1361 stock dispersal healthy mares from the north were sold.[49]

Foals were given by the king as tithes. Edward II granted the parson of Hadleigh every tenth foal from the Hadleigh (Essex) stud; each year his yeoman Roger Fillol was to have every eighth foal from the same stud.[50] Under Edward III ecclesiastics received every tenth foal from Windsor, Macclesfield and Princes Risborough. In 1332 John Neussom, Keeper in the North, was ordered to choose from John Brocas's pool in the south stallions that 'seem best for the king's profit'. In 1351 the Black Prince's stud at Princes Risborough received from his Master of Horse 'those horses in his keeping most suitable for being this year's stallions'; in 1359 the prince sent two destriers for the Risborough covering season. Courser stallions were also used on the Risborough mares.[51] The future Edward II's accounts show that Laurence of Chertsey, his Keeper of Horses at Windsor, received £85 5s 5d for the keep of 32 chargers and palfreys from 20 November 1302 to 14 May 1303, while at Windsor and *en route* to the prince at Roxburgh. Laurence and his groom received £4 8s in wages.[52]

IMPORTS AND OTHER ACQUISITIONS

In 1214 King John sent Thomas Britton to Spain with 200 marks, which secured eight horses. Henry III also imported from Spain,[53] and he acquired horses from Gascony in 1226 and from Lombardy in 1232, buying from a dealer selling in England; in 1232 the sum of 40 marks bought from St Ivo's Fair at Canterbury[54] horses that may have been foreign bred. In 1242 he paid 650 *livres de La Marche* for eight destriers;[55] in 1260 he confiscated three imported destriers from the rebellious Simon de Montfort. In 1251 the sum of 35 marks was given for a bay, Winchester diocese paying.[56]

Prior to his first Welsh war, Edward I imported 158 head and permitted his barons to bring in 45 more. These journeyed via the French port of Wissant to Dover. As the host mustered at Worcester on 24 July 1277, some stallions were no doubt used at stud in the early part of the covering season.[57] Otto de Grandison imported 2 destriers,[58] Henry de Lacy, Earl of Lincoln, had 30, and William de Bello Campo (Beauchamp) and others had 12. Many dealers were used: John de Graunt; Beneventutus of Bologna; Donelin de Florentia; the brothers Nutus and Burgess de Florentia; Galvanus de Ferrara. Mathew de Columbariis, the king's Sergeant, was often sent on buying commissions, including the purchase of 40 head from Philip III of France who had relaxed his export ban (see above) as Donelin was allowed to bring 18 Great Horses from France.[59]

Trade escalated as the second Welsh war loomed. In 1281 Edward was prepared to spend 1,000 marks on Spanish horses,[60] and a year later Nutus and Burgess de Florentia were given import licences for 80 foreign horses and various unnamed merchants brought stock into England from the Low Countries.[61] For his Flanders campaign in 1297, Edward bought nearly 100 head for his household knights.[62]

Single-item purchases and gifts to and from the king also feature. In 1275 his kinsman Maurice de Credonia (Craon) received Edward's Bayard.[63] During the Scottish wars Galliardo de Brinnak, a Gascon knight, received from the king a white horse costing £33 6s 8d; William, son of Glay, after being freed from a Scottish prison, received a covered horse worth £20 to ride in the Scottish wars.[64]

Gifts to kings came from many sources. One showing Edward's equestrian acumen was a Spanish horse.[65] From Stirling on 25 April 1304, he wrote to 'his good friend Borgeys le frere Pute, merchant' of his pleasure at the Londoners' gift which had been delivered to Borgeys, informing him that 'the treasurer, the Bishop of Chester, will see the horse wants nothing' and asking Borgeys 'to keep him in good condition and speedily inform him if he is suitable for him, of what kind he is, his height, age, and colour, and if his teeth are worn or not'.[66] The king needed assurance the gift was not 'long in the tooth'.

Confiscations swelled stables and coffers. After the 1298 Scottish raid into Northumberland, which was led by the Earl of Menteith,[67] among others, the earl's goods were sequestered, including two horses Person the Lombard sold for £40 on the king's behalf. A year later John de Insula reminded the Exchequer that the money was still due from Person.[68]

MOVEMENT OF HORSES DURING WARTIME

During the Scottish wars York was the seat of government.[69] It held numerous royal mounts, being used as a forwarding station.

Wardrobe accounts for 1299–1300 list important equestrian data. That year the king and Prince Edward travelled extensively. Edward ensured he was well mounted. In November Ade Riston took 13 horses, 5 being destriers, from York to 'Cestr next Dunolm', then accompanied other destriers, hackneys, palfreys and sumpters from York to Thorp, Boroughbridge and Berwick, destriers usually outnumbering other horses. From 4 May to 18 June John Riston and palfreyman Laurence de Certefie took 8 destriers, 10 palfreys, 2 sumpters and 2 of their own horses from Stamford to York, placed them at grass, then accompanied them to the king at Carlisle.

John Guillemyn rendered an account for shifting the king's horses from place to place, receiving others and eventually getting all to Carlisle; most were destriers and palfreys. At Bristol from 20 November to 25 March he had 16 royal destriers and 2 of his own horses; then 2 more destriers and 3 hackneys came from York. On 16 April the horses started to move. Between 18 April and 7 May, 4 destriers, 4 hackneys, 1 sumpter and his own 2 went from Bristol to Thorpe Underwood; between 16 and 24 May, 26 were taken from Thorpe to Carlisle. The Carlisle feed list[70] shows:

20–4 June:	43 horses (approximately equal numbers of destriers and palfreys); 2 more palfreys then arrived
24 June:	45
25 June:	46 (including John Riston's)
26 June:	43 (3 left for the Curia)
27 June:	47 (addition of 2 palfreys, 1 hackney of the king's, and 1 palfrey belonging to Lord John of Britain)
28 June:	55 (addition of 5 palfreys of Prince Edward's and 3 horses of the queen's minstrel)
29 June:	53 (with an extra sumpter)
1 July:	55 (with an extra sumpter)

The calculations begin by adding up, but towards the end go slightly astray; none the less it appears that between them the king and his son(s) needed over 50 destriers and palfreys. No doubt many were loaned to household knights. These entries highlight movement of horses northwards in readiness for military use.

The Prince of Wales spent lavishly. In 1302–3 chargers and hackneys for himself and his household cost £568 6s 7d. The highest price was 110 marks for a morel (black) with white hind foot and muzzle. Sir Guido Ferre and Sir W. Reginaldi received £10 in expenses for themselves and their esquires for examining and trying the animals before purchase over 28 days in January and February. The trying was described as 'running', which indicates that speed was a requisite. For himself the prince reserved four chargers who wore blue and russet housings.[71]

ROYAL STUD EXPANSION

Edward II imported heavily from Spain. In 1308 he sent William de Guerenum there for 30 horses. In 1310 the king's Sergeant, Dominic de Runcevalle, was sent to buy 6 and by December had bought 2 for 50 marks. In the same year his main agent, William of Toulouse, went there for more, number unstated; in 1312 he again went abroad, destination unstated; but in 1313 he visited Spain and Navarre to purchase 30 head, and in 1314 returned there. A merchant of Caen had a wide-ranging brief to buy horses and armour in France, Germany, Navarre and Spain in 1317, and Hugh le Despenser was asked to bring back destriers and other horses if he went to Spain. Towards the end of his reign Edward advanced 1,000 marks to two Spanish merchants, Andres Perez de Castrogeriz and Gonsalvus Guderitz; both Edward and Perez were dead before the transaction was complete.[72] Andalusian and Lusitanian horses were, and remain, elegant, impressive, short-coupled and up to considerable weight – a desirable quality for a covered warhorse whose armour could be one of many types – linen and canvas housings, leather, padded material, or mail. By the early fourteenth century horse armour similar to a coat of plates was in use, and by Edward III's reign (1327–77) was becoming more common.[73] Canvas was reasonably effective, and cuir bouilli tough enough to turn most weapon strikes.

Edward II needed constant warhorse reinforcements and had to maintain production. Imports brought fresh lines of proven breeds. In 1305 he purchased Earl Warenne's stud at Ditchling, Sussex, asking the Archbishop of Canterbury to loan him a suitable stallion to cover his mares. In 1309 his agents Philip and Bynde Bonaventura purchased 20 destriers and 12 mares in Lombardy. Lombard horses, probably so named because Lombard merchants sold them, almost certainly originated from Apulia or Sicily,[74] both areas noted for horse-breeding in Roman times.[75] The Carthaginians introduced oriental blood, and possibly Spanish; in the Muslim and Norman era much Barb and Arabian blood entered. Under Spanish rule stock continued to be influenced.

Studs expanded soon after Edward III began effective rule in 1330. His war needs were heavy. In 1330 his stable staff included 29 carters, 37 sumptermen and 92 palfreymen. By the start of the Hundred Years War in 1337, this had risen dramatically. In 1339 royal accounts show 41 carters, 63 sumptermen, 167 palfreymen, 99 grooms.[76] Huge numbers of horses were mustered, large reparations paid for lost animals. Carthorses, sumpters and hackneys feature, but destriers, coursers and palfreys stand out. In 1330 John Brocas bought three destriers: Pomers, a grey, cost £120; dappled grey Lebryt, £70; bright brown bay Bayard £50.[77] In 1332–3 Arnold Garsy de St John went to Spain to reclaim the 1,000 marks Edward II had advanced and to buy 50 head. Inflation meant 23 were purchased for £715 13s 4d.[78] Edward imported from Sicily early in his reign, and from 1358 onwards sent Edmund Rose abroad to purchase horses. In 1362 he bought 4 in Belgium. Prices spiralled. A sorrel from Liege cost £106 3s 4d. Irish horses were cheaper. In 1340 John Brocas bought 112, costing from £24 to 12 marks.[79] Although these horses were destined for war and general riding, any surviving import would eventually have been sent to stud.

Edward was not to be conned by crafty dealers. He sent William Mountcliff and his two partners from Antwerp, the war headquarters, to Luxembourg to search for already broken-in destriers. Landuch, a German horse-dealer, was often used. On 4 November 1339 he was paid for checking out destriers and other horses bought for the king. Edward also bought from Landuch.[80]

A horse was the 'right gift' in royal circles. In one year Edward III was given 21 horses – 9 destriers, 5 palfreys, 4 coursers, 2 trotters and a stallion (unspecified). Donors included the queen, magnates and knights, the Counts of Juliers and Guelders. Significantly a bay destrier came from Benefacii of the Peruchie Society (bankers) – maybe seeking court preferment![81] The 12 purchases shown are more interesting. Most were for gifts, some reciprocal. Salisbury, Beauchamp and Cobham had given the king valuable horses. Salisbury's horse cost the king £150! – a staggering sum. Five came from German dealers at more moderate prices, Landuch supplying 4 ranging from £22 10s to £40 10s.[82]

The most interesting items were payments for breaking horses. Ade Selby, king's archer, received 45s, as did Guido Lorimer. Hugo Lorgini and William Rokeford, king's archer, each received 22s 6d, but John Ravensholm, the king's scutifer, received £9.[83] Why did Ravensholm receive more? Did the payment reflect his expertise or social standing, or was the warhorse a particularly good one with an evil disposition that warranted danger money for sorting it out?

A few references to Edward I show equine personalities and dispositions, and possibly how a knight interacted with his horse. Certainly today's premium on civility and good temper was absent. Viciousness was tolerated to a marked degree – maybe expected in a battle charger. Several royal incidents show medieval equines were not always tractable, on occasion causing financial and physical damage. Some royal horses shared the Plantagenet temper.

When a horse bolted with Edward I, almost throwing him, it was quickly sold off and a replacement purchased for 100 marks, twice the sum received for the nervous/bloody-minded horse. At Falkirk Edward received two broken ribs, caused by an out-of-control horse's bad temper or bad manners.[84] In August 1300 his destrier Morello of Cornwall kicked Alemanni, a stable boy, at Kirkcudbright. The boy received 5s recompense and another 5s for his passage home. At Anand in Scotland a woman who was injured by one of the king's palfreys received 4s for recompense and medicines.[85]

Horses, falcons and greyhounds had a high place in Edward's affections. When one of his horses was sent to Adam de Riston at Newcastle, Adam was ordered to take good care of it, the king specifying exact amounts of food and 'other things needful to keep him in good condition' till the royal return from Scotland.[86] In a letter to the Prince of Salerno in 1279, Edward owned to a delight in greyhounds; but his special care was reserved for his falcons; when one of them fell sick he had a wax figure of it made and placed in front of St Thomas's shrine at Canterbury, asking the saint to intercede for its recovery. In 1304 he wrote a personal thank-you letter to the widow of John de Muk who had cared for his favourite falcon, Marmaduke.[87]

THE HUMAN ELEMENT

Cavalry was, and remained, the elite arm. It was drawn from three main sources.

1 The Household Retinue

Men in the king's personal service, his household retinue, formed the nucleus of Edward I's cavalry and included sergeants-at-arms, squires, knights and bannerets, mostly young men from senior landowning families in England, but with some from Gascony, Spain, Brabant and Holland. Members received annual payments for robes and fees, and maintenance when at court. A household position offered excellent career prospects, many members rising to high government office. Some held key military positions in Edward's Welsh and Scottish wars. The numbers receiving fees fluctuated, as shown in Table 1.2.

Table 1.2 Fees paid to members of the royal retinue

Date	Bannerets	Knights
1284/5	14	87
1285	20	56
1286	13	39
1287 + 1288	80	
1289	10	50
1297	10	26*
1300	30	50
1301	18	50
1303	23	31
1306	17	28

* Twenty knights not shown as receiving fees should be added to the total.

Most cavalry was raised from the retinue, each bringing his own attendants, to which was added other horse paid by the king for specific campaigns. Two individuals illustrate household service.

Eustache de Hache rose steadily through the ranks. In 1276 he was a sergeant-at-arms.[88] He fought at Falkirk as a banneret, losing a bay charger worth 100 marks in the battle carnage.[89] In 1299–1300 he received fees and robes, was stationed at Berwick and had a small retinue at Drumbou (Dornock) of three knights and six men-at-arms receiving the king's pay of £47 4s for 59 days from 4 July to 13 August. He again indented for horses – a black charger worth 50 marks and a dun rouncy worth 5 marks.[90]

Robert Clifford was more prominent. In 1297 he was posted to Scotland to help the King's Lieutenant, Earl Warenne;[91] he fought at Falkirk (1298) losing a *ferrand pommele* (dark dappled grey) worth 45 marks;[92] in 1298[9] early in February he was warden at Lochmaben;[93] a year later he was still at Lochmaben with Sir John de St John and 30 men-at-arms with covered horses.[94] From

12 January to 24 June he had to defend the Scottish marches, receiving 500 marks of pay from the king. Sir Thomas Hellebek and four men-at-arms of his troop had horses killed, with a total value of £41 6s 8d and later that year a black charger worth 50 marks and a dun rouncy worth 5 marks belonging to Sir J. de Crumwell and Thomas de Monteny respectively were indented for.[95] He next provided troops for war in Caerlaverock, Dumfries and Dalswinton.[96] In 1302 he was indentured to serve in Scotland from Michaelmas to Easter with 20 horse for 200 marks, to be paid by the Sheriff of Westmorland.[97] In 1303 he was ordered to join a *chevauchée* near Dunfermline with his own '*mednee*' and other named indentured men. The king warned him, and other captains, not to admit any strangers to the group on pain of forfeiting horses and arms, and getting a stretch in prison.[98] His final task in Edward's reign was to lead the men of the Liberty of Durham to the aid of Henry de Percy in putting down the Bruce's 1306 rebellion.[99]

2 The Feudal Levy

The feudal levy was of knights owing mounted service for a specified period, usually 40 days. It was sometimes difficult to obtain. Taking up knighthood was not always attractive. It was costly: a festive ceremony; purchase and maintenance of armour and mount, and a lifestyle possibly more expensive than a man's income could comfortably support. Once a man was knighted he owed military service to his liege lord. The levies for Edward's first Welsh campaign in 1277/8 raised sufficient troops from household, feudal and volunteer sources. Subsequently it became clear that ongoing military requirements needed a steady supply of cavalrymen and horses. Accordingly on 26 June 1278, distraint of knighthood was ordered for all landholders with a yearly income of £20 or more. Edward issued repeated summonses to mounted service but with income variations and certain exemptions. Commissioners were empowered to enforce knighthood. On 26 May 1282, the king ordered that any man with 30 librates of land should have one great warhorse with proper armour which could serve him in cases of emergency as often as necessary, but four weeks later the order was relaxed because of the 'great shortage of warhorses', allowing anyone owing service to compound for cash.[100]

3 Paid Men-at-arms

Paid men-at-arms were mostly a feudal lord's sub-tenants or small landowners. The Calendar of Patent Rolls for 1279–88 shows this system in operation: Reginald Fitz Peter was ordered to cease distraining his tenant Grimbauld Pauncefoot for four barbed horses as Grimbauld was already serving under Roger de Mortimer in Wales.[101]

In November 1282 the distraint to cavalry service was expanded to non-feudal levies of those holding less than 20 librates of land but skilled in arms. After the battle of Falkirk (1298), where many horses were killed, the scope was further enlarged. All parcels of land worth £3 or more were to be grouped in units of 30 librates to maintain one trooper and his barbed mount.[102]

Earls and barons – tenants-in-chief – had a quota of knights fixed for the number of knights' fees they held. For each knight two additional troopers were expected. If a knight quota fell short the discrepancy was remedied with two troopers per knight. Earls ordinarily served gratis and were expected to exceed 40 days, but a lesser known baron could leave after that period or, if he remained, expect pay.[103] Normal daily pay under Edward I was 4s for a banneret, 3s for a knight, 1s for a man-at-arms with a covered horse, and 6d for one with a horse not covered.

Most cavalry was English, but Edward also employed a considerable force of Gascon horse. In 1282 a few crossbowmen were mounted Gascons. Many Gascons, not of the household, are shown as losing horses in the king's service at Falkirk and elsewhere in Scotland in 1298.[104]

LOGISTICS

Raising, allocating and maintaining cavalry presented a complex problem. As well as putting cavalry in the field, strategic castles and forts were garrisoned with foot and horse, provisioned and with remounts supplied. Ancillary staff – farriers, who also doctored horses, carters, saddlers, etc. – serviced the equine population. The following indentures show stocking for a major garrison. Provisioning must have been formidable.

John de St John, Lieutenant of Galloway, commanded Dumfries Castle and the county, Lochmaben Castle, the Annand valley and the marches towards Roxburgh, seeing much action during his service. Of his own retinue he had 40 men-at-arms receiving pay of 700 marks. The king added, and paid the wages of, 20 men-at-arms, 50 crossbowmen at 3d a day, 150 archers at 2d, a bowyer and his groom at 6d, a blacksmith (farrier) and his groom at 5d, a carpenter at 4d and a watchman at 3d. The knights among the king's men-at-arms are listed with their retinues, totalling 20:

> Sir Montesin de Noillan – six barbed horses
> Sir Arnaud Guillaume de Pugeys – four barbed horses
> Sir Gaillard de Brignak – two barbed horses
> Sir William de Sowe – four barbed horses
> Sir Bernard de Bignoles – four barbed horses.

The indenture covered a truce from 9 November 1300 to Pentecost 1301. The king reserved discretion to add to or detract from the numbers under Sir John's command.[105] Two indentures issued on 9 November to Sir Richard Siward with 10 men-at-arms and Sir Richard le Mareschal with 3 to attend Sir John, show that the king immediately increased his complement. In the same document Sir William Latimer was appointed warden of Berwick's castle, town and county with 30 men-at-arms of his retinue and 200 foot paid at daily wages by the king.[106] Similar indentures run throughout the *Documents relating to Scotland*.

Most entries in Drokensford's 1299–1300 accounts deal with war expenses. Harness, horses bought, cost of messengers, horses hired and maintained, carthorses used to haul war victuals, etc., appear under *Necessariae, Equis Emptis*, *etc. Victualling* details everything required to stock a garrison; number of carthorses used, horseshoes and nails bought; oats, peas, beans purchased and sent by cart or ship. County sheriffs provided victuals and transport, each item and its source faithfully recorded. *Compotii* submitted by garrison commanders show how many foot and horse had to be paid and fed and what stores were issued. A large section lists royal gifts, other expenses and horses lost in the Scottish war. The king was liable for £1,765 12s 6d for 177 horses lost; most of these died in service but a few were lost to the Scots. Edward also occasionally gave horses and their equipment. He purchased from Drokensford mounts for Sir Thomas Morham at a cost of £26 13s 4d and two sergeants-at-arms each had a horse plus tack costing £10 per horse.[107] Other equestrian expenses shown are tips to grooms taking horses to the king on manoeuvres. The standard tip was 6s 8d. Expenses for couriers are also shown.

THE MILITARY HORSE

Warhorses were valued so that troopers could claim for losses. As it was customary to present only one for valuation,[108] were subsequent losses accounted for by the station commander entering replacement values in his accounts? Some horses were not valued and recompense seems to have been fixed at £2 whether belonging to a man-at-arms or a knight; knights usually rode better-quality horses. Non-valued rates were unchanged throughout the reigns of the three Edwards; £2 was the lowest value for a covered horse, though infrequently other riding horses appear in the accounts at less. In 1299–1300 John Hayward lost two horses, one valued at £10, the other non-valued at £2.[109] Norwell's 1338–40 accounts show William Kekenwyk losing two non-valued horses at a £4 total; Sir Robert Walford and Sir Richard Murymouth each lost one non-valued horse at £2 each. Throughout Norwell's accounts many horses appear with the word *appreciati* and recompense, with the exception of £5 paid to William Alderbury, appears at £2.[110]

Reparations were not made for horses lost during truce periods. This exerted restraint on garrisons who might otherwise have reacted if they felt provoked, or unduly bellicose. The cost of a replacement, if one could be found, was more than many earned in months at 1s a day.

The returns from Edinburgh on 28 February 1299[1300] show equine strength. The constable, Sir John Kingston, had 5 esquires, 7 chargers, 13 hackneys and 21 grooms. Sir John had one charger for himself, one for his *socius* Sir Walter de Sutton, one each for his esquires. The hackneys were used for general riding when not on a war footing. Other knights at Edinburgh were:

Sir Ebulo de Montibus with	1 esquire,	2 chargers,	3 hackneys,	5 grooms
Sir Gerard de Freney	2	3	4	7
Sir Thomas Morham	2	3	–	7
Sir Herbert Morham	2	3	4	7
Sir Henry de Cantelu(p)	2	3	4	7
Sir . . . Lees	2	3	4	7
Sir John Luda	1	1	2	3

A medieval carectarius, *with powerful shoulders and haunches, but no coarseness, portrayed by Leonardo da Vinci. This illustrates that there was little difference between saddle and cart types at this period. (Photo: Photographie Bulloz; reproduced by permission of the Institut de France)*

There were 12 men-at-arms with a charger and a hackney apiece, plus a spare hackney. Two men-at-arms were without chargers, but had a hackney each. The total number of horses is 156(?) of which 63 were chargers, 3 being 'insufficient'. There were 67 men-at-arms to mount so a few were either not horsed or underhorsed relying on hackneys. Among other personnel in the castle were Elias the Marshal and his shoer.[111]

Numbers varied according to retinues, garrison size, magnates' wealth, current needs, ability to supply stock and replenish losses.

The Hidden Horse: the Farmhorse and Provisioning

Rhuddlan Castle on the River Clywd was built by Edward I in 1277 as a base for his advance into Wales. It resisted Llewelyn ap Gruffyd in March 1282, and on 2 August of that year 750 cavalry and 8,000 foot mustered.[112] Rhuddlan accounts[113] show cavalry constables and over 1,000 archers in pay by the end of September, and highlight ancillary services. Analyses of the accounts and farming methods show what food stores were accumulated, their provenance and the heavy use of carthorses hired to haul war supplies.

Haymaking was spread over 76 days using, at each operational peak, 23 mowers, 160 spreaders, 24 rakers, 77 stackers. Three-horse carts ranged from 2 to 20 a day. Mowing took 398 man days. Prior to modern haymaking a mower could put an acre (0.4 hectare) a day in swathe; good land yields 2 tons (2 tonnes plus) per acre. Being conservative about land fertility, and medieval man's labour capacity on a poorer diet, at even half the output Rhuddlan had a minimum of 200 tons (203 tonnes); 29 three-horse carts were hired to collect litter (bedding), which suggests a grain crop. Six other rigs were hired for six days to shift castle dung and bring in roofing turves. Other supplies (some were of a luxury nature, but the bulk were war materials) were streaming in by cart. Building materials were sent to nearby Macclesfield Royal stud and to the river for shipment to key fortresses. Wheat by water, with a short haul to the castle, and from Ruthin (15½ miles away/25 km) and Chester (25 miles/40 km) accumulated to 598 quarters, roughly 100 tons (101.5 tonnes). Not included in the rolls were horse grains – oats, peas, beans – but these would have been stored, possibly appearing in a roll that has not survived. Other entries were saddlers and costs for mending horse harness, and three of the 'king's shoeing smiths' returning to the king. These would have been in addition to resident farriers and others in the locality so cavalry use was envisaged. Each smith would have had his apprentice(s). A farrier can shoe 8 to 12 horses a day. Presumably in war heavier demands (overtime) were made.

CAPACITY AND COST OF OUTFITTING CAVALRY

At the outset of Edward I's Welsh wars *servitium debitum* was owed from 6,081 knights. Technically Edward could call on that number plus the customary two troopers per knight, but it would not have been practical or possible to array the total.

Women and ecclesiastics holding knights' fees who did not send knights or men-at-arms were charged scutage at 40s per fee, enabling Edward to meet some of his war costs in hiring foreign mercenaries and paying knights after their obligatory service expired. Sometimes higher fees than required were paid, sometimes less. Payments were levied in arrears. For the 1277 campaign:

the Abbot of Tavistock paid £32 for 16 fees
the Bishop of Ely £160 for 40 fees
the Abbot of Peterborough £166 13s 4d for 60 fees
the Archbishop of York owing service of 20 knights sent 4
the Bishop of Hereford owing 15 knights sent 3 knights and 4 sergeants
the Abbot of St Albans owing 6 knights sent 1 knight and 10 sergeants
the Abbot of Sherbourne owing 2 knights sent 4 sergeants.

Equipping a knight was expensive. A destrier cost between £40 and £80; cheaper horses between 20 and 40 marks; men-at-arms had even cheaper mounts valued sometimes as low as £2. The highest reparation in 1299[1300] was 80 marks; many were 30 to 40 marks. Rouncies varied from 30 marks down to £2.

Fleur, a 15.2hh Lithuanian draught mare, at the Royal Armouries, Leeds. This type of horse was used as a Great Horse or destrier. (Photo: author)

John de St John's retinue, which was extremely well mounted, sustained heavy losses in the March of Cumberland, amounting to £244 for 13 horses – 3 destriers at 80, 60 and 40 marks, 10 rouncies at from 30 to 8 marks. As a group these horses were above average value.[114]

A knight's armour, weapons and horse equipment were a huge investment. In 1302–3 the Prince of Wales purchased three bascinets for £1; two pairs of 'jambers' for £1 6s 8d a pair; three helmets at a cost of £3, £2 13s and £15, the latter being a close variety. A pair of plate cuisses cost 6s 8d; a pair of poleyns and two pairs of 'sabaturs' came to 13s 4d; a pair of plate gloves cost 10s.[115]

The account roll for the Windsor Tournament in 6 Edward I sheds light on equestrian equipment and can be used, with care, for general war use. The horse is called a courser. This has been taken to mean a running horse. In Restoration England it meant racehorse. In Edward I's day it was just as likely to mean warhorse, but of a lighter stamp than destrier. Its trappings for the 'jousts of peace' with blunted weapons were: a well-stuffed saddle; a 'grete halter for the reyne of the bridell', three double girths with double buckles and a 'double singull' (surcingle) with two buckles at each end to go over the saddle; a martingale, a peytral, a neck covering of iron, a leather crupper for the hindquarters, and trappers to go over the lot. The horse was to be newly shod and wear a 'softe bitte', which can only mean a mild bit, most likely a snaffle; the medieval curb could not be called 'softe'.[116] The wealthy could afford a complete armour for the horse. A 1277 account roll has an entry of 16*s* for two linen coverings to prevent mail housings galling the horse.[117] Armour was varied; some covered the whole horse, as in mail, some the most vulnerable sections – head, neck, withers, chest, flank and quarters. The rider's saddle and saddle-cloth protected the mid-section to some degree.

GENERAL USE OF CAVALRY

Edward I's total *available* cavalry, as opposed to paper strength, was about 8,000. Of these, about 2,750 were knights, the rest men-at-arms. The full complement was never called out. Medieval chroniclers are notoriously inaccurate. Hemingburgh's '7,000 horse' at Falkirk was a force of 2,400.[118] Throughout hostilities in Wales and Scotland most cavalry use was in small groups patrolling marches and garrisoning forts, castles and Scottish peles. The unit could be as few as 5 men or as many as over 60, plus archers and other staff (see above). There were also indentures for impressive numbers, and instances when the king ordered officers to raise sizeable cavalry squads for a raid on the Scots.

In December 1297 a major push was organized after the disastrous battle of Stirling Bridge. The king ordered prests of £7,691 16*s* 8*d* from the subsidy for the Scottish war collected from the Province of Canterbury, for 700 covered horses – 200 from county cavalry, 500 from nobles:[119]

John de Warenne, Earl of Surrey, expedition captain, with 100	£1,538 6*s* 8*d*
Roger Bigod, Earl of Norfolk and Suffolk, with 130	£2,000 0*s* 0*d*
Ralph de Monthermer (Mortimer), Earl of Gloucester and Hertford, with 100	£1,538 6*s* 8*d*
Humphrey de Bohun, Earl of Hereford and Essex, with 90	£1,384 10*s* 0*d*
Henry de Percy, with 50	£769 3*s* 4*d*
William Beauchamp, Earl of Warwick, with 30	£461 10*s* 0*d*

In October 1298 Berwick garrison had 60 men-at-arms and 1,000 foot. The warden was warned not to foray on the enemy with fewer than 30 horse and 500 foot.[120] In December a foray was to be launched from Berwick by Sir Walter de Huntercombe, Sir Simon Fraser and other officers with 200 men-at-arms.[121] In November 1300 Sir Richard de Hastang was to hold Jedworth Castle with 10 men-at-arms, 30 archers and ancillary staff.[122] By February 1301[2] Jedworth's garrison was only 5 men-at-arms during a truce lasting till Pentecost.[123] The constant reparations for horses show it was essential to have well-run baronial studs; even simple knights must have had at least one broodmare, or enough to purchase a replacement for one that was past service. The king paid only for dead, stolen by Scots, or incapacitated horses, which can be identified in the Falkirk rolls as those 'sent to hospital'.[124] Drokensford's accounts refer to horses 'sent to the Karavan', the pool of horses administered by the Crown.[125] Once there, if sound enough for other than front-line duties they could be used either for pulling carts, if sufficiently sturdy, or as pack-animals. If slightly injured or temporarily lame they could be returned to war duty when fit.

A roll dated 1300–1 shows nearly 500 warhorses valued for use by members of the household. At least half were casualties, falling sick or dying in service or at Linlithgow horse infirmary.[126] The enquiry made when John Sampson lost Stirling Castle to the Scots in 1299 showed horse losses to theft, death, or surrender to the Scots. Several sumpter and hackney saddles, and a 'draps de cuir' with 'houces and appurtenances', which sounds like a leather bard, were lost. Because he was wounded in the king's service Sampson was fined only 60 marks from the £149 10s 3d claimed. The balance was paid from arrears of the papal tithe imposed by Boniface VIII due from the Abbot of St Mary's, York.[127] Edward often used the proceeds of other taxes as moneys for war costs. He and his grandson raised additional sums from the populace at tenths and fifteenths of movable property. Certain movables were exempt, warhorses among them.

THE HOBELAR

From 1296 a trickle of a new type of trooper – the hobelar, a light lancer – appeared, initially recruited from Ireland. The hobelar's partner was the small, relatively lightly built hobby, standing around 14 hh. Remains of the original wild horse have been excavated near Dungannon, County Waterford. Other pre-Christian equid remains come from Loughrea, County Galway and show oriental characteristics in the skulls, as do those from the Craigywarren Crannog, County Antrim, where the long bones (cannons) resemble those of Arabians; the height varies between 13 and 14 hh. Early commerce between Ireland and Spain suggests the oriental influence derived from Spain, though some authorities look to France and its Libyan stock.[128]

Down the centuries from Giraldus Cambrensis (c. 1146–1223) onwards, Irish horsemen and their ambling hobbies – swift, nimble, 'pleasant and apt to be taught' – were noted, as was the Irish weaponry: darts, light spears, axes and stones cast by slingers, all used in rapid skirmishing tactics.[129]

Skirmishers suited Edward I's purposes on the Scottish marches for reconnaissance, communications and the quick strike. In 1296 the king summoned the Irish, commanded by the justiciar Sir John Wogan, to serve in Scotland. Among the Irish forces were the Earl of Ulster, Richard de Burgh, 8 bannerets including Wogan, 26 knights, 285 men-at-arms, 260 hobelars, 28 crossbowmen and 2,600 foot. The hobelar was paid 6d a day. Each knight and man-at-arms in the Earl of Ulster's retinue had three horses; and in other retinues they had even more, but the hobelar had only one.[130] As an unarmoured mount the hobby was considered of less value, but he was potentially of greater use owing to his speed, nimbleness and ability to survive on less fodder. The hobelar had to conserve his mount by judicious use, not risk him in close combat where the killing danger was highest.

Some Irish hobelars remained in Scotland after 1296 being employed in various tasks. In July 1299 Robert Clifford, warden of Lochmaben Castle, wrote to Richard Abyndon, the king's treasurer at Carlisle, requesting him to pay either in food or money what was owing to Richard le Brut, who had been retained to spy on the enemy and who for the last six weeks had received no recompense. The matter was urgent as the warden feared the hobelar would 'take himself off for want of sustenance'.[131] The garrison defending Lochmaben Pele against the Earl of Carrick in August 1299 comprised four men-at-arms, six hobelars and nine foot.[132]

One of John de St John's earlier indentures included an additional 20 or 30 men-at-arms and as many hobelars for Galloway's defence,[133] but in March the troop was still not mustered because the locals were refusing to aid him. The document states that hobelars are to be hired 'if he can find enough'.[134]

Hobelar numbers were insufficient as Edward found in January 1300 when, for another Scottish expedition, he ordered the justices, chancellor and treasurer of Ireland to send 300 hobelars, plus a huge quantity of oats, wine and dried fish. Dublin, Cork, Drogheda, Waterford, Limerick, Kilkenny and Rospont were also required to send similar provisions.[135] Only a small number of hobelars actually reported for duty,[136] being stationed in small groups, the largest of which was 14 men, at Carlisle, Caerlaverock, Kirkcudbright and Twynham.[137]

English hobelars were soon recruited – 32 hobelars, foresters from Redesdale, were in pay in July 1301[138] – but Ireland still provided most, Edward demanding 1,000 in February 1301 with the postscript 'with more horse and foot if possible'.[139] Again numbers fell short, only 391 being listed.[140] In 1321 when directing the Bishop of Durham to raise men-at-arms, hobelars and infantry Edward II made a rare reference to mares, telling the bishop to make sure hobelars were mounted on horses, not mares.[141] In a scouting party mixed sexes were to be avoided for fear of the horses paying noisy attention to the mares.

CAMPAIGN PLANNING: PROVISIONS AND HAULAGE

Victualling was an ongoing drain on the country's agrarian and episcopal economies. It must have been hard to keep producing strapping horses in prime condition. The size of medieval *carectarii* was nothing like our modern carthorses. Weight was more important than height and it was practical to match teams, particularly as regards height, to ensure loads were evenly divided between the normal three- and five-horse hitches. Medieval illustrations are of moderate value. *Carectarii* appear to have been what we would term ride/drive types, differing little from saddle equines. I would suggest they were about 15 hh with robust, cobby conformation, similar to the Lithuanian draught horses described in the introduction.

When a campaign was planned all available draught animals were commandeered, but the king was not always satisfied with their quality. In July 1306 accounts went out concerning oxen, horses and carts supplied by county sheriffs and abbots of monasteries. They make illuminating reading. One assumes this was not tolerated on a repeat basis and that the Carlisle receiver, James de Dalileye, played down the animals' value. Most horses are described as of 'small value', some as 'weak and of little value', one was infected and 'worthless', two were 'totally dried up in mind and body'; 12 oxen were 'small weak and lean' and 42 were weak. Of a total of 108 horses only 21, and of 66 oxen only 12, did not have some deleterious remark against them.[142]

Baggage trains hauled food for horses and men, equipment and munitions. Consignments were massive. Early in 1300 various counties and towns in England were ordered to send grain to Berwick-on-Tweed by 24 June. Totals were: wheat, 5,600 quarters; oats, 6,500 quarters; malt, 3,300 quarters; beans and peas, 700 quarters (for horsebread); these were massive amounts. Ireland was also commanded to ship huge quantities to Skinburness from where *carectarii* hauled supplies to nearby Carlisle. Westmorland and Cumberland sent direct to Carlisle.[143] Hay is also mentioned but most was acquired, along with cut grass, nearer to various bases. Transporting the huge quantities needed was not cost-effective. Among necessaries from York were 3,000 horseshoes and 50,000 nails, a part load, in seven three-horse carts.[144] Shoes and nails are listed in the *compotus* of Jacob Dalilegh, king's victualler at Carlisle in 1300. Farriers throughout England made shoes that were sent to Scotland for distribution. Shoes were purchased in tens of thousands and nails in hundred thousands. The exact number is hard to reckon as some shoes were sold by weight in quarters and some by numbers.[145] A late medieval horseshoe used between 6 and 8 nails, usually the former.[146] Obviously provision was made for a certain nail wastage; some shoes were probably reset if the horse was operating in non-abrasive going and just needed a trim.

Drokensford's accounts show garrison supplies of munitions, and for horses and people foodstuffs that had a wide but basic range – grain, bacon, mutton, fish, wine, etc. Although most troops carried their own basic weaponry replacements, especially of arrows, part of the north-bound baggage was formed of bolts, bowstrings and lances. Frequently, as with specie, these were transported by faster pack-animals. In November 1302 three pack-horses delivered a small mixed load of 45 crossbows, 12 costa(?), 31 lances and 108 lb (nearly 50 kg) of canvas from Newcastle to Berwick. At that time Richard de Bremmesgrave was receiver at Berwick and was required to send on to Selkirk Castle, garrisoned by Sir Alexander de Balliol with 30 men-at-arms, 60 quarters of wheat, 10 casks of wine, 120 quarters of malt, 160 quarters of oats, 10 quarters of salt, 20 quarters of beans and peas, 20 crossbows and 5,000 quarrels, and 60 quarters of sea-coal. The sheriff of Roxburgh and Sir Alexander had to find transport, but Sir Richard was to pay for it.[147] The total weight of dry supplies was 430 quarters. For this, 144 horses, three to a wagon with a 1½-ton load, were needed, plus others for the wine and munitions. In the same document 14 Scottish garrisons are named, some with more men, some with fewer, but with more than 500 mounted troops overall.

Where terrain was difficult for wagons, sumpters were used. A sturdy pack-horse could carry 400 lb (180 kg) dead weight, but very slowly; a 200 lb (90 kg) load was the norm. In 1298 when a raid on Stirling was planned with 200 men-at-arms and no infantry, 300 pack-horses carried supplies.[148] No doubt these animals were more lightly laden and able to move at a smart clip.

THE HORSE AT THE FRONT LINE

Under the cavalry umbrella I include not only heavy cavalry who fought on horseback, but those who used the horse more intelligently. In Edward I's early army nearly all the heavy cavalry rode covered horses and worked best in open country. There were some large, wasteful battles that left many horses dead and injured, but these were rare; most campaigns were over difficult country, and this, coupled with his opponents' skirmishing tactics, forced the king to make changes in cavalry composition and use.

He made limited use of mounted Gascon crossbowmen,[149] but by his grandson's day most archers were mounted, which enabled them to reach the war zone rapidly and as rapidly to evacuate it. Hobelars were increasingly used. In autumn 1319 when Edward II's army besieged Berwick, of 8,080 men 1,040 were hobelars.[150] Under Edward III hobelar use increased, some garrison contingents often matching, and in some cases outnumbering, men-at-arms. In 1338 Roxburgh had 60 men-at-arms and 80 hobelars.[151] The Perth garrison was to be increased from 100 men-at-arms and 120 hobelars, only half mounted, to 200 men-at-arms, 200 mounted hobelars, and 400 archers, of whom half were mounted in wartime.[152] In 1339, from Cumberland and Westmorland alone, 1,200 hobelars were raised for the siege of Perth, but only 64 men-at-arms from the same counties are noted.[153] From 1337 many garrisons carried a complement of mounted archers.[154]

Massed cavalry use is not recorded in the Welsh wars.[155] To counteract Welsh guerrillas, cavalry was deployed to defend troops on the move and to retaliate and/or to harry an enemy in retreat. In other than really inaccessible places a man on horseback is faster than one on foot, so troop mobility was vital against enemies who moved unhindered on their own turf. Small cavalry bands garrisoning Welsh castles acted as territorial guardsmen protecting communication lines, baggage and specie convoys, and had the ability to foray rapidly into surrounding countryside.

Regular cavalry service was undertaken in small units. A series of attacks on English-held forts began in March 1282. By early April cavalry was concentrated on the Welsh borders, as it had been in 1277. The base at Chester had 600 horse, and in all Wales there must have been around 800. By mid-June Edward had taken over the Chester cavalry, and by the end of the month was dispersing it throughout Wales to combat flaring rebellion. In this war archers were first brigaded with cavalry.[156] In December 1282 the Welsh siege of Builth Castle was broken by marcher lords John Giffard and Edmund Mortimer. Prince Llewellyn's spearmen in a position on the hill above the River Yrfon blocked Orewin bridge. On 11 December, unseen, English foot crossed upstream and delivered a flank attack. Meanwhile the bridge passage was opened. Archers and horse combined, gaps opening in the Welsh ranks, the cavalry charging in and completing the destruction. Llewellyn, absent at a chieftains' conference, returned as the fight was ending and was cut down. Giffard also fought at the battle of Maes Madog on 5 March 1295,[157] where the Earl of Warwick commanded 119 lances from Montgomery with 2,689 foot, 26 mounted constables and a few crossbowmen. A night march ended by surrounding the Welsh, through skilled use of horse, foot and archery, plus efficient pursuit by cavalry.[158] Destructive harrying is an important cavalry duty, if not the most important. Horses relish a chase, and, especially if entires, can be dangerous, such danger having nothing to do with the rider, though he poses an extra threat.[159]

In the Scottish wars there were several massed charges. The battle of Dunbar, on 27 April 1296, was the first major engagement. Thinking the thinly stretched English were retreating across the Spott burn, the Scots horse broke ranks and charged, only to be overwhelmed when the English rapidly re-formed under Earl Warenne and drove them from the field. The Scots fled towards Selkirk Forest 40 miles away (64 km).[160] After Dunbar Edward progressed throughout Scotland; by June 1297 William Wallace led a Scotland in revolt. At Stirling Bridge on 11 September 1297, the Scots led by Andrew Murray and Wallace trounced the English under the Earl of Surrey and Hugh Cressingham, the English treasurer, at whose instigation one contingent had been dispensed with to reduce cost. Surrey, who did not regard the Scots as a serious threat, overslept, compounding his stupidity by sending cavalry across the Forth by a narrow bridge that allowed only two horses abreast, rather than detouring 2 miles (3 km) to cross over a wide ford and attack in strength. Wallace and Murray waited till half the English had crossed, then attacked, cutting the force in two and taking a heavy toll of the English, only a few of whom reached safety before the bridge was destroyed.[161] The Scots under Wallace then overran the border counties.[162] Edward ordered massive reinforcements, 29,400 foot being levied from the northern and midland counties, North Wales and the Marcher lands.[163] Early in March 1298 he returned from Flanders to take command. On 25 June cavalry mustered at Roxburgh, the king joining the army early in July; the English forces advanced into Scotland, devastating the land but unaware of the Scots' whereabouts. Food was short, the Welsh on the point of deserting to the Scots if things went Scotland's way, and Edward ready to turn back, when on 21 July news arrived that the Scots were only 13 miles away (21 km) at Falkirk. That night the English camped near Linlithgow, each man by his horse. Next day the armies faced each other, the English with over 15,000 foot and 2,500 horse, the Scots fewer, with only a few horse who held ready to the rear, trusting their schiltroms to turn the heavy cavalry by aiming their spears at the horses.[164]

The earls of Norfolk, Hereford and Lincoln were in the van, pressing the attack only to be turned by a burn that delayed impact with the Scots right. Bishop Bek of Durham led the English right and after skirting the loch both English wings and schiltroms connected. The Scots horse fled; the English cavalry charged repeatedly, annihilating the Scottish bowmen. Welsh longbowmen and foreign crossbowmen fired into the schiltroms; as they crumbled, the cavalry finished them off by a massed charge. Scots losses were heavy, thousands perishing on the field or drowning in the loch.[165] The English lost about 2,000 foot and only one knight, Master of the Temple, Brian de Jay; 110 horses valued for service were lost. As there were probably two or three times as many unpaid as paid cavalry in Edward's army,[166] the toll must have been hideous, if in the same ratio reaching 300–400, plus those injured.

In spite of England's repressive rule and heavy military presence, the Scots' resolve hardened. Robert Bruce was crowned on 25 March 1306, and during Edward's last year, 1306–7, a concentrated effort was made to search out and 'pursue the Bruce and his accomplices who are lurking in the moors and marshes of Scotland'.[167] Under Edward II (reigned 1307–27), the Scottish position strengthened and the king repeatedly received complaints that the Bruce's raids were putting garrisons under pressure. Requests for reinforcements escalated as battle came closer.[168] The Bruce and his captains, especially Randolph, Earl of Moray and James Douglas, the Black Douglas, were masters of guerrilla warfare, the swift hobby their mainstay. Knights and squires rode fine strong horses, and commoners small ponies. Irregulars followed on foot. They lived off purloined cattle and oatmeal cakes from a supply of meal carried behind the saddle. They covered 60 to 70 miles (95 to 115 km) in a day and night,[169] a perfectly feasible sustainable distance for a lightweight horse not overburdened.

By the summer of 1310 the Scots were trading with Ireland for foodstuffs, iron, steel, weapons, armour and horses. In the following years the Bruce struck repeatedly over the borders.[170] As the Bruce augmented his horse stocks, Edward's suffered heavy depletion. From a 1311–12 valuation of 840 horses at the garrisons of Dundee, Berwick, Bothwell, Livingstone, Lithco (Linlithgow), Strivelin (Stirling) and St John's Town, 132 were lost,[171] plus others lost elsewhere in constant raiding and skirmishes. Some appear in later *Restauro* documents. As well as the Bruce plundering, the *loyal* (to England) people of Scotland, in the English garrisons of Berwick and Roxburgh, were doing likewise. To a complaint of this sent in autumn 1313 Edward replied on 28 November that 'as soon as some pressing and weighty matters are disposed of' he would send redress, informing his people that he would lead an army to their relief the following year at midsummer![172]

BANNOCKBURN: 24 JUNE 1314

Stirling, one of the few strongholds still held by the English, was under siege. Edward finally began preparations as promised with summonses to earls, barons, knights and ecclesiastics owing feudal service for cavalry to muster at Berwick on 10 June 1314. The earls' response was scant, only Gloucester, Hereford and Pembroke serving; the rest sent minimum quotas. Lesser magnates and knights responded better, with cavalry numbering 2,000 to 2,500 plus a limited number of foreign horse.[173] Although Barbour inflates host numbers, he gives other details; he wrote that Edward's cavalry was enhanced by knights from France, Hainault, Gascony, Germany, Flanders and Brittany. He gives 3,000 horse barded in mail and plate.[174] As he wrote *c.* 1375, his information was probably derived from eye-witnesses. Since the English cavalry rode covered horses, he is not far out at 3,000 for total cavalry; we can ignore his fanciful figure of 40,000 infantry – there were *c.* 15,000 men, summonses having been sent out for over 21,000.[175]

Scottish morale was high after years of gaining the upper hand, the Douglas gaining 57 victories in 70 engagements.[176] Of an army of 5–6,000 only 500 were light cavalry.[177]

The approach to Stirling via wooded New Park or across the spongy carse was a trap for cavalry. Bordering the track through New Park small pits were dug and covered with grass;[178] here a falling horse would break a leg, or at best wrench limb or shoulder. The carse was lethal for heavily burdened chargers.

By 23 June Edward was close enough to Stirling to prevent the castle being surrendered. Its castellan warned him to wait as the Scots might now withdraw. Late in the day some Scots in front of New Park appeared to be so doing. Gloucester and Hereford, far enough from Edward not to hear any order, crossed the Bannockburn and charged uphill.[179] Henry de Bohun, Hereford's nephew, saw the chance of a lifetime. Ahead of him, setting his army ready, was Robert Bruce on a small grey palfrey, with a crowned helmet on his head, and armed with an axe. 'Seeing him horsed so ill' Bohun thundered down on the Bruce, thinking to use his charger to overthrow the Bruce's palfrey. Barbour describes the two men charging at each other. As they closed, the Bruce reined his palfrey aside, rose in his stirrups, clove Bohun's crest, helmet and skull in two, and was left with the shattered axe stump in his hand. It is tempting to think Bruce's palfrey was a Connemara; most are grey and are descendants of the type of animals ridden by Irish hobelars. The following English took heavy casualties; Gloucester was knocked off his horse before they withdrew. When 800 cavalry under Sir Robert Clifford and Sir Henry Beaumont tried to bypass the Scots to get to Stirling, a schiltrom under Moray forestalled them. The fighting was fierce, horses impaled on bristling spears. Some Scots nipped out from the schiltrom to stab horses and bring riders down. Eventually the schiltrom was surrounded, the English throwing everything they had into its heart – knives, spears, darts, maces.[180] But it held and Clifford's broken remnants dispersed, some to their ranks, some to Stirling, ending the first day's fight. Both armies stayed under arms overnight. Because their destriers were dehydrated the English stayed in the carse and overnight stripped nearby houses of planking, etc., using it to bridge the carse streams so that by morning they were on firm ground.

Next morning hostilities reopened with an exchange of arrows, followed by another impetuous cavalry charge led by Gloucester. In his pre-battle speech the Bruce noted how the English 'glory in their warhorses and equipment',[181] and ordered his infantry to spear the charging horses. The wounded horses rushed around in terror. Many were brought down; others unseated their riders, though some knights did manage to keep their seats. Other English cavalry was in a solid mass into which Scottish archers rained arrows, wounded horses running amok. The English archers, usually the backbone of their army, received a flank attack from Sir Robert Keith leading the Scottish horse, killing many and scattering the rest.

The Scots victory was of steady foot against cavalry used in the stupidest manner – massed on a limited field, unable to manoeuvre, or committed in wild rushes regardless of cost, recking the Scots at no military worth. Instead of being integrated with the cavalry, Edward's archers were stuck in the rear. Edward was led from the battlefield against his will – he was no coward, if no strategist – by Sir Aylmer de Valence, Earl of Pembroke, but Sir Giles de Argentan, acknowledged one of the era's ablest knights, refused to flee, charged Sir Edward Bruce and was brought down and killed, his horse impaled on Scottish spears. Two hundred spurs were taken from dead English knights. Douglas harried the English, capturing some of the king's rearguard; the rest reached the safety of Berwick.[182]

In the following years as the Scots ravaged England Edward continued inept. In July 1314 Sir Andrew Harclay sent a desperate warning that an army of Scots would cross into England on the 14th and that prior reinforcements could have prevented it.[183]

EDWARD III

Turbulence greeted the accession of Edward III (reigned 1327–77). The Bruce was ailing but the Douglas and Moray were still to be reckoned with as Edward found in the abortive Weardale campaign. Forces on both sides were largely mounted, the Scots on tough, small horses, the English with chargers for the men-at-arms and lighter animals for hobelars, who at this date, 1327, formed a quarter of the English forces.[184]

On 1 February, Edward III's coronation day, the Scots entered England and made an unsuccessful attempt on Norham Castle. Preparations were made to retaliate. On 5 April summonses went out. Meanwhile the Scots were mustering and arrangements were made to clear the northern English counties of non-combatants. In late May hundreds of cavalry arrived at Dover under John of Hainault, and 50 under William, son of the Count of Juliers. In mid-July Edward and his cavalry reached Durham. The foot had gone ahead.[185]

The sight of burning villages warned the English that the Scots had crossed into Northumberland. Three weeks of frustration followed for the young king. His army was moving through unknown territory of mountains, valleys, stony tracts, and treacherous bogs and marshes which cost men and horses. The Scots gave them the slip. With no baggage wagons the English and their horses went hungry. Rain set in for a week. The horses' tack became sodden, their backs developed sores; shoes loosened in heavy mud and could not be replaced, so

Fourteenth-century armour for horse and rider, Royal Armouries, Leeds. (Photo: author)

horses became lame as well as thin. The only English gains were Scots taken in sporadic skirmishes while the armies faced each other across the River Wear.[186] During the stalemate while the English, unable to bring the Scots to battle, hoped to starve them out, the Scots quitted their first position and relocated at Stanhope Park, from where the Douglas launched a furtive move with 500 men. 'Softly did he ride' till he was among the English and cut the royal tent ropes, accounting for 300 English before galloping away. By morning the Scots had slipped away. Froissart gives Douglas's troop as 200.[187]

After the Weardale disaster the Hainaulters returned home but first sold their valuable warhorses, claiming for lost mounts and for contract pay. Horse costs were £21,482 5s 6d; war pay £19,228 7s 3¾d.[188]

Again the Scots ravaged over the border, and when England sued for peace the treaty was sealed with the marriage of David, the Bruce's infant son, to Joan, Edward III's sister.[189] Edward was forced to acknowledge Robert Bruce as king of an independent Scotland. But Scotland still had to fear rapacious England when Edward achieved full power in 1330.

Dupplin Moor in 1332 was an English infantry victory. In command of the English forces was Edward Baliol, titular king of the Scots, having been foisted on them by Edward. The horses had been sent to the rear to be used in harrying, a pattern Edward repeated at Halidon Hill in 1333. Archers played the main role, firing into the Scots array till it fled, Edward leading the punishing chase. Frequent Scottish uprisings followed by raids meant a heavy war bill and a drain on resources. As most archers were mounted, lightweight horses were in demand. To suppress the rising of 1334, 3,900 men were mustered at Newcastle by November – 1,200 men-at-arms, 1,200 foot, 1,500 hobelars or mounted archers – with more troops arriving till mid-December.[190] In 1335 yet another army of 13,000–13,500 was mobilized. The mounted element from England, not including the household nucleus, was 2,400 men-at-arms including magnates; 251 men-at-arms, vintenars and ductores from shire levies. Magnates supplied 1,095 mounted archers; town levies 121; shire levies 2,128. Towns sent 31 foot archers; shires 3,342. Ireland sent 17 knights, including the paymaster, 472 men-at-arms, 291 hobelars, 805 foot. Of the 3,031 Welsh only 337 were mounted, most being foot archers.[191]

TWO

The Hundred Years War: Crecy, Poitiers, Agincourt

The preliminaries began in 1337 when the Earl of Derby landed at Cadzand, English archers routing Flemish opposition.[1]

In 1339 Edward III marched from Brabant to Vilvoorde with 1,600 men-at-arms among whom were the earls of Lancaster, Warwick, Suffolk and Northampton, and Sir Reginald Cobham and Sir Walter Manny. Many were still with him nearly 25 years later when he fought his last campaign.[2] Also present were the Earl of Salisbury and the Bishop of Lincoln. Edward's army was better equipped than those of his father and grandfather. The Tower of London, the national arsenal, stockpiled equipment.[3] The English warhorse was rarely used on the battlefield. His main contribution was the mobility which characterized the expensive but inconclusive preamble of the first few war years when Edward's armies wasted much of France. This stage ended when England made a pact with Flanders for mutual assistance against France. Edward returned to England in 1340 leaving the earls of Salisbury and Suffolk to man a garrison in Ypres. They spent the rest of the winter harrying Lille and its environs. In the summer of 1340 Edward's fleet destroyed French and Castilian sea forces, but as Flemish support weakened he made a truce with France. Both used it to re-equip for war. It expired in March 1345.

THE CRECY CAMPAIGN: 1346

Edward landed at Saint-Vaast-de-la-Hougue on 12 July 1346. In the ensuing six weeks he marched through the Cotentin and Normandy to Paris, then swung north back to the coast of Calais, devastating the land and amassing booty which was shipped to England, including valuable prisoners of war for ransom. Philip VI of France was dangerously close behind him until at Blanchetaque on the Somme a ford enabled the English to cross, not without a hard fight against defending French.[4] On 25 August the two kings faced each other at Crecy. The English host, estimated by modern count at *c.* 15,000 inclusive, was said by Froissart to be 4,000 horse, 10,000 mounted archers and an unstated number of Welsh and Irish foot.[5] The French, by modern count 40,000 strong,[6] had among them mounted units from Germany, Bohemia, Luxembourg, Lorraine, Saarbruck, Flanders, Namur and Hainault. The battle was a débâcle: English discipline against French impetuosity and wasted chivalry. The English were all dismounted, horses emparked in a ring of baggage wagons and carts. The French sent their Genoese crossbowmen in first. When, unable to prevail against English archers, they turned to retrench, their own knights rode them down calling them craven.[7] Among the French each knight wanted to be the first to the fray. Those behind forced the foremost on. Any chance of orderly retreat was denied. In all, the French are said to have delivered 15 or 16 charges.[8]

Le Bel, a Burgundian chronicler, gives a graphic picture of horse casualties. The Genoese were trapped between the French van and the English archers. The weaker horses, presumably felled by arrows, fell on top of the Genoese; others trampled these and fell on top of each other 'like a litter of piglets'. The horses then balked; some ran backwards, jibbing; some reared; some turned their hindquarters to the enemy; others let themselves fall to the ground – if denied flight, some frightened horses will collapse in panic. Among this heap of maddened, injured, dead and dying horses the English moved in for the kill.[9]

After the battle, horses were used in skirmish and round-up operations, 500 men-at-arms and 2,000 archers being detailed to deal with any French that might be re-forming. Froissart says more French were killed then than in the battle, in which he says 1,291 nobles perished, which is believable, and an exaggerated 30,000 of the rank and file.[10] English losses were slight.

Like the battle of Poitiers 10 years later, and Agincourt nearly 60 years after that, Crecy was a military landmark. Not so prominent were blitzkrieg *chevauchées*. The horse was indispensable to Edward III's son the Black Prince (1330–76) and to the victor of Agincourt Henry V (reigned 1413–22), both of whom scorched their way through France on softening-up raids. However, following Crecy (1346) an impartial enemy struck first France, then England: the Black Death, which wrought such havoc in the late 1340s that war ceased for nearly a decade. High mortality paralysed Europe. Commoners in crowded insanitary conditions suffered most, but the rich often found escape futile, death striking in town and countryside, peasant hut and noble household. Land lay fallow; crop production fell; armies could not be provisioned or fodder for horses found.

POITIERS: 19 SEPTEMBER 1356

By 1355 recovery was under way. Edward III again pressed his claim to the French Crown. His heir, Edward the Black Prince, raided southern France in 1355, pushing northward in 1356. Towards the end of September 1355, 1,000 men-at-arms, 1,000 horse and 300 to 400 foot archers, and 170 Welsh foot sailed from Plymouth. The prince indentured with the king for 433 men-at-arms, 400 mounted and 300 foot archers, needing a minimum of 833 horses, plus mounts for other magnates and their retinues, certain non-combatants and administrative staff, and cart and baggage animals. Some men-at-arms were allowed to buy horses in Gascony; replacements for horses lost in service were to be purchased there, all to be valued by the Constable of Bordeaux. Those shipped from Plymouth were appraised and marked, presumably branded, by John Deyncourt and his assistants; two farriers sailed with the army; Lambkyn Saddler supplied some of the prince's tack.[11]

Chandos Herald says that on landing the horses were 'well rested', the prince marching on 5 October with over 6,000 fighting men, boosted by Gascons and Bearnais including the famous Captal de Buch. Although he says that for 'four months' the army cut a swathe of devastation from Toulouse to Narbonne,[12] actually the raid ended on 1 December at La Réole in Guienne after the English had ridden 550 miles, not counting diversionary pillaging. Seven rest days were taken and stopovers of two or three days to reduce towns or castles, 'negotiate' terms (blackmail), etc.[13]

The raid was multi-purpose: retaliation against the Armagnac's aggression towards Gascony; the amassing of plunder and ransoms; crop-stripping, which denied retaliatory forces sustenance and the French Crown its taxes; pressuring the French, who were already threatened by Edward III landing at Calais – unexpectedly he withdrew, but not before France had drafted troops to that area. Travelling fast in English-held territory to Arouille, his son the Black Prince crossed into Armagnac. On some days he covered 25 miles (40 km), losing many horses, which, according to Chronicler Baker, was due to high mileage. Although a series of 25-mile days, each followed by a rest day, is not excessive, horses shipped in stuffy holds and starting out soon after landing had probably succumbed to what Hewitt terms transport fever,[14] more commonly known as shipping fever – strangles – a streptococcus bacillus that without modern drugs is often fatal; its incubation period coincides with the 11 October arrival at Arouille. Also horses are susceptible to stress when shipped, and most had been contained below decks for some time before sailing. From experience, even a 24-hour spell in a modern ship with excellent care meant horses needed nearly a week after landing before they were fully operational. The army was unopposed until occupying the town of Narbonne, when it suffered a missile barrage from the citadel. French troops were coming from Montpellier; the Count of Armagnac was on the army's heels. The return to Guienne was rapid riding in sodden winter conditions, crossing Armagnac's rising rivers. The French a few miles behind were also hampered. By 25 November Edward crossed the swollen Gers. Less than 30 miles (48 km) later he reached Mézin in Guienne.[15]

Edward wintered at Bordeaux quartering troops at La Réole, Sainte-Foy, Saint-Emilion and around Libourne. The Captal, Chandos and Audley wintered partly in open camp, partly in skirmishing for lodging around Agen and Cahors, taking Port Sainte-Marie and besieging Périgueux Castle.[16]

In early spring 1356, extra men and horses were ordered for the prince's army. In March 300 mounted archers were directed to be at Plymouth by 17 April; two weeks later this was doubled, 500 to be from Cheshire, the prince's own county. Sumpters were purchased, the receiver in Cornwall being ordered to buy 30 of the strongest baggage horses and provide 30 grooms. The earls – Warwick, Suffolk, Salisbury, Oxford, Stafford – had fresh mounts sent in two transports assigned for their horses and victuals.[17] As supplies were being raised for the king's Normandy campaign, equine and agricultural resources were stretched to the limit.

On 4 August 1356 the army rode north, successfully besieging Romorantin. It captured the lords Boucicault and Craon and turned first west to Tours, then south, reaching Poitiers on 18 September, 'bringing much booty for they had wrought much damage in France' and had gained valuable prisoners for ransom. John II of France (reigned 1350–64) had mustered his army at Chartres, and moving fast reached Chauvigny and Poitiers ahead of the prince. Scouting ahead of their army were 200 English on 'excellent horses' and a hot fight ensued when they charged the French rear taking a fresh haul of prisoners including the Counts of Joigny and Auxerre.[18]

Battle was inevitable. The Black Prince's raiding route south was blocked. From prisoners he learned that he was heavily outnumbered, the French having 8,000 cavalry, 2,000 crossbowmen and a mass of light infantry – in all, 16,000 men – while he had only 2,500 horse, 3,500 archers mostly mounted and 1,000 foot, totalling 7,000.[19]

Horses played a crucial but entirely adverse role for the French van. A formidable hedge lay across the road between the armies. Froissart's initial description is ambiguous; it was either a frontal barrier or two lateral hedges. To reach the English who were on foot the French had to pass through a gap of no more than four horse widths. The barrier was sown with archers in harrow formation. On their exposed side the English were protected by the concentration of baggage wagons and equipment. The horses were held ready. The French had learned somewhat from Crecy and from their Scottish knights, and had dismounted their cavalry apart from some 300 chosen by the French marshals Arnoul d'Audrehem and Jean de Clermont from the 'toughest and best fighters . . . fully equipped and mounted on superb horses', which included German mercenaries. These elite men were to smash through and break the English front. After fruitless attempts by the Cardinal of Périgord to mediate, the first blow was struck by the impetuous Sir Eustace D'Aubrecicourt charging from the English van, his challenge met by a German, Sir Louis de Recombes. Connecting at full speed both were unhorsed, five German men-at-arms pinioning Sir Eustace, who was then tied to a baggage wagon. He was later rescued and took part in the final onslaught.

The opening French charge was met by murderous fire from both flanks, horses falling injured, others swerving or turning tail, refusing to face the fire. A few riders battered their way through, but the majority were trapped, rendered impotent in the press. Those who turned tail were swamped by the oncoming French foot under the Duke of Normandy. Although French losses were heavy, the army was still operative but inexplicably the Duke of Orleans's contingent in the rear mounted and rode off. The English seized their chance, mounted all available horses, including sumpters and baggage beasts, and bore down on the French Constable's division, the battle breaking up into savage mêlées, many men being unhorsed in the crush.

Meanwhile 600 cavalry and mounted archers under the Captal de Buch had ridden round the eastern side of the French. The English horse charged from concealment and burst upon the foot, archers raking French flanks. As the French crumbled, King John, his son Philip and many rich knights were captured for ransom.

Poitiers was another longbow victory, the French and their horses not knowing which way to turn to avoid lethal shafts. The horse has been denied his due. Used at critical times in concerted frontal action by the Prince and in flanking attack by the Captal, he played his part. Equally sure is that the French horse usage was stupid, the best knights and choicest destriers being killed or maimed. Some destriers undoubtedly became English booty. The withdrawal of Orleans with a third of the French force remains unexplained. It cost France the battle, but for the French cavalry to fight on foot among despised infantry went against their cavalry tradition.[20]

AN UNEASY PEACE

By the land-grabbing 1360 Treaty of Brétigny, Poitou, Limousin, Quercy, Marche, Angoumois and North Ponthieu were settled on Edward III, who also reclaimed Aquitaine, retained Calais and got a huge sum agreed for King John's ransom. In return the English king relinquished his claim to the French Crown. Uneasy peace ensued for nine years. The English taxed their French 'subjects' to the point of rebellion. Both countries prepared for war. By the 1370s Edward III's military acumen was spent, his heir terminally ill. Slowly, under Charles V (reigned 1364–80) France whittled away at the English possessions until only Calais and a strip between Bordeaux and Bayonne remained. In 1377 the Black Prince's ten-year-old son, Richard of Bordeaux, succeeded his grandfather as Richard II of England; in 1380 the unstable Charles VI (reigned 1380–1422) became King of France. Under minority rule both countries suffered – peasant revolts and religious upheavals in England; family dissensions in France as Burgundians and Orleanists fought for power. In 1394 Richard II's marriage to Isabella of France extended peace. When Henry Bolingbroke, Duke of Lancaster, supplanted and murdered Richard in 1399, consolidating his position as Henry IV was paramount. On his accession in 1413 Henry V determined to regain England's losses in France.

AGINCOURT: 25 OCTOBER 1415

Henry dickered over truce renewal terms, reiterating the claim to the French Crown, and demanding the residue of John II's ransom, enlargement of Aquitaine's boundaries, and Charles VI's daughter Catherine in marriage.[21] The expected failure of talks gave him the excuse to launch war on France for which he had been preparing throughout 1414 and 1415. As the truce ended, the English at Calais overran the Boulonnais.[22]

Campaign preparations were impressive. A subsidy and hefty borrowing without interest from the Church, cities, towns and individuals raised cash. A fleet of 1,500 ships was gathered, from 20-ton minnows to the 500-ton flagship *Trinite Royale*. Many were commandeered, others hired, some provided by the Cinque Ports. Indentures with magnates and military leaders raised 2,000 men-at-arms and 8,000 archers, each contract's terms explicit. Transport to and from France was to be at the king's cost for retinues, baggage and horses. An estimated

25,000 horses were embarked. Dukes were allowed 50 each, earls 24, knights 6, esquires 4, archers 1. Combatants utilized over two-thirds of the total. Among them were the dukes of York, Clarence and Gloucester, 8 earls, 2 bishops and 19 barons, and if they took up their full allotment, they must have claimed much of the equestrian capacity. In addition were saddle-horses for many non-combatants, sumpters and carthorses; especially sturdy horses were needed for Henry's significant artillery train. On 11 April 1415 writs went out for supplies, including orders to Robert Hunt, Sergeant of the Wagons of the Household, to provide carpenters, wheelwrights, smiths and materials for carts; to Stephen Ferrour, Sergeant of the King's Farriers, for smiths and iron for horseshoes; and to John Southmede, cartwright, to provide 62 carts with harness, halters and collars. Sheriffs were to procure cattle and provisions to feed the army in its first weeks in France.[23] In Henry's retinue the largest group was his equestrian establishment – his Master of Horse John Waterton and his grooms; John Othvin, Surveyor of the Stable; Nichol Harewode, Clerk of the Stable; Ranulph Apulton, Clerk of the King's Avenrie (horsefeed); fodder purveyors; Gerard de la Strade, Groom of the Horses; Richard Hodel and Thomas Smith, yeomen smiths; Richard Bere and other saddlers; and the Clerk of the Marshalcy.[24]

The fleet sailed on 11 August arriving 3 miles (nearly 5 km) off Harfleur on the 14th. Harfleur was invested on 18 August, surrendering on 22 September; by 8 October, his back secure, Henry embarked on a *chevauchée* to Calais, but with an army reduced to fewer than 1,000 men-at-arms and about 5,000 archers. Many had died of disease, others been invalided home, and a large garrison was left at Harfleur. Hugging the coast to the River Eu they swung east on learning Blanchetaque ford was guarded by 6,000 French under Marshal Boucicault. The French shadowed Henry along the Somme valley. At Fouilloy he left the river, turning south to Nesle, where under threat of the burning of their houses peasants revealed unguarded crossings at Voyennes and Bethencourt. Repairs to the smashed causeway over the marshes delayed them but by nightfall on 19 October they were across, camping at Monchy la Gache, six miles from the French camp.[25] On 20 October heralds issued the French challenge, querying Henry's route and drawing a brusque response: 'Straight to Calais, and if our enemies try to disturb us in our journey, it will not be without the utmost peril.'[26] On 24 October Henry reached Maisoncelles to find the French blocking his route. The English had ridden 260 miles (420 km) in 16 days, had crossed several rivers and skirmished often, and were famished from tramping through stripped land now sodden with rain that rotted some of the archers' clothes; dysentery still raged. On the 25th Henry's depleted force faced over 20,000 French in a passage half a mile (0.8 km) wide between the wooded environs of Agincourt and Tramecourt.

Henry deployed his cavalry on foot in three units, integrated with archers somewhat to their fore and curving in on their flanks. Each archer carried a pointed stake. Under cover of the Tramecourt woods 200 mounted archers went to hit the French flank. Rain had softened the earth to a morass. The French were deployed in four lines to Henry's one, the first and third dismounted cavalry in full armour, the second archers. Mounted men-at-arms brought up the rear; mounted units were on both flanks.

The English, exhorted by old Sir Thomas Erpingham, advanced first; once within range they loosed a hail of arrows. To prevent arrows piercing their vizors, many of the French lowered their heads and lumbered forward. Casualties mounted rapidly; the crush in the dismounted ranks barred efficient use of weapons. The mounted units on the flanks swept forward, many horses being impaled on the hedge of archers' stakes. The 800 men under Sir Clugnet de Brabant, detailed to break the English line, were reduced to seven score. Horses ran amok maddened with pain, bolting into the advancing foot, breaking its line and creating such chaos that the rearguard cavalry fled. Seizing the opportunity, English archers wielded swords, daggers, axes, killing every downed Frenchman except those worth a ransom. But seeing the rearguard cavalry re-forming, Henry ordered that all prisoners be massacred, angering their captors who were thus bilked of profit. The resurgent 600 horse under the counts of Marle and Fauquembergue were almost all killed or captured. The French lost from 8,000 to 10,000 men, including 100 magnates and 1,500 lesser nobles. Henry's losses were small. Estimates vary between 500 and 125; many were only injured.[27]

After Henry's death nearly seven years later, the French slowly regained their losses. At the battle of Formigny in 1450 Sir Thomas Kyriel's 4,300 were massacred in an attempt to salvage Normandy for England. Three years later the old Earl of Shrewsbury, one of Henry's Agincourt generals, trying to hold Guienne led his army into French guns at Castillon.[28]

THREE

Encounters with the Orient and Africa

Western Europe echoed to the hoofbeats of acquisitive armies. Italy was under constant pressure. The Holy Roman Emperor controlled the north, the Pope was temporal lord of the Papal States, Normans held the kingdoms of Naples and Sicily. In 1198, Emperor Frederick II (1197–1250) had inherited Naples and Sicily from his Norman mother. During his reign flarings between the Guelf/Papal and Ghibbeline/Imperial factions caused the 20-year Lombard War. He was succeeded briefly by his legitimate son Conrad in 1250, and then by his bastard son Manfred, who fought for 12 years to keep his inheritance, losing his life at the battle of Benevento in 1266 to Charles of Anjou; the Pope had offered Naples and Sicily to Charles provided he drove Manfred out. Charles brought in Provençal men-at-arms and hired mercenaries in France and the Low Countries with papal money.[1] Charles of Anjou's harsh rule (Sicily 1260–82, Naples 1266–85) was exacerbated when a soldier raped a Sicilian girl on her way to Vespers on Easter Monday 1282, sparking a revolt. The islanders slew the French soldiers and then offered Sicily to Pedro III of Aragon (Aragon 1276–85, Sicily 1282–5)[2] starting the Franco/Spanish struggle for dominance in Italy. Ramon Muntaner's Catalan chronicle illustrates equine trade, breed provenance, mounted warfare, and the use of warhorses carried by Spain's predatory fleet.

The period was one of military change during which the warhorse's importance peaked; as cavalry became accustomed to fight on foot, the horse's role altered but was still vital, especially on long-range campaigns needing speed. It was the age of the professional soldier and the Free Companies with members from many lands – Germans, Hungarians, Catalans, Spaniards, French, English, Italians, etc. Many companies gravitated to Italy; others were raised there, friction between Italy's city-states fostering their growth from the late thirteenth century. They fought under a contract – a *condotta* – which stipulated length of service, pay, services and equipment required, numbers, types and value of horses. Once a *condotta* expired, *condottieri* could fight for another paymaster, but a contract usually specified an interim period before they could take up arms against their former paymaster.

Cavalry was the most important part of a *condottieri*'s force, but the roles of infantry and mounted archers gradually increased. Other sources used to raise

Albrecht Dürer's portrait of a man-at-arms showing the type of horse the average man could afford. This is a true representation of a horse used for war. (Graphische Sammlung Albertina)

The type of rouncy a less-well-off condottieri *would have made do with. Pisanello's drawing shows a raw-boned animal in need of good fodder. It also shows the horse with slit nostrils, a medieval practice intended to improve breathing (the horse was probably broken-winded). (Photo: R.M.N.; reproduced by courtesy of Louvre Departement des Arts Graphiques)*

troops were feudal levies in many lands, town militias in Italy, the *arrière ban* in France, but it was the day of the mercenary and the contract band was a two-edged sword. Offering superior fighting qualities, bands found ready employment. When unemployed they roved at will terrorizing whole areas, looting, extorting maintenance for men and animals. Harvest time was lucrative; mercenary leaders were almost guaranteed a hefty sum to stay away.

Examples of contract bands in and out of work occurred in 1351–3 during a period of sustained aggression between Florence and Milan. Targeted by the Visconti of Milan, Florence experienced trouble in raising the city militia for her defence. The Milanese army of 5,000 heavy and 2,000 light cavalry and 6,000 foot, commanded by Giovanni da Oleggio, included a German heavy contingent. They marched unopposed into Tuscany over the Appennines, reaching the environs of Florence where their scouts and foragers roamed at will. Threatened with industrial action by underpaid workers, Florence quelled dissident leaders by threatening mutilation. Only then would the city militia man the walls, but forces were insufficient to oppose the Visconti in the field. At most Florentine cavalry was 2,000, but was under strength and lacked a leader, for independent commanders feared fighting for the Viscontis' enemy. By September only 1,500 horse and 3,500 foot had been raised, but Scarperia in the fertile Mugello defended so stubbornly that as winter approached Oleggio withdrew. Throughout the winter of 1351/2 Florence, allied with Perugia, Siena and Arezzo, hired forces. Florentine cavalry expanded to 3,000; the four towns were obliged to keep an extra 3,000 horse and 1,000 foot; Florence negotiated with the Emperor Charles IV for 6,000 very expensive German heavy cavalry. Impressed by this threat, Giovanni Visconti concluded a peace with Tuscany in April 1353. Thousands of *condottieri* were now unemployed.

Concurrently the Grand Company of Fra Monreale, a renegade Hospitaller ousted from Naples by her *condottiere* captain Malatesta of Rimini in 1352, was ravaging its way north, its numbers rapidly expanding with ex-Milanese troops. In 1354 Tuscany was wasted. Perugia and Siena bought Monreale off; on 7 July Florence paid 25,000 florins for two years' immunity. Shortly after this, Monreale was taken and executed by Cola di Rienzo, but his successor Conrad of Landau was equally rapacious. Meanwhile Florence upgraded her forces, leaguing with Pisa, Perugia and Volterra, a joint force of 1,800 horse and 900 crossbowmen being agreed. Florence also raised 4,800 crossbowmen for city and countryside defence, 2,500 stationed at the Appennine passes into Tuscany ready for Landau's prompt appearance when the truce expired. Barred in 1356 and 1357 Landau appeared in 1358 asking permission to cross Tuscany on his way to aid Siena against Perugia. Florence restricted passage to a mountain route where Landau's company was ambushed by mountain folk, Florentine forces attacking survivors, but Landau had captured four influential Florentines who negotiated cessation of hostilities and led the company to safety at Imola where they were joined by German mercenaries who had deserted their paymasters at Perugia and Siena to exact vengeance on Florence. Landau's predations ended when Florence hired Malatesta who forced Landau out of Tuscany into Lombardy in 1359. The cost had been enormous in money, lives, agriculture and horseflesh.

In France after the 1360 Treaty of Brétigny many soldiers were unemployed. Branded *écorcheurs* – skinners – some drifted towards Italy, among them the German Albert Sterz's White Company of 3,500 horse and 2,000 foot. They were hired by Montferrat, Milan and then Pisa, which paid 40,000 florins for four months in summer 1363. The company ravaged around Prato, Florence and the Arno valley unopposed, then, laden with booty, drifted back to Pisa, which promptly renewed its *condotta* for six months at 150,000 florins. In spring 1364, now under Sir John Hawkwood, the company again ravaged Florentine territory.[3]

TROOP ORGANIZATION AND CAVALRY NUMBERS

Border defence increased the need for cavalry and as weaponry included greater use of crossbows after 1250, and eventually firearms, changes from mail and/or leather armour to plate accelerated. More horses were completely covered, the fatigue factor rising. Consequently cavalrymen needed more mounts; out of this grew the unit called 'the lance'.[4] Other factors not usually considered but allied to fatigue were heat build-up, dehydration, loss of body salts via sweat, and a syndrome called tying up (azoturia), a build-up of lactic acid which means a horse cannot function: myoglobin causes the urine to appear bloody, the hindquarters go rigid and there is often muscle damage. As most campaigning was in summer many such incidents must have occurred but the veterinary reason was not understood. The lance unit was to remain the cavalry unit until the end of the Renaissance. Its size varied at different times, its composition in different countries. The basic Italian unit was man-at-arms, sergeant and page – two effectives plus one groom cum servant. In a 1336 campaign a mercenary lance in Venetian employ comprised two men, each lance receiving 9 ducats a month, out of which they had to fund food and accommodation, and stabling for their horses (which included fodder). Horses lost in service were paid for. In 1373 the lance was increased by one; pay had risen to 18 ducats but, presumably because of the enhanced sum, horses lost had to be replaced at the rider's cost.[5] Though increased, such pay was hardly adequate if new horses had to be purchased as even a poor-quality nag cost at least 20 ducats,[6] the price prevailing a century later. However, inflation in horse prices was almost zero for many decades at a time.

In the mid-fifteenth century the lance grew to a four- or even five-man unit. There was not the same pressure on Italian cavalry to dismount to fight. The larger French lance included four effectives – a man-at-arms, a coutillier and two mounted archers.[7] Horse casualties increased as the trooper in his carapace became hard to despatch. Earlier it was considered 'bad war' to harm the horse, but by the late 1400s it was normal practice. Replacement needs spiralled. Early in the fifteenth century Milan was reliably reputed to have 20,000 cavalry and the same of foot. Venice fielded 9,000 horse in 1404 against Verona and Padua. In 1439 the Venetian chronicler Sanuto estimated Italy had 70,000 cavalry; in the three major armies the cavalry numbers were Milan 19,750, Venice 16,000 and Aragon (Sicily) 17,800. In 1456 the Milanese ambassador to France told Charles VII that Milan had 12,000 peacetime cavalry. This was higher than France's standing army, the *Compagnies d'Ordonnance*. Ludovico Gonzaga, Marquis of Mantua, was Milan's Lieutenant-General and kept 1,300 stand-by cavalry, boosting it to 3,000 in wartime.[8]

The numbers above give only a partial picture. Chroniclers note horse movements between countries; stud records spanning more than a century show Mantuan acquisitions. Added to combatants' mounts were horses for the lance's non-combatants, mail horses, gun-carriage teams (see Chapter 5), carthorses and pack-horses. The largest contract companies resembled ambulatory cities with foragers, provisioners, etc. Home breeding could not provide enough animals so horse-dealers had a lucrative international trade.

THE ALBANIAN STRADIOTS

Philippe de Commynes compared Stradiots to Spanish *jinetes*:

> Stradiots dress as Turks except for the head . . . They are hardy people, sleep in the open year round as do their horses. They are all Greek, and they come from the places which Venetians own in Greece, some from Nauplia in Argolis, in the Morea, and others from Albania around Durazzo, and their horses are strong and are all Turkish horses.[9]

Stradiots are linked to the rule of Scanderbeg (1443–67). Albania had fallen to the Ottomans but Turkish custom permitted chieftains autonomy provided they swore allegiance to the sultan. One such was John Castriot of Kruje, north-east of Tirana. To ensure his loyalty his sons were taken hostage and trained to Ottoman service; one son, Gerji, rose high and was created Skander Bey, but in 1443, after a Hungarian victory over the Turks at Nish, deserted, took his father's fortress at Kruje and in the ensuing years united Albania, freeing it from the Turks. He bequeathed it to Venice, which kept it till 1501, relinquishing it to the sultan after decades of fighting. In the interim Albanians settled in Sicily, Naples, Venice, Calabria and Greece. Venice rapidly took advantage of Albanian light cavalry's fighting qualities in her 1463–79 war against the Turks. Stradiots were renowned for their courage, ill-discipline, tendency to desert for better opportunities, and dishonesty when collecting pay in Italy while back home relatives were also claiming on their behalf; on balance, however, Venice found them indispensable, especially in policing her overseas territories and guarding coasts and borders against Turkish raiders.

They fought unarmoured, except for a shield, breastplate and Turkish-type helmet, armed with double-ended lance, shorter javelin, sword, mace or club; some used crossbows. Their uses were many – reconnaissance, harrying after battle and attacking the enemy's rear and baggage train during a march (when the desire to pillage often overrode military orders).

They were soon sought by other military leaders, their numbers increasing dramatically. After Fornovo (1495) Charles VIII of France recruited 8,000. The Emperor Maximilian (reigned 1493–1519) hired 400, his grandson Charles V (reigned 1519–55) enrolled them *en masse*. In England they served under Edward Seymour in Henry VIII's vicious 1545 autumn campaign against Scotland.[10]

The Stradiots' Turkish horses were lithe, tough, swift and considerably brainier than the ponderous equines beloved of northern armies. Some Stradiots must eventually have resorted to other light breeds.

HORSES IN THE OCCIDENTAL SPHERE

Since the Roman era Italy had bred and imported quality horses. Spain and North Africa produced ancient and contemporary warhorses. In Hannibalic times Spanish cavalry went to Carthage and North African horse to Spain with inevitable crossbreed spin-offs. Spanish horses were also brought into Italy by Hannibal at Cannae (216 BC) and by Julius Caesar for his campaigns in Gaul (58–50 BC). Later Spain received much Barb blood via Moorish cavalry, whose officers from Damascus introduced some Arabian, Anazeh Arab and Turcoman blood; the Arabs had looted horses since the early days when they raided from the peninsula to Turcoman territory.[11]

From this amalgam of the oriental and the indigenous Spain produced the Andalusian, coveted by all European noble houses. It was the tap-root of much of Italy's medieval stock.

The dispersal of warhorse breeds/types can be traced mostly through the passage of armies and changed ownership via booty, tribute and, occasionally, sale. Sometimes the breed was named, especially in the Orient and India, but in Europe it was normal to judge a horse by price, which is no true guide to 'a well-bred horse'. However, from the fourteenth century onwards we have journals written by travellers, some of whom were keen observers and able horsemen. Distinctive qualities emerge; from type we move to specific breed. But apart from pure Arabians in Mamlūk studs and India there was no fanatical adherence to purity, although one Italian stud came close: the 'Gonzagas'.

THE GONZAGAS

The Gonzagas of Mantua were Italy's premier horse-breeders exporting to many countries. Gonzagan fascination with quality horses dated to at least 1329 when Luigi Gonzaga started racing at Mantua. The ducal stud specialized in perfecting certain strains, Margonaras successfully outstripping imported Barbs in 1462. Mantua was a magnet drawing horses from many lands. Gift horses came from Naples; agents scoured Sicily, unsuccessfully in 1470 but with better fortune in 1477 when they bought 16 entires priced from 12 to 17 Venetian ducats. Other sources from the 1450s onwards were Spain, Barbary, Sardinia, England, Ireland, France, Italy. Orientals came from the Ottoman Empire, some described as Turkish, others as Arabians. Lady Wentworth, while doing sterling work, and using Mantuan archives, nevertheless frequently *assumes* all orientals to be Arabians. However, significant numbers of Arabians were bred in Mamlūk territories, which fell to the Ottomans in 1517. Other tribes by transhumance and horse-breeding activities, notably the Anazeh, put Arabian stock into the Ottoman sphere. In 1488 the Mantuan stud held 650 horses, each breed being kept separately. From the 1497 stallion list a clue to breeds emerges as the custom was to name a stallion for its donor, breeder, or place of provenance; the records hint that Frisian horses also stood at Mantua – the King of France gave one called Frisonello, and another was named Frisone.[12] France had long used Frisian horses in her armed forces (see p. 14). Other magnates would have tried emulating the Gonzagas. *Condottieri*, many of whom were wealthy landowners, also bred for their own war needs.[13]

THE ORIENTAL IMPACT

During the Crusades Europeans evaluated Turcoman horses, a lively trade existing in 'Turkish' stock (i.e. Turcoman/Turkmene). There was an influx of Turcoman stock into eastern Europe (see below). In the Balkans Ottoman influence clamped down, was broken, was reimposed, and 'Turkish' stock came into Venetian territories. Indeed there is evidence from Venetian sources that Persian horses infiltrated Ottoman armies and therefore were involved in their land conquests when the Grand Turk fought on occidental and Persian fronts. Venice, the major trading syndicate, kept diplomatic contact throughout the Mediterranean, Anatolia and Persia. Envoys to the Persian court left detailed reports from which the equestrian situation regarding Ottoman and Persian cavalry can be seen, as well as equine and equestrian interaction between eastern Europe, the Orient and the Tatars (see below).

In 1471 Uzun Hassan of the Ak Koyunlu Turcomans, and ruler of Persia, sent his ambassador to Venice 'to comfort the Signoria to Folowe the warres against the said Ottamanno'. Venice's answer was to send Josefa Barbaro and the ambassador back with the fleet gathered to attack the Ottomans in Corcyra (Corfu); it carried much military *matériel* for Uzun Hassan. There were 99 galleys, mostly from Venice but with Spain, Cyprus, Rhodes and the Pope contributing, which contained 440 horses, most Stradiots' mounts, 200 crossbowmen and handgunners, their officers and various officials. Artillery included bombards, springards, *schiopetti* (handguns), powder, shot, wagons (gun-carriages) and lesser artillery of 'divers sorts'. After Corfu fell the ambassadors continued by sea to Adana where they struck inland to cross the Euphrates into Uzun Hassan's territory, reaching Tabriz after a hazardous journey: Kurds killed the Turcoman ambassador, Barbaro's secretary and two others, injuring the rest who fled on horseback, losing pack-horses and all their baggage.

Barbaro observed a Turcoman muster and was impressed by the numbers and types of cavalry, but said the only horses for sale in the ambulatory city following the army were 'nags worth between 8 and 10 ducats that come out of Tartarie which the merchants bring at 4 or 5,000 at a clappe . . . being sold for 4, 5, or 6 ducats being litell and serving onlie for carriage [pack]'. He also noted the quality horses from Baghdad presented to Uzun Hassan.[14]

Ambrogio Contarini left for Uzun Hassan's court in 1473 travelling via Germany, Poland, Lower Russia, the steppes and the Black Sea. He presented a German saddle-horse to Governor Pammartin in Polish Russia and was asked to leave his other horses there, as they were entires, and to proceed with Russian horses. At that time Russia needed sizeable breeding stock. Unloading at Caffa, as the condition of his nine horses had deteriorated, he saw mounted slave-catchers under a *subasi* (Turkish officer) rounding up captives. He travelled through Georgia during the rebellion of Uzun Hassan's son 'Gurlumameth' (Oghurlu Muhammad) who was raiding with 3,000 mounted bandits up to Tabriz.[15] There Contarini, the Burgundian and Muscovite envoys and two 'Turkish' ambassadors were told to return and to inform

> their sovereigns and the Christian princes that he [Uzun Hassan] had intended fighting the Ottomans but because of his son's rebellion his forces were split, some against his son, some to 'annoy the Ottoman' but at a future time he would be ready to attack the Ottomans.

Barbaro informed Contarini that Uzun Hassan had over 20,000 cavalry with 'good and handsome horses'.

Contarini and the Muscovite returning via Georgia and Mingrelia had horses, money and arms stolen and found Caffa taken by Ottomans; they stayed almost a year in Astrakhan, beset by money troubles and Tatars, and left on 17 August 1476, with a caravan of almost 300 riders and 200 led horses for use as food and for sale in Russia. The Tatar ponies were wild, timid, unshod and small. *En route* they saw 400 horses from the previous year's caravan roaming loose, escapees from Tatars who preyed on travellers. Once past Riazan, Contarini felt safer as Duke Zuanne of Moscow (Ivan III) had a border patrol of Service Tatars. Contarini went by horse-sled from Moscow to Warsaw, there purchasing horses for travel to Frankfurt.[16]

Caterino Zeno and Giovan Maria Angiolello also travelled to Anatolia and Persia. Both give details of Ottoman and Persian armies from the time of Uzun Hassan to that of his grandson Ismail. Angiolello appears to have been a roving envoy at one time in Mustapha's Turkish camp, much later in that of Ismail. They note the huge booty from engagements between Persian and Ottoman forces; Angiolello especially comments on the 1,000 horses that the Ottomans acquired from Tabeada alone after their defeat of the Persians in 1473.[17]

Venice sent Vicentio d'Allesandri to the Persian court of Shah Tahmasp in 1571. His task was to get Persia to attack the Ottomans by land, so drawing off their attack on Venetian Cyprus. Tahmasp declined; the Cyprus war ended in peace between Ottoman and Venice, but Persia lost out, Murad, Selim II's son (reigned 1566–74), taking Media, much of Greater Armenia and Tabriz. D'Allesandri gives the most informative description of Persian horses:

> The horses are so well trained and are so good and handsome that there is now no need to have them brought from other countries. This has happened since the arrival of Sultan Bayazeth who fled into Persia with some magnificent Caramanian and Arab horses, which were given away throughout the country, and afterwards he was executed by order of the king. There were 1,000 horses and mares in existence. On this account there has never been so fine a breed, and the Ottomans even have not got one like it.[18]

For centuries Persia exported horses to India, sending pure Persian and Gulf Arab (Persian cross Arab) so it would seem the Arab was used earlier in Persian studs. It also appears that Persian blood was widely dispersed via the Ottomans. In ancient times Persia was renowned for superb horses. Carmania (Cilicia) was next to Cappadocia, also famous for excellent horses.[19] Clearly these areas continued producing good stock.

IMPORTS AND DEALERS

A regular feature of a medieval army was the horse-trader(s). Fairs attracted itinerant horse-copers who carried on a significant international trade. There were embargoes (English, French and Spanish bans have been noted above, and Hungary banned exports until the Hapsburg era[20]) but export licences could be obtained, and the frequency with which bans were reiterated shows they were constantly flouted. Hungary and Germany were main suppliers of warhorses, German dealers prominent. Pandolfo Malatesta bought four great Hungarian warhorses at 200 ducats each from Hermes Bentivoglio in 1507 when the cheapest mount cost about 20 ducats.[21] De la Brocquière described Hungarian horse-trade in the 1430s:

> Zegedin is a large country town. Many wild horses are brought thither for sale . . . should any one want 3 or 4,000 they could be procured within the town, and they are so cheap that a very good road horse may be bought for 10 Hungarian florins . . . From Zegedin I came to Pest . . . the country from one town to the other was good and level and full of immense herds of horses . . . Pest is inhabited by many horse-dealers and whoever may want 2,000 good horses they can furnish the quantity. They sell by stables full containing 10 horses; and their price for each stable is 200 florins. I looked into several, where two or three horses alone were worth that price. They come for the most part from the mountains of Transylvania . . . The country is excellent for breeding them, from the quantity of grass it produces.[22]

The Spaniard Pero Tafur doing his Grand Tour in the mid-1430s visited horse fairs at Cologne, Frankfurt and Medina (in Castile) but reckoned Antwerp the largest with horses of every type.[23] In the late thirteenth century Domingo de la Figuera of Saragossa grew wealthy on regular sales of Castilian horses, 20 or 30 at a time, in Gascony and Navarre, doing particularly well in Toulouse and Bordeaux.[24] After every major battle demand would be heavy. At Caravaggio, on 24 September 1448, 10,000 horses were killed. Whatever the level of hostilities, from a skirmish to a full-scale battle, horses succumbed, and some of the new military had nasty reputations in their treatment of enemy mounts, the Stradiots for stabbing them, the Almugavars for disembowelling.

THE CHRONICLERS

Ramon Muntaner recounted Aragon's thirteenth-century exploits, Philippe de Commynes those of fifteenth-century France. Both observed the equestrian context.

Pedro III of Aragon was rarely at peace. Boaps of Tunisia withheld tribute; Pedro determined to exact it. Fief-holders were ordered to raise mounted contingents, ships and horse transports (*tarides*) were built, arrangements were made to ship wheat and oats to Collo (Constantine) on the North African coast. Armourers worked feverishly, engineers produced siege engines, quarrymen cut ballista stones.

In June 1282, 20,000 Almugavar mountain infantry, 8,000 crossbowmen and 1,000 knights landed at Collo, but Boaps had died. His son Bugron requested Spanish aid against the Saracens. When Bugron offered to turn Christian and swear fealty to Pedro, he was assassinated. During the fortifying of Collo daily *razzias* (raids) for animals and captives were made. The Saracen host was reputed to have shot from 30,000 to 100,000 horse and innumerable foot. With conflict imminent, combatants were ordered to arm at dawn, the knights to armour their horses. Muntaner has the Aragonese victorious, the Saracens fleeing unharried for fear they would return to pillage. In fact the Spaniards failed to hold Collo and were left camped on the shore. In the interim the Sicilians revolted against their Angevin king, sending to Collo for Pedro's aid. Responding he embarked troops and horses for Trapani, then Palermo, where he was crowned King of Sicily, provoking war with King Charles who besieged Messina, which 2,000 Almugavars went to relieve. After heavy losses Charles raised the siege, the main Aragonese force harrying him to Reggio, costing him many horse and foot and firing many of his ships and horse-transports. In several sea and land battles the Spaniards took much booty including 200 French horses.[25] The Almugavars then attacked Charles's nephew, Alençon, at Catona, looting goods, horses and mules which were brought to Messina. Subsequently Pedro led a 15-day *razzia* into Calabria, leaving 500 Catalan and Aragonese cavalry to hold it, before returning to Catalonia.[26]

DE LURIA

In 1283 and 1284 the Spanish admiral Roger de Luria won many sea fights against Charles, and successfully raided Malta, Calabria, Apulia, Naples and Corfu, capturing massive French and Angevin tonnage; at one time he secured 300 warhorses and palfreys being shipped for Charles's knights who were sailing to Sicily. Off Naples in 1284 Charles of Taranto, Charles's heir, was captured. He spent the first four years of his reign a prisoner of Aragon.[27]

Around 1285 de Luria harried coastal Provence, raiding inland with 100 horse and many Almugavars, targeting Béziers, Agde and neighbouring territories. Much French shipping, much booty and many horses were taken.[28] He continued his profitable piracy, raiding the Barbary coast, Crete and Candia, and scouring Romania (Byzantium), until his campaign of terror reached Matagrifon (Akova) where 500 French horse and a large body of foot opposed him. He unloaded 150 horse from his galleys and a fierce fight ensued. Victorious, the admiral then sacked Patras and pillaged Cephalonia and the duchy and island of Corfu before sailing for Apulia, landing at Brindisi to be met by 700 French horse. True to their custom his Almugavars attacked the French by disembowelling horses and killing their riders.

The admiral's own horse was killed and he mounted another. His troop accounted for some 400 French horse and considerable foot, garnering much loot.[29]

De Luria's raiding shows how an interchange of horses was possible between mounted pirates and land-based enemy. Although Muntaner downplays Catalan losses, both sides suffered them. Horses were taken as booty, so the troopers' new mounts would have included Barbs, Turcomans, Arabians, Spanish, Neapolitan and French animals. This interchange goes unmarked in history but must have accounted for much mixing, especially as Muslims often rode mares.

ARAGON AND FRANCE

The Pope interfered in the wars, creating Charles of Valois, the second son of Philip III of France, King of Aragon. In 1285 France invaded Aragon with French and papal cavalry, reportedly 18,000, plus many foot, going via Roussillon to the pass of Panisars. The Almugavars repulsed them, despatching 1,000 horses and riders, some of whom fell down the mountainside, but with reinforcements coming up and local monks guiding the French over the pass of Manzara they camped in the plain of Peralada. At dawn Infante Alfonso attacked with 500 horse and 2,000 foot killing over 600 mounted French guards.[30] A woman of Peralada, hearing small harness bells, discovered a French knight trapped in the trench between her garden and that of her neighbour. She thrust at him with a lance, the point going through his thigh and saddle into his horse's side. The horse bucked and reared but, chained to his saddle, the knight could not be thrown. She continued her attack, wounding the horse in the head and stunning it, then seized its reins and demanded the knight's surrender. Escorting him to Peralada she was awarded the knight, his arms and his horse. The knight ransomed himself for 200 gold florins.[31]

At Peralada, King Pedro of Aragon with 200 Almugavars met in combat 400 French knights under the Count of Nevers. Fighting ferociously, Pedro broke his sword, but unhorsed Nevers with a mace blow on his helmet, to be despatched by a squire. The Almugavars wrought such havoc among the horses that none escaped unharmed; the king accounted for over 15 French knights, but was temporarily hampered when his reins were cut (here Muntaner advocates double reins, one of chain, the other leather). As the horse barged about, four Almugavars seized it and tied its reins, rendering it controllable. In this part of the engagement over 300 French knights were killed, the king (*supposedly!*) accounting for over 60. Their horses were so badly mauled that none was worth taking: all had at least seven or eight lance wounds.[32] The French host was reduced to only 3,000 horse by the three killers: sickness, battle and famine. Philip III died on the way home and although his son Philip IV was granted safe passage his rearguard was annihilated, his pack-train pillaged.

AFRICA AGAIN

In new African hostilities Tunis attacked Jerba; Sicily sent 100 horse and 1,500 foot to Jerba's aid, but undisciplined Catalans lost 72 horses and most of the foot in an attack by the Saracen cavalry who now held Jerba, receiving a 300-horse boost from Tunis. Muntaner, sent in with a victualling fleet, found the castle still held for Sicily but its disordered garrison reduced to 30 heavy and 15 light horse. The Saracen leader Alef refused to surrender the island so Muntaner shipped in 200 mercenary Arab horse, raised a further 200 on Jerba and systematically raided Saracen enclaves till the Saracens were driven to one end of the island. Alef then raised 8,000 mainland horse, the first wave arriving in 14 barges and routing the Christians. His captains Jacob ben Atia and Selim ben Margan, holding back on the mainland as Muntaner's sea-attack sank 17 of Alef's transports, negotiated to ransom the Saracen horsemen stranded on Jerba, guaranteeing no further assaults. Muntaner agreed the ransoms of all but Alef and his retinue, awaiting the decision of Fadrique of Sicily (reigned 1296–1336). He sent in 200 horse and 2,000 foot and on Ascension Day 1310 the battle for Jerba was fought. Alef, strong in foot but weak in cavalry, was ground down by repeated Catalan charges and a day-long slogging mêlée in which the horses were the highest casualties – 60 killed, another 60 fatally injured, others wounded though surviving; 17 Catalans died, over 300 were wounded, but Alef's losses were huge and thousands of captives were sold into slavery, the revenue from Jerba and the neighbouring Kerkennas Islands being awarded to Muntaner for three years.[33]

War then erupted between Fadrique and Robert I of Naples (reigned 1309–43) sparked by Fadrique's raid on Calabria. Robert retaliated in a two-pronged attack on Sicily with a host of horse and foot, and on Muntaner's Jerba with 400 horse and 404 siege-engines, but found that by splitting his forces he weakened his attempt on Jerba. He was unable to cope with Fadrique's 60 galleys and the threat of Arab cavalry, now allied, waiting to cross to Jerba's aid. Disease struck his host; most of his cavalry horses also succumbed. A treaty was struck, but was broken in 1325 when Naples attacked Sicily to be repulsed by Fadrique's cavalry and Almugavars.[34]

Sardinia too flared. Pisa claimed it, Aragon invaded and Cagliari sought Pisan aid. Some 1,200 heavy horse, 800 of whom were Germans under Count Nieri, and 6,000 foot, many from Tuscany and Mantua, were defeated by Aragon, and Sardinia and Corsica passed under Aragonese rule.[35]

The main equestrian features running through Muntaner's chronicle are the colossal numbers of horses raised by antagonists and the regularity with which they were shipped across the Straits of Messina, going from Sicily to North Africa, or from Spain to Sicily, mainland Italy and North Africa. Battles and skirmishes accounted for many losses, especially due to Almugavars, but sickness also raged in cavalry lines. The cavalry was drawn from many sources, mostly mercenaries from the Arabs and the Papal States, and *condottieri* from Germany, Provence and the Italian city-states. Estimates of cavalry in the hundreds are believable, but multiples in the thousands need treating, as usual, with caution. Suffice to note that Spain's conquests were largely due to her splendid horses.

BURGUNDY

Philippe de Commynes, born in 1447, entered the service of Charles of Charolais at 17, but transferred from Burgundy to Louis XI of France in 1472. He was present at many military engagements. His analysis of Charolais's character shows him as choleric and rather stupid, with too many aggressive irons in the fire to manage: 'he disdained every piece of advice in the world but his own' and 'was never lacking in courage but was frequently deficient in organization'.[36] Louis was the opposite: wise, cautious, devious, willing to listen to advice, fighting only if guile and diplomacy failed, but gradually expanding French territory at Burgundy's expense.[37]

In 1464 Charolais ordered the seizing of a French warship, imprisoned the Bastard of Rubempré and told Louis's ambassador to inform his king that 'he had given me a good dressing down by the chancellor, but before the year has passed he will have reason to regret it'. Charolais resented France's retaking the Somme towns, relinquished by his father Philip for a hefty price. He marched for Paris in 1465 when Louis was occupied with rebellious nobles in 'the War for the Public Good'. His 1,400 men-at-arms were 'poorly trained, poorly armed', but 'well mounted . . . few could be seen who did not have five or six large horses in their equippage'. All 8,000 archers were mounted, the army accompanied by a large artillery train and enough baggage carts to encircle the entire army. Skirmishing *en route* was followed by fighting up to the gates of Paris. Charolais billeted at Longjumeau, his army at Montlhéry. As Louis's arrival was imminent the Burgundians arrayed for battle. Orders to fight on foot were countermanded. In the confusion of mounting, Louis's forces arrived and archers from both sides started harvesting casualties. French archers were in 'excellent condition', Burgundian 'without order or commandment'. Of Burgundian men-at-arms fewer than 400 had breastplates, and 'not even 50 knew how to lay a lance in rest'; no servant was armed. In the chaotic engagements the balance of power swayed from one side to the other. Burgundians under St Pol crumbled and fled, but those under Charolais broke the French and pursued them hotly until warned that the French were regrouping. On Charolais's return a fleeing French infantryman poked him with a pike, then 15 French men-at-arms charged, inflicting many wounds, and with his gorget lost Charles was in dire straits until 'a stout, heavy, coarse man mounted on a horse of the same proportions' thrust into the mêlée and saved him. Neither side won but as Charolais was on the field when night fell he claimed victory, ordering out 50 lance teams to espy the king's night-quarters. At dawn Burgundy was ready to re-engage when a carter said the French had disappeared. De Commynes had 'a tired old horse who drank a bucketful of wine . . . I never found him in such fine shape or so refreshed'. The Burgundians marched to Etampes. Reinforcements flooded in, the army rising to *c*. 50,000 (de Commynes says 100,000): French nobles, furious at Louis's confiscation of their lands; a huge mounted contingent under the Duke of Brittany; 800 men-at-arms previously in the French *Compagnies d'Ordonnance*; 900 men-at-arms from Burgundy; the Duke of Calabria with 120 fully armoured men-at-arms from Italy, among them the *condottiere* Count of Campobasso; 400 well-mounted crossbowmen, and 50 Swiss foot.

Skirmishes were constant but Burgundy's cavalry slowly evaporated, only 2,000 lance teams remaining and these not as strong as the 2,500 equivalent in Paris. Although Charolais, Calabria and Brittany were strong in artillery it caused 'more fear than losses'. After much wastage of men, mounts and *matériel* Louis appeared at a muster of Burgundy's forces and became reconciled with his disaffected barons. The Treaty of Vincennes was agreed,[38] but by 1470 Charolais, now Duke of Burgundy, was conducting his war of attrition for the Somme towns.

The army mustered at Arras was 'the most powerful and handsome he had ever led for he had 1200 ordinance teams, and they had three archers for one man-at-arms, all of them well armed and well mounted. And in each company they had 10 extra men-at-arms . . . his lands [Burgundy's] were very rich at this time.' The army marched by way of Péronne, Roye and Montdidier into Normandy. Roye fell and its garrison surrendered, leaving behind their horses and harness, except that men-at-arms were each allowed one *courtault* (a horse with cropped ears and docked tail, after the disgusting French habit; the same mutilation was seen in the artillery horses in Charles VIII's invasion of Italy). Subsequently Beauvais was bombarded for 15 days but proved so obdurate that the siege was lifted. Eu, Saint-Valéry-en-Caux and Neufchâtel-en-Bray were taken, the Caux region to Rouen burned. Carelessness cost Burgundy his foragers so the army went hungry, and with winter approaching it retired. The French retook Eu and Saint-Valéry.[39]

In 1474 Burgundy's wealth drew Campobasso back with 1,000 men-at-arms, exceptionally well mounted. He had 3,000 English men plus his own troops 'well mounted and well armed' and with 'long experience' also mustered. The artillery train was large and powerful. All this was launched at Neuss while Burgundy awaited word from England where Edward IV was mustering forces to assail France.[40] By this time de Commynes was on Louis's payroll and commented on his tactic of avoiding open conflict against Burgundy by putting strong garrisons in the towns, knowing that the inertia of a siege would cause Burgundy's inactive army to deteriorate.[41] The siege of Neuss dragged on for a year. The emperor, Louis and Burgundy tried to outfox each other, but eventually an accord was reached, the town surrendered to an apostolic delegate and Burgundy was free to give his much delayed assistance to England in the form of 500 barges (*schuiten*) sent to ferry Edward's horses and *matériel* over. Edward had raised 1,500 men-at-arms and 15,000 archers, all mounted, plus the mounted retinues of each man-at-arms.[42]

Edward's army was indeed impressive but de Commynes's arithmetic somewhat optimistic. A payroll for the French expedition of 1475 shows fewer than 1,000 men-at-arms and *c.* 7,000 archers, not counting 2,000 for Brittany under Lord Audeley and Lord Duras, and 1,000 to be raised by John Sturgeon, Master of the Ordnance, to aid the duke. The *schuiten* must have been crammed. A lance in Edward's army meant one man-at-arms, plus servant(s). All combatants were mounted, the nobility with several horses, men-at-arms ordinarily with three, archers one; plus hundreds for baggage and artillery. John Sturgeon, who commanded the pikemen guarding the artillery, oversaw a huge staff for its transport of 4 officers each having 6 chariotmen and 30 carters. William Rosse, Comptroller of the Ordnance, could impress manpower for the artillery train including harness-makers, wheelwrights and cartwrights, chariotmen (drivers), and collect bolts, stones, gunpowder, etc., and the raw materials needed – leather and seven kinds of wood, plus everything required for crossbows and longbows. He could commandeer shipping over 16 tons to transport them all.[43]

Landing at Calais, Edward expected Burgundy to be there with a large army of men-at-arms, but although Burgundy arrived the bulk of his army was plundering the Barrois and Lorraine. When Edward arrived at Saint-Quentin he anticipated a welcome but found his army assaulted by artillery and cavalry from the garrison; he lost men killed or taken prisoner. Burgundy's aid being lukewarm, Edward struck a deal with Louis. For nine years Edward was to receive annually 50,000 ecus, then the revenue of Guienne. Louis sweetened the deal with '300 carts of the best wines', and Edward's brother the Duke of Gloucester received many gifts including 'well equipped horses'. Edward returned by forced marches to Calais losing many men to a furious Burgundy's ambushes.[44]

Ever rash, Burgundy spent his last two years in a futile war, losing territories in Lorraine and three disastrous battles: Granson and Morat in 1476, Nancy in 1477 where he was killed.

FRENCH INVASION OF ITALY

De Commynes was with the young Charles VIII, King of France (reigned 1483–98) when he invaded Italy. Ludovico Sforza, the usurping lord of Milan feuding with the Neapolitan relatives of the legitimate lord, Gean Galeazzo Sforza, encouraged Charles, as an Angevin descendant, to secure the crown of Naples for France.[45] Seizing Naples proved easy. Leaving Vienne on 22 August 1493, Charles swept down through Italy. On 9 September he reached Asti, acquired by the Duke of Orleans through his marriage to Valentina Visconti. Less than five months later the French reached Naples. Capua, Aversa and Naples negotiated. Aragonese rule had been harsh; women were abused, church authority disdained; loans forced from the nobility; agriculture and animal husbandry exploited for successive kings' profit. In particular the lucrative and militarily important equine industry suffered, for the Aragonese

> took away from them their breeds of horses, of which they had several, and they kept them for themselves and they took care of having them trained, and in such great numbers, whether horses, mares, or colts, that they were estimated at several thousands, and they sent them to graze in various places in the pastures of the lords and others to the great detriment of these people.

One of the nobles' first acts, after opening Naples to Charles, was to pillage Ferrantino's extensive stables, the Spaniard having fled to Ischia.[46]

After staying a year in Naples, losing many troops to disease, Charles left but his return was blocked by a federal Italian army – the first time such an alliance had gathered – under Venice's *condottiere* general Francesco Gonzaga of Mantua. Charles needed to reach Orleanist territory but Gonzaga set a trap at Fornovo on the Taro. On 6 July 1495, a battle was fought, mostly by cavalry. The French were badly mauled, but though the Italians claimed victory, the casualty list negated the claim: Gonzaga had 2,400 men-at-arms, 2,000 light cavalry including 600 Stradiots (not 1,500, as de Commynes said), 10,000 foot; Charles *c.* 900 men-at-arms, *c.* 7,000 foot.[47]

Marshal de Gie's strong vanguard of 350 men-at-arms, 300 dismounted archers from the king's guard, 3,000 Swiss and some mounted crossbowmen drawn from Charles's personal guard of 200 men rode forward as it was feared the Italians would launch an early attack. Great difficulty was experienced in getting the artillery over the Ligurian Appennines near Pontremoli. Artillery horses had to be boosted by baggage animals and by bands of up to 200 Germans (Swiss) who added their muscle power to hauling guns over the mountains and, with the horses, to braking them on the further slopes. Stradiots plagued de Gie's scouts as they descended into the Lombard plain, skirmishing and pricking at the camp periphery throughout the thundery night prior to battle, and looting the huge baggage train estimated at 6,000 mules, horses and donkeys.

The main attack was to be launched on the French rear by Gonzaga, his uncle Rodolfo and Fortebrazzi with 600 fully accoutred men-at-arms, Stradiots and mounted crossbowmen. No doubt Gonzaga's stud provided mounts for his retinue. Back-up was supplied by 200 men-at-arms under the bastard son of the late Duke of Urbino. The Count of Caiazzo with some 400 men-at-arms and a large number of foot fronted de Gie. Bentivoglio of Bologna's son, at the head of 200 men-at-arms, was to lead a second charge after Caiazzo's initial shock. A reserve remained in the Italian camp, but in the event this engaged first. The main battle and rearguard were not close enough to give mutual aid; Gonzaga's contingent had crossed the Taro and come on the French rear. De Commynes wrote that Charles was mounted on a one-eyed black horse called Savoie, 'the most beautiful horse which I have ever seen', which must have been rather small as it made Charles, who was short, appear tall. De Commynes left the safety of the Swiss unit, three of his retinue being killed as he went to join the king. At this juncture Stradiots attacked and pillaged the French baggage killing several guards and at least 100 stablemen. By the time de Commynes arrived Italians were within 100 paces of a vulnerable Charles, his rearguard behind him on his right with 120 lance teams and 100 mounted archers of the Scots Guard who fought as men-at-arms. To his left was cavalry under the Count de Foix.

The Italians, lances in rest, 'came on at an easy gallop'. The French and Scots charged, the king among them, the left hitting the Italian flank. Both sides attacked boldly. Stradiots to the Italian rear, seeing (or thinking) that their side was winning, took off after the baggage mules that were hightailing it towards the distant French van, leaving their men-at-arms in the lurch. These once their lances were spent fled.

The Italian horse under Caiazzo attacked de Gie, but 'when the time came to lay lances in rest, they took fear and broke up in disorder by themselves. The Germans [Swiss] took 15 or 20 of them by their bridles and killed them. The rest fled.' Those around the king routed the Italian horse who fled, strongly harried, though most of the killing was done by valets and servants using hatchets and longswords.

Charles, attended by but one ill-armed *valet de chambre*, was set upon by several men-at-arms but 'the King had the best horse in the world for himself, and he moved around and defended himself' till help came. This suggests the horse was adept in work on the haunches, able to pivot rapidly, avoiding contact.

At this period crude horsemanship was giving way to sophisticated manoeuvres where the horse was more a nimble partner than a steel-clad battering ram.

Meanwhile the men whom de Commynes called 'our group' harried almost to Fornovo before drawing rein to let their tired horses blow before returning to Charles. In all, about 3,500 Italians died, among them several Gonzagas and 60 men-at-arms of Gonzaga's own feudatories. Allowing for numerical licence Italy lost *c*. 3,000, France 200. It was the last of the great *condottieri* cavalry battles, but though victorious the French had hazardous travelling ahead, with the threat of the re-formed Italian army at their back. But as the Italian horses 'were armoured they were not able to catch up . . . and were never within 20 miles of us'.[48]

In 1499 an altogether tougher French king, Louis XII (reigned 1498–1515), invaded Italy, which became the battleground for renewed French and Spanish claims to Italian territory.

FOUR

Eastern Europe and Russia

In eastern Europe horses and steppe ponies were essential partners in war. Cavalry, with rare exceptions, was the senior arm. Over centuries steppe tribes infiltrated eastern Europe – Avars, Magyars and Cumans in Hungary; Bulgars, Pechenegs (Patzinaks), Khazars, Cumans and Mongols in Russia and the lands bordering the Black Sea and the Crimea. Crimean Khans plagued Russia for centuries; Mongols invaded in the 1220s and 1230s, occupying Russia for two hundred years; Lithuania and Poland were frequently raided. Later via eastern Europe and the Balkans the Osmanlis continued their drive for Islamic power. The Baltic arena became the Teutonic Knights' battleground.

The reasons for war varied: the Mongols' territorial and plundering acquisitiveness; German trading proclivities; Russia and Poland/Lithuania's need for Baltic ports; the Teutonic Knights' proselytizing zeal cloaking their land-grabbing aims. War was not only a matter of keeping shamanistic Mongol or Islamic Turk at bay; power-bases within the Christian eastern bloc changed often. When not themselves repulsing Tatars Christian armies used them against their Christian enemies. And Batu Khan's Golden Horde fragmented among warlords within the Russian and Crimean confines.

THE NEED FOR CAVALRY

Eastern Europe's sheer landmass demanded horse armies; much of warfare was raiding so speed was essential; for example, after Moscow won independence from the Tatars in 1480, the Tatars raided Muscovite territory almost yearly until the diplomacy of Grand Prince Ivan III (1462–1505) won a respite, but in the first half of the sixteenth century 43 raids are recorded.[1] Between 1558 and 1582 while Ivan IV (1530–84) committed most of his forces against Livonia for access to the Baltic, Crimean Tatars raided in all but three years. The worst raids were in 1564 against Riazan; in 1569 with a Tatar/Ottoman campaign against Astrakhan; and in 1571 and 1572 against Moscow. In 1571 Devlet Girey fired and looted Moscow's fringes taking 100,000 captives. The Nogay Tatars raided Kazan; in 1572 it took 20,000 Russians to defeat Girey who retreated to the Crimea after huge losses; 1576, 1577 and 1578 saw raids on the Volga Basin in Muscovy.[2]

When the Crimean khan led his horde it numbered 80,000 effectives; his personal retinue was over 1,000. 50,000 or 40,000 respectively marched when the army was led by his second- or third-in-command. In 1501 Mengli Girey ordered that each man should have three horses, plus for each five men a cart; on distant raiding into Poland, Lithuania, Hungary and Moscow baggage was on pack-horses and camels. To maintain speed mounts were changed often.[3] Their 'Christian' enemies, who often turned allies when Orthodox and Catholic considered it expedient to use Tatars in their confused warrings, also required vast herds of horses.

The Russian army was predominantly cavalry, and at the end of the sixteenth century 80 per cent were still mounted gentry.[4] Lithuania originally had 100 per cent cavalry; in 1528 she could raise 200,000; infantry formed a sizeable proportion only after army reforms in 1563, 1565 and 1567 demanded that nobles owing military service send one foot soldier for every two horsemen.[5] Poland had a high reputation throughout Europe for effective cavalry.[6] Moldavia gained freedom from Hungarian overlordship in the mid-fourteenth century and from no more than 50,000 families raised *c.* 50–60,000; most were mounted but fought on foot.[7] Other nations purchased warhorses from Moldavia and Wallachia. In 1569 Devlet Girey bought 700 Wallachian horses to boost Crimean herds, which were often under strength.[8]

THE RUSSIAN AND EASTERN EUROPEAN EQUINE MATRIX

Horse supply can be traced more readily from the Mongol and Osmanli periods, with specific breeds often noted in contemporary sources. Two main sources were steppe pony types, and oriental breeds that came largely as a result of Ottoman incursions into Hungary, Poland and the Crimea, and by direct trading with Osmanlis by countries subject to the Turk. Arabian, Turcoman and Persian could be found, plus the crosses bred for numbers rather than quality.

RUSSIA

Higher-ranking Tatars had superior horses. One was the Argamak, variously and contradictorily described as: a fine warhorse; a special breed of horse but no good for war; a thoroughbred; a horse able to cover 100-plus miles (160-plus km) a day.[9] It appears as a horse of exceptional endurance capabilities, but was a type, not a distinct breed, although a superior specimen could be designated an Argamak. A Kabard Argamakern crossed with a Khirgiz steppe mare gave nineteenth-century Ural Cossacks a superb mount.[10]

The Kabardin comes from the Caucasus: 'its origin is lost in antiquity and the breed is in fact a complex hybrid produced as a result of crossing horses of the Mongolian root with eastern breeds'. It is hardy, sure-footed, enduring, fast and recovers rapidly from excessive exertion. It stands *c.* 15 hh; conformation assets are deep chest, hard legs and excellent hooves that often require no shoes. This means good heart-room and sound legs and hooves, vital in modern endurance horses and history's warhorses.

The Karabair, indigenous to Uzbekistan and Tadjikistan, is another ancient breed with input from Mongolian and oriental stock. Raised by an equestrian people where lush lucerne and ample barley grow, the Karabair has endurance, strength and a sound constitution. It stands an inch or so less than the Kabardin.[11]

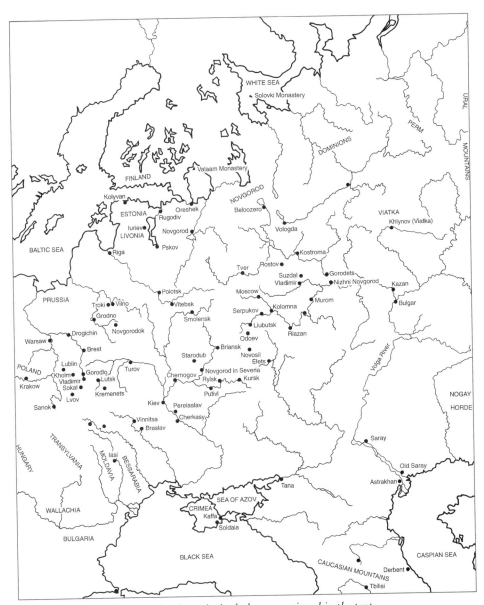

Eastern Europe and Russia, showing principal places mentioned in the text.

These breeds were located in the Mongol empire of the period of Russia's fall to Batu Khan and lay also in the pathway of Seljuks and Osmanlis, only the southern tip of the Caspian Sea separating Turcoman homelands from their paths to conquest. A backtrace to Russia's early equine supply is very revealing. The Mongols brought their own and allied Turkic ponies, but just prior to General Subudei's probe into Russia the Mongols conducted a campaign in Khwarazm in 1219–20. Its capital Samarkand and other cities, among them Bokhara, Khojend, Otrar, fell to Subudei. Tabriz bought safety with tribute in silver and thousands of horses. Other herds would have supplied droves of additional mounts from areas rich in quality horses: Samarkand was not far from Ferghana; Persia, Khorassan, Fars, Kabul – areas producing superb horses. Kabul was a major medieval horse-trading centre (see Chapter 8). Tribute was regularly paid in horses.[12]

The Russians also needed horses by the drove and in the sixteenth century largely depended on herds driven annually from Astrakhan and neighbouring districts after a deal was struck in Moscow between Tatar and Muscovite. A contingent of Tatar service cavalry and *c.* 200 *streltsy* musketeers escorted the drove, which during Ivan IV's reign was well over 50,000. Once in Riazan province it was considered safe to dispense with all but a few dozen protective cavalry. In Moscow up to 8,000 prime head were siphoned off for the Imperial stable. The drove would have been mostly steppe types but have included some Argamaks.[13]

Russia had its indigenous wild horses/ponies as did Poland and Lithuania; these differed little from Mongolian ponies. Later all would have drawn from the same sources.

Grand Duke Vladimir Monomach (1115–25) boasted of his equestrian skill:

> at Chernigov I even bound wild horses with my bare hands or captured 10 or 20 live horses with the lasso, and besides that, while riding along the Rus river I caught these same wild horses barehanded.

Horse- and cattle-breeding was a large part of the Kievan economy, the nobility raising horses to mount retainers in the constant feuding between various houses, or to repel nomadic inroads. A Master of the Stables oversaw an estate's equestrian enterprise; the largest estates boasted huge herds. In a raid by the Davidovichi on the Olgovichi 3,000 mares and 1,000 stallions were lifted. Although Turkish nomads from the east and the Cumans constantly pestered Kievan Russia she also employed independent Turkish warriors and whole tribes as mercenaries, many of whom settled in South Russia. Their mounts added to equine resources; others came from Russia's oriental trade and from steppe nomads, particularly the Pechenegs who sold whole droves attended by herders, mostly from the Khop tribe. From this came *khop*, 'a herder', later transmuted into *kholop*, 'a slave'; a prince's herder was usually his slave. Many grooms and herdsmen were of Turkish extraction.[14]

The *De Administrando Imperio* of Constantine Porphyrogenitus (905–59) shows the position Pechenegs held in regard to Russia. The Byzantines bought their friendship to use as a shield against possible Russian inroads around the Dniester and Dnieper. Byzantium also retained friendship with the Alans to use against the

Khazars in the Sarkel around the confluence of the Donets and Don, and the Chersonnesus in the Crimea.[15]

The Arab historians Gardezi, Ibn Rusta and Al Bekri wrote of the tribes inhabiting the periphery of early medieval Russia: the Volga Bulgars (Bulkars), the Khazars, the Burtas (Burdas) astride the middle Volga between the Bulgars and Khazars, and the Pechenegs (Bajnaks, Bajanakiyya). The Bulgars were hostile to the Burtas, who were subject to the Khazars and had to pay them tribute of 10,000 horsemen. The Khazars levied military service on their own tribesmen according to personal wealth, and yearly raided the Pechenegs. They could thus field 10,000 horse raised from the Burtas, paid troops and their own tribesmen owing mounted service. Some were 'experienced men' – mercenaries; others wealthy men with retinues and horses equipped with weapons 'complete' spears, and mail armour.[16]

From these glimpses of Turkic horse-power within what is now Russia, and from Kievan Russia under Rurik of Novgorod (862–79), which was also the period of Magyar movements through southern Russia, it can be seen how important horses were.

HUNGARY

A Hungarian chronicle of 1380 described Magyar horses as small, strong and swift, those of the nobility as tall and handsome. Medieval terms were 'capital; hand-picked; handsome; fit for a lord',[17] denoting type not breed. Hungarian horsemanship and warfare resembled the Turkic style, but because of contacts with western Europe by the fifteenth century her heavy cavalry was *equipped* in the western style.[18] Matthias Corvinus (1458–90) summed up Hungary's preferences:

> We have no desire for horses that hop about with bent hocks in the Spanish fashion, we do not want them even as a pastime, still less for serious business. What we want are horses that stride out and stand firm when required.[19]

De la Brocquière described Hungary's large-scale horse-breeding (see above, p. 57).

When Turkish power gripped much of eastern Europe most superior horses came via the Ottomans. John Hunyadi's victory over the Turks at Belgrade in 1456 added booty horses to Hungary, but at Mohacs in 1526 Turkish victory initiated 150 years of Turkish overlordship and a steady increment of Turcoman and Arabian stock into Hungarian (and Polish) horse-breeding.[20] Not all Turkish cavalry rode 'capital' horses and it was sometimes difficult to spirit away a superior booty mount.

THE NADASDY ARCHIVES

Thomas Nadasdy requested Ferenc Bebek to send him two horses picked from Turkish booty, one good racker and one capital. Ferenc replied: 'There is nothing of that description, but if we have nothing of the sort in hand we have some Turkish prisoners from whom we can demand as ransom the stamp of horse required.' Oriental horses came via the Caspian and Black Sea territories through Transylvania, Moldavia, Bessarabia, Podolia, Circassia and Tartary.

In 1548 Lady Majlath told her son his father was sending him a 'Saracen horse from Bethlehem' indicating a direct Arabian import. In 1556 Thomas Nadasdy's correspondence illustrates the range of horses repeatedly purchased by him on behalf of Archduke Maximilian. In one consignment sent to Vienna there were three Moldavian walking horses, three pacers, a grey spotted Turkish horse, a Szegh from Moldavia and a chestnut from 'beyond the Alps'.

In 1570 Nadasdy's accounts show three types of horses: capital, rackers and common. Huseain and Harambasha were capital horses and the Nadasdy clerk, Adam, noted Harambasha's provenance:

> there is an order that the captured captains and their horses are to be sent to the King and his son. As we have to do with the Germans [Hapsburgs] things are not easy. Of good horses suitable for a lord there are only two; one of them is with Andras Perhö. We have sent secretly to Kapuvar with orders to tell no one that it belonged to Harem Pasha and let no one see it.[21]

The Hungarian Szekely's forebears came from Sicily[22] which had long had oriental, Italian and Spanish strains.

POLAND

Poles have been known for centuries as expert horsemen and lovers of good horses. This is reflected in old Polish proverbs:

> A man without a horse is like a body without a soul.

> A Turkish foal, a German partridge dog, and a highborn child are the best to breed from.

Polish preacher Piotr Skaga (1536–1612) rebuked the Poles:

> Ye love the son of the mare more than the Son of God.

Poland's stocky Hucul pony came from the Carpathians (also in Hungary) and continental trade supplied horses from Hungary, Germany, the Low Countries, England, Spain and Italy. Oriental and steppe stock came via Tatar and Turk and by purchase. Today Poles excel in breeding Arabians. The earliest *accurate* references to *pure Arabs* in Europe are Polish. In 1506 Prince Sigismund visited Buda bringing Badavi (Bedevi-at) Bedouin horses. King Sigismund Augustus II (co-reigned 1530–48, reigned 1548–72) started a purebred Arabian stud at Knyszyna; in 1570 his equerry published a book, *O Swierzopach i Ograch* ('Of Mares and Stallions'). Master of Horse Adam Micinski was to aim at a fixed type of horse using only selected purebred stock. Stephen Batory (reigned 1575–86) kept the stud going and sent his equerry Podlodowski to Arabia to purchase new stock; on the return journey via Constantinople the horses were stolen, his equerry murdered. Henry of Valois (1573–4) fled from Poland arriving in France on a black mare from Knyszyna, then offered to sell her for 2,000 crowns to Max Fugger who wrote a book on stud and cavalry matters. She was described (imprecisely as she was an Arabian) as 'Turk mare, blaze on face, black mane, three white socks, eel stripe'.[23] Nobility and magnates followed suit operating large studs of oriental horses; Arabians were most desired as sires.[24]

THE BALTIC BLOC

Warhorses from Germany and indigenous breeds featured in the Northern Crusades. Backed by the Pope, who was never shy of distributing lands he did not own to crusaders, Livonia was targeted for conversion, but the real lure was land, power and trade – especially the last-named. Denmark, Sweden and Poland were Catholic, the Novgorodian dominions were Greek Orthodox, others with a Baltic outlet were pagan. Into the Baltic flowed many rivers. The most important carried the bulk of trade goods. The Oder served Saxony, Poland and Bohemia; the Nieman served Lithuania; the Narva divided parts of Estonia and Novgorod; Novgorodian waterways were the Volkhov, the Neva and Lake Ladoga. For the most part the climate was excessively cold, the most valuable commodity fur; others were slaves, fish, amber, wax.[25]

Cross-border raiding and invasion also acquired goods. This often escalated into full-scale war, land acquisition and settlement protected by garrisoned forts. The horse was part of the framework, but not always easy to procure in watery, cold and densely forested regions subject both to natural hazards and to those inflicted in war. Sea-raiders could bring only a limited number; rivers and marshes were dangerous to cross; forests hampered cavalry and invited ambushes; waterlogged ground grows sour, tough grasses so horses went hungry; constantly sodden, spongy hooves break down under heavy burdens; hide saturated in raw, muddy conditions produces rain scald and mud fever, conditions that render horses unsound and inefficient.

LIVONIA

Henry of Livonia's chronicle gives much military information for the years 1198–1225. Scarcely a year went by when Livonia and its Germanic interlopers were not assailed by Russians from Polotzk, Lithuanians or Estonians, or under Germanic leadership retaliated in kind. Prior to Henry's arrival an earlier mission persuaded Livonians to accept baptism in return for showing them how to build stone-walled forts at Uxhull and Holm. When they recanted the Pope authorized forcible conversion. In 1198 'the bishop went to Livonia with an army'. Livonia resisted and fighting ensued, followed by a truce during which some Germans gathering horse fodder were killed. Retaliation by cavalry was swift but the bishop, 'restraining his horse badly', was killed; the Germans 'with both horses and ships, fire and sword' wasted Livonia's crops. The Livonians accepted baptism and the army returned home. In 1200 they rebelled and stole the monks' property and horses so that fields remained uncultivated. The Frisians then fired the Livonians' crops. Albert of Buxtehude was despatched with 500 warriors in 23 ships, returning to Germany every year until 1224 for recruits. In 1202 Albert's protégés, the Brothers of the Sword, arrived. Their main duty was to organize crusaders and levies of Livonians for summer campaigns. Riga was their headquarters and other 'convents' housed smaller numbers as this military order grew. Livonia's King Caupo and half the population became Christian,[26] but Christianity was unwelcome; Livonians regularly apostatized rebelling against harsh German rule.

In 1203 a Russian attack was bought off; the Prince of Polotzk then besieged Holm fortress and the Germans fought back, wounding many Russian horses and routing the prince's army. The next year Livonia and Lithuania allied, raided Riga and were repulsed, the Germans recovering purloined flocks. In 1205 Lithuania, going via Livonia, raided Estonia with 2,000 cavalry, capturing huge booty of men, flocks and horses. The raiders were resting in Livonia on their return when German knights struck. The Lithuanians lost *c.* 1,200 men and their booty to the Germans and Livonians who had joined in. In 1206 to gain Russian friendship Bishop Meinhard sent an armoured warhorse to Vladimir of Polotzk but its escort was bushwhacked *en route* by Lithuanians. Recanting, Livonians stole horses and destroyed crops around Riga drawing retaliation from the Sword Brothers. A short peace was brokered by the bishop, but no sooner had he left for Germany than Russians and Livonians allied to besiege Holm. In renewed fighting the Livonians were bested, their horses' hooves pierced by caltrops scattered around the fort. Henry's pious comment, 'quite properly theological doctrine follows the wars', meant Christianity clamped down again.[27]

In 1207 the Sword Brothers pressured the bishop for a third of Livonia and for (lands of) tribes not yet converted. The bishop agreed to the first, but said the second was not in his gift. On Christmas Day 1207 Lithuanians crossed the River Aa to ravage and loot herds of horses and flocks, their depredations halted only by the combined forces of crusading knights, Sword Brothers, Rigan merchants, the bishop's men and levies of Livonians and Letts. In 1208 the Sword Brothers raided Estonia with Livonian and Lettish levies, and Lithuania with pagan Semigallians. Henry, averse to criticizing Germans, gives a slightly comic description:

> the Lithuanians flew around on their speedy horses. As was their custom they rode about here and there, sometimes fleeing sometimes pursuing, threw their lances and staves and wounded many. The Germans, however, grouping themselves together into a single wedge and *protecting the army from the rear, permitted the Semgalls to go ahead* – the Semgalls fled . . . thus the whole weight of the battle was turned against the Germans. [emphasis added]

The Lithuanians sent the 'few' Germans scurrying back to Riga.[28] Master Wenno then led a blitzkrieg against Estonia, calling halt only when his horses were lamed; he returned to base and a reprimand from the magistrate Hermann who was in the midst of peace negotiations with Estonia.[29] In 1211 Estonia and

Livonia clashed again. Estonia had 'many thousands of cavalry and several thousand foot', Livonia had infantry and knight cavalry. When the 'knights charged . . . the trappings of the horses threw terror into the enemy', which suggests the horses were armoured. While the cavalry harried, Livonian and Christian foot quitted fighting to seize 'many thousands of horses'. Raiding went on unabated; in one raid alone Germans lost 100 horses from overwork, and in 1214 a mounted army of Germans, Livonians and Letts raided Estonia for horses, exhausting theirs in the process. Resting until Lent they again raided first Estonia then Russia for horses. Eventually the Germans who had taken Fort Odenpah were besieged by Estonians and Russians; food and fodder ran short, starved horses ate each other's tails. The siege was lifted on condition the Germans returned to Livonia. In 1218 war erupted again; Germans, Livonians and Letts routed and harried Russians until at a stream-crossing the Russians regrouped and made a stand. Barely 100 of the 200 German knights remained; many had dropped out – presumably their horses were blown – yet although the Germans took the brunt of Russian arrows only a single knight was wounded and one Lett killed, but 50 Russians died. Henry claims the Russian army was 16,000 strong! Retreating via Livonia and Estonia the Russians learned that Lithuania had attacked Pskov in their absence.[30]

In 1222 Estonia was partitioned between Denmark and the Livonian (German) bishop. The Brothers appropriated part of the Danish holdings; the Livonians revolted against their oppression; the Mongols probed Russia; the Russians sued for peace to avoid war on two fronts. In 1225 a papal legate toured Estonia and Livonia warning the Brothers to curtail their harshness and restore Denmark's Estonian lands. When he left the Brothers retook the territory and by 1230 were such a menace that another legate with his retinue of knights was sent to retake Reval and return it to the Danes; he was captured and imprisoned. Master Folkwin's request to the Teutonic Knights to accept his Order was refused; in 1236 the Brothers, with Russian help, invaded Lithuania, but the crusading knights balked at fighting, scared of losing their horses in the bogs. The Lithuanians annihilated them; Folkwin and 50 Brothers perished. In 1237 the reduced Order was subsumed into the Teutonic Knights under the rule of Grand Master Herman Balk. Restitution was made to Denmark. In 1227 the Danes had stabling for 250 warhorses and 200 hacks at Reval.[31] Undoubtedly the Brothers looted both stables and farmlands with breeding stock.

THE TEUTONIC KNIGHTS

When Acre fell to Islam in 1291 the Teutonic Knights' headquarters became eastern Europe where they had already made military inroads. Between 1211 and 1225 they had defended Hungary's Transylvanian border against the Cumans, but were then sent packing. In 1226 Conrad of Masovia sought their aid against incursive Prussians; by 1230 they were ensconced on the Vistula, building Torun (Thorn) fortress. Conrad offered Chelmno as a fief. The Order, which had other ideas, appealed to the Emperor Frederick II (reigned 1215–50) who authorized them to hold Chelmno province and future conquests as lordships of the Order.

Sanctioned by charter from emperor and Pope, Prussia became an independent state governed by the Order. During the 50 years of war to conquer it Prussia was a proving ground for Brothers posted to the Holy Land. Samogitia and Lithuania were gripped between Sword Brothers and Teutonic Knights,[32] native Prussians enslaved or exterminated, German immigrants encouraged to settle, eventually arrogating to themselves Prussian nationality. The Pope granted crusader indulgences. The Order offered tangible assets. In 1236 Grand Master Balk enfeoffed a knight in Prussia with a fort, 300 Flemish hides (1 hide equalled 53 acres/21.5 hectares), fisheries, and tithes from three villages. In Livonia in 1261 knights were offered 40 hides, squires 10, and tithe exemption for six years to fight against Curonia. Later fiefs were smaller. The general rule was military service – a fully armed knight(s) with one or more destriers, or a light horseman, according to fief size and income. Fighting ability not status determined a man's worth.[33]

THE ORDENSTAAT'S EQUESTRIAN ESTABLISHMENT

The Order's commanderies were in strategic locations. Some had direct access to the Baltic – Riga, Memel, Elbing, Danzig, Konigsberg on the Frischeshaff. Tilsit and Ragnit were on the Nieman, the Prussian/Lithuanian border. On Poland's Vistula were Marienburg, Graudenz (Grudziadz), Torun (Thorn), 30, 40 and 60 miles (48, 64 and 96 km) upriver. Strassburg was 30 miles (48 km) east of Graudenz, Tuchel 20 miles (32 km) into (modern) Poland's north-west border; Osterode 40 miles (64 km) south of Elbing, etc.

Each commandery had its own studs provisioned from local resources and taxes in kind. Some raised just enough horses for their own use; larger commanderies – Konigsberg, Brandenburg, Balga, Christburg and Mewe – had studs in their demesnes. Konigsberg had 4 *pfleger* (sub-commanders); each ran a stud and smaller establishments. In 1404 at its peak Konigsberg (in total) had 95 great horses, 394 broodmares, 235 stallions and 650 farmhorses, not counting foals. Saddle types were heavy Germanic horses and light, native Prussian,[34] range-bred, pony-sized horses. In his 1557 travelogue Count Heberstein said the East Prussian horse was mouse- or ash-grey with an eel stripe and striped legs (grullo colour with markings denoting affinity to the Tarpan indigenous to eastern Europe and western Russia, now extinct in its original wild state). In old Prussia the wild horse was *Paustocaiacan*, a domestic horse *Schweike*, but in Marienburg records *Schweike* meant wild in the medieval sense of range-bred.[35] The Konigsberg numbers, apart from draught horses, would have been mostly destrier-breeding stock, the 235 entires, used as servants' mounts, a 'mixed bag'.

The Order often bought horses from peasants. Marienburg records for 1412 show villagers sold 46 horses for 229 marks;[36] averaging 5 marks, these would have been native ponies or low-value farmhorses. Germany produced heavy warhorses. Henry of Livonia mentions the best German horses sent to Vladimir of Russia by the Prince of Kokenhausen to gain his support against the Germans.[37] Around 1275 Mindaugas of Lithuania made a trade agreement with the Riga burghers and the Order, horses being valuable trade goods,[38] and the

Germans leading medieval horse-copers (see above). Several German states produce heavy saddle breeds: for example, the Holstein, traceable to the sixteenth century, or the Mecklenburg, the Brandenburg and the lighter Trakehner of East Prussia. Most come from areas in or adjacent to the Order's erstwhile territories, or from recruiting areas. Secular knights returned home after serving their term; many would have been on 'Order'-bred stock or gift horses. It is fair to suggest that the well-regulated studs had some input into the earliest foundation stock.

A postulant had to bring three horses worth 40 *gulden*, or the cash equivalent, armour and weapons and 25 marks for his journey to Prussia. The Teutonic Order accepted only German nobility – counts, barons, knights and service noblemen; peasants and townsmen were barred. If bribes were accepted (and detected) the man was sent back to Germany.[39] Once admitted, a brother knight was allocated two, three or four horses. He did not own them – pretty hard as initially he supplied them. Grand Master Winrich von Kniprode (1331–82) standardized this at three: a destrier and two light horses for travel. Higher-ranking officers could have more:[40]

> if the brother knight has four horses, the other brothers serving in arms should have two; if he has two or three the brother in the major offices should have three or four respectively . . . the brothers should have two squires . . . on the march the squires should ride before him or beside him with their horses.[41]

The highest officers had even more. In 1416 Elbing's commander had 17 chargers and 16 stallions farmed out in demesnes. Elbing's stocks were considerable. They ranged from 606 in 1404 to 395 in 1412. Between 1384 and 1432 they averaged 494.[42] Was the low 1412 figure due to Tannenburg losses? Or only to that year's widespread horse sickness?[43] Elbing had demesnes at Preussich-Holland, Mohrungen, Ortelsburg, Liebstadt, Bordehnen, Locken, Workallen, Machwitzhof; studs at Drausenhof, Neuhof, Weesenhof. In 1414 stud stock was as follows: mares 154; foals 46; two- and three-year-olds 39; aged mares 17; draught horses and letter ponies (*Schweiken*) 121; being trained 19. With the commander's 33 this agrees with 429 as Elbing's 1414 total, but in 1428 the 513 total shows distribution: Drausenhof 146; Weesenhof 87; Neuhof 104, the balance at Bordehnen 116; Mohrungen 19; Workallen 31; Machwitzhof 10. As no horses are shown for Elbing headquarters other demesnes were not recorded as having horses, and numbers do not always tally, this suggests stocks in excess of recorded numbers and that much evidence, recorded or not, has not survived. Between 1441 and 1451 Elbing had 40 brothers. A decade earlier an inventory noted 17 separate offices, from Commander Heinrich Reuss von Plauen down to Oberstolz the master gardener. All brethren had two or three horses each.[44] This gives Elbing headquarters 80–120 horses, not counting extras for senior officers.

In spite of huge numbers bred, bought, rounded up from indigenous stock, brought in by Crusaders and imported from Germany, stock was hit hard by death, whether in battle, to disease, or by injury. No horse would be kept unless serviceable. Some were lost to the enemy, others run off in raids, a percentage enticed away by truly wild stallions – a fairly common occurrence where range-bred and wild herds were common. In the period 1406–15 Christaburg commandery's stock went from 1,254 to 275.[45]

In the fourteenth century there were *c.* 2,000 knight brothers, and 3,000 priests, nuns and serjeants of the Order, giving at least 6,000 knights' horses, plus serjeants' mounts and those from fief-holders, peasants, mercenaries and secular knights whose first contingent – seven Polish dukes – arrived in 1232, followed in 1233 by Margrave Henry of Meissen with 500 knights, and knights from Brandenburg, Austria, Bohemia. Between 1323 and 1344 contingents came from the Rhineland, Bohemia, Alsace, England, Flanders, Austria, France, Bavaria, Holland, Hungary and Burgundy, and after 1350 there were Occitanians, Scots and Italians. In 1390/1 and 1392/3 Henry Bolingbroke, Duke of Lancaster and Earl of Derby (later Henry IV) came. His retinue of *c.* 100 included 13 knights, 18 squires, 3 heralds, 10 miners and engineers, plus about 50 volunteers. It cost over £4,360 to outfit and run, with wages, gifts, boat hire, horses, wagons.[46] His accounts for 1390 show 21 horses purchased locally – eight draught, six saddle, two sumpters, the others not designated. The cost totalled £43 3s 4d and 110 ducats. On 22 August Danzig merchant Lankow sold four mounts at 40, 24, 24 and 8 nobles respectively; Henry Maunsell sold Derby one for the trumpet at 16 ducats; two sumpters cost 21 and 24 ducats; a horse for Count Virtutum's farrier 21 ducats. Purchases were also made at Prake, Wene and Portgruer. Retinue members bought and sold among themselves. Other replacements came from booty. On 28 August a battle against Lithuanians yielded much booty including 200 saddled horses.[47]

A plan of Marienburg between 1410 and 1420[48] shows an external walled area of 7,560 square yards/1.75 acres. Within the castle complex an area 407 × 230 ft (124 m × 70 m) contained five stable blocks, a foundry for artillery and possibly housing farriers, blacksmiths' and armourers' shops, and a long building for tack. An oblong courtyard much larger than the walled paddocks but partly filled with buildings included more stables. The clear area was roughly the same as the paddock area – ideal for training and exercising mounts in security. In standing stalls a 16 hh stocky horse needs approximately 7 × 14 ft (2 m × 4 m), which includes rear space walkway for mucking out. Maybe only warhorses were stabled, the walled paddock used for safe containment of palfreys and *Schweiken*. If so the complement of warhorses was considerable. As with Elbing, Marienburg had territory from which it drew necessaries for Marienburg's equestrian establishment including its stud at Kalthof.[49]

Horse feed was hay and oats with grazing for horses at stud. Oats were bought compulsorily at 2s a bushel, levied at 6 bushels per hufe (42 acres/17 hectares). Good oats can weigh 56 lb (25.5 kg) per bushel. In addition, peasants contracted voluntarily for oats in excess of purveyance demands. The Order also demanded labour services from peasants with draught horses and wagons; usually native Prussians not incomer Germans bore the brunt.[50]

THE ORDER ON THE PROD

With Livonian and Estonian bases consolidated the Order's main target was Lithuania and Poland. Poles and Lithuanians were enemies until a treaty of 1305; the Order fought to strengthen borders against Russia and Lithuania and to prevent Poland regaining Danzig and Pomerania.[51] Lithuania's grand duke sometimes warred against the Order, sometimes allied with it, accepting baptism and recanting as it suited him. Other members of the ducal family allied with the Poles. Between Mindaugas (d. 1263) and his descendants Olgierd (d. 1377) and Kenstutis (d. 1382) Lithuania expanded from a 120-mile (193-km) radius centred on Vilnius to a 400-mile (644-km) radius to south and east, and bordered by Poland and the Order's lands to west and north.[52]

The Order's methods included summer and winter raiding, a harsh military presence in conquered territories, aid to warring nations if in the Order's interests, and as a sovereign state unwarranted war on other nations to expand its territories. Some fighting occurred almost every year; retaliatory raids were the norm. The local populace suffered capture, looting, farmsteads and crops burned, etc. Terrain and climate governed military undertakings. Marshes, forest, constant rains in spring and autumn, heavy snows and biting winter cold hampered action. Campaigning seasons were short – high summer and hard winter. Outside these times, soft ice broke under a horse's weight; spring thaw and autumn rains turned ground to a bog.

A winter *reysa* (raid) was short and swift with from 200 to 2,000 men carrying iron rations for man and horse at the cantle, loot and implanting terror the objectives. On a nine-day raid into Lithuania in 1378 Livonian brothers lifted 531 cattle and 723 horses, but their studs bore the brunt of Lithuanian raids. In 1376 Kenstutis stole 50 mares and 60 stallions from the Insterburg stud, and took 900 captives. A summer *reysa* was larger, usually designed to expand territories and seize horses as valuable plunder. In 1365 for a month's raiding each man carried rations, but horses were to subsist on grazing and grain from harvested or standing corn. Risks to horses were high. Lithuania lost 1,000 when raiding the Order's lands in the harsh 1376 winter. An over-ambitious summer raid in 1314 cost the Order men and horses. They raided 100 miles into Lithuania stashing food and pack-horses along their return route. Duke Gedymin's brother David counter-raided lifting the lot. The Order's starving troops ate their horses and men died of hunger. On forays the Order was ruthless. In 1311 Commander Gerhard von Mansfeld slaughtered captives and cattle to prevent their falling to the Lithuanians; in 1377 the commander of Balga, hampered by a sudden thaw when returning home, murdered 200 prisoners; the valuable 100 horses and 1,000 cattle survived.[53]

After the death of Kenstutis in 1382 civil war flared in Lithuania. Olgierd's son Jagiello took supreme power, Kenstutis's son Vitold fled to Prussia. The knights on the pretext of reinstating Vitold invaded Luthuania. Jagiello sought Poland's help, in 1386 married Queen Jadwiga of Poland (reigned 1383–9), and was crowned king as Ladislaus II (reigned 1386–1434); Lithuania turned Catholic. Vitold returned to Lithuania but, angered at the small appanage given him, again defected, triggering another German invasion, which was repulsed due to Polish reinforcements. In 1392 the breach healed; Jagiello gave the administration of Lithuania to Vitold, but the Order constantly tried subverting him, and he, thinking to conciliate them, in 1398 ceded them Samogitia, a Lithuanian province with a Baltic outlet separating Livonia and Prussia. The Order ruled the

Samogitians so harshly that in 1409 they revolted. Poland joined Lithuania and the carefully planned 1410 campaign was under way. Polish and Lithuanian forces with Ruthenian, Czech, Tatar and Hungarian contingents amounted to *c*. 150,000. The Order under Grand Master Ulrich von Jungingen fielded *c*. 80,000. Jagiello's army, apart from Polish heavy cavalry, was mostly light horse, the Order's mostly heavy lancers, a few crossbowmen with the new steel bow and artillery from Marienburg. On 15 June they met at Tannenburg (Grunwald). First blood went to the Order, its heavy cavalry shattering the Lithuanian and Czech left wing and nearly smashing the right wing as well; but the Polish horse held the centre, and their allies rallied. Before the Order's left wing re-formed, the whole of its reserve charged, but it had been weakened by the desertion of the Kulmerland Junkers. The Polish horse held stubbornly; after repeated charges the Teutonic Knights were outflanked, the battle degenerating into a sword-and-axe mêlée, surrounded by stinging Tatars. The Grand Master refused to yield and was cut down. It is estimated 18,000 fell, including 205 knights, with 14,000 taken prisoner. Heinrich von Plauen, left to guard Pomerania, galloped with 3,000 horse to hold Marienburg which withstood a 57-day siege until the Poles withdrew, their artillery ineffective, their army racked with dysentery. The Order never fully recovered. In February 1411 at the first Peace of Torun the Order kept land it held before 1409, returned Samogitia, and had a war indemnity to pay of £850,000.[54]

In Prussia the Order's repressive rule continued and in 1440 a Prussian league was formed which began by defending the rights of the nobility and towns. In 1454 open revolt flared, 56 of the Order's castles being seized. The league placed Prussia under Casimir of Poland (reigned 1447–92). He granted the Prussian Estates participation in electing Polish kings and the nobility many privileges, receiving in return yearly 2,000 *gulden* and three days' maintenance for his retinue. A new court and stables for 200 horses were to be built at Danzig. For 13 years Poland and the Order fought, first blood going to the Order at Chojnice in 1454 where it was aided by mercenaries. When the knights could no longer pay them they sold Marienburg to Poland. In 1462 Polish armies steadily pushed the Order towards East Prussia and in 1466 the second Treaty of Torun loosened the Order's grip. Prussia was partitioned, the west going to Poland, the east to the Order as a Polish fief. The Grand Master was to render military service with his knights, do yearly homage and admit Polish nobility to the Order, taking up to 50 per cent. Poland's territories were restored – Danzig, Pomerania, Chelmno province and the part of Prussia that included Elbing. Konigsberg became the Order's capital. Polish territory now stretched from the Black Sea to the Baltic, but in the next half-century much Polish military energy was wasted forcing the Order to obey the peace terms. In 1525 the unexpected happened. The Lutheran Albrecht von Hohenzollern, Margrave of Brandenburg Anspach, not the Grand Master, did homage at Krakow and signed a treaty agreeing to hold East Prussia from Poland. The Order was finished in Prussia; some brothers turned Lutheran and married, others left for Germany.

In Livonia the Order remained viable till Ivan IV's Livonian war. The Knights fought the Russians, at first with some success, but in 1560 Grand Master Kettler was captured and taken to Moscow. The struggle ended with the Knights ceding all their lands to Poland at the 1562 Treaty of Vilnius and the Order was disbanded. The Poles, Swedes, Danes and Livonians combined to drive Ivan out.[55]

THE MONGOLS IN RUSSIA

The Mongols returned to Russia under Batu, son of Juchi, and Subudei. From 1236 to 1240 Subudei master-minded a blitzkrieg with an army bulked by troops from Chingisid princes. First move by Mongke and Budek was against the Volga Kypchaks. In spring 1237 Batu and Subudei attacked the middle Volga Bulgars. That winter they crossed the Volga and systematically reduced Russian provinces; first Riazan, then Suzdalia fell; in 1238 Moscow, Vladimir and Kozelsk. The army then split, Subudei going north to take Yuriev, Rostov and Yaroslav, and Batu north-east to reduce Dmitrov and Tver. In March Torzhok fell; Novgorod city was spared as spring thaw ended the campaign. Mongol horses grazed and recuperated in the Russian steppes west of the Don; Mongolian remounts were driven in, herds captured from the Cumans and other nomads, others taken from Kazakhstan. In 1240 the assault on the remaining provinces began; it ended when Kiev fell on 6 December. When the Mongols assaulted Europe they left three *tumen* (30,000) to keep Russia subdued and guard their backs.[56]

Mongol Administration

Batu was the first khan of the Golden Horde, his capital Sarai on the Volga to which Russian princes, now appointed by the khan, came to pledge loyalty. Refusal to do so, or negligence in paying homage, was followed by the wasting and looting of the princely territory. Mongol garrisons were placed in towns, taxes in kind and of horses levied, military recruits raised.[57]

From Uzbeg (1313–41) onwards a Mongol commissioner resided in each provincial capital; a census was taken and taxes set at a tithe of men and horses (and other commodities). An early levy on Riazan under Batu demanded horses in batches of specific colours – black, dun, sorrel, skewbald – as each Imperial Guard unit used horses of a different colour. Horse theft carried the death penalty; Andrew of Chernigov was executed for exporting horses without licence.[58]

Discord in the Golden Horde

In the 1280s and 1290s cracks appeared in the Golden Horde. Nogay of the Mangkyts, Batu's great-nephew, became in fact if not in title co-ruler under Tuda Mangu and Tele-Buga, expanding his horde to include Cumans, Volga Bulgars, Alans in Moldavia, Russians from the lower Danube and Dniester. In 1285 he extended his interests to Hungary. In the winter of 1285/6 Tele-Buga attempted to invade Slovakia but lost so many men and horses in the Carpathians that he was forced to return to Galicia to boost his army and have herds of remounts driven in from the Kypchak steppe. The Mongols then looted Volhynia and Galicia while the remounts grazed throughout spring and summer wrecking agriculture. Aware of possible Polish aid to Hungary, Nogay and Tele-Buga's Mongols, with Russian contingents under the princes of Galicia and Volhynia, attacked Poland wreaking havoc and looting around Krakow and Sandomir, but did not subdue the Poles. Returning to Russia, the Mongols again devastated Galicia and Volhynia. In 1291 Nogay invited Tele-Buga to a meeting then turned him over to Tokhta. The Russian princes split into rival groups: Andrew, titular Grand Duke of Vladimir, the Rostov princes and Duke Fedor of Smolensk adhered to Tokhta; Dmitri, acting Grand Duke of Vladimir, Michael of Tver and Daniel of Moscow sided with Nogay. Tokhta mobilized, looting Vladimir, Moscow and other cities. The split deepened. Nogay taunted Tokhta:

Our horses are thirsty and I want to let them drink from the Don river.

The ensuing battle went to Nogay and Tokhta fled, but two years later (1299–1300) Tokhta defeated Nogay, who perished in battle on the Kagamlyk river in Poltava province.[59]

In 1357 Berdibeg murdered his father Janibeg, and from 1357 to 1362 there were eight khans, each of whom succeeded after exterminating his rivals. Into this discord came a non-Juchid Mongol general, Mamay, who ruled through Khan Abdullah (d. 1370) and his successor Muhammad Bulak.[60] In central Asia Urus Khan, a Juchid, came to power in southern Kazakhstan, and Timur arose in Samarkand. Urus Khan made a bid for the Golden Horde against Mamay. Tokhtamysh, nephew or cousin of Urus Khan, defected to Timur, but at Urus Khan's death he too made a bid for the Golden Horde. However, Mamay had first to be overcome.[61]

MOSCOW THE UNIFIER

Mongol control lasted for a century in western Russia until Galicia was annexed by Poland in 1349, and Ukraine and Belorussia came under Lithuania. Eastern Russia continued under Mongol domination. Unification began at Moscow when Ivan I (reigned 1328–41) added to his ducal title 'and of all Russia'.[62] While the Juchids fought each other, Moscow and Tver jockeyed for supremacy; Dmitri Donskoy of Moscow won. To defuse growing Muscovite power Mamay attacked Moscow's ally, Dmitri of Suzdal, at Nizhni Novgorod; most of his 1,500 horse were annihilated. Reprisals followed and Mamay mustered troops to counteract an imminent Muscovite revolt. In 1378 Muscovites and Suzdalians using Mongol envelopment tactics won decisively over the Mongol general Begich on the River Vozha in Riazan. Dmitri then raised 30,000 troops from the Grand Duke of Vladimir; Mamay an army of Golden Horde cavalry, Genoese foot and Riazan allies. They met on 8 September 1380 at Kulikovo Pole. Though the two sides were numerically equal, Mamay had more cavalry. The battle opened with a mounted combat between a Mongol prince and a Russian monk. On impact both were killed. Mongols cut the Russian foot down, their horse were hard pressed. Two horses were killed under Dmitri, but as the Mongols launched a final assault the Russian cavalry reserve, held in the forest, struck, turning a Mongol near-victory to a rout. The Mongol camp was looted but harrying was short – horses and men were exhausted. Mamay's Lithuanian allies *en route* to Kulikovo beat a hasty retreat. In 1381 Mamay was killed fighting Tokhtamysh on the Kalka. Tokhtamysh reimposed Mongol authority with help from Olgierd of Lithuania. In August 1382 he failed to take Moscow, but offered a truce in return for 'small gifts'. Lulled Muscovites opened the gates. The city was given over to looting and killing, then burned.[63]

TOKHTAMYSH VERSUS TIMUR

Tokhtamysh now turned on Timur seizing Tabriz in 1385/6, but after clashing with Timur's vanguard he withdrew into the steppes. In 1388 they clashed again on the Syr Daria near Khojend. Arabshah says that although Timur prevailed it was a near thing. Timur now took the offensive, mustering 200,000 men at Otrar in February 1391. Ahead of him was an 18-week march of nearly 1,800 miles. Potentially Tokhtamysh could muster twice Timur's number and, as the Golden Horde tribes were gathering, Timur's task was to find his evasive enemy. On the Tobol river were found the remains of 70 fires lit a day or so earlier, plus horse tracks. A Turcoman scout brought in a man who had seen 10 armoured riders camped near his dwelling and 60 Tatars set off with spare horses to catch them; from these prisoners Timur learned that the Golden Horde was camped a week's ride to the west. Tokhtamysh retreated as Timur marched through the Ural valleys until, gaining open ground, scouts confirmed they had come up with the Golden Horde rearguard, but not with Tokhtamysh. Rain halted the army for a week, then by a forced march they reached Samara in the Middle Volga region. On 18 June 1391 they clashed, Timur routing Tokhtamysh who again escaped into the steppes. Thousands of his men were left on the field. Timur's army looted Tokhtamysh's camp, harried the enemy to the Volga marshes, then gathered in herds of horses, cattle and grain, a mule-load of booty to each man, and a string of unshod colts; the victors were so overburdened that much was abandoned on the forced march back to Samarkand. Tokhtamysh still controlled the Golden Horde, and making concessions to Moscow Grand Duke Vasili was granted the principalities of Gorodets, Meschera, Tarusa and Nizhni Novgorod. On 15 April 1394 Tokhtamysh faced Timur in the Caucasus; he was decisively beaten and fled north harried by Timur, but again escaped. This time Russia was hit hard. Timur marched north up the Don; Riazan province was devastated; Elets city taken, its prince captured, the inhabitants killed or enslaved. Moscow prepared. Instead Timur turned for home and on the return looted Azov and burned Astrakhan and New Sarai. The Golden Horde received such a blow in economic and military terms that it never recovered, but Russia was not free of it until 1480 when Ivan III (reigned 1462–1505) broke the Mongol yoke.[64]

IVAN IV

In 1547 Ivan, dubbed the Terrible for atrocities committed on his people, nobility and foreigners, was crowned tsar of all the Russias, aged 17. At his accession Muscovy was ringed by actual and potential enemies: Tatar khanates – East

Kazan, South-east Astrakhan, South Crimea; to the west were Lithuania and Poland, to the north-west Livonia. In his regrettably long reign (1533–84) Ivan warred on all. His conflict with Livonia and Lithuania was intermittent but went on for decades at enormous cost.

CAVALRY SERVICE IN RUSSIA

Land tenure was *votchina*, or hereditary ownership, and *pomestie*, or fiefs awarded in return for mounted military service. In 1556 service was made obligatory for all landowners. The Russian army relied on cavalry, and although firearms were used they were unpopular. The bow was still supreme for long-range fire and far more accurate when used by skilled archers. From each 100 quarters of good arable land (*c.* 400 acres/162 hectares) one man with a horse and full armour was demanded – two horses for a distant campaign. A bounty was awarded for bringing more than the minimum. Obligation to service started at 15 years old. In principle it was seasonal, but the continuous wars meant most served lifelong. Wealthy landowners mustered with fine warhorses – Argamak – and poor men with a 'nag', no doubt a scruffy steppe-type pony. The richer cavalrymen provided horses for servants who were drafted into active cavalry use at need. Provisions for man and horse were also required, although some inadequate stores were provided. The norm was to purchase or pillage what was needed when supplies ran out. Meat on the hoof was driven and/or acquired by the army. Pay was mostly booty. Although the government considered 10 households adequate to provide man, armour, horse and arms, in practice 50 were needed. The cost was 20 per cent of the rent extracted from *c.* 400 acres[65] i.e. a fifth of a man's *total* land income. A huge estate on fertile land was needed to serve with a retinue of men, horses, spare mounts, servants, provisions, etc.

Figures for cavalry numbers given by contemporary authors range from 150,000 to 300,000, although the latter includes men of all arms; *c.* 110,000, not counting recruits, is more realistic.[66] Tatar units from allied and/or conquered tribes also served. Russian writers' propaganda obscured accuracy when quoting vast numbers of enemy killed to minimal national losses.

Most cavalrymen looked little different from Tatars. A contemporary woodcut shows Muscovite nobility on small, coarse, unarmoured mounts. Fletcher confirms this:

> Their horses are but small, but very swift and hard. They travel them unshod both winter and summer.[67]

Troopers were also equipped as for Tatar heavy cavalry in scale armour and with Tatar bows, side-arms and Tatar tack including snaffle bridle and knouted whips. Tatars also used lassos. There had been an early precedent: in 1245 Daniel of Galicia went to Sarai to swear allegiance to Batu. Thereafter he reorganized and re-equipped his army Mongol fashion in steel cuirasses, his horses protected by chamfrons and chest armour. This had to be as for heavy cavalry as most Mongols

did not aspire to steel armour or horse armour. Daniel stuck to flash Russian gear
– brocade coat with gold lace, green leather boots, gold-encrusted sabre; his
magnificent horse wore a gilded saddle.[68]

PRINCE ALEXANDER KURBSKY

Kurbsky was a general who fought in the Kazan and Livonian campaigns.

The Kazan war had several stages. In 1547–9 it failed due to severe winters.
In 1551 the Russians built Sviyazhsk fortress as a supply depot and base for
future campaigns moving supplies and artillery down the Volga. A diversionary
Crimean raid against Tula delayed the 1552 push. Kurbsky was sent with
15,000 horse and Tula's garrison, seeing Kurbsky coming, drove the Tatars off,
leaving him to mop up the Crimean rearguard. Then the army split, the tsar
going via Murom with the main army, Kurbsky with 13,000 cavalry via Riazan
and Meschera; they joined up at Sviayaga. The five regiments – great, right,
left, van and rearguards – and an advance guard, the *yartaul*, took two days to
cross the Volga, then three days to cover 4 miles (6.4 km) of watery wasteland
before reaching Kazan, deploying troops along the Volga as they went. Between
the Volga and Kazan lay a mile (1.6 km) of meadows. Kurbsky's right wing had
12,000 horse and 6,000 foot archers and Cossacks positioned between bog and
forest; they were open to Cheremisian Tatar cavalry attacks from the forest,
artillery fire from Kazan. The other regiments took up position between the
Bulak and Kazan rivers east of the Volga. The Khan of Kazan had 60,000
warriors divided between fortress and outlying detachments, plus 2,000 Nogays.
The first attack came as the second Russian wave crossed the Bulak. In three
weeks of skirmishing with Tatar cavalry attacking from the forest losses were
heavy on both sides. The Russians lost men and horses to musket and arquebus
fire and foragers to cavalry attacks, the Russian cavalry screen proving
powerless. Sleeplessness and hunger weakened the ranks so the decision was
taken to divide the army, half to guard the guns and remain in position outside
the fort: 30,000 cavalry and 15,000 foot and Cossacks were ordered to wait
concealed behind hills. Next morning Tatar cavalry attacked; the Russian horse
fell back on their trenches, drawing the Tatars on until Aleksandr Gorbady
brought his massed foot into a flanking movement. When the Tatars turned to
flee the Russian cavalry harried hard, Muslim corpses littering the ground for
1½ miles (2.4 km); 1,000 were taken alive. For 10 days Russians ravaged the land
piling up booty in grain, fruits, herds, but the campaign was not over.
Cheremisians lifted many Russian herds of horses, cavalry being sent to retrieve
them. After seven weeks the walls of Kazan were mined and blown up; five
and a half hours of fighting ensued until the khan surrendered; other Tatars
shot their way out and Kurbsky with 200 horse chased them to the river.
Hampered in the crossing, they made a last-ditch stand as Russians attacked
their rearguard. Kurbsky had

> an extremely swift and excellent horse. I struck my way into the middle of that
> Mussulman army and I recall how thrice my horse jibbed while I was fighting

and how the fourth time it fell, badly wounded, in their midst and I recall how I lost consciousness as a result of my great wounds . . . afterwards I learned that all those noble men . . . who agreed to gallop with me . . . had gone back and struck the Muslims from behind.[69]

Ivan garrisoned Kazan and a week later left:

all the horses were driven on difficult tracks along the Volga going over great hills where Chuvasians [Tatars] live, and as a result of this he [Ivan] destroyed the horses of all his army at that time, for if anyone had 100 or 200 horses, barely two or three of them survived.[70]

In 1553/4 Ivan attacked Kazan again with 30,000 horse and in 20 midwinter skirmishes harried the Muslims for a month as far as Bashkir territory. The vastness of steppe and forest is shown by the hide-and-seek campaign of 1555. Informed that Girey was raiding the North Caucasus, Ivan sent 13,000 horse under Sheremetev against Perekop (the Crimea); instead Girey was heading for Russia unaware of the tsar's army. Sheremetev had good scouting patrols and flank guards out and was coming up on Girey's rear to attack as the Tatars dispersed on their raid. A third of the Russians were sent against the khan's baggage train a half-day's ride from his route

for it is always the habit of the Khan of Perekop to leave half the horses of all his army five or six days journey behind, in case they should be needed.

Unfortunately Girey intercepted a courier, learned Sheremetev's plan, turned about and two days later defeated him at Sudbischi, 150 versts (about 100 miles/160 km) from Tula. Unaware of this reverse Ivan went against Girey to find he had evacuated the area two days earlier to return to Perekop.[71]

Astrakhan was hit in 1554 and 1556 and was annexed by Muscovy. In those years the Nogays lost droves of horses and cattle to pestilence; Perekop, which was also struck, lost 10,000 horses, prompting Kurbsky to recommend it as a good time to attack Girey. Ivan 'took little notice' sending only 5,000 horse against a Crimea forewarned by Sigismund of Poland.

In 1558 Ivan entered Livonia at Pskov reconnoitring in strength for a month on a 40-mile (64-km) front. That year Kurbsky took over 20 German fortresses and towns, Russian cavalry commanders besting the Germans (Teutonic Knights). This time Girey was misinformed – thinking Ivan still in Livonia his son set off to raid Muscovy, then, finding Ivan had returned to Moscow, turned for the Crimea, but

that winter was very cold and much snow, and they lost all their horses and a great number of Tatars themselves perished from cold.

The Russian Chronicle notes that Girey's son attacked Riazan, Tula and Kashira in December 1558.[72]

Kurbsky stayed in the Livonian theatre until 1564, then defected to Lithuania with good cause. Ivan's vituperative litany accused him of unwillingness to fight in Kazan; giving bad advice; wanting to return home when stores were sunk (in the Volga); leaving warriors behind to return home quickly; destroying soldiers by fighting at the wrong time; plundering Kazan when it fell; letting Tatars escape, and

> even if you suffered many wounds, none the less you achieved no brilliant victory, and how was it that at our town of Nevel with 15,000 men you were unable to conquer 4,000?

Ivan's diatribe ran to many pages. Kurbsky refuted accusations in the

> extremely bombastic epistle of the Grand Prince of Moscow . . . understanding it was belched forth in untamable wrath with poisonous words.[73]

PESTILENCE

Kurbsky and other contemporary authors writing of eastern Europe, Asia and Asia Minor mention huge animal losses to 'pestilence'. Noting the era, methods of animal husbandry and the tracts over which massed animals passed and repassed poses the question – which pestilence(s)? It is impossible to positively name the disease(s), but a suggestion, made after consultation with my veterinary surgeon, is that a pestilence attacking all species may have been anthrax, the ground so contaminated that fresh outbreaks occurred when armies campaigned, as they frequently did, over the same regions, and that a disease attacking only equines may have been strangles, a likely killer (see Chapter 9, p. 162).

What is certain is that animal health governed the capabilities of cavalry nations.

THE OPRICHNINA

In 1565 an unhinged Ivan abdicated, moving to Aleksandrova Sloboda because of the 'disloyalty and dishonesty' of his princes and boyars. He was persuaded back to Moscow on condition he be allowed a separate state within Muscovy with absolute power. The *Oprichnina* state flourished in 1565–72. Originally it contained 1,000 men, the number rising to 6,000, drawn from princes, boyars, their sons and the *Dvor* (court). In its later years foreigners were included. Large land-grants to *oprichniks* were made by confiscating estates of the *Zemschina*, landowners who lived outside the *Oprichnina* state. They were either banished to outlandish parts, killed on trumped-up charges, or forced into monasteries so their lines died out, Ivan clawing in their patrimonies. Around 9,000, almost a third of the gentry nobility from whom cavalry were raised, were ruined. *Oprichniks* wore black and rode black horses, with a broom and a dog's-head attached to the saddle – to sweep away treachery and signify loyalty. They ruled by terror.[74]

Heinrich von Staden, a crude, violent German mercenary, served as an *oprichnik*. His description of his own and Ivan's rapaciousness highlights certain aspects of equine acquisition for the army:

Ivan plundered his own people, land and cities. I accompanied him with one horse and two servants. Because every city and road was guarded by soldiers I could not get away with horses or servants. I finally returned to my estate with 49 horses, 22 pulling sleighs full of goods which I sent to my house in Moscow. I exchanged his former estate with Johann Taube for the village of Spitsyno one mile [1.6 km] from Moscow . . . I kept horses in this village so I could have them on hand when I needed them, I continued to live on my estate in the *Oprichnina* . . .

When the Grand Prince plundered his own country . . . several thousand teamsters were readied with horses and sleighs . . . I now began to assemble a lot of retainers, especially 120 menials who were naked and destitute . . . undertook my own expedition. When I took a captive I politely asked where money was, and when I took one from some other place asked where there were good horses. If the prisoner did not want to respond nicely they held him and tortured him.[75]

From Staden other snippets of horse supply can be culled; the Nogays were accustomed to sell several thousand (annually) from which the Grand Prince took a tenth. Persia and Bokhara, both suppliers of superb horses, were traded with. Sir Jerome Horsey was provided with Persian horses by the tsar when he was sent as English ambassador to Moscow. German warhorses were part of booty from Livonia after Wesenberg was taken.

Mercenary troops provided excellent cavalry: in 1581 Ivan invaded Swedish territory capturing many Swedes and mercenary troops whom he sent to Moscow:

among other nacions there were four score and five Scots soldiers left of 700 sent from Stockholme and three Englishmen in their company . . . Ivan tortured many Swedish prisoners.

Horsey interceded for the Scots, suggesting they be used against Crimean Tatars:

shortly the best souldiers and men at arms of these straingers were spared and putt apart, and captaines of each nacion appointed to govern the rest. Jeamy Lingett for the Scottish men. Money, clothes, daily allowance for meat, drink, horses, hay and oats, swords, peece [guns] and pistols were they armed with. Twelve hundred of them did better service against Tatars than 12,000 Russians.[76]

Ivan's death came as a relief to his beleaguered subjects; his Livonian wars had ended with his losing all he had previously gained. Sweden took Narva; Poland/Lithuania was in the ascendant, and Feodor, Ivan's weak-minded son, was governed by Boris Gudonov, his Master of Horse, soon to be tsar.

FIVE

The Tudors

After 1485 England's equine stocks were severely depleted due to the disastrous Wars of the Roses, and to nobility exporting valuable animals to prevent their being impressed for service. As armour became heavier, the mount to carry it became unwieldy as more cold blood was infused in its breeding. The full panoply escalated in cost as efficiency declined. Artillery and handguns ended the need for ponderous mounts in favour of speedier animals who were not such inviting targets.

Continental powers were building permanent armies in which cavalry played an important part and was increasingly evolving into light horse – mounted arquebusiers and pistoleers – although some heavy cavalrymen remained, notably in the German and French forces.[1] England, however, still depended on levies raised at need, and horses and men were often sub-standard. The Tudors undertook no *major* foreign wars, but stocks were to be drained further by Henry VIII's extravagant French campaigns and by the badgering of Scotland, with incessant border conflicts where horses were vital both to the reivers and to the moss-troopers detailed to stem cross-border hostilities. The deficiencies in horses for war resulted in legislation and forced Henry VIII (reigned 1509–47) to hire mercenary horse for French and Scottish expeditions.

Much Tudor correspondence concerned strenuous efforts to improve horse-breeding by domestic enhancement and importing stock.

Although horses were used for pleasure, the main thrust in sixteenth-century equestrian literature was the Right Mount for War. The catalyst was Italy where notable horse-trainers and treatises abounded. Some were translated into English. Blundeville adapted, expanded and presented as his own Federico Grisone's work. Italy exported well-bred horses heavily infused with Barb blood; when these were sold to England, Italian riders often accompanied them, taking up temporary residence there. Elizabeth's Master of Horse was Robert Dudley, Earl of Leicester, in whose household Claudio Corte was employed and who appointed Prospero d'Osma to manage Elizabeth's studs.

LEGISLATION, HOMEBREDS AND IMPORTS

Tudor legislation partly reiterated earlier laws, treated indigenous range-bred stock harshly and enforced stock enhancement.

By the 1530s Henry VIII had long been a major importer by purchase and gifts from Italy and Spain. James IV of Scotland (reigned 1488–1513), a few years prior to Flodden (1513), also imported warhorses and broodmares from continental sources.

In 1496 Henry VII (reigned 1485–1509) banned export of entires and of mares worth 6s 8d or more. Mares sold had to be at least three years old. A duty of 6s 8d was levied. Law evasions entailed stock forfeiture. Travellers could get licences to take stallions abroad for their personal use, but it was remarkable how many ran off or were stolen![2] In 1550–1 Henry VIII re-enacted this ban. Contravention was now a felony. A year later export to Scotland was banned.[3] In 1547 a fine of £40 was the penalty and in 1559 a year's imprisonment was inflicted. The law was reiterated in 1562 and in 1580 it was made March treason, a capital offence, to export to Scotland[4] in an attempt to boost supplies of mounts for border patrols.

In January 1580 the Privy Council ordered Lord Scrope, warden of the English West March, to investigate reasons for the 'great decay of horses' and to state how many horsemen were in service in Elizabeth's first regnal year (1558–9), how many now and how furnished. Scrope replied that he could find only a muster book from Mary Tudor's first regnal year (1553–4), which contained all horsemen, including 'bow and bill men with nags only to bring them to service'. Similar requests must have gone to wardens of the East and Middle Marches. Subsequently the Earl of Huntingdon, President of the North, surveying border matters, found 'daily sale of horses into Scotland' and the breeding of cattle for profit instead of horses.[5]

Prohibition was flouted long-term. The restrictive measures did bite but not very effectively. In June 1597 a lengthy investigation into alleged sales began. Lord Eure, warden of the Middle March, was accused of selling two grey geldings to Sir Robert Kerr. Eure denied it, referring enquiry to Raphe Mansfield, Captain of Harbottle. Finally in October Mansfield also denied selling to Kerr.[6]

Scots obtained horses over many years and in many ways; they had done so for at least 20 years to Sir William Selby's knowledge, as he told Cecil in May 1601:

among other causes that weaken our borders, selling horses to the Scots is not the least; for three of every four . . . are English . . . This is done in two ways; by the wardens conniving at English sellers, or winking at Scots coming in to Yorkshire fairs, etc. Another way is practised under Her Majesty's plaquettes granted for indefinite times; so that they will buy 60 horses with a plaquette for two, and never fill it up. I have known horses bought 20 years after the date of one. Such should be called in, and hereafter none granted but for 40 days or two months only and books kept . . . showing particulars of each sale. Berwick.[7]

In raiding over the years thousands were stolen by the Scots. A 1596 report on 'Decays of the Borders' since 10 Elizabeth I noted: East March lost 540; Middle March and Northumberland 1,245; bishopric of Durham 257; West March and Cumberland 146; Westmorland 95.[8] From June to September 1596, the West March lost 169 to Buccleuch raiding from Liddesdale, among other thefts, burnings and murders.[9]

Raids were retaliatory, largely cancelling each other out, but damage was done to farms, houses and livestock. Equine losses exacerbated the dearth by discouraging breeders from raising horses.

In 1592 the Scottish Crown complained of English raids in Falkland, Fife, in aid of the Scottish rebel Earl Bothwell. Borderers domiciled in England, mostly Musgraves and Grahams, stole 483 horses, some extremely valuable, from James VI's horse guard and wealthy subjects. Gold and silver boosted the value to £12,000 sterling. The guard lost 12 horses valued at £414, but gentlemen of Calder lost 150 horses and mares.[10]

THE HOMEBRED SCENE

England's topography governed whether horses were bred and reared or reared only in certain areas according to the availability of nutritious pasture for economical feeding.[11] Many old locations are still equine strongholds – Yorkshire and Leicestershire for hunters, the moors and mountains for native pony breeds. Laws aimed mainly at military stocks were brought in under Henry VIII. In 1535–6 (27 HVIII c.6) any owners of an enclosed deer park with a circuit of at least 1 mile (1.6 km) was required from 1 May 1537 to keep two broodmares of 13 hh minimum; any owner whose park had a circuit of 4 miles (6.4 km) or more, four mares. Covering stallions had to be at least 14 hh. Contravention cost a fine of 40s, half to the king, half to the informant.

In 1540 (32 HVIII c.13) in 25 specified counties no entire above two years old and below 15 hh was to be depastured in any forest, chase, moor, marish, heath, common or waste ground where mares and fillies were normally kept. In northern shires the minimum height was 14 hh. An informant on contraventions would gain the undersized stallion. Such stallions were allowed an annual break-out and four days for recovery. Escapees could be very busy during the grace period! Each autumn, mares, fillies, foals and geldings were to be rounded up. Any female unlikely to grow and be able to produce sizeable stock, and any horse or gelding unlikely to perform 'profitable labours', was to be killed and buried or otherwise disposed of to prevent 'noyance' (stink). But undersized animals could be privately owned and were not barred from stud, which rather negated the Act.

In 1541–2 (33 HVIII c.5) the wealthier were required to keep stoned (entire) trotting saddle-horses of at least 14 hh at three years old. Archbishops and dukes had to maintain seven, lesser personages five, three, two, or one, according to means. Clergy with between £100 and 500 marks and any layman whose wife wore silk, a french hood or bonnet of velvet had to keep a 14 hh minimum entire.[12]

CAERSWS

A document *c*. 1540–1 entitled 'A Declaration unto the king's highness for th'encrease of horses within the Principalitie of Wales' concerns the 'parcke of Caersous' in the Severn valley. The preamble refers to the 'grete quietnes' now in Wales which permitted safe pasturing of 'almaner of Catell'. From May to 'Holly

Rede' (a movable feast, but usually on 14 September), 1,000 head grazed for 4*d* or 6*d* a head (presumably according to size), but ate less than 10 per cent of the pasture, the rest rotting. An unnamed party suggested the king should set up a stud for an annual rent of 8*s* 4*d*, fence it, run 100 mares, allot to each 10 a stallion – a 'jennett' or some other 'grete horse' – and 'there to encrease that kynde of horsses which his Grace pleaseth to have contynuance thereof'. A keeper was to be appointed either at a fixed salary or at one-third of the annual increase, provided all stock was to be redelivered at the king's pleasure. If culpable the keeper was liable for the value of any losses. When a horse died a piece of its hide with the king's brand on it had to be sent to the appropriate official. Mares were to graze on the mountains and pastures 3 miles (4.8 km) away. At weaning, colt foals were to be sent where directed, especially to Wigmore, which cost £8 a year and had pasture, park and stabling; filly foals were to remain to breed from. Records and descriptions were to be made of each year's foals, which should be branded. Because Caersws afforded cheaper keep, it was able to accept yearling fillies from the king's Warwick stud.

The interest lies in the stud system. Mares ran free, stallions did not. Presumably mares were within the park at covering and foaling times, ready for re-covering on foaling or subsequent heats. The fillies from Warwick injected new blood; 10 mares were considered a stallion's 'book'.

A later document shows Thomas Phillips of Ludlow deputed to investigate sharp practices at Caersws during the tenure of keeper Thomas ap Rees who cared for 120 to 140 mares and who had kept no records for eight years. Some mares had gone missing. Called to account, Thomas passed the buck to drover Jenkyn Penllan, but Phillips could find no mares where Jenkyn lived. This shows how easy it was to purloin stock without records and as mares did not always conceive, barrenness could be blamed for fewer offspring.

The Caersws stud operated long-term. In 1571 the Earl of Leicester was granted the manor of Arywstley, which included the parks of Caersws. A previous master of horse, the Earl of Pembroke, had been lord of Arywstley. Tenure was probably on condition of keeping the monarch's stud. In 1888 the area was known for horses larger than native pony stock, locals attributing this to Spanish horses introduced by Leicester.[13]

Edward VI (reigned 1547–53) went further, requiring that imported stallions be 14 hh minimum and mares 15 hh.[14] In 1547 (1 EVI c.12) horse-stealing was made a felony without benefit of clergy.[15] In 1555 (2 and 3 P&M c.7) toll books were introduced. Sales had to be entered with the horse's colour and at least one particular mark, plus names and locales of buyer and seller. Horses had to be on view at least one hour prior to sale. This law was reiterated and amplified in 1589 (31 EI c.12); sellers now had to be known to the toll-gatherer or bring a referee to guarantee their honesty.[16]

In 1565 (8 EI c.8) Elizabeth lowered stallion height to 13 hh in fen country because spongy terrain caused miring of heavier stock. The earlier law had resulted in covetous men removing poor men's smaller horses so that they dared not pasture their stock 'to the utter subversion and decay of all tillage and carriage'.[17] Elizabeth inherited some of her father's laws and some from her half-sister Mary. Under Mary (4 and 5 P&M c.23) the community was divided into ten income groups, ranging from £5–£10 a year up to £1,000 plus. The latter were to supply 6 horses for demi-lancers with armour for at least 3 horses; 10 horses for the light cavalry, 4 corselets, 40 Almayn (German) rivets, 30 longbows, 30 sheaves of arrows, 30 steel caps, 20 each of steel caps, halberds, hagbuts, morions. Less equipment and fewer horses were required of those less affluent. Anyone not already obliged to maintain a horse must now do so. Those worth 100 marks a year had to provide an equipped horse; a missing bow cost a fine of 10s and a missing horse £10.[18] Considering the horse was probably worth considerably less than the fine this penalty would have promoted horse ownership.

Though Elizabeth passed no Acts enforcing provision persuasion under threat of the queen's considerable displeasure operated. Volunteers were to provide an equipped cavalryman or the cash in lieu. The cost was assessed at £25 rising to £30. The Irish wars of 1594–1603 yield information on the raising of Elizabeth's cavalry. Voluntary participation was in practice a direct order. The Church, recusants and lawyers were tapped: the Church provided men and horses or cash; cash and/or horses were levied from recusants; and in 1601 lawyers were asked 'as proof of their affection' for £25 each (they raised £2,000). A warrant of 1598 authorized a levy of 36 horses from the clergy and recusants in the provinces of Canterbury and York, and another 26 horses from recusants countrywide. On another occasion 36 named recusants were ordered to pay £15 each. Six drafts from Yorkshire, Cumberland and Durham were left blank for the Archbishop of York to decide who should pay the levy. In 1595 other levies were applied to raise small sums from subjects. In Derbyshire John Manners paid £2 13s 4d; in 1601 a further levy for three horsemen was ordered and John Manners was levied one 'sufficient' horseman provided with 'a good horse, saddle of Morocco or some other good leather, cuirass, casque, lance and good long pistol, or a sword and dagger, and a horseman's coat of good cloth'.[19]

THE IMPORTS

Scotland

Although Scotland had hobbies, galloways and Highland ponies, much of her warhorse foundation stock was foreign. Royal acquisitions are recorded, but common sense suggests baronial studs were similarly supplied. Royal studs were located throughout Scotland; the more important royal residences including Doune and Newark had stables. James II (reigned 1437–60) used hill runs in Mar for breeding and grazing. From there stock went to Dundee and Edinburgh. Horses broken at Strathavon went to Invernochty. Horses belonging to the household of James IV (reigned 1488–1513) grazed at Raploch near Stirling.[20] James I (reigned 1434–7) bought stallions and broodmares from Hungary.[21] In 1508 Henry VII of England presented armoured horses to his son-in-law James IV,[22] who was already making strenuous efforts to import warhorses. Parallel with his purchases were acrimonious letters to and from Henry VIII, their relationship souring until war was inevitable. Despite small cavalry participation at Flodden, no doubt English studs benefited by booty of defeated Scottish noblemen's warhorses.

From a breeding and military standpoint James IV's acquisitions are interesting because the stock came from many countries.

In 1506 James thanked Louis XII of France, saying he was deeply indebted to Louis for sending him *again and again* the best horses. James inspected the horses each day and made much of them. In return he sent Louis four hackneys. The next year James wrote to Ferdinand of Aragon that he hoped 'ancestral goodwill' would induce Ferdinand to allow James to purchase six horses in spite of Spain's embargo. In 1508 James thanked Ferdinand for allowing his agent, Andrew Mathesoun, to obtain horses, anchors and ropes – all war *matériel*. In February 1508–9 James again thanked Louis for horses, and for the kindness by which *on these two occasions* he transported the beasts, 'excellent of their kind', reciprocating with hackneys. Clearly French horses were regularly imported. The year 1508–9 marked the most active horse-hunting period. John of Denmark was requested to allow purchase of ships' masts and warhorses, and for information as to where horses could most readily be purchased. A similar letter for ships' masts and warhorses went to James's 'dearest uncle' the Duke of Holstein. James informed Charles, Duke of Guelders, that he was sending bearers 'in various directions' to seek out, select and purchase horses for transport to Scotland. The bearers were told if they visited Guelders to approach the duke for instructions to facilitate their task. A similar request was sent to Sigismund I of Poland asking that the bearers seek out and select 'those already for sale' and 'bring them back unhindered'. In 1512 Benedict Hawsang, a citizen of Danzig, was asked to help James's servant Thomas Forret in choosing and buying some horses, to lend Forret money if necessary and to arrange transport of the horses to Scotland. The Polish and Danzig connections are particularly interesting, possibly the Holstein one as well; the territory into which James had sent purchasers had in the past belonged to the Teutonic Knights and although the Order had long since gone into decline, the legacy left by its studs (see Chapter 4) would have influenced Polish stock. In 1509 John of Denmark told James his envoy had bought horses in Denmark and John was adding a gift of six. For various reasons the purchase of the Spanish horses had been delayed and in 1510 James asked for a renewal of permission, and for the number to be increased to 12, some at least to be mares. According to King James's letter to Dominic de Belisquis (Velasco), Constable of Spain, he gained permission but a later letter to Ferdinand reiterates a request for export of six horses.[23] As the correspondence with Spain spans several years it is unclear if one or more purchases were involved but clearly Spanish horses were proving difficult to obtain, probably because Henry VIII was now married to Catherine of Aragon.

Despite Holinshed saying only small nags existed there,[24] Scotland had long been tapped by English buyers. In 1347 Edward III had licensed Nicholas de Emeldon and Richard de Newtoune to purchase broken and unbroken horses, mares, oxen and cows and to import them to England over a four-month period.[25] Marcher garrison troopers were supplied on both sides so Scotland's situation was not that bleak.

Later under James VI and I (reigned 1567/1603–25) exports continued. Reporting on Scottish affairs Woddryngton told Walsingham that the Duke of Guise had sent James six horses, landed at Leith on 9 May 1582. Later James asked for licence to purchase horses in England, because 'he hath over huntyd all hys horsys'.[26] A good hunter was suitable for light cavalry.

England

Although Edward III led in upgrading stock, Richard II (reigned 1377–99) was reputed to have kept a fine stable of imported horses, but abuse of the system of royal impressment made inroads into English horses. Because thieves commandeered horses and disguised the theft under the cloak of royal need, a remedial statute (20 RII c.5) was passed.

England was tapped by Italy during the reign of Henry VI (1422–61). Borso of Este, Duke of Ferrara, and his successor and half-brother Ercole I benefited by drafts of English and Irish horses. The House of Este was connected to the Gonzagas of Mantua, Isabella d'Este marrying Gian Francesco II. Margaret, Henry VI's queen, sent to the Estes horses from the royal stud at Eltham. The Eltham strain was still prized in Ferrara and Mantua when Henry VIII began his programme of breed enhancement.[27]

A Barb, or rather a Berber, horse from the Duke of Newcastle's Méthode de Dresser les Chevaux. *(Photo: John Clark)*

Henry's acquisitions included hot-, cold- and warm-blooded breeds and types – prestigious saddle-horses and draught horses to counteract English deficiencies. In 1544 he negotiated, peremptorily, with Queen Marie of Hungary, regent for the Emperor Charles V, for thousands of Low Country horses. Henry, who was 6 feet 2 inches tall (1.9 m), with, at first, an athletic build, loved magnificence and ostentation. His reign was punctuated by shows of martial splendour, as at his meeting with Francis I of France at the 1520 Field of the Cloth of Gold, when sabre-rattling was toned down into jousts of peace. Some imports were distinct breeds, others really crossbreds like the Neapolitan and *some* Gonzagan stock infused with Andalusian and Barb blood. Draught horses that entered the royal studs would have had an impact on the breeding of English cold- and warm-bloods. At Henry's death the inventory of royal horses included several Flemish mares.[28]

Excessive demands were made on stock raised in royal and noble studs and parks. However, while still importing for upgrading, England began to emerge as a major equestrian country.

Italy and Spain

In 1514 Henry's agent Thomas Sieno went to Mantua to select horses from the Gonzagan stud of Marques Gian Francesco II who graciously sent a draft of four, mares and stallions. On 20 March Giovanni Ratto, the Gonzagan envoy, presented them to Henry informing him the marques had a stud of Barbary mares, jennets and great mares of which Henry could avail himself. A bright bay which Ratto rode in the Spanish fashion was reputedly worth its weight in silver. Altobello and Gobernatore particularly pleased Henry. Six more arrived that autumn with a promise of more when trained. In 1517 a fresh consignment arrived for Henry and Charles Brandon, Duke of Suffolk, Henry's brother-in-law and boon companion. A year later Henry's envoys were again horse-hunting in Italy. The dukes of Urbino and Ferrara also gave Henry horses. In April 1519 Sir Gregory de Cassalis was commissioned to purchase the best horses from Spain and Italy. He visited Ferrara where Duke Alfonso I apologized for deterioration in the breed of horses in 'his country'; Sir Gregory chose two of the breed of Isabella, Duchess of Milan; in 1520 he obtained a horse reputed to be the best in Italy. Mantua continued providing Henry with horses; his privy purse for 1530 shows travelling expenses for three horses and their handlers coming from 'Mantwaye'; in 1533 Henry wrote thanking Federigo II for his gift of horses.[29]

Henry often reciprocated with English animals. Hobbies were the usual equine gifts. In 1523 the Marques of Mantua received English horses in return for falcons and Mantuan stock; in 1526 mastiff hounds and hobbies were sent. Francis I of France received six horses and eight hounds in 1526.[30]

Agents scoured other sources for horses, especially those suitable for war. In 1517 Sir Griffith Donne acquired mares from Naples and Turkey and in 1519 Sir Gregory purchased 19 warhorses from Naples. Ten years earlier, when he married Catherine of Aragon, Henry asked her father Ferdinand for a Spanish jennet (Andalusian), a Neapolitan and a Sicilian.[31] Spanish horses continued to

Quesso, é pur anchor lin Armato da guerra, cō le barde d ferro Eʒ lo Arma tutto. cē bello, er
vtile, modo. parte mediuo adorato. parte talinto. Eʒ aqua Forte. in argēnto. cē
la sella d ferro adornta. er argentata. cē l spenachii.
come qui sotto si vedde : –

Orso's depiction of a warhorse in decorated armour and a silvered saddle. Though showing the extremely ornate war/parade armour and tack for a warhorse, it does little to illustrate what the horse was really like, except to confirm that it was of moderate weight. (Victoria & Albert Museum)

Sixteenth/seventeenth-century impression of a Turk (turcoman) horse from the Duke of Newcastle's Méthode de Dresser les Chevaux. *(Photo: John Clark)*

arrive, Ferdinand sending two valuable animals in 1515, followed by Sir Gregory's horse-hunting in 1519; 20 years later the Emperor Charles V sent 25 Andalusians.[32] Undoubtedly other imports also arrived.

D'OSMA'S REPORT, 1576

Appointed to 'find fitting remedies for past shortcomings', Prospero d'Osma compiled a report on the royal studs at Malmesbury and Tutbury.[33] Horses fell into three categories: coursers, small coursers and jennets. Courser still meant warhorse, from the old Italian term *corseiro*, 'battle horse',[34] most Neapolitans being so classified. Naples supplied equestrian excellence – coursers, studmasters, trainers. Federico Grisone opened the first academy in Naples in the 1530s and in 1550 published his *Ordini de Cavalcare* on training, emulated thereafter by trainers, some his pupils, and other authors. One of Elizabeth's stallions was named Grisone – whether for his colour or in honour of Grisone is uncertain.

There were two types of Andalusian: a larger, heavier animal and one smaller and more finely made,[35] so the royal mares were of Neapolitan and Andalusian blood, which did not preclude unrecorded outcrosses. D'Osma's remedial measures enabled the genetic breeding-out of 'bastard' blood. Stock lists show 34 mares, 21 fillies and 10 colts at Malmesbury; 32 mares, 22 fillies and 21 colts at Tutbury; plus an incomplete list of mares not to be covered at Tutbury. All were of potential warhorse use either in battle or at stud. Irish mares are noted at Malmesbury but with no mention of purpose or breed; presumably they were hobbies.[36] At Malmesbury 12 mares were not in foal; at Tutbury 15 of 20 courser mares foaled; small courser and jennet mares show no offspring. D'Osma planned to breed foals in alternate years; with 44 mares covered in 1576 he expected 10 not to conceive; in 1577 these and 21 others, 4 of which were maidens, would be covered. With the new 'ideal', fillies entered the mare band at five years old. Colts were backed at five, trained for a year and ridden for seven, then returned to stud aged 13. D'Osma considered that six stallions were ample for these studs. He advised using like on like, indicating there were more courser than small courser or jennet stallions. Five are known by name: the grey courser Grisone; a small courser, Abbot; a bay courser of Naples, Il Superbo; a *great* grey courser of Naples, Non Piu; and the jennet Argentino. Each breed was to bear its own brand. D'Osma condemned riding three- and four-year-olds and the prevalence of bad horsemanship. He surveyed pastures; detailed a feeding and care regime; recommended stud residence for covering stallions to save their energy travelling from stable to stud; and recognized that natural service achieved higher fertility than 'in hand' covering, although his reasonings are unscientific.[37]

NOBLES' STUDS

Aristocracy followed the royal lead. Land-grants were often made for raising horses for service. In 1509 'the King ordered fiftie gentlemenne to be speres, every one of them to have an archer, a demi launce, and a custrell, and every spere to have three great horses, to be attendent on his personne'.[38] A 'spere's' duties at court centred on providing horses on ceremonial and military occasions.[39] A similar body, the Gentlemen Pensioners, was set up in 1539.[40]

Many abbeys and monasteries such as Jervaulx raised excellent horses. Royal holdings mushroomed when monastic sites suitable for studs were confiscated. Land-grants increased, particularly to Gentlemen Pensioners: Sir Francis Knollys received Caversham Manor, including its park; and Ralph Fane received land belonging to the Order of St John of Jerusalem in the Tonbridge/Hadlow area, and lands forfeited by the Duke of Buckingham's attainder. Later Fane provided 30 horsemen for the 1543 French campaign. The Gentlemen Pensioner Nicholas Arnold, from Gloucestershire, had an equestrian career that spanned three reigns, his stud boasting Flemish and Neapolitan stock. Other nobles aided Henry, either surrendering land to raise warstock, or taking royal mares at grass livery. Marillac, the French ambassador, informed Francis I that in 1542 Henry could draw 150 head annually from his studs in Nottinghamshire and towards Wales alone. The pressure to breed warhorses continued under Edward VI and Elizabeth with musters of horses for service regularly held and the Henrician laws enforced. In 1580 Elizabeth set up a commission 'for the increase and breed of horses and for the keeping of horses and geldings for service'. Dates were set when sub-commissioners inspected all horses and mares in each county. The earlier laws about horse-breeding in parks were enforced.[41]

Despite Elizabeth's parsimony new blood continued to enter England, not only from Flanders and Italy. Her Master of Horse imported Barbs and jennets and, in 1581, six Hungarian greys.[42] Her subjects spread the net. In 1599 Lord Willoughby, commander at Berwick, complained that Captain Boyers was attending more to private enterprise than to his border duties:

> it is here geven forth that Boyers imployment is by some others for horses and other sutch persian and turquish stuffes.[43]

THE HORSE AT THE TUDOR FRONT

Throughout the Tudor reigns even though the equine population grew and improved, numbers were insufficient. A look at Henry's military extravagances and the interminable Tudor border problems shows the horse in Tudor war. Every aspect of equine usage is shown in *The Border Papers*.

Scotland suffered more than France, yet Henry's French expeditions loom large, once in peace, thrice in war. Scotland was hammered with full-scale battle and constant raiding, albeit much was retaliatory. Both Scots and English used Border light horse. For France England supplied few heavy horse, forcing Henry to hire mercenary cavalry. Henry's extravagant French wars added no significant military glory; from 1542 to 1547 they cost over £2 million, exhausting the monastic windfall of the 1530s. Wriothesley reported to Secretary Paget in 1545 that he was 'at my wits end how we shall possibly shift'.[44]

Henry VIII meeting Emperor Maximilian, showing all the pomp and circumstance of the fat and futile monarch – all show and bluster. (Photo: © Her Majesty the Queen, Royal Collection Enterprises)

In 1511 England had joined the Holy League – the Papacy, Venice, Spain, England – to prevent France dominating Europe. A year later the Pope stripped royal power from Louis XII of France and conferred his realm on Henry, and in 1513 Henry went to war.[45] His army was *c.* 24,000 strong, of which *c.* 3,000 were cavalry, mostly northern light horse, javelins, demi-lancers and mounted archers, plus 6,000 German pikemen and 1,000 Burgundian heavy horse.[46] The army was split into vaward, rearward and middleward, and the latter subdivided into right, left and a centre of 6,700 of whom 3,200 were an avant-garde and 3,500, including much of the cavalry, were gathered protectively around the king. Artillery was to front and rear, baggage and ordnance on the flanks. Ahead rode light cavalry scourers; behind were light horse to alert against rear attack.[47] While laying siege first to Thérouanne, then to Tournai, Henry never once risked his person.

DRAUGHT HORSES

Acquiring sufficient draught horses from England and the Low Countries was a massive task. Excessive drain on domestic stock hampered agriculture and subsequent grain supplies. Low Country stock cost Henry dear. For the 1513 war home supplies were bought from April 1512 onwards. Parishes supplied from five to ten horses each; individuals usually one, occasionally four or even six. In 1513 Oxfordshire supplied 312, Berkshire 243; eastern counties from Lincolnshire to Kent 2,566.[48] An estimated 2,000 vehicles were needed. Each ward had 90 for spare equipment and weapons; for example, bows used 13 wagons, bowstrings 2, arrows 26, spears and demi-lances 17, pikes 8, etc. Each ward had over 60 guns and 40 multi-barrel guns – organs. Victualling transport increased the numbers. Each cart had two to four horses, wagons four to eight. Middleward accounts for August and September show 600 carters and 120 wagoners as in pay. Artillery required most horses: 30 for each Apostle gun; 21 for lighter guns. Each bombard (two per ward) needed 24 Flanders mares; smaller guns ranged from 10 horses for a demi-culverin down to 2 for a falconet. There were over 500 tons of powder for initial bombardments.[49]

In 1544 even more animals were required. Accountants who had reckoned that English horses and vehicles were cheaper than hiring Flemish equipages found that a Flemish horse did the work of seven English horses under field conditions.[50] Often 15 English horses per wagon were required.[51] Lengthy correspondence between the Regent of the Netherlands and Henry's secretariat over supply of wagons, limoners (artillery horses) and draught horses ensued. Henry *demanded* 11,000 horses and was offended at the small number offered, then proceeded to tell Queen Marie how to raise his requirements, saying the emperor could get his horses from near the German border.[52] He got a sharp reply via Chapuys, Spanish ambassador to the English court. Marie stated he was ill-informed and ought to consider

> that in furnishing the 2,000 horses of the men of war [for the emperor's auxiliaries loaned to Henry] and 6,000 for artillery and wagons she will furnish more horses than the king will have for the rest of his army, *which is nowise reasonable*.[53]

He was cautioned that horses were raised in the Netherlands by consent.[54] He actually received 9,660 draught horses, 2,460 limoners and 1,800 wagons.[55] When *ordering* horses in 1545 and 1546 Henry was told to buy them at Oldenbourg Fair.[56]

Henry increased his supply by underhand means, buying, without licence, several drafts of mares, which occasioned Marie's bitterness when they were detected at the port of exit, 200 being arrested at Dunkirk. Chapuys was deputed to seek passports for them,[57] which were obtained with difficulty, Marie sarcastically remarking that she had refused passports for 2 and it seemed 'a mockery' now to ask for 200; that farm economy depended in part on rearing horses, and such a number exported would harm this, especially as Henry had already taken 700 mares out of the country without licence. Her parting comment was she 'hoped he would order his subjects to abstain from transporting any more to which she could not consent'.[58]

At the end of the campaign this episode still rankled, plus the fact that Flemish carters and victuallers were abused by the English. The Bishop of Winchester dismissed it saying:

> order would be taken [and] so few mares were transported as not to be worth speaking of, and that how they [the English] had enough ado to pass their own horses, and as to carters and victuallers that in every large camp there would be some disorder.

He accused Flemings of drunkenness, malice and letting the French capture their artillery, etc.[59]

Impressment was felt long-term. As most cart animals were mares, production was doubly hit. Prime mares went uncovered, mares unfit for service foaled. War wastage was higher than in farming, plus there were losses at sea and to French ambushes. Over 3,000 Flemish horses died, plus uncounted English animals.[60]

In 1544, to reduce hardship, Henry ruled that only such horses and carts could be taken 'as might be conveniently spared without disfurniture of necessary tillage and husbandry of any man',[61] but as an ally the Netherlands suffered. His complaints about horse provision did not stop but became a continuing litany of ungrateful, ungracious gripes.

CAVALRY DUTIES

Cavalry duty in 1513 included protecting daily victual trains from Calais to Thérouanne against stronger French cavalry, which included several companies of Albanian Stradiots. An ambush occurred on 27 June. The unarmed Flemish carters cut the traces and fled on draught horses. The outnumbered English, after an initial riposte by cavalry and archers, fled to Guines Castle, horses, carts and contents falling to the French.[62] Accounts varied, losses ranging from 24 to 100 carts. A month later it took 700 cavalry to recapture the St John Apostle gun which mired near Saint-Omer being taken by a French raiding party.[63] Cavalry was fully engaged at Guinegate, near Thérouanne, on 16 August at the Battle of the Spurs, the only real battle in Henry's exploits, although he was absent from the fray. Stradiots, backed by French cavalry in their rear, and a diversionary troop to keep the English engaged north of the River Lys, tried to deliver victuals on horseback to starving Thérouanne. The plan misfired: English 'border prickers' observed the French movements and Henry, warned, advanced 1,100 middleward horse. While Stradiots circled the main body intent on their mission, skirmishing began between French and English cavalry. Dismounted English archers shot the gendarmerie's horses, which, maddened with pain, wheeled; troopers fled, and the rout was exacerbated by returning Stradiots who had been turned by cannon shot *en route* to Thérouanne. The few steadfast French guarding the Lys bridge were captured. Henry's expensive Burgundian cavalry came in at the last moment, the lure of ransoms spurring them on. So hot was the chase that French armour and horse bardings littered the fugitives' path.[64]

The log of Grufydd Elis, a Calais soldier, describes the 1523 and 1544 campaigns – the cold, sodden conditions, mouldy sparse rations, the stink, filth and dysentery in camp that bedevilled the common soldier. Evident is strong criticism and hatred of most officers, and an indictment of Henry for using untrained soldiers who on occasion had to be beaten by their officers to force them to fight. In Suffolk's expedition to Montdidier Elis served under Sir Robert Wingfield, deputy of Calais.

Suffolk arrived at Calais at the end of August 1523, which was late in the year for a campaign. His army consisted of 10,688 foot and horse, and 1,648 in ordnance, transport and support services. About 600 were light horse; heavy horse were few; many archers were mounted. Draught horses would have outnumbered saddle-animals. At the end of September Suffolk was still in Calais waiting for Imperial reinforcements under the Count of Egmont-Buren. Only 500 heavy horse and 3,000 landsknechts arrived, fewer than anticipated. The campaign was costly in animal and human resources, the aims large – to thrust at Boulogne and then at Paris. But the army only temporarily reaped a clutch of towns – Bray, Roye, Montdidier, Nesle, Bouchain – and devastated the surrounding territory.[65]

Elis estimated the army at no more than 14,000, including wagoners, 10,000 with Suffolk, 5,000 with Buren. Desertions and wastage contracted numbers. At Montdidier horses and men fed well on ample provisions including the 'fattest pigs I ever saw', but there were too few English to hold the captured towns; a slow retreat was undertaken. At Bouchain Castle, which fell on 15 November, Henry ordered the army to remain for the winter, saying pay, provisions, artillery and ammunition were on their way. But cold winter set in with a vengeance, temperatures plummeted, the army grumbled. Elis says men were too lazy to fetch food, straw for beds and firewood. Disobeying the king's order, the army marched in the 'hardest frost known to the oldest in the army', many of whom were over 60 years old. Although many were said to have died of cold, Elis himself saw none die or freeze but said that 'in this company old and young men were on horseback from 6 a.m. to 9 p.m.'. Suffolk continued on to Bruges, shipping horses in two hoys, which broke up in a storm; all were lost.[66] Suffolk had to face a Henry irate at his disobedience.

In 1544 an unwieldy Henry and the Emperor Charles V essayed the enterprises of Paris and Boulogne to crush France – Henry to take Boulogne and Montreuil, Charles Luxembourg and Saint-Didier. The Army Royal of 28,000 foot and 4,000 horse – at most 200 men-at-arms, the rest light horse and mounted archers – was to be augmented by Imperial auxiliaries and mercenary horse and foot to a total of 42,000.[67] Henry's agents scoured Europe for mercenaries. Two rogues were Hans von Sickingen and Christopher von Landenburg. Landenburg received 16,000 florins conduct money and dickered over his pay, demanding 'emperors rates' but without supplying the requisite numbers of barded horses; he said that 200 had refused to bard horses, as promised, because it had been found too cumbrous. Eventually it was agreed that he would receive top rates only if horses were barded. Landenburg then demanded an excessive number of deadpays. Much correspondence ensued over his 'predatory' ways, and Henry finally refused to have him even though warned he would enter French employ. Charles had spent 100,000 florins to stop his landsknechts doing the same.[68] Egmont-Buren and Thomas Lightmaker supplied numerous top-quality troops, though Henry was disappointed that not all the horse were men-at-arms but included 'boresperes and short handgonnes'.[69] Eventually Frederic Spedt spoke for Landenburg's horse saying they would serve, many being capable of leading as well as or better than Landenburg,[70] five companies arriving at Boulogne:

the emperor's auxiliaries, 2,000[71]
Buren's Clevelanders, 706[72]
Thomas Lightmaker's Dutch, Westphalian and Danish *reiters*, 500
the Germans: Ytelwolf de Goetenberg, 470
               Hillemer von Quernem, 127
               Chrystoffel von Prysborch, 415
               Hans van Winsigenroot, 321
               Albert Bysscop, 36
               Philippus van Heur, 50
               Otto of Rytberch, 41[73]

Alexandro Gonzaga offered 300 mounted arqubusiers; Joergen van Lesken and Borges van Moncke from Gotha, Germany, each offered 300 or 400 horse. About 50 Stradiots were willing to serve. Mercenary bodies brought their own commissariat, wagoners and wagons. Buren had 208 carthorses and 37 mounted messengers.[74]

With mercenaries, especially Germans who were sticklers for conditions of service, much more was involved than 1,000 horse suggests. The richer Germans came with six or eight horses each.[75] For every 12 cavalry, a four-horse wagon and driver was needed; for every 50 horse, a conductor; for every 100 horse, a smith with wagon for shoes, nails and portable forge; for every 500, a standard-bearer and page, priest, clerk, surgeon, trumpeters, Master of the Camp, trusheman (interpreter) and 'fureyour' (harbinger)[76] – all to be provided with mounts.

From the start things went badly: insufficient military supplies and food for horses and men; inefficient carthorses from England, and not enough of them;

acrimonious demands to and replies from the Netherlands.[77] Discipline was atrocious, hygiene non-existent, profiteering rampant. Sickness and hunger ravaged the lines. Of Buren's contingent over 700 cavalry died, mostly from sickness.[78] Horses were eaten in starving Montreuil.[79]

Grufydd Elis's graphic account covers Montreuil and Boulogne. The Duke of Norfolk's vaward started landing at Calais on 6 June, followed by Lord John Russel's rearward 12 days later. Suffolk's foot and horse followed. The main battle force landed with the king in mid-July. Cavalry numbers reported at 16,000 were 'strongly doubted' by Elis who noted the rancour between Norfolk and Russel. Depredations started early, a Picard stealing baggage horses as the English camped before Bourthes. Light horse chased him and recovered the animals. Baggage trains were attacked. Even with artillery protected by foot and horse, and cavalry scouting ahead for a safe site, two draught mares were killed as Norfolk pitched camp before Montreuil.

Elis noted the taking of the 'old man' tower and the lower town of Boulogne three days after Henry invested it (19 to 21 July); the main town did not fall till 14 September. His carpings from his Montreuil post flowed fast and rancorously. The heavy cavalrymen and mounts appeared in gilded armour; the new Italian 'pardisans' were faulted for brittleness; the English were so lax that the town was not sealed; the camp soon ran short of food and drink, sending to Saint-Omer 30 miles (48 km) away on a fortnightly rota; conveyers consumed a third of the total; much else was lost through leaky barrels; wagons overturned. What arrived lasted only four days. To save pay some soldiers ate green fruit. Dead horses, mares and stallions rotted and stank; entrails and offal littered the ground; pestilence flared. Foragers dared not leave camp without protection of light horse and scouts. Those the French caught they hanged. Local people were allowed in to sell produce, but before long dysentery raged (Elis calls it lientria).

In one episode Elis is at his critical best – justifiably. There was a warning that 700 French horse would attack the victualling train under Captain Hussey who was 'a fat bellied lump of a man, big in body and in authority, lacking in sense and a coward at heart'. Ignoring Lord Durre's order to await reinforcements, he left Saint-Omer with his men in disorderly array, his baggage beasts unprotected. The French swooped, killing some leading victuallers; others fled to warn those following, hotly pursued by the French. The English horse riposted gaining a brief respite; the French attacked again as Hussey tried to restore order. The Flemish victuallers unhitched their horses and fled to Saint-Omer. The French charged both flanks and artillery train, killed some gunners, cut the traces and stole the horses. Hussey 'helpless and senseless' was ordered by one of Henry's servants to get into the centre of his unit and encourage his men rather than appear to be fleeing. Finally English horse feigned flight luring the French into range of their archers and handguns where some French horses were killed, others crippled; most pursuers veered off; a hardy few kept up the chase. In the débâcle Elis saw a French horseman spit a wagoner with his sword. Eventually Lord Durre's relief cavalry arrived to find men devouring the victuals; over one-third of the wagoners and draught animals fled and over half the victuals were destroyed. Soldiers hauled the ditched wagons into Lumbres where they sold victuals for half their value. Six French were killed or taken prisoner; English losses were over 400 killed and wounded. Two days later, with victuals replenished, the train set out protected by artillery and Burgundian horse, yet as it was traversing a narrow section much was lost through fear of attack, 'everybody running and trotting over everybody else . . . so that they upset their carts'.

Officers profiteered by sending their own carts and those seized from the king's baggage train, selling victuals for personal profit. Victuals which arrived at Boulogne were spoiled before distribution.

Elis accused the king of having no real intention of taking Montreuil, but using that siege to enable him to take his ease at Boulogne. Consequently the French foot and horse emerged from Montreuil 'to bicker with the English' while the lax guard dozed and slept. Daily skirmishes occurred with Italian horse and foot in French pay. The siege dragged on, then to Norfolk's fury he heard of the emperor's peace treaty with the French (signed on 18 September). Help was summoned from Suffolk at Boulogne, Montreuil abandoned and stores destroyed – but not before some soldiers got so drunk they were killed by incoming French. At Etaples where they camped overnight before burning it men and horses drowned in the Canche in their haste to cross, harried by French; Norfolk's men and Suffolk's relief force fled; fearful of a trap the French did not press their advantage. Their work was completed for them in a cold and hungry Boulogne where animals starved and died refusing mouldy fodder. Eventually *en route* to Calais, when the English were feeling secure in their own territory, French cavalry struck the artillery train. Gunners were killed, powder barrels emptied, horses seized. The English reached Calais at midnight but only the leaders were admitted, leaving many to die outside. This disgraceful episode was capped by a French attack on Boulogne. The walls were breached in a night attack, both sides suffering high casualties. The French were eventually repulsed largely due to precipitate looting.[80] The English were left with an expensive trophy to garrison. Before he died Henry agreed to relinquish Boulogne in eight years' time for an exorbitant cash demand.

SCOTLAND AND ENGLAND

Amicable relations between Henry and James IV, married to Henry's sister Margaret, soured in 1511 when Henry joined the Holy League against France, Scotland's ally. In 1512 James offered Louis a treaty for mutual military aid against England provided England broke any truce in force.[81] James had other grievances. On 6 August 1512 Henry wrote to the Earl of Surrey with commissions of array for musters of horse and foot from Yorkshire, Northumberland, Cumberland, Westmorland and Lancashire:[82] the Borders were to arm against the Scots. On 15 August James complained to Henry over his refusals to grant a universal peace with his allies' consent, and of safe conducts for Scots ambassadors to work for it. James stated he had overlooked and forgiven the 'inconvenients' committed on his subjects, and thought Henry should have done likewise; that wardens and commissioners could deal with Border matters; and that he had been ready to make reparation for outrages and 'never was mindit uthirways to yow than your manifest dedes give us occasion to be'.[83] Lord Dacre, warden of the East and Middle Marches, warned that Scots fortresses were well fortified, the English side needing the like.[84] In January 1513 James wrote to John of Denmark for aid as Henry had decided to war on Scotland, since he could not invade France with impunity if Scotland were let alone. James feared for Scotland if Henry should win in France.[85]

In June the Pope interfered, threatening to excommunicate James if he warred on England.[86] The acrimony deepened to insults, James accusing Henry of having 'no intention of keeping good ways of justice . . . shown by injuries suffered by James and his subjects'. These included the slaying of Scots warden Sir Robert Kerr on a day of truce, harbouring his killer, imprisoning Scots subjects in chains, etc.[87] Henry's reply included insulting James's ancestors 'which never kept longer faythe and promise than pleased them'. This was written just prior to Flodden.[88]

Incidents multiplied. In August, retaliating for an English raid, Alexander Lord Hume, Lord Warden General of the Scottish Marches, forayed in Northumberland with (variously estimated) from 3,000 to 7,000 riders, burned seven villages and rounded up a great herd of geldings, but was so hampered by plunder that Sir William Bulmer had time to circle ahead and ambush the Scots with fewer than 1,000 men. Over 500 Scots were cut down, over 400 taken prisoner, booty and horses recaptured.[89] On 7 September Surrey wrote from Wollerhaugh that he had sent Rougecroix Pursuivant to warn James he had come to resist his invasion of England.[90] Two days later James was dead on Flodden Field. Scotland lost over 10,000 dead, the English c. 1,500. The only cavalry actions had been Scottish prickers overriding the English opposed to them, and Lord Dacre's English borderers charging the rear of the main Scottish battle. Hume's borderers kept as clear of the fighting as possible, plundering the dead the night following; the reivers of English Tynedale and Scottish Teviotdale plundered the English tents and baggage and stole their horses; the Bishop of Durham was angered by the borderers' lack of national interest. However, many borderers on both sides fought bravely, and it was the Borders that suffered the most.[91]

THE BORDERS

The marches incorporated six areas: the English East, Middle and West Marches, and the Scottish East, Middle and West Marches, each controlled, sometimes less than efficiently, by a warden, his deputy and the Border garrison captains. As early as Edward I's day the Borders were seen as set apart. In a case over a 'furtively lifted' horse Edward I asked about Border law and custom prior to judgment.[92] Thereafter a fascinating equestrian picture emerges through contemporary documents, especially in Elizabeth's reign.

Scottish law predated Tudor equine requirements. In a statute of 1214 every Scot of property was to own at least one horse; in 1327 Scotland could muster 20,000 horses for service.[93] During the sixteenth century service usually meant Border warfare. Raiders, variously called reivers, prickers, riders or moss-troopers, were invariably mounted. Most horses ranged between 15 and 16 hh; others were *c*. 14 hh; a few reached 17 and 18 hh,[94] showing how improved breeding techniques had raised the average height. Most information comes via English documents. Horses crossed borders freely through reiving, capture, or sale, which was usually illegal, both countries prohibiting, ineffectually, such sales. A sense of Border community prevailed with intermarriage and sharing of problems. Its extreme was seen in Somerset's 1547 invasion when, according to the Englishman Patten's records, English and Scottish borderers were seen talking to each other; they made no real attempt to inflict serious injury but only went through the motions of attack.[95] This sense of community did not prevent a century of feuding and raiding among themselves. Often Scot fought Scot, English fought English, but most families acknowledged a national allegiance and banded together for cross-Border fighting. Among the Scots the main riding families were: Laidlaws, Jedforests, Pringles, Elliots, Crosiers, Scotts, Kerrs, Turnbulls, Armstrongs, Irvines, Carvilles, Maxwells, Johnstones, Jedburghs, Youngs, Taits, Rutherfords and Careys (wardens). The main English families were: Fosters, Robsons, Ogles, Dodds, Fenwicks, Musgraves, Bells, Ridleys, Tailors, Charltons, Selbys, Herons, Carnabys, Grahams, Collingwoods and Burns.[96]

Following Flodden, English borderers raided from Annan to the Merse, Lord Dacre's brother Christopher heading a raid that lifted 4,000 cattle, insight and horses. The Scots retaliated and the next spring for every beast lifted by the Scots, Dacre took 100, for every English village that was burned, six Scots villages flamed.[97]

There were continual flare-ups along the Borders until in 1603 James VI of Scotland became James I of England, a twist that would have enraged Edward I and Henry VIII. Before the linking of the crowns, uneasy truces were regularly broken. In spring and summer 1523 the Borders erupted. Jedburgh was sacked by Surrey in September; Lord Dacre then captured Andrew Kerr of Ferniehurst after much hot fighting; under cover of night Scots entered the English camp and loosed 1,500 horses, which galloped through the camp, maddened by pain as guards shot blindly into the dark. Two hundred of them thundered through the burning town, 50 plunged over a precipice; in all the English lost 800. Surrey did not dare credit the Scots, reporting to Henry that it was the devil's work.[98]

During the 1540s the Tudors attacked Scotland repeatedly. Not only the Borders but the capital itself was burned. In 1541 Henry made a royal progress. It resembled an army with 5,000 horses, 1,000 soldiers and an artillery train. Halting at York he waited for James V of Scotland to join him in a meeting designed to cajole the Scots king into remaining neutral if England went to war against France. James, mistrusting Henry, never arrived. In 1542 Henry tried again, *demanding* James's presence, either in York or in London, at Christmas, and backing up his 'invitation' by threatening 'some notable exploit' against Scotland.[99]

In autumn 1542 war threatened. The Borders boiled. Liddesdale erupted. Anton Armstrong led a foray into Bewcastle Waste in which seven Fenwicks were massacred, enraging English borderers. Henry's commissioners countered, pressuring the English riding clans of Redesdale and Tynedale to retaliate, but found the Charltons, Dodds and Milburns would not attack Liddesdale men, both because they were often their accomplices, and also because they were strong. Robert Bowes, warden of the English East March, launched a foray against Teviotdale with the men of Norham and Berwick garrisons, Redesdale and Tynedale. The foray was intercepted by the Scots under George Gordon, Earl of Huntly, at Haddon Rigg on 24 August, and became a rout as Scots rode the English down, capturing Bowes and Heron. Furious, Henry despatched an army under Norfolk who crossed into Scotland on 21 October, conducting a campaign of devastation for six days before returning to Berwick, while Hertford raided Teviotdale with 2,000 riders. With the west wide open James sent 18,000 men under Lord Maxwell, warden of the Scottish West March. On 23 November the battle of Solway Moss was fought. Thomas Wharton, Maxwell's opposite number, who had a scant 3,000 men in Carlisle, augmented his forces with William Musgrave's prickers, and in the ensuing fight used reivers' tactics of charge, hit, run and recharge, especially on the flanks. The Scottish army crumbled, or, as Wharton said, 'our prickers gatt them in a shake all the way'. In the rout Scottish borderers harried, killed and pillaged their own compatriots. The English booty included 3,000 horses, 24 cannon, 4 cartloads of spears. On 1 July 1543 an uneasy peace was agreed, the infant Mary Queen of Scots being affianced to Henry VIII's son, young Prince Edward. On 11 December the Scottish parliament annulled all the Anglo-Scottish treaties and renewed Scotland's alliance with France on the 15th.[100]

Enraged, Henry planned a massive campaign to destroy Scottish power. Starting at Coldstream in the Scottish East March, Douglas and Maxwell lands were 'to be harried with fire and sword and all that cannot be brought away destroyed'.[101] In January Suffolk advised an early invasion to destroy the remaining corn supplies and 'to let [hinder] the sowing of grain, bygge [barley] and haver [oats]'. Such privations would prevent the Scots from raising sufficient men for defence and bar timely French and Danish aid. Non-capitulation would incur wasting from the Borders to the Firth, except the fortresses of Edinburgh, Stirling and Tantallon. The Merse was to be spared to provide fodder for English cavalry and draught horses. Suffolk envisaged six weeks as sufficient, stressing that adequate provisions must be secured in English Border garrisons and 2,000 extra garrison troops supplied to devastate 16 miles (25 km) into Scotland. The army needed was estimated at 20,000. A three-month truce was to be denied, but a one- or two-year truce granted – time for Henry to defeat France and prevent aid to Scotland.[102]

Henry approved Suffolk's plan and suggested a March launch, asking how many cavalry were included. Yorkshire, Leicestershire, Nottinghamshire and Lincolnshire were so well stocked with wheat, malt, peas, beans and other 'haver' that an army could be sustained for six months. If Suffolk was not satisfied with victualling an estimate for 14,000 foot and 2,000 horse for up to a month was to be made. Edinburgh town was to be sacked if the castle resisted. On the return the Merse and Teviotdale were to be burned. Because Suffolk was to accompany Henry to France, he advised his replacement, Hertford, on conduct of the campaign. He reckoned that Henry's proposals allowed insufficient time to gather carts, wains, draught horses, oxen and provisions, etc., informing Hertford that grass and fodder were already gone in the Merse and on the Borders where the Scots would devastate their land rather than let their enemy profit.[103]

From Yorkshire came 140 carthorses to draw supplies and artillery, 9 of them, which belonged to Henry, coming from parks where they had been left at grass after Norfolk's raid in 1542. The purchase and transit of 131 draught horses to Newcastle cost £146 18s 8d; purchasing 7 horses and a cart to haul 'treasure' from London cost £21 3s 6d plus £43 6s 8d for hay. Suffolk estimated a peck of grain a day (2 gallons/9 litres) for each beast, needing 8,000 quarters and 800 carts per 20-day supply. To remedy shortages in draught stock and carriages Hertford resolved to use the worst cavalry horses as pack-animals and purloin carriages and horses from the Scots.[104]

In 1544 the Privy Council's orders to Hertford were harsh. He was ordered

> to burn Edinburgh town, so deface it as to leave a memory for ever of the vengeance of god [for which read Henry] upon their falsehood and disloyalty; do his best without long tarrying to beat down the castle, sack Holyrood House, and sack, burn and subvert Lythco [Linlithgow] and all the towns and villages around, putting man, woman and child to fire and sword where resistance is made, then pass over to Fife and extend like destruction . . . By a month spent thus this journey shall succeed most to the king's honour.

There were 15,000 foot to land at Leith; 3,000 in Border garrisons to occupy the local Scots; 4,000 horse, under Lord Eure and his son Sir Ralph, from the East and Middle Marches, to burn Haddington, while Wharton with 3,000 horse and foot should burn Hawick, as they returned to their garrisons after the bulk of the army re-embarked. The earls of Westmorland and Cumberland were to guard the Border territories in the wardens' absence. Jedworth was also to be burned.[105]

At Edinburgh and in its environs 400–500 Scots died; English losses were small, but the toll in horseflesh was high. Many East March horses were decayed (spoilt/overridden/injured); one garrison alone, John Carr's, lost 40 horses; Scots took others when capturing their riders. In the burning of Jedworth town and abbey horses were hard pushed, especially 500 that raced for the Border when the sight of smoke warned that English villages too were burning, 14 miles (22.5 km) off where 900 Scots horse and 100 foot were retaliating. All but 80 horses were spent; these gave chase, capturing many Scots, but the horses were so overridden that no further enterprises could be undertaken for more than a month.[106]

SPOILS

The 1544 assault was only part of the Tudor blitzkrieg. From 9 September 1543 to 13 March 1544 sanctioned raids yielded 3,285 cattle, 4,710 sheep and goats, 408 Scots prisoners and 35 dead, 124 villages, towns and hamlets burned, 324 horses taken. The haul from 7 July to 17 November 1544 was huge: 192 towns, etc., burned; 403 Scots slain, 816 taken; 10,386 cattle; 12,492 sheep; 1,296 horses.[107] War-spoils were similar in content. Edinburgh yielded cattle, money and plate; Jedburgh, 500 horseloads of booty; a September foray into the Merse by garrisons from Warke, Cornell, Norham and Berwick, 1,000 bolls (over 63,000 kg) of corn – in one night alone 400 horseloads were lifted – plus a clutch of cattle, nags and 16 good horses, and many Scots killed and captured.[108] No doubt pack-horses were part of the 'liftings'.

At Ancrum Moor in 1545 the Scots hit back with a vengeance. To chastise Scots who had sided with the English, such as Crosiers and Nixons, the Earl of Angus led 300 lances against Ralph Eure at the head of 3,000 Middle March riders. Feeling confident, Eure was lured into the hills where Angus was reinforced by Scott of Buccleuch and Fife cavalry which dogged Eure's heels without striking. At Ancrum Moor Angus dismounted his riders, concealing them in rough ground. Eure ran smack into the ambush. His charge became a shambles, then a rout. His Scottish allies deserted to Angus. Over 1,000 English were killed and captured,[109] bringing reprisal by Hertford. His army was bulked by foreign mercenaries, who landed in England from March onwards. They included 1,300 Spanish arquebusiers, horse and foot, under Pedro de Gamboa; German lancers under Mathew Lightmaker, Peter Hoen and Vollard van der Lughe; and Albanian Stradiots who had deserted the French.[110]

PINKIE CLEUCH: 10 SEPTEMBER 1547

In 1547, after the failure of negotiations with the Scottish regent, Marie of Guise, for the marriage of the young Mary Queen of Scots and Edward VI, now King of England, Hertford, now Lord Protector Somerset, invaded with 16,000 men. He had 4,000 cavalry – an unusually large proportion – including 2,000 northern light horse; 500 heavy horse from Boulogne; Pedro de Gamboa's 200 arquebusiers; an Italian troop and the Gentlemen Pensioners. The Earl of Arran's Scots numbered $c.$ 25,000; only 1,500 were light cavalry who, the day before the battle, manoeuvred in sight of the English to draw their cavalry out. Initially Somerset prevented his cavalry charging, but Lord Grey of Wilton, English cavalry commander, persuaded him and charged with his 500 'Bulleners'. In a short fierce fight the Scots horse were mauled so badly that they played no part in the battle on 10 September.

After crossing the Esk the Scots three-schiltrom formation appeared wedged into one unwieldy mass inviting a flank attack from both English cavalry wings and frontal fire from the 15 sakers. The first charge of heavy horse was against the Earl of Huntly's division at the north-east section, the next against Arran. The schiltrom pikes cost the cavalry dear, but the charge bought time for the sakers to be brought up at the gallop and they blasted windrows in the Scottish phalanx from point-blank range. Gamboa's arquebusiers galloped by, firing into the schiltroms. Helpless the Scots came under the fire of English bowmen before the final charge of Wilton's horse. They broke and made for the river. At Pinkie Cleuch over 10,000 Scots died, 1,500 were captured. The English lost $c.$ 500, mostly heavy cavalry.[111]

Somerset garrisoned many Scottish fortresses; Lord Grey was given dual command of the North and the East March. In the next two years Border warfare was the worst suffered as Scots retaliated for years of English savagery, each side committing appalling atrocities. Slowly the English were expelled and in 1549 withdrew their garrisons giving assurances that Scotland would never again be attacked.[112]

Border forays were not quelled for another 50 years, but conflicts were contained mostly within the marches. As England prospered under Elizabeth Border diplomacy grew, though each side ensured fortresses and peles were well garrisoned. National warfare descended into clan and family feuding, with organized warden forays when the Borders boiled too fiercely.

Elizabethan Equestrianism: Training for War

In 1584 Bedingfield translated and published Claudio Corte's work on training horses for private and military use: at first a trainer should be patient and kind and the bridle equipment humane, but a tougher regime is advised for horses of 'evil habit'. A horse that rears or yarks (kicks out) should get a good whipping, but not about the head as that makes horses head-shy and 'feared of the sword and cowardly'. If a horse is too restive and runs backwards, a 'footman' is to prod his quarters with a hot brand on the end of a pike; other means of control, such as tying cords to his testicles or cats to his tail, are 'ungentlemanly'. A stubborn runaway is to be harshly dealt with by being galloped along a ditch blocked at the end with a footman to belabour his shoulders with a cudgel. Failing that, burning wisps or arquebuses should be used (presumably the arquebus's report stunned the horse to a standstill). The cowardly horse that will not run should be forced by 'great and sharp means', being beaten on his quarters by a second rider behind him and by his own rider, who also shouts at him.

Warhorse exercises lacked the above cruelty. Corte advised keeping the animal fit by running it up and down hills, and over broken (rough) ground, and by jumping hedges and ditches. Sham fights defused his fear of weapons, especially about the head, and a fleeing mounted opponent engendered courage, or more accurately, aggression. If when incited he attacked a foot soldier, he should be rewarded with a titbit. The training should accustom him to warlike noises – shouting, horns, drums, trumpets, firearms, rattle of armour, etc. Hunting got him used to many of these and to the press of other horses. He was to be 'ridden among various wheels', which presumably means artillery caissons. Night-riding, training a horse to wait while the rider dismounts and remounts (more difficult than it appears) and swimming – many horses balk at water – were included.[113]

John Astley's work covered warhorse training for skirmishes and hand-to-hand combat, concentrating on the latter. He stressed working for a true partnership between horse and rider, and outlined such abhorrent abuses as horses with 'raw noses; bloody mouths and sides; curbed places galled [chin grooves]; misuse of the chaine, cavesson and musrol and such like, which were first devised to save their mouths, not to mar noses and muzzles'. Misuse necessitated harsher restraints at which the rider then complained the horse hung on the hand and needed spurring, blaming the horse whereas it was his insensitive use that spoilt the animal. Astley admits the need for several types of bit for temporary correction, but denounces the practice used to force a recalcitrant charger to the trooper's will – gum callouses formed by rough handling cut off, tongues cut out, and the nostril and gristle cut away.[114]

This list of horrors shows that in Europe warhorses were first given humane, repetitive training, but that resistance frequently incurred brutality, which must have caused some horses to revert to 'evil habit' and become a liability in battle. However, it is possible to brainwash *some* equines so totally that they will perform tolerably under any circumstances with robotic obedience, lacking what a partnership with a horse allowed to think for itself can elicit, and which must have saved many a trooper's life.

In 1587 with war rumblings from Spain Sir John Smythe was commissioned to help raise and train in Essex and Hertfordshire at least 2,000 men, with 100 horse for every 1,000 foot. Smythe bragged that captains from wars in France and Flanders learned much from his 'trainings'. He noted that colonels and captains of horse used to remain mounted in battle, while customarily mounted officers of foot, even the 'Lt.General and the King himself', dismounted to fight if the army was preponderantly foot. Now all who could do so remained mounted and officers of foot, once their men were drawn up in sight of the enemy, would 'upon their horses of swift careers' either stay on the foot's flanks or rear, or join the horse, thinking it below them to serve on foot, or – an even more caustic note – be more ready to 'save themselves with the force of their heels and spurs than with any dint of sword' which is why so many foot perished and 'never any chieftain'.

Infantry arquebusiers faced with a cavalry charge needed nerves of steel to hold their fire until cavalry were within 8 to 12 paces, and not 20 times that distance as had been taught 'by our men of war'. With a gallop pace of 16 feet (4.8 m) and a trot pace of 12 (3.6 m), the chance of being spitted by a lance or shot by a cavalry pistol was great. Only one in five guns worked and of shots that connected only one in five killed, but the rest caused injury, some permanent. Smythe thought the bow, now almost totally eclipsed, more accurate and lethal against cavalry, recommending that archers in 50-strong bands under 'skilful' officers be mounted. Crossbowmen should have a 'two and a half pound [1.1 kg] bow with crooked gaffles hanging at their strong girdles . . . that they might bend their crossbows the more easily and readily, with 24 quarrels in a case at the pommel'. Archers and their captains should be mounted on 'good cold geldings of mean size'. The men's armour should be of Spanish fashion. Archers were to be trained to fire 'galloping upon the hand, and in other motions of their horses'. Smythe reasoned that an arrow's barbed head would lodge in a horse's flesh and the animal fall 'a yerking, plunging and leaping as if mad'. Its troop would panic, the disorder escalating until all enemy riders were thrown; whereas a gunshot could kill the animal outright if it hit the horse's vitals, or incapacitate it, breaking its bones or its back so that it fell, but if the bullet passed through, the animal, though shrinking at the entry into its flesh, would still be of use. Smythe had seen the results of gunshot and heard the same of arrows from English witnesses. He notes the failings and uncertainties of firearms, and the distance accuracy of arrows over arquebuses and calivers.[115] The bow was still valued in Border forays for its silent delivery.

BORDER WARFARE

Queen Elizabeth (reigned 1558–1603) needed light horse on the Borders; conditions caused perpetual friction between the monarchs of England and Scotland. The Bishop of Durham writing to Lord Burghley in November 1597 describes the ideal Border trooper:

> when we speak of horsemens furniture this means every horse to be of 15 or 16 handfuls high, good and sufficient sadle brydle and gyrthes; for the man a steel cap, a coate of plate, stockings and sleeves of plate, bootes and spurres, a skottish short sworde and a dagger, an horseman staffe and a case of pistolls.

He complained that of 80 extra Yorkshire horse allowed, which cost the county £1,600, only £800 was delivered from Yorkshire and not above 40 of the promised 80 horses had appeared.[116]

The ideal was rarely met. Complaints of insufficient horses and lack of equipment were themes running throughout the *Border Papers*. Constant forays depleted stocks, and Elizabeth's parsimonious ways, saving money while still expecting her wardens to maintain peace, were added burdens.

Wardens and Days of Truce

The long-term, mid-reign English wardens were Lord Hunsdon for the East March; Sir John Forster for the Middle March, succeeded by Lord Eure when Forster in his late nineties was hardly able to stir from his Alnwick base; and the Lords Scrope (father and son, Henry and Thomas) for the West March. Their Scottish opposite numbers were Lord Hume for the East March, the lairds of Cessford and Ferniehurst by turns for the Middle March; and Maxwells and later Johnstones for the West March.

In the early 1580s England suffered heavily from Scots raids and 'loose men' spoiling both sides of the Border. Scrope and Forster complained constantly of Liddesdale raiders and Cessford's procrastinations over march meetings where bills were 'fyled'; justice was supposed to be done and redress made. Cessford counter-claimed against English inroads.[117] The customary warden meetings were delayed – according to Scrope, for five years and to Forster, for eight. This contravened 'Regulations for the Borders' in force since 1556, which stipulated that meetings were to be held not on the Border but at a town several miles within it. Each warden was limited to a retinue of 100, and was to receive/give assurances to his opposite number.[118]

Days of truce often went awry. Many lawbreakers ignored summonses, and the truce often ended with assaults. In July 1585 when Forster met Ferniehurst, Sir John Russel in Forster's retinue was shot dead. In place of the unknown murderer Ferniehurst should have stood hostage, but refused to be delivered.

Ferniehurst had come to the meeting with 3,000 armed men flying his own ensign 2 miles (over 3 km) into England. At the fatal shot the Scots rounded on the English and took many prisoners; Ferniehurst drew his sword and a mounted chase ensued, a further 100 horses and men being taken.[119]

Musters

In 1579 the Privy Council issued a memorandum on the Borders concerning the decay of the English marches, especially Northumberland. Several key points were listed: private quarrels between Herons and Carres, 'who would rather overthrow each other than face the enemy'; spoils by the Scots; the long peace bringing neglect of horses and furniture of war; castles and keeps in the hands of unfit keepers, and absentee landlords.[120]

Light horse were crucial to 'keeping the borders' because of the rough terrain and the speed with which forays were launched. Border musters of the 1580s and 1590s illustrate deficiencies in horses and weaponry.

Forster mustered the Middle Marches on 26 March 1580. A total of 1,670 tenants were liable to serve with horse and equipment. Only 1,145 presented so furnished; 525 had no horses. Those lacking horses gave a variety of reasons: landholdings were too small to support horse and armour; oats and hay were dear; there were too many fines; West Marchers were selling horses into Scotland.[121]

In 1583 the West March light horse muster showed many troopers were 'unfurnished'. In Bewcastle Waste alone where 92 should have come on horseback only 36 did so; 27 lacked horses because of feuds, raids and spoils, and 28 for no cause given. (Figures as in original document.) In his summation Scrope requested special consideration from the queen for Bewcastle as tenants were 'so impoverished they are not hable to bye horses and furniture by reason of their manyfold hereschippes [raids] as before is elleged'.[122]

In November 1595 horse stocks plummeted further. The Middle Marches, which should have mustered 1,137 horses, managed only 136 light horse and 8 horses for petronels; 993 were disallowed because the horses were either 'insufficient' or absent. Only two years previously 920 light horse had mustered, showing the damage cross-border raiding caused. Each town, village, or holding listed men liable to serve with a description of horse, armour and weapons. Few were completely equipped.

The summary for Coquetdale and Redesdale shows 257 troopers viewed. Only 88 had suitable light horses: nags of 14 hh, 27; of 15 hh, 33; mares (no height given), 10; geldings of 16 hh, 17; gelding of 17 hh, 1. In Castle and Morpeth wards most horses were unsuitable and disallowed. Only 19 light horse mounts and 30 suitable for use with petronels passed inspection, but the men lacked the petronels; 364 horses were disallowed as 'the Scots spoil them continually of these and other goodes'. Many men had no spears, few had coats of plate or light horsemen's caps.[123]

At Berwick in June 1594, the condition and supply of equipment were deplorable. Almain and Flanders corselets were in various states of repair; there were only 9 'chaffornes' (chamfrons), 4 pieces of old leather barbes for horses, 82 'galtroppes' (caltrops), 251 lb (114 kg) of horseshoe nails. At Newcastle the only armour in store – 29 pairs of mail sleeves – was old and decayed, and the 24 'jackes' (buff coats) were rotten and 'myce eaten'. However, there were 27 'steele saddles' (war-saddles with partial armour for riders' legs) showing that the man-at-arms was still considered of use.[124]

A constant complaint was a lack of oats and fodder for horses, and the penurious condition of troopers. Horses were issued with beans, peas, or oats only from Michaelmas to May Day,[125] grazing thereafter; this was normally possible as most ridings occurred when horses were at 'hard meate' (corn-fed). On 22 December 1597 Sir Robert Carey complained from Berwick. He found the country 'in better state' than he expected, with a partial lull in frays, and wished to improve conditions but could not as the garrison horses were weakened from hunger. Pay was overdue and insufficient for man and horse at 8d a day and oats costing 8s or 9s a week.[126]

Eure and Scrope also complained. Soon after his appointment in 1595 Eure campaigned for 100 extra horse to serve the garrisons and secure the country against the ridings in the wintertime. After three months' nagging he was allowed to levy 80 extra suitably equipped horse in Yorkshire and the Bishopric of Durham. Owners of the horses were promised their return 'if otherwise they dy not'. Scrope also pleaded 'for a few horsemen to keep down outrages, for footmen are not so good to defend and pursue'.[127] By January 1596 Eure was desperate. The promised 80 had not yet come. He had only foot unable to prevail against the 200 'good Scots horses' rumoured to be waiting to strike from Annandale, Ewesdale and Liddesdale. He asked for 18d a day as the minimum cost for man and horse. By the end of February he had no horses, no troopers, no extra pay, and warned Burghley that if underpaid the men 'will learn border fashion' how to supplement their lack.[128] He dropped his demand to 16d but to no avail; the queen would not budge from 12d and he had to subsidize the deficit.[129] On 20 March 70 horse arrived lacking armour. Eure intended to increase the shortfall of 10 to 20 local men serving for half-pay if the pay was allowed. A canny man, he planned to rotate his locals so that in four months 160 would have served, breaking any 'kindness they have with the Scot'.[130] In April only 71 light horse and 31 horses of lower stature fit for petronels were mustered, some sub-standard. On 2 May the 10 Durham horse arrived and Eure quickly noted successes in capturing the Davisons' 'headsman' and meeting Sir Robert Kerr to agree a day of truce for 2 June.[131]

In June Teviotdale Scots stole all the work-horses from the Earl of Northumberland's town of Dennickle. In retrieving them the Alnwick constable shot James Burne, the leader, but pursuit was impossible as the earl had fewer than 30 fit horses. A feud now blazed up over Burne's death. By February 1597 the situation had deteriorated. Sir William Bowes warned Burghley of imminent war; to 3,000 Scots horse the English could oppose only 1,000 scattered along the Borders.[132]

Ravages committed since the Border Commission of 1587 totalled £92,989 6s 1d of which Teviotdale under Kerr and Liddesdalers under Buccleuch were responsible for three-quarters. Buccleuch was responsible for over 20 murders, Kerr about 16. Later in a revenge raid against Sir Cuthbert Collingwood, who was retrieving his own goods and killed a Scot in the process, Kerr killed 35 Collingwoods, and entered into a feud with Sir Robert Carey for executing Burne, a thief.[133]

Warden Carey

Sir Robert Carey, Lord Hunsdon's son and Queen Elizabeth's cousin, became deputy warden of the East March in October 1596. On Eure's resignation he was made Middle March warden and in 1598 a member of the Council of the North. He was a great horseman, courtier and ambassador and 'kept men and horses far above my rank'.[134] On the Middle March he kept at his own expense '40 good horses and good men able to ride them'. In Border cleansing he hanged or beheaded highwaymen and about 17 of the most notorious Border Scots. In summer 1601 he ran a warden raid or 'Hot Trod' against Liddesdale with over 200 horse. Outlaws fled to Tarass Moss threatening to stay there till Carey gave up, and then to keep him 'waking the next winter'. Adopting ambush tactics he bested 300 Scots horse and 1,000 foot, taking many prisoners, among them five principal outlaws. During the Tarass Moss siege Scots raided his lands, then sent him one of his own cows so he might have 'English Beef'.[135]

In March 1603 Carey was the link between the Tudors and the Stuarts. Repairing to London, he was at court when Elizabeth died at 2 a.m. on Thursday 24 March.

Carey's ride to Edinburgh with news of James's accession is famous. He rode 397 miles (639 km) on foul March roads in three days. Starting on the day Elizabeth died, he stopped at Doncaster overnight and at Widdrington on Friday met his deputies with orders to keep the Borders quiet and proclaim James king on Saturday morning. At noon on Saturday 26 March he was at Norham, then galloped on; when his tiring horse fell, Carey was kicked in the head, but weak from loss of blood he reached Edinburgh that night, the first to kneel to James VI of Scotland and I of England.[136]

The Stuart era began and with it horsemanship expanded. Hunting and racing and the consequent great improvement in light-horse breeding under royal patronage took centre stage.

PART II

The Orient and the Near East

SIX

The Mongols and the Mamlūks

The Mongols, Il Khans of Persia, Mamlūks of the Middle East, Ak Koyunlu Turcomans and Ottomans all had an equestrian background.

The assassination of the Ayyubid Sultan Turanshah by his Mamlūk guard in 1250 ushered in the Mamlūk sultanate. The commander-in-chief Aibek (1250–7) married Turanshah's widow and ruled as Malik al Muizz Aibek.[1] Within 10 years Mamlūks faced Il Khans at Ayn Jalūt.

THE IL KHANS

The first Il Khan was Great Khan Mongke's brother Hulegu (ruled 1256–65) who served as supreme army commander, aided by General Kitbugha, in the campaign to bring Persia, Iraq and Syria under the Mongol yoke. In 1253 he organized supplies along the route to Persia, reserving all pasturage for the cavalry mounts. His army moved fast. He reached Samarkand by September 1255, crossed the Amu Darya (Oxus) in January 1256 and reduced over 100 castles and fortresses controlled by the Batiniya (Assassins). In 1258 Baghdad fell. Hulegu was helped by Golden Horde troops from his cousin Khan Berke who asked for Azerbaijan in return. Hulegu refused, constant discord resulting between the two. Azerbaijan included the Mughan steppe, vital for grazing the Il Khan herds. In 1261 at Derbend and 1263 on the River Terek Hulegu and Berke fought. Although Berke won, he was not strong enough to oust Hulegu's people from Caucasia. The Il Khans retained the Mughan steppe until 1307 when they moved from Tabriz to a new capital, Sultaniya, 200 miles (322 km) south. By then under Gazan (1295–1304) the Il Khans had formed an independent state.[2]

AYN JALŪT: 3 SEPTEMBER 1260

In 1259 Hulegu marched on Syria. His troops sacked Aleppo in January 1260; Homs, Hamah and Damascus yielded. In April Hulegu returned to Iran leaving Kitbugha to hold Syria. Many Khwarazmian, Ayyubid and Kurdish soldiers defeated by Hulegu on his march to Syria fled to Egypt swelling the Mamlūk forces, but they came poorly equipped due to loss of arms and horses.

The all-cavalry Mamlūk army consisted of *c.* 14,000–24,000 Mamlūks and 10,000 *halqa*. Mamlūk cavalry differed from the forces that the Mongols were used to fighting. Lacking the great pastures used by nomadic tribes to equip each soldier with many mounts, the Mamlūk government relied on a more highly trained cavalry with superior arms.

At Ayn Jalūt near Afula in the Plain of Esdraeleon 20,000 Mongols under Kitbugha met 12,000 Mamlūks under Sultan Qutuz.[3] The Mamlūks had the advantage of riding downhill as the plain fell sharply to the Jordan. Kitbugha led the first charge, swept away the Mamlūk advance guard and overran their left flank. The Mamlūk right and centre held and worked round the Mongol flank. Fighting was savage, Kitbugha galloping back and forth encouraging his men and initiating many new charges. Risking all, Qutuz, surrounded by his Mamlūk guard and backed by the rest of the army, plunged into the thick of the fight. General Baybars fought at his side. Mamlūk discipline and weight broke the Mongols who were swept from the field. Kitbugha's horse was killed. He was captured and before decapitation was brought before Qutuz who reviled him. Kitbugha defiantly boasted that a year's increase in Mongolia would replace losses in horses and men. The Mongols were harried 10 miles (16 km) to Beisan (Bethsan) where they turned. Close order fighting began again led by Qutuz until the enemy collapsed.[4] Mamlūk firepower was superior to that of the Mongols, their bows having a more powerful cast. Once the Mongols were worn down by straight, fast Mamlūk shooting, the fresher, larger Mamlūk horses enabled them to attack.[5]

On 10 September 1260 Qutuz entered Damascus in triumph. Baybars was sent to despatch Mongols still in the region, and Mamlūk cavalry columns visited every city as far as the Euphrates. The rule of the surviving Ayyubid prince, Al Nasir Yusuf, was ended, and from Egypt to the Euphrates Mamlūk power was established.[6] Ayn Jalūt and successive victories were due to initial selection and tough training in the Mamlūk barracks and hippodromes.

Under Baybars (1260–77), Al Mansur Qalaoon (1279–90) and Al Nasir (or Al Nacer) Muhammad (1298–1308 and 1309–41) the Mamlūks became the most sophisticated military equestrians.

THE MAMLŪK CAVALRY

Composition

Mamlūk cavalry was comprised of the Royal Mamlūks, the Amirs' Mamlūks and the *halqa*. The Royal Mamlūks were inherited from Sultan Malik who as Salih Ayyub purchased young boys, mainly from Kypchak Turks, to be trained as his personal mounted guard. His Royal Mamlūks were based at Cairo on a Nile island and were called Bahri-river-Mamlūks. Initially they were *c.* 1,000 strong[7] but the numbers eventually rose to 12,000 housed in 12 *tibaq*, the military barracks of Cairo citadel.[8] The Amirs' Mamlūks were purchased to serve in Amirs' personal retinues.

By 1260 the numbers had jumped to 4,000 Royal and 10,000 Amirs' Mamlūks.[9] Merchants visited steppe camp-sites purchasing youngsters of 10 to 12 years for sale to the sultan and his amirs. Even though sold as slaves, the youngsters went willingly, for a Mamlūk cavalryman's life offered good prospects, especially to those bought by the sultan.[10] During the Bahri period, up until the accession of Al Dhair Barqūq (1382–9 and 1390–9), Kypchak Turks provided most Mamlūks, but Mongols, Caucasians, Alans and Russians – indeed boys from any steppe tribe with an equestrian background – were also purchased.[11]

Halqa were allotted fiefs to support them. Many were Egyptian-born sons of amirs and Mamlūks and were known as *aulad ul nas*, 'sons of the people'. Cavalry numbers fluctuated, but the cavalry strength from the reign of Al Mansur Qalaoon is shown in Table 6.1. Up to 10,000 other cavalry were raised from Turcoman tribesmen and Bedouin Arabs.

Table 6.1 Cavalry in the time of Al Mansur Qalaoon

	Royal Mamlūks	Amirs' Mamlūks	Halqa
Egypt	12,000	5,000	12,000
Syrian viceroyalty towns			
Damascus		2,000	12,000
Aleppo		1,200–1,500	3,000
Smaller viceroyalties (e.g. Gaza; others were Hims, Hamah, Safad, Tarabulus [Tripoli])		80	1,000

Loyalty of individual Mamlūks was to their patron, not the state. After manumission they remained in the service of the sultan or of the amir who had first recruited them. On his death they could become mercenaries or farmers. If the former they owed no loyalty, other than their hire agreement.

Land-grants and Promotion

Land-grants were tied to a trooper's rank. If the sultan wished to reward a soldier, the man was raised to officer rank with a fief for the Mamlūks he was required to equip and maintain. Basic ranks were amirs of 10, 40, or 100. Occasionally amirs of 5, 20, or 80 were created, but usually only when a small fief was given to the son of an important man. An amir of 40 was known as an amir of drums as he was allowed a small military band. In war an amir of 100 commanded 1,000 men made up of his own guard and *halqa*.[12]

Government land was set aside outside Cairo for growing lucerne (alfalfa, sometimes incorrectly translated as clover), an ancient crop still grown in Egypt and a food of exceptional nutritional value. From this the sultan made a yearly grant to his amirs and Mamlūks for feeding their horses. For the three-month growing season each Mamlūk received half a feddan (1 feddan = 0.5 acre/0.2 hectare) for each *aliq* (fodder ration) entitlement. No barley, the bulk of the *aliq* ration, was received during this season. In the 1488 regulations each Royal

Mamlūk received three *ala'iq*. The higher the rank, the larger the award. Grants fluctuated, but some must have been very large because in 1512, after sustained drought, the commander-in-chief lost 200 feddan; amirs of 1,000 lost 100, amirs of 40 lost 40, amirs of 10 lost 15.[13] Usually, though, after the Nile's annual inundation, growth was rapid, nutritional value high, multiple cuttings possible.

Horse Supply

The *iqta* (fief) system by no means provided enough horses. Another source was large-scale breeding of high-class stock. Abou Bekr outlines purchases, stud policies and management system of Al Nacer's famed stud of Arabian horses. He details training for all disciplines including war, although his main concern was racing, a consuming passion among the Mamlūks. Bedouin tribes, especially those that raised the high-priced and highly esteemed Faras horses, sold to Cairo as did Barqa in Cyrenaica, which also made tribute payments. The Maghreb also supplied horses.[14] The Maghrebin kings sent the Mamlūk sultans large presents of horses, Al Nacer receiving 500 in one convoy. Repeated repressive raids against rebellious Bedouins in Upper Egypt in 1301 yielded a punitive levy of 6,000 horses, 22,000 camels, 110,000 sheep and goats, plus cattle and donkeys. When a campaign was imminent extra horses or cash equivalents were levied on districts. Any amir not serving on a campaign had to pay a levy in horses.[15]

The sultanate inherited horses from Syria, which had bred quality horses since the days of the Seleucids.[16] The principal breeds used by Mamlūks were:

Arabians:	the Faras were purebreds, the Hedjin halfbreds with an Arabian sire, the Moukrif halfbreds with an Arabian dam
Berdhun:	a non-Arabian horse of mixed breeding
Berber or Barb:	from North Africa, the Maghreb: the superior Berber resembled the Arabian, as infusions of Arabian blood had taken place before the Mamlūk era. The indigenous mountain stock was tough, enduring and an easy keeper. A native Barb has a ram (convex) head, and a sloping croup, which assists balance in tricky going. It is shorter-coupled than the Arabian, which itself is shorter in the back than most breeds.[17] Because of infusions of outside blood in the post-Mamlūk era the modern Barb differs from the ancient breed, and many were so named because they were exported via the Barbary states
Turcoman/Turkmene:	horses from Turcoman tribes hired as mercenaries.

Abou Bekr describes various breeds. Several were purebred Arabians from different tribal zones. Faras from the Hejaz had beauty, good feet and limbs; those of the Nejd had superior conformation – a long neck, large shoulders, full belly, strong thighs and fine limbs. The Yemeni had coarser bone and an angular frame, with a heavy body, thick legs, pointed shoulders, slender flanks and a short neck, and were fine horses, although this source was virtually, though temporarily, wiped out in AD 1327–8 by epizootic diseases.[18] Jezira horses had excellent hindquarters, large shoulders and forelimbs and were either purebred or heavily infused with Arabian blood. Barqa horses were heavy-bodied, fleshy-chested, big-headed and thick-legged with huge feet. Egyptian horses were plentiful, with a long neck, weak limbs, long pasterns, big feet and an ungraceful (weak) chest. The Berber/Maghrebin had a strong neck, thick legs, round knees and cannon (lower limbs) and was usually a proud horse, but lacked wide, large nostrils.[19] The Khorassanian Chahri (Shihry) was tough and insensitive to wounds and severe bits, but was so vicious that a fallen rider had to be on his guard. In war it fought for its rider with hooves and teeth, but 'was very risky to approach'.[20]

Other points concerned superficial looks, but those noted indicate what was significant, particularly in a warhorse. The Faras were far superior by both ancient and modern standards. The Egyptian was a 'weed'; the Barqa clumsy but up to weight; the Barb without much Arabian blood was stocky but lacked an efficient respiratory tract for sustained speed – it can go at high speed only in short bursts but keeps going indefinitely at a steady pace. Most accolades are reserved for the Faras, which were reserved for gifts to the sultan. Al Nacer owned thousands of Faras broodmares[21] from which future racehorses and warhorses were raised and distributed among his amirs and high officials. Being a racehorse did not exclude the horse from use in war. Knowledge of racing and all it encompassed was also part of the Mamlūk *Furusiyya* training. Maqrizi stated that only horses and camels used in war were authorized to race.[22]

Baybars, a superb rider and warrior, did not favour one particular breed,[23] but he and his immediate successors imported a yearly quota of Barqa horses. When in the reign of Al Nacer the quota was not delivered one year, he sent an army against Barqa.[24] Al Mansur Qalaoon, Al Nacer's father, preferred Barqa horses, commenting on their utility; the Arabian, he said, was for parades.[25]

Barqūq, the first Circassian sultan, also favoured Arabians.[26] On the death of Al Nacer 4,800 horses were found in his personal stables, plus 5,000 racing camels. On the death of Barqūq it was estimated his personal studs held 7,000 horses and 15,000 camels; alternative figures were 6,000 horses and 5,000 camels, or 2,000 horses and 5,000 camels.[27]

Twice a year, at the end of the spring grazing period and in the polo season when the sultan attended military games at the Hippodrome outside Cairo, he awarded gifts. Amirs of 100 received horses equipped with lavish saddles, bridles and gold (fabric) housings – some as many as 100 a year; amirs of drums got horses without apparel.[28] Amirs of 10 received horses only as a personal, not traditional, gift from sultan to subject. Governors of Syrian provinces received horses according to rank at the second distribution.[29] An amir was obliged to keep four horses in training. The *Amir Akor*, Master of Horse, was responsible for many of the sultan's horses in training;[30] they were primarily trained to race, the racecourse being a testing ground for war use. Indeed all mounted activity was geared to eventual warfare.[31] Ordinary Mamlūks received their war mounts on finishing their training. If a Mamlūk's horse died, he received a replacement on furnishing proof of its death and a piece of its flesh.[32]

AMIR AKOR

Al Nacer created the post of *Amir Akor* whose responsibilities were:

administration of stables, studs and *manak* (camel stations)
purchase and acquisition by levy of grain, beans and fodder for horses and
camels
organization and payment of staff
purchasing horses.

Al Nacer was personally involved in many purchases, paying huge prices for
exceptional individuals. The related Bedouin tribes of Beni Mouhanna and Beni
Fadl bred the best Arabians and came from Syria, although originally from the
Nejd.[33] Other Arabians came from Bahrein, Iraq, the Hejaz, Haca and Katif,
fetching 10,000 to 30,000 *dirhams*; exceptional animals might make from 70,000 to
1 million *dirhams*. Ordinary stock purchased for Mamlūk cavalry was much
cheaper, though this information comes from the end of Mamlūk rule, when
5,000 *dirhams* (13–14 *deniers*) bought a cavalry mount; 3,000 *dirhams* a pack-horse.
The trooper could have either the horse or the cash[34] to choose a suitable charger
for a forthcoming campaign.

TRAINING

Furusiyya Exercises

Superb facilities for *Furusiyya* training and practice in mock battles were
provided by hippodromes or *maydans*. Most were built during the Bahri period
(1250–1382), but then fell into disrepair. In 1503 Sultan Kansuh al-Ghawri built
the only *maydan* of the Circassian period. *Maydans* were self-contained, with
palace, gardens, training, race and polo grounds and complete stud facilities.[35]
Here, the *faris* (cavalryman) received intense individual and group training in the
military arts, called *Furusiyya* exercises. The successful trainee possessed
Furusiyya, meaning all a horseman had to master to become an accomplished
knight.[36] Once trained he was manumitted, given a horse and military
equipment[37] and served in the personal guard of his ex-owner.

Horsemanship and horsemastership incorporated a vast body of knowledge,
each element having its own specialized field. A Mamlūk cavalryman had to
doctor his horse, make its tack, at a pinch shoe it or tack in an extra nail if a shoe
became loose,[38] craft his own shooting equipment and handle all weapons with
absolute control. *Furusiyya* equestrian exercises included training with lance,
mace, bow, crossbow and sword, plus polo, hunting and horseracing.[39]

Equitation

The Mamlūk's most important accomplishment was in riding his horse
instinctively, leaving him able to wield weapons efficiently and/or place his horse
to advantage in a massed charge or hand-to-hand combat. Coming from a steppe

background Mamlūks were natural horsemen used to riding well before recruitment, but there was a great difference between untutored riding and disciplined riding with the aim of fighting cohesively in the most renowned cavalry of the medieval period. The apprentice first learned to mount a dummy horse both with and without a saddle, and with and without full military equipment. Next came a live horse wearing only a horse-cloth, called *jull*, made of wool or bristle. To mount, taking his whip in his left hand, he placed his right thumb on the *jull*, his right palm on the withers, and when mounted he hit the horse with his right hand on the offside (right) of the neck. Training progressed on a saddleless horse at canter, trot and gallop,[40] or so says Ibn Qayyim al Jawziya (d. 1356) but this sequence does not accord with other sources or make much sense – it is normal to progress via walk, trot, canter, gallop – so one is left wondering if he had understood correctly. Ibn Hodeil's description has a more modern ring: he advises a bareback sequence of walk, slow trot, faster trot, very slow canter, faster canter only when the rider has an independent seat and does not need to hook his feet under the horse's elbow,[41] and finally full gallop. To maintain contact with the stirrup tread Abou Bekr recommends placing a coin between tread and boot sole.[42] Horses destined for lance work were to be galloped only on short stretches.[43] This ensured that they erupted explosively, lending poundage to the thrust.

Abou Bekr describes several saddles, from the lightweight shallow one used on youngsters to 'national type' saddles for different equine backs. He preferred the *Naceri* saddle for its pommel, cantle and shallow seat design which assisted trainee cavalrymen; this must be the low cantled 1293 design of Al Baysari.[44] It was easier to get into and out of; the rider could lean back to avoid an incoming weapon and had more flexibility in his own movements when delivering a blow.

Lance Exercises

Introduced on a large scale into *Furusiyya* training, lance exercises performed in the *Maydan al Kabak* throughout the Bahri period enjoyed a temporary resurgence in importance under the Circassian Barqūq. An elite 40-strong lancer corps, the *Al-Rammaha*, under a *mu'allim* and his four subordinate *bashat* officers paraded in the twice-yearly *mahmil* procession. Men and horses were armoured as for battle, the horses in steel caparisons and head armour.[45] The *Al-Rammaha* formed two teams, each led by a *muqaddam*. Formalized exercises ridden in parallel lines and concentric circles finished with Mamlūks in opposing lines, each man engaging in single lance combat with a designated opponent. Starting with individual training a young lancer had to master exercises that made him so expert he could wield his lance travelling fast, attacking, circling, fleeing. Group training involved simulated battle.[46] Targets varied. Two resembled ring-spearing and tent-pegging. The former used a post, a *dari'a*, raised to a rider's height; on top was a ring or cord loop. As he galloped past he either reversed his lance to extricate it from the loop or could let its thrust carry it through the ring and retake it as his horse galloped past.[47] Both methods had risks, the first if he did not disengage cleanly, the second if the horse galloped too fast for him to grasp the lance. Tent-pegging targets were scattered cones, to be collected on the lance tip. Variations

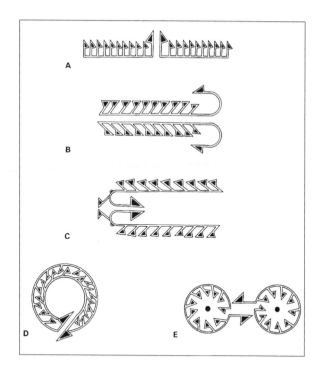

The intricate manoeuvres of the Furusiyya exercises that every Mamlūk had to master, and one reason why they were such excellent cavalrymen, far outshining any occidental counterpart in equestrian skill. (Reproduced by kind permission of the School of Oriental and African Studies, University of London, from War, Technology and Society in the Middle East, V.J. Parry & M.E. Yapp (eds), Oxford University Press, 1975)

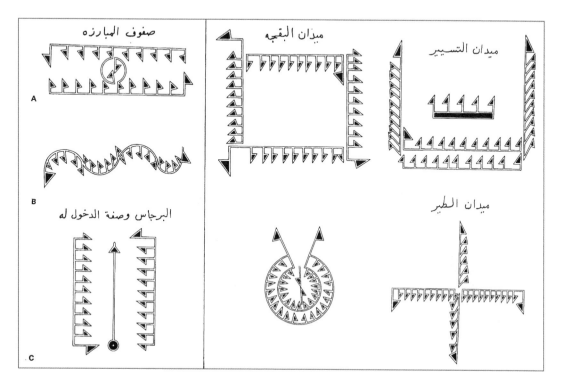

were 12 rings fixed to a rod, or a ball placed on a man's head, to be speared as the horse galloped by. The *Birjas* game used a target of seven segments placed on top of each other and encircled by metal, into which the charging Mamlūk threw his spear; if he was successful, the target toppled; if not, the lance fell to the ground.[48]

Archery

Qabak was a game in which a gourd was mounted on a mast in the centre of the arena and an archer galloped towards it and shot upwards. Care was needed to avoid collision with the mast. Taybugha relates an incident when the viceroy of Tripoli's Amir of the Hunt momentarily lost concentration; his horse swerved, hitting the mast, and both died of their injuries. This shows the horse's speed. An Arabian or Turcoman could reach more than 30 mph (48 kph) over a short distance. Common or Berdhun horses would have been too slow. Many horses travel crooked unless the rider corrects deviations. Taybugha advises novice archers to practise with a gourd suspended from a rope attached to two masts, one at each side of the arena. An unfamiliar mount was to be tried first at a walk without any shooting, then at the same pace aiming at the gourd, using the *Qighaq*, or slanting-down technique, before working at speed. The method was to canter the first third of the pitch, full gallop for the next third and shoot at the target, remain at the gallop for the last third. The pitch distance was a minimum of 131 yards (120 m), a maximum of 284 yards (260 m), given by Taybugha in arm spans – from 60 to 130 spans.[49]

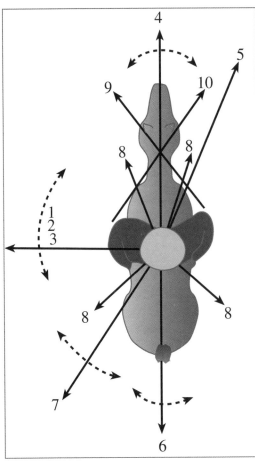

Overhead view of the operational field of fire, showing the many shots perfected by oriental archers. (After Taybugha al Baklamishi al-Yunani, Saracen Archery, tr. J.D. Latham and W.F. Paterson, Holland Press, 1970)

A short range presented difficulties in control and smoothness of gait as there would have been scant room for the horse to lengthen stride and lower his topline to give a steady platform for the archer to nock, draw, switch rein hand, turn in the saddle, and loose over his horse's rump before he reached the end of the pitch and veered to the left, where Taybugha says the exit was. This suggests the horse would gallop on his left lead or risk bringing himself down on his turn. On the left lead if the horse swerved he would have headed away from, not into, the mast, thus avoiding collision. Wind direction also had to be taken into account.

POST-TRAINING USE OF MAMLŪK AND MUSLIM WARHORSES

I have concentrated on the Mamlūk and his charger because there is so much evidence. The basics apply to other oriental cavalry training. Once the Mamlūks were entrenched, enemies loomed – first the Il Khannate Mongols, then Timur; by the mid-fifteenth century they faced the Ak Koyunlu of eastern Anatolia and the rising power of the Ottomans against whom they had a long, bitter and inconclusive struggle in the 1480s before being defeated in 1516 by Selim I (1512–20) at Marj Dabik north of Aleppo where Sultan Al Ghawri died

Mamlūk weaponry, as shown in G. Rex Smith, Medieval Muslim Horsemanship, *fol. 136a. (Photo: Oriental & India Collection, British Library)*

in battle,[50] and their last-ditch stand on 22 January 1517 at Ridanieh outside Cairo. By their neglect of firearms the Mamlūks had encouraged Ottoman aggression.[51]

Muslim armies still gave precedence to cavalry and Umar ibn Ibrahim al-Awsi al-Ansari's *Muslim Manual of War* outlines its use, as does Ibn Hodeil's work.

Horses and mares were used. Ibn Hodeil says mares were best for fast expeditions, night attacks and 'secret warfare'; stallions for open conflict, battles and extended marches; geldings for ambushes and patrols because they could sustain effort[52] – a remark that appears inaccurate, as although on the whole geldings have a more equable nature than stallions, so can be pushed further because they argue less, they are no more enduring. Al-Ansari does not mention geldings, but sensibly advises single-sex groupings for ambushes[53] and ensuring horses were neither stubborn nor sexually restive and had sound hooves and backs. For scouting parties securely shod racehorses were best.[54] His warnings were apposite: mares in oestrus can be a pain in the backside, some of them stubborn or bad-tempered, and some stallions in the covering season are bloody-minded even if a mare is not present.

Mamlūk weaponry, as shown in G. Rex Smith, Medieval Muslim Horsemanship, *fol. 136b.*
(Photo: Oriental & India Collection, British Library)

Scouting was carried out either by an individual or a pair of scouts, or by a small patrol under a general, *al-muqaddam*. A single scout reconnoitred, reporting to base; a pair of scouts split up, one staying on watch to see what transpired while the other reported back; in a group the *muqaddam* decided dispositions. A returning scout brought his horse in calmly to avoid raising alarm. Pre-arranged signals were: if he dismounted the enemy was camping; walking to right or left of his horse indicated the side the enemy was approaching from; galloping into base warned of imminent attack.[55]

Marching orders were that scouts went first, then experienced trackers, pioneers to smooth rough tracks, cavalry vanguard. The 'rest' followed; the cavalry rearguard, *saqah*, protected the army's back.[56] A camp was surrounded by so many protective layers of cavalry – mounted guards at entrances and three lines of horse at strategic distances from the camp perimeter – that a surprise attack or infiltration should have been impossible.[57] When marching into territory where the enemy's whereabouts were unknown scouts and cavalry protected all sides, cavalry surrounding baggage and treasure chests.[58] Five lines were deployed against a numerous enemy. Vanguard cavalry used the most experienced warriors arrayed right, centre, left, subdivided to give nine detachments, each under a *muqaddam*, with spaces between units for officers to sally out for single combat. The second line of highly rated cavalry was similarly organized. The third protected the baggage, assisted by light armed horse of the fourth. The fifth, also aided by the fourth at need, repelled attacks from the rear and protected baggage against looting.[59]

In battle infantry went ahead to protect cavalry and break the enemy; cavalry's main duty was to harry but at no time should it act recklessly or waste horses' energy. Massed cavalry was to proceed steadily against an enemy that stood fast after the first assault. Troopers were not to risk themselves by being lured into single combat by a fleeing enemy or into an ambush, or by going too far out for a safe return to ranks. Concerted harrying was to be done only if sure of success, initially by a direct chase; the enemy should be allowed access to water and its flight not be impeded, for a cornered enemy fleeing for his life would fight hardest, but allaying the fear of being cut down made them easier to surround and capture. Half the cavalry harried, half looted the enemy camp.[60]

Infantry were to receive the brunt of a surprise attack giving cavalry time to mount and engage. A cavalry reserve guarded the army while they were mobilizing.[61] Complete obedience to superiors and strict discipline were maintained, especially if night fell forcing temporary withdrawal; cavalry officers were not to retire until all was secured for the night. If battle formations had to be kept overnight the army contracted, a cavalry screen guarding the perimeter until day when battle was resumed.[62]

SEVEN

The Ottoman Empire

Ertogrul (d. 1289), a Turkish chieftain of only 400 horse, served the Sultan of Rum, holding a small fief at Soegud on the Kara Su river. His son Othman (reigned 1289–1326) expanded his father's land in Bithynia at the expense of the Byzantines. Two important factors in Ottoman (Othmanli) progression were Othman's line of seven able descendants and strategically sited territory opposite Constantinople.[1]

In 1301 Othman defeated 2,000 Byzantine cavalry at Baphaeon. By 1345 the Ottomans faced Europe. Ten years later they were based at Gallipoli and in 1361 Edirne (Adrianople) fell to them, threatening Christendom. Under Murad I (1362–89) they expanded into the Balkans and consolidated in Anatolia; in 1387 they defeated the Karamans at Konya; they occupied Bulgaria and in 1389 defeated the Serbs at Kossovo, where Murad was killed. His son Bayezid I (reigned 1389–1402) succeeded him and thrust further into Anatolia and the Balkans. Hungary felt Bayezid's might; he occupied Mamlūk Malatya and Elbistan, and encroached on Timur's territories.[2]

Between 1399 and 1401 the Mamlūk, Ottoman and Timurid empires clashed. Although Mamlūk and Ottoman paid heavily, Timur's course was almost run. Arabshah notes the infighting among Bayezid's sons: Suleiman murdered Isa; Musa killed Suleiman to avenge Isa; Mahomed killed Musa. In 1421 Murad II (reigned 1421–51), son of Mahomed, succeeded and regained all losses occasioned by Timur's invasion. Arabshah says Mustafa was lost; to ensure his death 30 of his name were executed.[3]

The essential oriental equine content had largely been fixed; indeed oriental breeds today differ little from their medieval ancestors, while occidental breeds are constantly evolving. Military documents, reports by European ambassadors and travellers, and the history by the Mamlūk Abu-l-Mahasin ibn Taghri Birdi show the horrors of war, the means that enabled its perpetrators to inflict it over such a wide area, and how news travelled so rapidly ahead of the cavalry's hoofbeats.

Although infantry was used by all, it was relegated to an inferior role; the only exception was the small Ottoman Janissary Corps, and this was not expanded to a 12,000-strong force until the reign of Suleiman the Magnificent (1520–66).[4]

CAVALRY AND LAND-GRANT SYSTEMS

The 'Sipahis of the Porte' were the elite paid cavalry of the sultan's personal guard drawn from non-Turk, non-Muslim origins – war captives, purchases and,

Stylized depiction of warrior lassoing his opponent, a typical Mongol tactic. (Photo: Oriental & India Collection, British Library; BL OR. 13859, f. 147)

in large measure, the *devshirme* child tribute, levied on Christian subjects, especially on Slavs and Albanians, the boys being raised as Muslims in Ottoman training schools. Most provincial cavalry were feudal *sipahis*. *Akinjis* were light cavalry armed with sword, shield, scimitar, lance, mace. Organized in units 10-, 100- or 1,000-strong, and commanded by a *sanjak bey*, they were used mainly in frontier zones. On campaigns they went ahead of the army as scouts and raiders to disrupt and destroy enemy supplies and take prisoners for interrogation. Each *akinji* normally took two horses on expedition. His motives were booty and the hope of eventually getting a *timar*.[5]

The feudal *sipahi* was tied to the *timar* system. At the top was the *Beylerbeyilik* incorporating several smaller units, *subasaliks*, which made up a *sanjak*, the main administrative unit. A *subasi* commanded *sipahis* who were allotted *timars* in his *subasilik*. Only men from the military class were eligible for a *timar*, gained via the *sipahi*'s commanding officer who petitioned the sultan for a land-grant on his behalf. A successful *sipahi* then waited till a *timar* fell vacant. A *sipahi* owed military service reckoned on the value, not the size, of his *timar*. In the fifteenth century lower-grade *sipahis* averaged revenue of *c*. 2,000 *akçes* per annum; *sanjak beys* 200,000 to 600,000; *beylerbeys* from 600,000 to 1 million. The system aimed to provide a standing cavalry force, each *sipahi* equipping himself with horses, bow, sword, shield, lance and mace. If his *timar* revenues were sufficient he was to be armoured. For each 3,000 *akçes* of income he also had to provide a *cebelu*, a fully armoured horseman. According to *timar* value each *sanjak bey* built up a contingent of light cavalry. Regular service was required. If seven years elapsed without a *sipahi*'s serving, he lost his *timar*; if he resumed military duties, his commanding officer could petition for its reallocation. *Timars* were not hereditary until the later empire. A *sipahi*'s sons were awarded smaller *timars* in varying locations, thus preventing strong family coalitions threatening authority.[6]

DE LA BROCQUIÈRE

De la Brocquière, who lived among the Turks in 1433, describes the Ottoman system. The Turks were 'tolerably handsome', of moderate size and strength. They were hardy and ate sparingly, letting nothing go to waste – mortally sick horses and camels were killed and eaten.

> Their horses are good, cost little in food, gallop well and for a long time. They keep them very poor, never feeding them but at night and then only giving them 4 or 5 handfuls of barley and double the quantity of chopped straw . . . At break of day they bridle, clean and curry them, but never allow them to drink before midday, then in the afternoon every time they find water, and in the evening when they lodge or encamp; for they always halt early, and near a river if possible . . . during the night-time they cover them with felt . . . All their horses are geldings; they keep some others for stallions, but so few, I have never seen a single one . . . Their saddles are . . . hollow, having pummels before and behind, with short stirrup leathers and wide stirrups.

He twice saw cavalry kitted for war at the ceremony where 'Greek renegadoes' converted to Islam on entering Turkish service:

> they wear very handsome coats of armour like to ours, except that the links of the mail were smaller; the vambraces were the same . . . On their head they wear a round white cap, half a foot high, terminated in a point. It is ornamented with plates of iron on all sides to ward off from the face, neck, and cheeks, blows of the sword . . . they usually wear another over it, namely a bonnet of iron wire . . . some cost from 40 to 50 ducats, whereas the first are bought for 1 or 2; although not so strong . . . they resist the cut of a sword. I have spoken of their saddles in which they sit, deep sunk in them, their knees very high, and with short stirrups, a position in which they cannot support the smallest blow from a lance without being unhorsed. The arms of those who have any fortune are a bow, a tarquais [shield], sword, heavy mace with a short handle, the thick end of which is cut into many angles. This is a dangerous weapon when struck on the shoulders, or on an unguarded arm . . . a blow given with it on a head armed with a salade would stun a man. Several have small wooden bucklers with which they cover themselves well on horseback when they draw the bow . . . *having seen it myself*.[7]

Successes were due to obedience to commanders and to a good spy and reconnaissance system enabling the sultan to lay ambushes ahead of a (Christian) army. At a drum signal they rode off in silence and perfect order:

> without the file ever being interrupted from the horses and men being trained to this purpose. 10,000 Turks will make less noise than 100 men in the Christian armies. In their ordinary marches they only walk, but in these they always gallop; and as they are beside lightly armed, they will thus advance further from evening to daybreak than in 3 other days; and this is the reason why they cannot wear such complete armour as the French and Italians. They choose, also, no horses but such as walk fast, and gallop for a long time, while we select only those that gallop well and with ease. It is by these forced marches that they have succeeded in surprising and completely defeating the Christians.

Territory dictated their manner of fighting. In woods or among mountains many small units would attack the enemy at different points. Elsewhere ambushes were sprung after well-mounted scouts had gone ahead. If faced with a massed enemy they surrounded it and when a bowshot off poured fire in on horses and men until the enemy was in total disarray. If harried they fled and were then at their most dangerous, shooting unerringly over their horses' quarters. Each trooper had a *tabolcan* (small drum). When any officer saw a disordered enemy a drum signal called troopers to him, then they either charged as a group or split into small units attacking at different points. In battle fireworks were thrown among enemy horses, and bold vicious camels driven ahead to attack enemy cavalry. Horses' behaviour can be very contradictory – brave and antagonistic against men and other horses, but scared witless by strange animals (a friend of mine had a horse that was terrified of donkeys, although he had seen them many times).

Greece annually supplied 30,000 horse (i.e. from Greek and Byzantine lands under Turkish rule) and Turkey 10,000. If more were needed, Greece could supply, for pay, up to 120,000, half of which were miserably accoutred foot. Crushed territories were obliged to render service – Serbia had supplied 3,000 horse in a recent war. Among the Ottoman armies were Christians from Greece, Bulgaria, Macedonia, Albania, Slavonia and Wallachia; de la Brocquière thought they would desert if a good well-mounted French army half their number were to march against them! *But* the Europeans would need 'a general well obeyed by his troops'.

Another traveller was Pero Tafur, who, during his 1435–9 'grand tour', had an audience with the Grand Turk Amurath (Murad II). He noted that 'all go on horseback, on very small and lank horses'. He was impressed by the great number of horses but surprised they could carry their masters, not appreciating their qualities as had de la Brocquière, and said he would 'as lief ride on one of our asses'. In Kaffa he marked the slaves on offer – Russians, Mingrelians, Caucasians, Circassians, Bulgars (from Russia), Armenians. A Tatar slave was worth a third more than any other. Major buyers were Egyptian agents purchasing for the Cairene Mamlūk army.[8]

NICOPOLIS: 28 SEPTEMBER 1396

In 1393 Bayezid annexed the Dobruja and occupied Tirnova, the Bulgarian capital. Ivan Shishman the vassal tsar evaded Bayezid's summons and on his return from raiding Hungary Bayezid captured and executed him.[9] Sigismund of Hungary now sought European aid to combat Turkish aggression.

In February 1396 Bayezid warned that he would invade Hungary by May, but Sigismund waited on the defensive until September. His Hungarians and vassal troops from Bohemia, Styria, Carinthia, Wallachia and Transylvania mustered at Buda. Foreign contingents included 6,000 Germans, 1,000 English, a few Italians and Poles, and 10,000 French; in all, c. 100,000. Sigismund crossed the Danube into Bulgaria and captured Widin and Rahova, massacring the Rahova garrison. He arrived at Nicopolis on 10 September and besieged the fortress for 15 days before scouts brought news that Bayezid's army was only a day's march away.

Four miles from Nicopolis in terrain fissured by ravines Bayezid concealed flanking forces, his reserves masked by the slope on which his army was drawn up. *Akinjis* swarmed ahead; foot archers were set behind a row of sharpened stakes; and behind them were the feudal horse. Concealed on one flank were Bayezid and the *Sipahis* of the Porte. The Serbian horse of his vassal Stephen Lasarevitch were also concealed. Bayezid's plan was to use the *akinjis* as 'cannon fodder' then the *sipahis* would take the full force and the reserve come in on a flank attack. Sigismund proposed using Magyar warfare – clouds of archers on Bayezid's periphery to soften the Ottomans up, the heavy cavalry coming up in support. French pride dictated otherwise. Enguerrand de Coucy led a scout patrol, which skirmished with a Turkish advance unit and annihilated it. Confidence boosted, the French refused to allow Sigismund first blood; although de Coucy himself and Admiral Jean de Vienne advised sticking to Sigismund's plan, the French Constable the Comte d'Eu, Philip of Artois, Jean sans Peur of Burgundy, Boucicaut and the Count of Nevers demanded that the French lead the attack and d'Eu claimed the right.

Hans Schiltburger, a man-at-arms in Lienhart Richartinger's retinue, which was in Sigismund's division, left an account. He says Nevers led the attack, with Burgundy in the first ranks. The French fought their way through two corps, being surrounded by a third. Over half were unhorsed, Turkish archers aiming at the horses. Other chargers were wounded and/or impaled. Initially breaking through *akinjis*, archers and stakes, the French thought they had the upper hand, not realizing that only part of the Turkish forces were as yet engaged. Then the *sipahis* stationed over the hill came in view, rode them down and cut them to pieces. Sigismund's troops, which should have led, fought a successful engagement a mile from the town *en route* to the main battle and, warned by maddened, wounded and riderless horses plunging past them, pushed on, engaging 12,000 regrouped Turkish foot (archers). Schiltburger says that when Richartinger's horse was shot, 'I Hans Schiltburger rode up to him in the crowd and assisted him to mount my own horse. Then I mounted another which belonged to the Turks.' Sigismund pressed on with cavalry and

> when the Turkish king saw this he was about to fly, but the Duke of Irisch [Lasarevitch] went to the assistance of Bayezid, and the Despot threw himself on the King's banner and overturned it.

Lasarevitch's flanking attack signalled the end, but the carnage continued with mass executions and thousands led into slavery, among them Schiltburger.[10]

TIMUR

Timur (1336–1405) was born at Kesh in Transoxiana to Teragai of the Barlas Turks. His great-grandfather Karachar Kevian was commander-in-chief to Chagatai, one of Genghis Khan's sons whose patrimony ran from the Amu Darya (Oxus) towards China and Mongolia. Timur's early military career was under Kazan, the power behind the throne of

Chase scene from the Zafar Namah. *This picture demonstrates the elegant proportions of oriental horses. (Photo: Oriental & India Collection, British Library; BL ADD. 7635, f. 152r)*

Samarkand. After Kazan's murder Timur entered the service of Tughluk Khan of the Jat (Chagatai) Mongols, being made head of the Barlas clan and *tuman bashi* (leader of 10,000). In 1360–9 he was embroiled in internecine Tatar warfare. After Tughluk's death, he clashed bitterly with Ilias, Tughluk's son, captured his brother-in-law Hussein of Herat, a grandson of Kazan, and emerged as ruler of Samarkand. From there he launched successive campaigns, becoming the most feared Asiatic conqueror. In the next 30 years the Timurid hammer fell on Chagatai territory, Khwarazm, the Kypchak steppes, Khorassan, Persia, Seistan, Kandahar, Mazanderan, Sultaniya, Azerbaijan, Georgia – the list goes on. Any failure spurred him to greater efforts; rebellion brought terrible revisitation. In 1393/4 he invaded Iraq. Many cities fell, but Sultan Ahmed of Baghdad eluded him, escaping to the Mamlūk sultan in Cairo. Baghdad surrendered and paid tribute. In 1398 Timur invaded India. The Mamlūks reinstated Ahmed in Baghdad as governor for Egypt.[11]

In September 1399 Timur left Samarkand; ahead lay three years' intensive warfare. He based himself on Tabriz using the plains of Karabagh as a remount depot for his army's vast herds of horses. Arabshah gives 800,000 as the number entered on the army rolls, only a portion of which was under arms at any one time. They were raised from subject territories, including drafts from his Indian conquests. At Baghdad alone, 100,000 mustered under his son Shah Rukh after he had been in the field over a year. In addition to horses, camel trains, elephants from India and the meat on the hoof of all Tatar armies had to have grass and water. For this Timur enquired of geographers and merchants, and sent scout patrols ahead.[12] Tabriz had access to the best breeds of the area. Indeed Timur's heartland included the Turcoman breeding grounds, and the contingents drawn from his subject peoples supplied a varied equine content. His path of future conquest was into the heart of Mamlūk territory with its famed Arabian studs. From Tabriz Timur sent divisions against the Georgians. Marching via the valley of Erzurum, by midsummer 1400 Timur had taken all the towns as far as Sivas, the gateway to Asia Minor. Ottoman frontier forces retreated in haste. Bayezid's son Suleiman held Sivas, which fell and was sacked after an 18-day siege.[13] Suleiman fled to Bayezid, who shelved his war with the Mamlūks and in a *volte-face* asked the young Mamlūk sultan Faraj for an alliance against Timur; this the amirs refused.

On 15 September Cairo learned that Malatya had fallen; on the 16th, that Timur's advance guard was at Aintab. On the 29th Timur's ambassador warned Damascus that

> the previous year Timur had warred on Iraq to punish those who had killed his ambassador . . . Then when he received word of the incivility of that boy, Suleiman ibn Abi Yazid ibn Uthman, he had set out for Asia Minor that he might twist his ears. He had gone to Sivas and had done there and elsewhere in Asia Minor the things of which they had reports, then he had turned toward Egypt in order that he might strike coins there and his name be mentioned in the Friday sermon [i.e. become ruler]; thereafter he would return home.

In answer, Sudun, viceroy of Damascus, had Timur's ambassador executed by cutting him in two at the waist.

As Timur neared Aleppo, Asanbugha, the Mamlūk executive secretary, and viceroy of Aleppo, urged Cairo to send the army to Syria. Meanwhile the viceroy of Tarabulus with 700 horse skirmished with 3,000 Tatars. Four were captured and halved at the waist at Aleppo where troops gathered from Damascus, Tarabulus, Hamah, Safad and Gaza, but leadership and opinion of how to meet Timur was divided. Timur's ambassador to Aleppo ordered Viceroy Damurdash to seize Sudun of Damascus, in return for which Damurdash might continue in office. Damurdash beheaded him.

Syria prepared to fight having lost hope of Cairene aid. On 28 October Timur surrounded Aleppo, next day assaulting the city. Two days of skirmishing ensued. On the 30th Timur opened the battle offensive with a cavalry charge; at first the Mamlūks stood firm but then they crumbled and the left wing was routed, though the right wing held, supported by troops of Tarabulus. A mighty but brief battle raged; Timur's troops rode down the broken Syrian forces as they fled to Aleppo where many were smothered in the crush to reach the citadel. The city was looted, its people raped and killed, its buildings burned; the suffering continued for four days, during which the citadel was mined, forcing Damurdash to ask for an amnesty. He was given a robe of honour with the request that prisoners be exchanged; some Aleppans were pardoned, but the killing went on. Timur raised monuments at Aleppo: towers built from the skulls of over 20,000 dead. He 'left it a lonely solitude where only the owl and the vulture took refuge'.

On 2 November Hamah surrendered to Timur's son Miran Shah who garrisoned the city. As he left the citadel, defenders killed two of his men. Hamah then suffered Aleppo's fate.

Amir Asanbai az Zahiri, warden of the Mamlūk armoury, was captured by Timur and later made warden of Timur's armoury. Timur told him he had never seen armies like those of Egypt and the Ottomans; the former were a mighty force that lacked direction, because of the youth of Faraj and the lack of military knowledge among the amirs; the latter had a sagacious, adroit, energetic leader in Bayezid but lacked sufficient forces.

Damascus prepared. Some were for quitting, some for resistance. On 19 November Amir Timraz, Egypt's interim viceroy, organized the collection of 1,000 horses and 1,000 camels to send with enlisted troopers being mustered and reviewed. Arabs from northern and southern Egypt were summoned. On the 26th the Cairene army mobilized, not reaching Damascus till 21 December. Two days later Timur's vanguard of 1,000 horse approached and in a skirmish outside Damascus 100 Mamlūks scattered the Tatars, some submitting and warning of Timur's craft. Disinformation followed; Turcomans allegedly seized Aleppo, killing over 3,000 Tatar horsemen; those sent to Tarabulus were wiped out; five of Timur's soldiers said half his army was ready to defect to Faraj. But on 1 January 1401 (Taghri Birdi's ms says 1 February, a scribal error) Timur was at Qatana, 14 miles (22.5 km) away south-west of Damascus. With battle at Damascus joined, the sultan's left was quickly routed, Gaza troops fleeing to the Hauran. Timur's attack on the sultan's right was pushed back 'at the point of the lance'. Hard-pressed, Timur twice asked for an armistice and exchange of prisoners; twice Faraj's amirs refused, but the rot had set in. Some Cairene amirs and some of the sultan's Mamlūks deserted, hightailing it back to Cairo to enthrone the usurper Shaikh Lajin al Jarkasi. Faraj's amirs now hustled him back to Cairo, the Mamlūk collapse continuing with a general exodus of the Cairene army, but only those who had swift horses made it, Tatars capturing the rest. On 8 January Damascus surrendered; 10 million gold *dinars* were demanded. The citadel held out for 29 days. When the tribute was paid Timur bled the city of all movable property and arms, torturing the inhabitants for more.[14] It had taken Cairo 66 days to muster troops after hearing Timur was at Malatya, a further 27 days to reach Damascus – too little and very much too late!

The Mamlūk sultanate was in chaos, young amirs squabbling among themselves for power in the name of the 12-year-old Faraj. Even after Timur ravaged Syria the infighting in Cairo continued. Maqrizi calls Faraj 'the most ill-omened of all the rulers of Islam. He brought ruin on Egypt and Syria.' He definitely ruined his voracious amirs. In his last few years 630 of them were executed and in May 1412 he was deposed and assassinated. He was only 24 years old.[15]

Timur moved slowly eastwards to Baghdad, his army hunting for meat. A terrified Sultan Ahmed and his ally Qara Yussuf of the Qara Koyunlu Turcomans fled to Bayezid whom Timur, in a vituperative letter, threatened with war if he gave them asylum. Couriers galloped to Shah Rukh with orders to bring in 10 divisions, and to Prince Muhammad to bring the Samarkand troops. Baghdad was invested, its suburbs stormed and levelled, siege-engines bombarding the city for a week until on a blazing June day it fell. The city was razed, only its religious buildings left standing. By July Timur was back at Tabriz.

Bayezid, confident and eager to fight, baited Timur with insults about winning in Persia and Hind by deception, and in Syria due only to the Mamlūk squabbling, and finished by boasting of the Turkish army. Timur returned insult for insult saying Bayezid was mad. From winter quarters he prepared for war.[16]

COMMUNICATIONS IN THE TATAR AND MAMLŪK EMPIRES

Timur's courier system enabled him to keep in touch with his sons and commanders in the field, with his Tabriz headquarters and with his capital at Samarkand. Ruy Gonzalez de Clavijo, Castile's ambassador to Samarkand in 1403–6, who travelled safely through Timur's dominions, described how from Tabriz to Samarkand post stations were situated at regular intervals and 100–200 horses kept ready at each. Couriers rode flat out day and night and had the right to demand a traveller's mount; refusal cost him his head – Timur's troops and even his sons were not exempt. Clavijo saw many dead horses killed by overriding, which was approved if it meant a faster delivery. On the day of Clavijo's audience with Timur 300 gift horses were paraded, and Timur pronounced summary judgement on an amir who had been left in charge of 3,000 horses and could not produce them all: even though he pleaded he would produce 6,000 if given time, Timur had him hanged.[17]

In Egypt and Syria a similar system, the *Al Barid*, operated. There were 28 routes, some of which had the same start and finish but variant routes. The longest, 966 miles (1,554.5 km) from Cairo to Mecca, had 57 stations. Cairo–Gaza–Damascus–Aleppo was 688 miles (1,107 km). The horses were provided by enfeoffed Bedouin Arabs and changed monthly. Established by Baybars in 1261, the *Al Barid* functioned till Damascus fell to Timur. It took four days – at a push three – to ride the 475 miles (764.5 km) from Cairo to Damascus. After Damascus fell dromedaries replaced horses.[18]

ANKARA: 20 JULY 1402

Bayezid's army was *c.* 85,000, one-third infantry and cavalry of feudal *sipahis*, Lasarevitch's Serbian horse, and Tatar auxiliaries. Timur fielded *c.* 140,000, mostly horse archers, some infantry and elite Tatar-Turkic armoured horse – Timur had brought Damascus armourers into Persia, and Samarkand had a large armour industry. Bayezid made his main camp at Ankara and there the Turks waited for eight days, but Timur had disappeared. Then Timurid scouts descended on a Turkish outpost and carried off prisoners; anticipating Timur's arrival, Bayezid crossed the Halys to give battle, waiting within a bend in the river, but Timur, seeking good cavalry ground, had gone beyond the bend. When his scouts reported that Bayezid's camp at Ankara was deserted, Timur covered 100 miles (161 km) from Kuch Hissar in three days and camped in the Ottoman tents. A river leading into Ankara was rerouted behind the Tatar forces and Timur laid siege to Ankara's Ottoman garrison and poisoned the local water supplies. After a week-long march in mid-July heat, Bayezid appeared 12 miles off (19 km), the energy and fluids sapped from horses and men. He was outsmarted, beaten before he engaged.

On 20 July 1402, the thirsty Turks met the rested, refreshed Tatars on a front stretching over 15 miles (24 km) across the plain. The Turks came on with drums reverberating; the Tatars waited in silence. Suleiman, Bayezid's son, launched a cavalry charge on the Tatar right, hurtling into a hail of arrow and naphtha fire. Disordered, the Turks then received successive charges of Tatar horse and in the first hour went over from offence to defence. Now by pre-arranged agreement the Tatar auxiliaries defected to Timur. The Serbian mailed horse, embroiled in the hardest fighting of the day, struggled for life on the Tatar right. Their despot was killed. Bayezid's right crumbled. He was left with a corps of foot surrounded by Tatar horse. He fought grimly till late in the afternoon, then mounted a horse to escape, but his horse was shot by arrows and fell, and he was captured. Suleiman made good his escape, and Timur harried the fleeing Turks throughout Asia Minor.[19]

THE AK KOYUNLU

Mehmed II (1451–81) revived Bayezid's empire. In the interim the Turks had taken care to avoid confrontation either with Christendom or with Shah Rukh (d. 1447). The strongest of Mehmed's enemies was Uzun Hassan (1450–78) of the Ak Koyunlu, whence comes much military equestrian detail. Some has been noted above (pp. 55–7); more comes from other Venetian reports and from the 1476 review at Fars, showing the equestrian and equine capacities of the late fifteenth-century Persians and Turcomans. There was much similarity between all oriental armies – breed of horse, equipment, armour for horse and man – as the Turcoman influence pervaded; many of the horses came from Turcomans through trade, loot and tribute, and the men themselves fought in the wars between Turcoman dynasties and in the Mamlūk sultanate through purchase from Turcoman tribes.

Venice sent its ambassador Caterino Zeno to Uzun Hassan, to offer Venetian aid against Mehmed II. Zeno describes Uzun Hassan's army for his 1472 campaign into Ottoman territory:

> His warriors were c. 100,000 including attendants who accompanied their masters. Some of them and their horses were armed after the manner of Italy, and some with strong thick hides . . . others were clothed in fine silk with doublets quilted so thickly they could not be pierced by arrows; others had gilt cuirasses and coats of mail with so many weapons of offence and defence . . . Servants were

Maksat, an Akhal Teke stallion presented to Prime Minister John Major to mark his 50th birthday by the president of Turkmenistan. Maksat is here ridden by WO2 Jerry Watkins, RAVC, of the Defence Animal Centre at Melton Mowbray, Leicestershire. (Photo: Ground Photographic Section, RAF Cottesmore)

also excellently mounted with cuirasses of polished iron. In place of bucklers they have round shields . . . and make use of the keenest scimitars in battle. The masters made a total of 40,000 men . . . their servants 60,000, and finer cavalry were never seen in any army.[20]

Uzun Hassan sent 40,000 horse into the Boorso (Bursa) region. Mustapha, Mehmed's son, arrived with 60,000 horse. The Persians (Ak Koyunlu) were routed by a flying column 4,000 strong. The Ottomans renewed war at Malatya on the Euphrates in 1473 when the Ak Koyunlu, at first victorious, were routed in resumed hostilities, Uzun Hassan fleeing on an Arabian mare. The Turks acquired huge booty including at least 1,000 horses from Tabeada alone.[21] Uzun Hassan and most of his army survived due to the extreme mobility of their Turcoman horses, but 3,000 troops were captured and executed.[22] In a peace treaty with Mehmed, Uzun Hassan promised to abstain from incursions into Ottoman territory,[23] but according to Zeno he intended to war on Mehmed again the next year.[24]

Persia could still muster impressive numbers. In 1474, accompanying Uzun Hassan to his summer quarters at Sultaniya, Barbaro further describes his host, saying that 'there were so many horses mustered that they covered 30 miles in circuit' (to count them Barbaro let a bean fall into his pocket for every 50 that passed); of the horses in service

there were 3,000 covered with certain armour of iron made in little squares and wrought with gold and silver tacked together with small mayle, which hanged down in manner to the ground . . . the rest (18,000) were covered with some leather after our manner, some with silk and some with quilted work so thick an arrow could not have passed through it. The horsemen's armour was of the same sort . . . Among the horsemen there were about 1,000 spears, 5,000 targets, 10,000 archers, the rest some with one weapon some with another . . . all told there might be about 25,000 good horsemen.

There were large contingents of foot and an impressive back-up service utilizing 30,000 camels and 12,000 baggage horses, mules and donkeys. Shoemakers, smiths, saddlers, fletchers, victuallers and apothecaries accompanied the army, plus the glitz without which no oriental sovereign went to war – leopards, hounds, various birds of prey, etc. Feeding a horse cost 3*d* per day, shoeing 12*d*. Horse tack was in short supply.[25] This muster was probably preparatory to the Georgia campaign of 1475.[26] Barbaro notes that some troops had come from Fars, but 'great numbers also remained behind'.

Davani, recording the 1476 review held by Sultan Khalil, Uzun Hassan's son and governor of Fars, uses typical Islamic hyperbole to describe the right, left and centre formations (Table 7.1).

Central Asian lamellar armour for horse and rider, which was used from the fifteenth to the nineteenth century. (Photo: author's collection. Royal Armouries, Leeds)

Table 7.1 Ak Koyunlu troop review 1476

	Men in armour	Archers	Servants	Totals
Right wing	2,392	3,752	3,900	10,044
Left wing	1,931	3,721(?)	1,718	7,370
Centre	932	3,014	1,716	5,662
	5,255	10,487	7,334	23,076
plus				
Inaqs	583	2,928	3,098	6,609
Boy nokars	810	2,420	–	3,230

In addition to the 33,000 shown in Table 7.1, there were 340 Kurdish amirs, 350 Shul chiefs (an Iranian tribe) and 494 guards of fortresses and highways. The *inaqs* were the prince's companions and their retinues; the *boy nokars* fighters belonging to the Bayundur division of Uzun Hassan's sept. Each division was led by a high-ranking personage: the right wing by Sultan Ali Mirza, who led an 'army of young lions all plated in iron from the tops of the riders down to the

Medieval oriental armour, showing the full panoply for man and horse. (Photo: author's collection)

hooves of their steeds'; the left wing by the Supreme Noin (the term for a general, taken from the Mongolian *noyan*, Amir Mahmud Beg, Uzun Hassan's uncle; the centre by Sultan Nur al-din Alvand Mirza, 'who looked like a mountain of iron at the head of his men similar to fire concealed under iron'. Both the princes, Sultan Alvand and Sultan Ali, were young children. Alvand gave his father a horse 'swift as a thunderbolt'; Ali rode a piebald charger and gave his father 'an excellent horse with gem-studded saddle'. The senior amirs also presented horses, the great Amir Ismail Muhrdar one 'the likes of which has not been seen since they tied Pegasus [the star] in the stables of the Milky Way'. Each civil servant had a retinue of mounted archers and servants. The Darugha of Kazarun, Chalabi Sayf al din Mantasha, had 240, including 38 in armour (in Russia a *darugha* was a Mongol-appointed tax collector; many Russian words were derived from Turkish and Mongolian). Back-up services included 168 stable attendants, 34 stirrup-holders, 38 postmen and 184 messengers.[27]

Khalil succeeded his father and the family wars erupted immediately. His cousin Murad ben Jahangir Mirza revolted, supported by some of the Qara Koyunlu Turcomans with whom there had been bitter warfare. Murad defeated Khalil's forces at Sultaniya, but was shortly overcome and beheaded. Murad's brother Ibrahim was also defeated, but then Khalil and his young brother Yaqub met in battle on 15 July 1478, and Khalil was hacked to pieces. His sons both submitted to Yaqub, Alvand dying the same year, Ali surviving till 1490 when he too was murdered to safeguard the throne for Yaqub's son Baysunghur. Khalil had reigned less than seven months.[28]

NUMBERS AND DISTANCES

From an equestrian perspective the most remarkable points to note in the Mamlūk, Ottoman, Timurid and Persian wars are the huge numbers of horses and other animals that were repeatedly mustered; the way that constant warfare caused heavy animal losses and needs for replacements; the tremendous distances that armies covered – one can appreciate that an army's passage must have seemed like a plague of locusts to the populace unfortunate enough to live in its path, for not only were there the military animals and trains of baggage beasts, but also herds of cattle and sheep, goats, etc. Barbaro noted 20,000 small cattle – sheep and goats – and 2,000 great cattle at Khalil's review. All these needed grass and water till it was their turn for the pot.

PART III
India

EIGHT

The Warhorse in India: Military Background

Our period opens with the invasions of Mohammed Ghuri of Afghanistan. Sind fell to him in 1182, Lahore by 1185, Delhi by 1192. Thereafter much detail about India's equestrian history is available, which includes her massive use of imported stock. Much predates the medieval era.

The Indus valley civilization used the horse.[1] The ancient port of Lothol, Gujarat, yielded horse bones dating back 4,000 years.[2] This bears directly on equine development explored later. Around 1,500 BC the Indus civilization was overrun by mounted nomadic Aryans from eastern Iran. After Alexander the Great's campaigns into India in 326–325 BC Greeks were present in the Punjab, north-west Pakistan and the Kabul valley. From the Greek-governed province of Bactria invaders reached as far as Pataliputra (Patna) early in the second century BC. In the first century BC the Sakae (Scythians) invaded, conquering the Punjab as far as Mathura, later occupying the Indus valley, Gujarat and Malwa, with Ujain their capital until the fourth century AD.[3] India's early kingdoms of Magadha, the Nandas and Mauryas made extensive use of horses. *The Arthashastra* of Kautilya, advisor to the Mauryan Chandragupta (c. the fourth century BC) instructed on horses and chariots.[4] Thus the Turcoman horse was in India much earlier than is usually thought, its presence strengthened by the Sakae. In Alexander's day Bactria's capital was Zariaspa, and this and another tribal capital he subdued, Arimaspi, are both guides to horse breeds. *Aspa* in Persian means horse (*asva* in Sanskrit): Zariaspa, 'golden horse', Arimaspi, 'well-schooled horses'. Many Akhal Tekes are golden-hued. Zariaspa was later called Balkh,[5] and Abou Bekr ibn Bedr noted that horse-trainers from Balkh were highly esteemed. From early Islamic times neighbouring Khorassan's Chahri (Shihry) warhorse was renowned, even if of evil temper.[6] Bactrian, Turkmene and Khorassani horses were linked to an ongoing production line. Medieval writers charting India's history mention these and a great many other horses.

Many writers were world travellers, some ambassadors, occasionally horse-dealers selling to royalty. Their information is valuable, often sketchy, occasionally misleading. In the 1200s Marco Polo observed horses in many lands and noted the huge numbers imported by India. He stated that Malabar bred no horses.[7] Athanasius Nikitin misleads by saying no horses were bred in India.[8] The emphasis on imports and the lack of data on domestic breeds gives an unbalanced view of Indian equine production. Fortunately some court historians give a little evidence. India had several early veterinary treatises, the first by Nakula, *c*. 1200 BC.[9] Translations into English are rare. Luckily a work not available in England was produced in India by my host Shri Raghuraj Sinh Jhala: the *Asva Sastra* ('Science of Horses') by the fourteenth-century Jain author Hēmasūri. I went to India on a quest to locate information on Indian-bred warhorses during the Delhi sultanate and early Moghul periods. When armies marched to the war-drums of indigenous kingdoms in conflict and of invading conquerors, the great distances involved meant that success depended on mobility,

Raja Bhupat Singh of Jodhpur riding a grey Kathiawari stallion. (Photo reproduced by courtesy of Raja Bhupat Singh)

which in turn meant cavalry in huge numbers: a repeat of the earlier influx of invaders' horses, plus droves of imports. Hēmasūri's *Asva Sastra* shows that India had a wealth of homebreds, and it outlines both desirable and undesirable characteristics.[10]

In addition the evolution of two superb Indian warhorse breeds dates from this era: the Kathiawari and the Marwari. I was privileged to see these distinctive horses and to visit breeders who are striving to preserve this valuable heritage; but the threads of lineage are slender, the bases for both breeds delicate. To preserve the Kathiawari and Marwari breeds, which gave unstintingly on the battlefields of India, an injection of state and national interest is needed, backed by adequate funding.

THE ASVA SASTRA

Despite a title meaning 'Science of Horses', Hēmasūri's work may appear unscientific, because some of the characteristics that he states had an influence on horses' suitability are illogical, owing much to the superstition that affects many oriental texts. But the practical information shows much of medieval India's equine picture, listing 153 breeds/types: their conformation, temperament, frugality, gaits, courage, sexual behaviour, etc. Six categories – three desirable, three not – are used. Breed localities indicate that several had long been widely dispersed, enabling India to horse her *kshatriyas* suitably even if wealthier nobles rode imported stock. Although medieval historians generally overestimated army numbers, India had a vast population and army numbers were greater there than in other nations, even allowing for exaggeration. Arabia, Persia, Badakshan and Turkmenia collectively would have been unable to export enough to meet India's total needs. According to Marco Polo, most horses imported into Malabar died within the year from lack of care,[11] but this was surely an exaggeration, though no doubt mortality was high.

Hēmasūri's 91 desirable horse types are noted by localities in India, adjacent countries and islands. Common sense prevails in the introduction and in an extensive list of undesirable traits. His classification of pure and mixed breeds would not now be recognized, but the basic principles used for selective breeding are sound. Purebreds were from prime native stock using stallions and mares of equal merit and age. Aged horses with similar assets were said to produce inferior stock classified as mixed breeds. These had some undesirable traits. Assets were: beauty; intelligence; tractability; eagerness and courage in war and hunting; endurance coupled with power and speed. Preferred were taller horses that were lithe, sure-footed and handsome. Slower horses of moderate stature and heavier build, with an imposing way of going, were also desirable if they possessed most of the given assets. The worst faults were a weak constitution; 'tottering', i.e. a stumbling and/or unsound gait; laziness; a tendency to be highly strung, rebellious and stupid. A warhorse had to be an easy keeper surviving and working on short rations; it must endure thirst, heat and other climatic disorders, and if entire be tractable and quiet near mares. Hēmasūri encouraged kind treatment of young horses. Training started in the second and third years. Hard work was deferred until four or even five years of age, continuing until the fifteenth year; masters were enjoined to care for the horse as its strength declined – Hēmasūri was a Jain with respect for all life. The reality, though, was different; retirement for spent warhorses was impracticable.

A pre-purchase examination was advised in which age, gaits, strength, performance and other qualities relevant to war work were checked, as in a present-day veterinary examination. Other points, irrelevant and superstitious to the modern eye, were the position and shape of curls and marks, the colour, and noises made when neighing. General conformation and behaviour are covered in an additional list of 117 points. Important categories concern dentition and eyes; various types of impaired vision are indicated. From a list of bad points ideal conformation can be deduced: refined head and neck; well-proportioned body and limbs; moderate chest with good heart-room; medium withers; wide loins and croup; resilient hooves; profuse but fine mane and tail; lack of coarse hair on ears, chin and fetlocks. Desired performance assets were energy coupled with strength; docility; willingness; and a liking for other horses' company so that wandering off to graze crops was unlikely.

THE MILITARY BACKGROUND

Medieval Hindu India was not a consolidated empire. Many kingdoms within India fought for power, but the greatest danger was Muslim invasions via the north-west frontier (through which warhorse breeds flooded). After the Ghurid invasion northern India was dominated by the Afghan and Turkic rulers of the Delhi sultanate, 1206–1526 and 1538–55; the gap occurred during the split reign of Humayan (1530–8 and 1555–6). The Delhi sultanate comprised:

1   the Qutbis 1206–90
2   the Khaljis 1290–1320
3   the house of Tughluq 1320–1413
4   the Sayyids 1413–51
5   the Lodis 1451–1526
6   the Surs 1538–55

The sultanate sought territorial expansion, especially under Alauddin Khalji (1296–1316) who from 1293 to 1310 captured Devagiri, attacked Gujarat and Malwa, then took Warangal and Dvarasamudra.[12] The Tughluqs continued the expansion into Warangal, Bengal, Orissa and Pandya. Many provinces proclaimed independence as Delhi fended off Mongol incursions; in 1229–41 the Mongols gained control of the western Punjab, continuing their attacks until 1306, when they were threatened in central Asia, and returning repeatedly in the fourteenth century.[13] In 1299 Alauddin Khalji's general Zafar led his troops against the Mongols; the Mongol left wing feigned retreat and was chased some 36 miles (58 km) by Zafar's right wing, which was then surrounded and annihilated by troops from the main Mongol army; Zafar was killed. The sultan stood firm at Delhi and, as they often did when odds were against them, the Mongols withdrew. Cavalry numbers, grossly exaggerated, were said to be 200,000 Mongols versus 300,000 Muslims.[14] The worst Mongol/Turkic raid came in 1398 when Timur sacked Delhi, installing Khidr Khan as governor of the Punjab; he subsequently proclaimed himself the first Sayyid sultan.[15]

Meanwhile the south was turbulent. A check to Islam's campaigns came around 1344 as three Hindu states – Warangal, Dvarasamudra and Anegundi – combined to throw off Delhi's yoke. Anegundi grew into the powerful kingdom of Vijayanagar, which dates its foundation in 1336. Its northern border was the River Krishna. Its supremacy was often challenged. With the Delhi Muslims repelled from the Deccan, the Bahmani kingdom was founded in 1347, Gulbarga its capital, the River Tungabhadra its southern border. Throughout its 180-year history, especially under Muhammad Shah (1358–75), it fought Vijayanagar over territory between the confluence of the two rivers – the Krishna and Tungabhadra – centring on Raichol (Raichur). In 1365 a tremendous battle was fought and Vijayanagar was beaten, her army harassed for three months, her capital besieged for a further month, before the Bahmanis retreated, drawing the Hindus after them and then turning to renew the battle, in which 10,000 Hindus were killed. Eventually peace was agreed, but conflicts repeatedly erupted. Other Muslim kingdoms rose to power within Vijayanagaran territories and fought both Vijayanagar and their co-Muslims. The Adil Shahs of Bijapur overthrew the Bahmanis to gain independence under Yusuf Adil Khan (1489–1510). In 1490 the Nizam Shah of Ahmadnagar seceded from Bijapur with Vijayanagar's aid. Thereafter Vijayanagar declined; in 1512 Sultan Quli Qutb Shah of Golkonda seceded, and the Vijayanagaran lands were steadily eroded until on 23 January 1565 at Talikota her troops faced the might of Bijapur, Golconda, Ahmadnagar and the Gujarati Muslim sultan of Ahmadabad. Vijayanagar's army was destroyed and its ruler Rana Raya, almost a centenarian, was captured and beheaded, thus ending the power of this southern kingdom.[16]

Contemporary chroniclers noted that infantry was calculated in multiple *lakhs*, or occasionally as 'uncountable', but it was the exploits of huge numbers of cavalry that drew from them their descriptive passages. Other influences affected the equine matrix. The Portuguese landed in 1498 at Kapukad in Malabar and soon controlled key ports – Daman, Bombay, Chaul, Honavar, Cannanor, Quilon, etc. – giving them a stranglehold on equine maritime trade. In 1515 they took Ormuz, the port from which Gulf Arab and Persian stock was shipped.[17]

This battle scene from the Zafar Namah *shows hot-blooded oriental horses in a variety of armours. (Photo: Oriental & India Collection, British Library; BL ADD. 7635, f. 359v)*

The Turkish Sayyids were ousted by the Afghan Lodis in 1451. Afghan nobles resented central authority and carved out what were virtually independent principalities.[18] Babur, descended from Genghis Khan on his mother's side and Timur on his father's, a ruler of Mongol/Turkic extraction, was building his power base in Afghanistan. He looted across the Sind in 1505 and again in 1519. In 1524 when Daulat Khan Lodi of Lahore and Alauddin Alam Khan of Dibalpur appealed to Babur for help against the repressive regime of Ibrahim Lodi (1517–26), he invaded Hindustan, beat Ibrahim's general Bihar Khan and placed his own amirs in key positions: in Lahore his Master of Horse, Mir Abdul Aziz; in Dibalpur, with Alam Khan, Baba Qashqa Mughal; in Sialkot, Khusrau Kukyldash; in Kalanur, Muhammad Ali Tajik. Daulat

Khan, dissatisfied at receiving only Jalandhar and Sultanpur, retreated to the hills and gathered an army; he defeated Alam Khan in Dibalpur and marched on Sialkot but was beaten by Babur's Lahori amirs. Subsequently Ibrahim's army marched on Lahore to oust the Moghuls, thus bringing about Babur's fifth expedition into Hindustan and the fateful first battle of Panipat, 20 April 1526, where the Lodis were soundly defeated and Babur ensconced at Delhi as the first Moghul emperor. He was succeeded first by his son Humayan, then by his grandson Akbar (reigned 1556–1605), whose reign was one of constant military activity, consolidation of the empire and army reforms. Consolidation never went smoothly: provinces proclaimed independence; others remained to be drawn into the Moghul net. Mewar never submitted.

THE COURT HISTORIANS' AND TRAVELLERS' CHRONICLES: HORSE SUPPLIES

Court historians collated data on equine supplies. Ghiyath-u'd-din Balban (1266–87) constantly fended off Mongol incursions. Ziya al-din Barani quoted this as the reason why he did not expand the sultanate further southwards into Hindu territories. One son governed Bengal, another Sind. Balban acknowledged that Hindu principalities depended on warhorses and elephants, but felt his supplies of both were secure and adequate – Bengal sent elephants, and through Sind came Tatar and sea-borne horses. There were also numerous excellent countrybreds from Sivalik, Sannam, Samana, Tabarhind, Thannesar and the camps of the Khokars, Jatus and Mundahirs, so he did not need horses from Mongol territories. The above shows that all the East Punjab to the north-west of Delhi and westward from the Jumna was a major horse-breeding area; that horse breeds were feeble in the extreme south; that north-western and western India bred horses from Vedic times; and that countrybreds were militarily inferior to imported horses.[20]

Balban's supply through Sind shows the routes into the sultanate. For Tatar read Turcoman (later he refers specifically to Mongol horses); 'sea-borne' alludes to the Arab/Persian trade.

The first European to give any details was Marco Polo, whose data are given country by country; many involved India. Turkey bred high-priced horses and fine mules; Baghdad maintained a huge cavalry; Iraqi horses appear in many chronicles. Persia's excellent horses fetched extremely high prices equal to 200 *livres tournois* of red gold. Persian armourers produced matchless armour for horse and man, their styles influencing Indian production throughout the period. Badakshan (Afghanistan) bred a tough, enduring, first-class cavalry horse, so hard-hooved that shoes were unnecessary; it was speedy, exceptionally sure-footed and inured to cold – Babur noted the terrible cold in his Afghan winter campaigns. Excellent stock came from Karajang (Yunnan, China) and from Anin (Burma). Marco Polo knew the Malabar coast, which traded with Arabia and the Persian Gulf. They sent Arabians, Gulf-Arabians (Arab cross Persian), Persian, Abyssinian and Syrian horses.[21]

A SAMPLE OF NUMBERS

Delhi sultans, state governors, independent rulers and wealthy nobles kept huge private stables and could muster vast numbers for war. Alauddin Khalji kept 70,000 horses in Delhi alone. Feroz Shah (ruled 1351–88) maintained five separate stables at Delhi and pastured thousands of horses around the capital. He gave hundreds as diplomatic gifts – 500 to Sultan Sikandar of Bengal at a peace treaty. Annually 10,000 Arabians and 'incalculable' homebreds were given to nobles by his predecessor Muhammad bin Tughluq (reigned 1325–51). He could raise 900,000 cavalry of Indians, Persians, Khatis, Turks. The Damascene author Abbas Ahmed says their horses were excellent.[22] As he served Al Melik al Nacer Muhammad ibn Qalaoon of Egypt, he knew fine horses. The complete record of Al Nacer's superb stud was logged by Abou Bekr ibn Bedr.[23] In 1398 Timur ordered his Master of Horse to supply 30,000 remounts to Pir Muhammad Jahangir's cavalry as theirs had perished from rains and fatigue when the Sulaiman mountains and the River Indus were crossed, Uch and Multan besieged, and many engagements fought. Later when the king of Kashmir wrote abjectly to Timur, over a massive tribute of 30,000 horses and a *lakh* of silver *tankas*, Timur promised to lower his demands.[24]

SUPPLY TO THE SOUTH

Vijayanagar depended on imports and piracy to boost supplies. The Kanarese sea-captain Timmaya robbed Muslim ships at Vijayanagar's order, but in 1502 a Portuguese fleet under Vasco da Gama was ordered to block Muslim trade between India and Arabia and divert trade to Portugal. Muslim Calicut was attacked and seven ships left to guard the coast. Da Gama returned to Portugal, but thereafter regular fleets were sent. In 1505 Francisco de Almeida was appointed first viceroy and ordered to develop good relationships with Vijayanagar. Gersoppa, subject to Vijayanagar, sent Timmaya as envoy to Almeida, seeking amity. Any good intentions soon broke down: the Portuguese, having chased a Muslim ship until it ran aground off Honavar, claimed its cargo of horses; the Gersoppa chief also claimed them as Honavar was in his territory. Almeida attacked, burning Honavar and many of its ships. Timmaya was prominent in subsequent peace negotiations. In 1509 Portugal established supremacy in the Indian Ocean by victory over the combined fleets of Egypt and Muslim Gujarat. This denied the Muslim north its Arab and Persian imports, and Portugal now controlled imports into southern India. Alfonso de Albuquerque succeeded Almeida and in 1510 captured the island of Goa from Muslim Bijapur aided by Vijayanagar. Albuquerque rewarded Timmaya with the post of *Aguazil Mor* for the territories of mainland Goa in return for 400,000 rupees and military aid for territorial defence. However, Timmaya did a little business on his own account, attacking three ships in Portuguese waters, one of which came from Ormuz carrying horses.[25] Portugal became a major force in Indian trade and politics, monopolizing the horse trade. Albuquerque used it as a bargaining counter between Hindu Vijayanagar and Muslim Bijapur; he put it up for tender between them, asking 30,000 *cruzados* per annum. He offered help to Vijayanagar against Bijapur if she would pay for his troops. To Bijapur he offered all horses that came to Goa if Adil Shah would surrender to the King of Portugal a portion of the mainland opposite Goa. Before the matter was settled Albuquerque died. From the chronicles by Paes and Nuniz we learn of regular trade through Portuguese horse-dealers and, belatedly, by a treaty of 19 September 1547, Vijayanagar got its exclusive permit to purchase all horses shipped through Goa, promising in return to deny landing rights to Muslim ships. Any that landed were to be seized and sent to Goa.[26]

IBN BATTUTA

The Maghrebin traveller Ibn Battuta spent considerable time in India in Muhammad bin Tughluq's reign (1325–51). He accompanied an ill-fated embassy to China, which included diplomatic gifts of 100 thoroughbred (high-class) horses; the embassy never arrived in China but Ibn Battuta did. He was a connoisseur of and kindly towards horses. When he escorted Khatun Bayalun, Sultan Ozbeg's wife, to visit her father the Byzantine emperor, she gave him many horses, some for consumption; he always spared them. His mount for three years was a Khwarazmian black to which he gave preferential treatment. He gives excellent information on India's trade in Turkish horses. A good Turcoman, at source, cost a negligible 50 to 60 Turkish *dirhams*. Turcoman tribesmen made a living by raising horses, which were exported to India via Sind in droves 6,000-strong. Horse-dealers repeatedly bled this source, each purchasing 100 or 200, sometimes more, employing a mounted drover for every 50. The journey to Sind whittled away their flesh so they were pastured on arrival to achieve marketable condition, yet the greater part died or were stolen. Sind levied a tax at Multan on crossing the Ravi. Duty amounted to 25 per cent; even so traders raked in profits as the cheapest sold at 100 silver *dinars*, and quality horses at 200–500. Purchasers valued strength and stride expecting a horse to carry a mailed man plus its own armour housing. The purebred Arabian valued at 1,000 to 4,000 *dinars* was used for racing. In 1340/1, two years after Ibn Battuta entered India, the sultan lowered taxes to 5 per cent for Muslim and 10 per cent for non-Muslim traders. To facilitate his affairs Ibn Battuta presented the governor of Multan with costly gifts, including a horse. An audience with the sultan required a substantial gift. In Ghazni he bought for the sultan 30 horses from an Iraqi trader from Takrit and a camel loaded with arrows, and in Sind additional horses, camels, etc.[27] Iraqi horses were first-class; many had Arabian blood as the annual peregrinations of some Arab tribes reached Syria and Iraq. Early in the Arab conquests great military bases were established in both countries and land reserved for horse-rearing. Syrian horses were also prized in India. Using Arabians to upgrade stock stems from the time when the Arabs consolidated their breeding principles, before the Prophet's era, although it took centuries to raise production to a level at which the Arabian horses in the peninsula and tribal transhumance territories could sustain the drain that Indian and other markets exerted.[28] Ibn Battuta also noted trade in Nubian horses to Sumatra, which had strong links with India.[29]

STRUCTURE OF THE HORSE TRADE

The Kudirai-Chettis (horse-dealers) had merchant guilds at Malai-Mandalam (Travancore) in the twelfth and thirteenth centuries.[30] Hindu horses had long been graded according to caste: *brahman* – brave in battle; *kshatriya* – if it breaks down it keeps going till the end; *vaishaya* – gallops and shies; *shudra* – a coward, throws its rider and flees.[31] Hēmasūri's classifications reflect this. Ibn Battuta noted four grades in the Muslim north.[32] The Delhi horse-market was well organized under the sultanate. Prices of countrybreds and less valuable imports were based on military values. In Alauddin Khalji's reign, three of the four classes were suitable for war. Prices were reckoned in *tankas*, equivalent to *dinars*: first-class, 100–20; second-class, 80–90; third-class, 65–70; *tattus* unfit for muster, 10–25. Comparisons show a good pack-mule cost 4–5, an indifferent one 3; a milch buffalo, 10–12; a buffalo for eating, 5–6; pound for pound the buffalo was cheap, weighing at least double a horse's weight. By Feroz Shah's reign horse prices had rocketed tenfold; a mule, once 4–5 *tankas*, now cost 30–40 due to inflation and currency debasement.[33] The best would have been snapped up before reaching market, and although officialdom exerted price control no doubt crafty dealers and availability influenced prices.

Tribute horses had to meet specifications. The Jam of Thatta's annual tribute to Feroz Shah was 50 horses worth a *lakh* of *tankas*, or 2,000 each. The horse-trading Muqta of Multan was obliged to send 2,500 animals; provincial governors with *jagirs* on trade routes paid heavily. As Feroz Shah's control weakened, horses were diverted from Delhi, dealers going further afield[34] – good news for restive principalities in need of remounts before seceding from the sultanate, as frequently happened.

Most sea-travellers' accounts cover the Hindu south, the Deccan and Gujarat. The north is illustrated by travellers coming overland and by Indian Muslims, though the latter's accounts can be biased and so flowery that to extract facts is difficult; occasionally they defy common sense.

ALAUDDIN KHALJI'S CAVALRY

Amir Khusrau's history of Alauddin Khalji covers most of his campaigns, fought in the north and as far south as Malabar and Pandyan Madura.[35] Nowhere does Khusrau hint Alauddin was ever beaten. The facts are not so simple. The Mongols twice besieged Delhi, and many gains won under the leadership of the Gujarati Hindu convert Malik Kafur disappeared as Gujarat, Chitor and Deogir broke away. Incessant campaigning needed a huge standing army and a constant supply of remounts. Khusrau highlights equine acquisitions. Alauddin's victories were as follows:

AH 695 taking Deogir in the Deccan
AH 697 four engagements in which tens of thousands of Mongols were slaughtered and vast numbers captured for ritual execution, graphically described by Khusrau

AH 698 campaign against Gujarat, Malwa and the Rajput fort of Ranthambor
AH 700 Malwa defeated
AH 702 Chitor fort taken
AH 705 Mandar fort taken
AH 706 Deogir taken (again)
AH 708 Siwana, Bihar campaign
AH 709 Tilang (Warangal) campaign
AH 710 Malabar and Pandya campaign
AH 711 returns to Delhi loaded with spoils.

Khusrau boasts of huge amounts of booty and vast numbers of tribute horses, and describes certain breeds' military qualities. The sultanate's remount needs were largely met from booty and tribute, which had the added benefit of immobilizing a defeated enemy. Alauddin's preferred chargers were 'well-bred desert-roaming horses', i.e. Arabians. Some spoils entered race training, many were given away, other Yemeni, Arabian and Indian horses were used to turn infantry into cavalry. Mongol mounts were also captured.[36] By this time Mongols had acquired horses from the widespread territories they plagued; their cavalry would have used Mongolian ponies, Turcoman and Persian horses, etc. – even Iraqi Arabians. In the campaign against Malwa, cavalry numbers were high on both sides. Malwa fielded 30–40,000 horse (and uncounted foot) against a 'choice' Muslim army. When Deogir revolted (AH 706) 30,000 horse marched from Delhi to put it down; after choice horses and elephants had been reserved for the sultan,[37] the troops shared the Deogir spoils. During the Warangal campaign men and beasts suffered hardships and losses. Desert horses' hooves remained unchipped, but the weaker laminae of pack-horses' hooves split on stony tracks. Five rivers were forded in a six-day march and in mountainous tracts many exhausted horses fell to their deaths. Finally a flying column of 1,000 cavalry was despatched to Warangal, two groups of 40 scouts galloping ahead to reconnoitre. The town was invested, but the Hindus attacked by night only to be counter-attacked and savagely harried, this being repeated at the siege of Sabar fortress in Tilang by 3,000 heavy horse under Qara Beg Maisara. The army commander ordered daily cavalry raids on Rai Luddan Deo's nobles and after a severe battering Warangal surrendered, relinquishing 20,000 Bohri and Kohi warhorses and hundreds of elephants. Each Bohri (sea-borne) was superb, economical to feed, nimble, indefatigable and fast. The Kohi from mountain areas[38] could represent the trade in horses that Marco Polo noted from Yunnan, and Hēmasūri from Kamarupa (Assam), Nepal, the Himalayas, China and Kambhoja (Tibet), entering eastern India without going through the sultanate. Jusjaini, an early thirteenth-century chronicler, comments on the 1,500 head sold daily in Krmbtn in Tibet; he says Bengal there bought quantities of Tanghan horses, which entered Bengal via a tortuous mountain trail through Assam, and were known from the seventh century for comfortable paces.[39] In Akbar's time Tanghans were considered strong and powerful.[40]

The year-long Malabar campaign provided further details. Malik Kafur's men were mounted on soft-mouthed, hard-hooved horses. More horses were captured in Pandya and Malabar. The horses described at the fort of Bir of Dhar Samandar were clearly Arabians as they had several characteristics peculiar to the breed: 'black eyed' (collyrimmed) and with a pronounced jibbah. Other qualities were stamina, courage, speed and a palette of coat colours – blacks with bonnet (white) faces, silver-, rose- and dark-dappled greys. At the sack of deserted Madura, Khusrau fantasized describing the haul of 5,000 horses from Yemen and Syria. In modern terms they were horses that dreams are made of, ethereal beauty combined with speed and perfect action. Captured horses were branded on the thigh and sent to Delhi for a victory parade. The account ends by noting that only a few of Alauddin's campaigns have been listed.[41]

BHAMANI SUPPLY

The Russian merchant Nikitin travelling in 1468–74 visited the Deccanese Bhamani kingdom. His stallion, presumably Russian, was impounded to coerce him to convert to Islam but returned on the intercession of a Khorassanian. On the Bhamani court at Bedar (Bidar) he noted, rather loosely, 'the rulers and the nobles in the land of India are all Khorassanians', saying they held all important army posts and armoured both themselves and their horses; the commander-in-chief was Melik Tucher, a Khorassanian 'boyar' who kept a stable of 2,000 head and commanded a great army, which Nikitin credits as having over a million horse in the campaign against Vijayanagar. Much of Bedar's cavalry rode Khorassanian, Turcoman and Hegostani imports, which came in via Dabul and from the largest Indian horse-fair held at 'Shikhbaludin Peratyr', a Russianized name for a mart not far from Bedar, which itself sent 20,000 head. Nikitin also mentions common horses – countrybreds – and remarks that his stallion sold for a good price.[42]

SIXTEENTH-CENTURY TRAVELLERS

Ludovic Varthema travelling in 1503–8 set down sparse but enlightening notes on the Indian horse trade. He gives a believable figure of 40,000 for Vijayanagar's permanent cavalry, and says how few mares the rai's kingdom had, due to an embargo on their entering – no doubt to deny his nobles the means of breeding large numbers and so to prevent formidable and possibly rebellious retinues forming. The kingdom maintained trade and customs dues payable to Vijayanagar. Cannanor had friendly links with Portugal. A reputed 200 ships a year from many countries put in there. Persia used it to land horses, 25 ducats per head being levied before despatch to Vijayanagar. Further south Quilon had sizeable imports, maintaining a 20,000-strong mounted force.[43]

Duarte Barbosa, c. 1518, said that at Goa horses from Ormuz were capped at 40 *cruzados* each, earning the Portuguese king 40,000 ducats annually. Indian factors bought better, bigger, more valuable horses from Aden and Dhofar. Their value in India was 500–600 *cruzados* each.

At last a European ventured into the heart of the sultanate and commented on the large numbers and good quality of horses raised around Delhi.[44] Domingo

Paes (d. 1520) travelled with factor Christovao de Figueiredo to Vijayanagar with 320 horses for the rai.[45] Later his compatriot Fernao Nuniz described Vijayanagar's equestrian complement and how it was employed. Much of his information came from Figueiredo who was present at Krishna Deva's war against Adil Khan of Bijapur over Raichur. A passage in Nuniz's chronicle shows the Rai of Vijayanagar's astuteness over horse-trading. Annually he bought 13,000 from Ormuz and the country. He paid 1,000 *pardaos* for 12 to 15 countrybreds, retained the good Persian horses, sold the countrybreds to his captains at five for 1,000 *pardaos* and purchased purebred Arabians from the Portuguese at no cost to himself. This highlights the standing of Arabian, Persian and countrybreds. Another passage shows him buying 600 horses from the Portuguese at 4¾ head for 1,000 *pardaos* when he was marching to relieve Raichur from the Adil Khan.[46] Unfortunately it does not state whether they were imported or countrybred. If the latter, inflation had set in due to the war. By 1520 the Portuguese controlled mainland Goa so could profit by buying and selling countrybreds.

En route to his posting, Tome Pires (*c.* 1512–15), scrivener to the factor at Malacca, visited many countries and acquired knowledge of Portuguese and Indian equine trade. He noted the density of military horses and gave details not shown by earlier writers. Prime horses were sent to many destinations, especially Cairo and India. Aden traded for horses *from* Zeila and Berbera across the Bab el Mandeb in Ethiopia, and *from* Suakin in Sudan, and *to* Ormuz in exchange for Malabar spices and drugs. Horses went direct to Goa from those bred near Aden and from Cairo.[47] Throughout the Mamlūk period Cairo had a great variety of horses, and several strains of purebred Arabians from Hejaz, Nejd, Yemen and Jezira; some partbreds came from the Jezira. Heavier horses came from Barqa (Cyrenaica) and Barbs from the Maghreb. Until 1327 the Yemen was a major supplier to Cairo (and India) but an epizootic disease almost wiped out its entire stock and time was needed before numbers recovered.[48] The horse yards at Aden must have been filled with a greater variety of breeds than noted by historians who mention only Arabians. All found a market in horse-hungry India. Pires confirms the value order: Arabians, Persians; and those from Cambay. Although he promised to return to the latter, he failed to do so. Were they lower-grade imports, or countrybreds collected for shipment to southern ports? The Persians, the Rajputs of Cambay and the province of Delhi are noted as neighbours of the Nodhaki (Baluchi) nomads who owned many horses and mares used in raids. As they were Rajput allies no doubt Baluchi horses and those stolen by them filtered into Cambay. Pires said Rajputs preferred mares as warhorses for guerrilla raids against Muzaffar Shah II of Cambay whose 30,000 cavalry, many riding caparisoned horses, included mercenaries from Macaria, Arabia, Turkestan, Rumes (Anatolia), Persia, Khorassania and Abyssinia. Many would have their own breed of horse. The Gujaratis had factors in Calicut and Malacca, which were then Portuguese. He said the Portuguese stifled the trade of the Deccan and of Cambay.[49] He knew trade throughout India and the East Indian islands, commenting on the military value of and trade in horses from Siam, Pegu,

Cambodia, China, Bali, Lombok, Sumbawa, Madura and Java, which was militarily strong, acquiring many horses from those areas. East India was well supplied with horses, especially Bengal whose ports controlled trade. It was at war with Sikander Lodi of Delhi who although powerful was a dry 15 days' march from Bengal.[50]

NINE

Cavalry and the Moghul Empire

Prior to establishing himself at Delhi in 1526 Babur struggled incessantly in Kabul, Samarkand, Ferghana, etc. Cavalry appears regularly in the *Bābur Nā ma*, but no specifics of breed or performance for horses brought into India with his army. Significantly an isolated comment says how he perceived Indian equines: 'Hindustan is a country of few charms . . . There are no good horses, no good dogs, nor grapes, musk melons or first-rate fruits.'[1] There are several references to Tipuchaq horses trained in special gaits. A Turki word, *Topchaq* meant a long-necked Turcoman horse.[2] Other equestrian notes concern skirmishes for loot or tribute. From the Jigrak of Andijan, between Kashgar and Ferghana, Babur took '20,000 of their sheep and between 1,000 and 1,500 of their horses and shared all out to the men' in 1494/5. For well over 1,700 years Ferghana raised elite horses.[3] Babur spent most of his pre-India years being pushed around and trying to establish himself; his followers were often few, their resources constantly depleted, and to augment them was a major part of his campaigning. In his first ranged battle in AD 1499/1500 (AH 905) he fought a successful cavalry engagement against Ahmed Tambal who was trying to take Andijan, Ferghana's capital, from him; subsequently he lifted Tambal's herds of horses.[4]

The composition of Babur's cavalry can be gauged by his 1504/5 exploits. He raided the Hazaras (Afghanistan) who had refused to pay 'large tribute of horses and sheep'; plundered the Indian plains for Afghan traders' livestock, including 'tipuchaqs and horses bred for trade'; then returned to Kabul,[5] which like Qandahar was an important trading centre, the latter being the main place for Khorassani trade. Kabul received goods from Kashgar, Ferghana, Turkestan, Samarkand, Bukhara, Balkh, Hisar and Badakshan. All raised horses valued in India. Kabul had up to 10,000 head per annum which Hindustani traders vied for. The Kabul valley and the foothills, mountain slopes and other valleys around it abounded in good pasture where Turk and Moghul clans grazed their horses.[6]

Court historian Abul 'Fazl 'Allami's *Ain-i-Akbari* covered Akbar's administration. Cavalry received detailed treatment. Akbar loved horses, insisting

India, showing principal places mentioned in the text.

on good care of horses awaiting sale at markets. Prices were fixed according to quality, and efforts made to curb dealers' malpractices. Merchants brought good horses from Iraq, Turkey, Turkestan, Badakshan, Sirwan, Qirghiz, Tibet, Kashmir, and other countries. India bred high-class horses; some could not be distinguished from Arabian or Iraqi horses. The finest, which came from Kutch (the Kathiawar peninsula), were on a par with Arabians. In the Punjab were bred Sanuji horses resembling Iraqis. Pachwariyas were bred in Pati Haybatpur, Bajwaral, Tihara in Agra district, Mewar and the Suba of Ajmir. In the North Hindustan mountains was raised a small strong horse called a Gut, and in Kuch Bihar the Tanghan, which was ranked between the Gut and Turkish horses, suggesting a strong but reasonably refined type. Akbar's own stables held 12,000 choice horses.[7]

THE RANKS OF AKBAR'S HORSES

There were two classes: *khasa* horses were in the first class, others in the second. *Khasa* horses comprised six stables, each with 40 superb Arabians and Persians; horses in the princes' stables; Turkish courier horses; horses from Imperial studs. Each stable had up to 30 horses. The description is confusing as apart from the six stables of Arabians and Persians we do not learn how many 30-horse stables there were. Second-class horses were divided into stables containing horses worth 30, 20, or up to 10 *mohurs* each.[8] The horse's value governed its nutrition; the more valuable it was, the greater allowance it received. Rations in winter were peas or vetch, in summer grains called moth and gram; two types of peas good for fattening; flour, sugar or molasses, ghi, cut green wheat or barley, and cut grass according to season.[9]

There were seven grades of cavalry horses: Arabs, Persians, Mujannas, Turki (Turcoman), Yabus, *tazis* and *janglahs*, plus the low-grade *tattu* that 'is now altogether thrown out'. The first two included horses that resembled Arabs and Persians in looks and ability, no doubt partbreds. Mujannas resembled Persian horses but could be of Turkmene or Persian blood and were all geldings. Turki horses came from Turan and were strong with good conformation but not as good as the first three grades. The Yabus – Turki cross Indian bred horses – lacked size and strength and were inferior in performance. *Tazis* and *janglahs*, Indian bred, were types, not breeds, good mares being rated as *tazi* and bad ones as *janglah*. Akbar's ordinary troopers mostly rode fourth- and sixth-grade animals. Akbar forbade export of horses.[10]

HAZARDS AND HEALTH

Encompassed within extensive southern sea-coasts, with mountain ranges on its north-west, north and north-eastern borders, India still often found her position uncomfortable. Once the north-western sectors were breached she lay open to constant and vigorous invasion. To conquer, reconquer and hold land, horses were essential to an army's mobility. Although India continuously imported horses and bred them at home, the constant warring in and over the land drained her resources. Battle caused high mortality and incapacitating injury. Minor trauma such as galls and temporary lameness hampered cavalry efficiency. Comments about heavy losses from rains, fatigue, starvation and accidents recur. Piracy and shipwreck took a toll of horses coming by sea. Theft was endemic in land transit. But most losses were from epidemics, the bane of medieval (and later) cavalry. In Feroz Shah's campaign against Thatta, an epidemic reduced his 90,000 cavalry by three-quarters.[11] When Babur's uncle, Sultan Ahmed Mirza of Samarkand, tried to wrest Ferghana from his nephew in 1494, he faced a major setback: 'a murrain broke out amongst their horses then massed together; they began to die off in bands.'[12]

India's equines succumbed to fatal diseases not met with in the Occident. Horses concentrated in cavalry depots, dealers' yards, and breeding herds were susceptible to epizootic lymphangitis, which strikes in cool weather; to equine encephalomyelitis (paraplegia); to equine peroplasmosis (biliary fever); to surra, a trypanosome parasite, which can be hosted in cattle, buffaloes and camels (which succumb more slowly than horses) – the monsoon season is the most dangerous time;[13] and to dourine (VD). Comments on rains causing deaths probably indicate one or other of these killers. Another disease usually fatal in medieval times is 'shipping fever' or strangles, a streptococcus bacillus that runs rife among animals kept in close proximity. Many horses loaded in Arabia and Ormuz must have perished from this scourge, as well as horses from the concentrations noted above.

THE BLOODHORSE AS CHARGER

The elite Indian charger was a bloodhorse. The breeds catalogued were either 100 per cent hot-blooded or had a high proportion of hot blood. A heavy-fleshed, cumbersome horse with the large soft hooves characteristic of colder, wetter climates could not have survived India's climatic excesses or negotiated the wild territory that passed for 'cavalry country' – land interspersed with nullahs, rocky outcrops, thorny scrub and searing desert. Nimbleness, excellent limbs and hard hooves are vital, plus a wariness that alerts a rider to danger. The ability to survive on scant fluid is an asset. Oriental horses lack the water-laden tissues of some western horses, and are less prone to severe dehydration. While essential for sustained efficiency, water was often short in India, except in monsoons which brought their own hazards.

THE KATHIAWARI AND THE MARWARI

The Kathiawari, which predates the Marwari, was one of several influences in the evolution of the Marwari warhorse, especially around the time of Mewar's major struggle for independence from Akbar, and from neighbouring Gujarat and Malwa. However, the two breeds did not merge, nor become divergent strains. The Arabian is the only breed with any claim to pure ancestry – and even that claim is open to serious question.[14] Kathiawaris and Marwaris have some similarities; there are also many differences between them. The obvious influence

Members of the Katti people mounted on their Kathiawari horses, which appear much as they would have done in the period covered by the text. (Photo: author)

in the Kathiawari is Arabian, in the Marwari Turcoman. The two breeds streamed in over several centuries – the Arabian through heavy trading, much of it via Kathiawar and Gujarat, the Turcoman through trading via the north-west frontier and through successive invading armies. Kathiawari and Marwari history is linked with that of the Katti and Rajput clans.

Katti and Kathiawari

Akbar extolled the horses of Kutch.[15] In the late twelfth century the Katti, a people of Scythian origin, migrated from the Punjab to Kutch, then known as Saurashtra. Recorded in Arrian's *Campaigns of Alexander*, the Katti were noted as 'excellent soldiers and brave men'; they fought gallantly against Alexander when he attacked and captured Sangala (near Amritsar) not long after the battle of the Hydaspes in 326 BC.[16] They were reckoned more cruel and braver in battle than the Rajputs, but unlike the Rajputs, who never retreated even if outmatched but fought to the last man, the Katti would retreat to fight again.[17] Nomads, graziers and dacoits, they settled throughout Kutch and there found an indigenous dun horse with a dark spinal stripe and the dark banding on legs and withers that is typical of wild horses. The Kattis crossed the indigenous dun with their Punjabi horses, and thus arose the breed named after them.

The present maharana, Darbar Satyajit Khacha of Jasdan, traces his Katti lineage to the late twelfth century in unbroken line. Three brothers settled at

Tajun, a 15hh Kathiawari mare ridden by the author. She possessed all the surefootedness and superb disposition of her breed. She had previously been in the Mounted Police stables in Gujarat but is now owned by Raghuraj Sinh Jhala, IPC, Retd. (Photo: author)

Hingolgadh Fort, overlooking the Panchal, Saurashtra. This fort dates to the seventeenth century and is typical of the Indian forts built through the medieval period. It is now the country residence of Darbar Satyajit Khacha of Jasdan. (Photo reproduced by courtesy of Darbar Satyajit Khacha of Jasdan)

Arun, a prize-winning stallion belonging to Darbar Satyajit Khacha of Jasdan and pictured in the courtyard if the Jasdan palace. Arun is an excellent example of the breed. (Photo reproduced by courtesy of Darbar Satyajit Khacha of Jasdan)

Chotila and in the mid-seventeenth century moved to Hingolgadh and Jasdan, and from them stem three main Katti clans: Khacha, Kuman and Wala. Hingolgadh fort commands a position over the Panchal, the heartland of Kathiawari breeding, and is a prime example of how both Kattis and Rajputs built for defence. In Khacha defensive actions and feudal wars great use was made of Kathiawaris. The present maharana is vice-president of the Kathiawari and Marwari Horsebreeders' Association and owns fine Kathiawaris that exhibit the characteristics that made them ideal cavalry mounts when Kathiawar became a major supplier of warhorses. Indeed Kathiawaris might be a cause of war: when Jasdan's ruler coveted a mare belonging to one of his own clansmen who refused to give her up, the man sought refuge in the small principality of Bhimora, whose ruler refused to surrender him; war ensued, and Jasdan defeated Bhimora and won the mare. It is worth noting that Kathiawar warriors preferred mares and that the breed is traced through the female line, as was the Arabian in its homeland – possibly the only two breeds to be so traced.

Breed Characteristics

Horses are an intrinsic part, even today, of Katti village life. Kathiawaris average 14 hh to 15 hh. Duns predominate; chestnut, bay, brown and grey occur, but black never; piebalds and skewbalds are rarely seen and are not esteemed. The horses are short-coupled, often rather narrow but not weedy. Advantageously raised, they will reach the upper height of 15 hh, with a moderately fleshed appearance. One criticism made of the breed is that its quarters slope too much, but judging by many representative groups I saw, this was not so, for most had strong, rounded quarters, others quarters that were moderately angled, which, combined with well-let-down hocks, indicated power. The short, well-crested neck is carried high. The head is dry and clean-cut, in some appearing rather long. Narrow at the poll it widens to a broad forehead with huge, wide-set eyes. The profile is either straight or slightly concave. Thin flaring nostrils allow good air intake. The upright sickle-shaped ears, almost touching at the tips, are a hallmark of the breed. Their extreme mobility intensifies hearing. Legs have clean hard tendons; hooves are so dense that shoeing is rarely necessary, even with sustained travel on abrasive going. Temperament is equable and Katti stock learns quickly. They are incredibly sure-footed on the most dangerous terrain. Though considered small by western standards they are up to weight, and would have easily carried an armoured trooper in battle. Katti tribesmen rode light and rarely wore armour, instead using padded cotton protection, with a metal helmet worn under a turban. Arms were sword, lance and a small, round, rhino-hide shield. Spurs were not used.[18] Bitting was mostly snaffles, sometimes with mild burrs on the cannons.

Marwari and Rajputs

Marwar (Jodhpur) was the largest province of Rajasthan, home to the Rahtors, the warrior Rajput mercenaries, who originally came from Kanauj in 1212, led by Rao Siha Rahtor. Many other Rajput clans settled in Rajasthan and neighbouring provinces. In harsh terrain and searing climate a courageous horse was needed to negotiate the hot, choking conditions of arid Rajasthan, surviving on scant rations and water (annual precipitation is less than 4 inches [100 mm] as against Delhi's 24 inches [600 mm] and the Western Ghat areas's 157 inches [4,000 mm],[19] and to carry fully accoutred warriors into battle. Medieval Rahtors were noted horse-breeders who produced an enduring breed by judicious use of native stock and infusions of Arab, Turcoman and Kathiawar blood. The *Shalihotra*, a medieval equine treatise, records the Sambhar, a Rajasthani breed.[20]

Marwaris range from 14.3 hh to 15.1 hh, but many are considerably taller – up to 16 hh. All colours occur; many are black. Skewbalds and piebalds are numerous, though for obvious reasons undesirable in battle. This multicoloured hide may be inherited from long-ago Persian imports. Apparently Marwari ancestors were already present in the days of Alauddin Khalji as Khusrau gives vital clues noting several elements: the 'lily-/scissor-eared' hallmark; hard cuplike hooves; endurance in long journeys under desert conditions[21] – all part of Marwari make-up, though it was not then classified as a breed. Other characteristics are strong limbs with clearly defined tendons; spare frame; thin coat; ability to cope with heat and cold without excessive dehydration, and well-developed senses of smell and hearing – very useful in desert conflict. The

Marwari stallion. (Photo reproduced by courtesy of Raja Bhupat Singh)

Marwari head is narrow, with the profile either straight or slightly ram; the eyes are soft but not over-large, and have exceptionally long lashes acting as dust filters. Overall appearance is of a very strong, medium-weight animal with good paces.

Paces and Gaits

Both breeds have walk, trot, canter and gallop paces, and each has a special gait that gives a very comfortable ride. The Marwari performs the *rewal*, which incorporates different speed elements – the slow *ralla*, medium-paced *saagum* and fast *madri*.[22] The Kathiawari performs what is confusingly called the *revaal* – a slight difference in spelling but a completely different gait. The *rewal* is identical to the American gait known as the *rack*, and the Kathiawari performs the equivalent of a *running walk*. Each has its own timing of hoofbeats.

Raja Bhupat Singh of Jodhpur mounted on a typical Marwari stallion. (Photo reproduced by courtesy of Raja Bhupat Singh)

A 16 hh Marwari mare owned by HH Mahipendra Singh, Maharana of Danta, Gujarat. (Photo: author)

STUD PRINCIPLES AND SODAGAVARS

In peacetime Kattis and Rajputs expanded their stocks. The size of *jagir* for a Marwar village thakur depended on how many Marwari horses and armed troopers he raised for the ruler's service. Marwaris were maintained ready for war, the cost borne by the village cultivators. Should a horse die, either in battle or peacetime, the thakur must supply a replacement or risk losing his *jagir*.

Mortality or injury in battle meant recourse was often had to the *sodagavar* (horse-dealer). Many were established in Gujarat and Kathiawar. The Mir were from an Islamic community who kept stallions for service and traded in horses. The Dhadi were Muslim horse-dealers and the Charan bards also had a sideline in horses for sale and service. In medieval times horse-dealers of princely states went to Kathiawar for stock as Kattis produced good warhorses. During the Raj Colonel Stanhope and the officers of the 17th Dragoons were mounted on Katti horses and were reckoned the best mounted in HM's service. In both warrior communities it was considered reprehensible to stand a stallion at stud for gain so mares were taken to the local *sodagavar* for covering. However, no stigma attached to selling the offspring, especially colts, the Kattis retaining mares for their own wars and for breeding. The Rajputs preferred stallions for battle, although mares were also used.[23]

Mares and stallions in the same fighting unit could cause havoc, especially as there would always be some mares in oestrus. Some stallions are readily governable, others are a liability, so Rajputs used a drug called *katha* which depressed the clinical state in mares and deprived the stallion of libido. An unwelcome side-effect was that it did not disperse but rendered the horses less capable of breeding. Henna was a multi-use drug: as a dye on manes and tails to satisfy Rajput love of colour; as an anti-irritant against heat rashes and allergies; as a deodorant on 'in season' mares, and a suppressant to maintain a mare in the anoestrus state; as an antiseptic on wounds.[24]

It is perhaps relevant that in Kalliawar, a Gujarat dialect, the word for stallion is *ghoda*, for mare *ghodi*; *wacharo* means a colt foal, *wachari* a filly foal. There is no word for gelding.[25]

BATTLE MOVEMENTS

In sixteenth-century Europe there was a revolution in training horses. Schooling became an art when high school equitation was born. Today's equivalent is the exquisite performance by the Spanish Riding School of Vienna, which traces its history to 1580 when Archduke Charles founded the Royal and Imperial Court Stud of Lipizza on the Karst.[26] Yet this picture of Europe leading equestrianism is false. India was using 'airs above the ground' in cavalry warfare by the time of the Delhi sultanate.

Three movements executed by Indian chargers have been shown in Moghul art. They are the levade, the courbette and the oran (variously known as the uraan or udaan); which comes from the Hindi verb *urna*, 'to fly'. Other movements evolved from the volte (circle), canter pirouette, and turn on the forehand, which Indian warhorses did at three-quarter speed.

The Levade

By raising his forehand and shifting weight on to his haunches the horse is placed to rein around in a 90° or 180° turn, and immediately leap away or surge forward. The levade was used to evade attack, or to turn rapidly and take the offensive in a different direction. Done rapidly and successively it enabled a surrounded trooper to maintain momentum and minimize the target for attackers.

The Courbette

The horse leaps vertically, hocks well underneath him acting as a propellant. The courbette was used only in combat against an elephant, the horse's forefeet striking the elephant's head. It needed a courageous horse and a skilful rider who could place the horse accurately, as the elephant's tusks often wore extensions of sharp swords.

The Oran

Related to the capriole, the oran was used only against elephants by a lancer, or swordsman, whose target was the armed warrior in the elephant's howdah. Great athleticism and propulsion were required in the oran as the target, mounted in the howdah, was over 13 feet (4 m) above the ground. For maximum damage the lance-thrust was made at the point of highest aerial extension when the speed and power of the horse's leap were harnessed to the attack, which could be delivered from either a direct or a three-quarter angle.

Hand-to-hand Fighting

When forward movement was hampered in the mêlée, hand-to-hand fighting was often done with opponents warily circling at a canter while still facing each other, forcing the horses into half and full pass movements as they circled. As antagonists closed for the kill the circle contracted to a canter pirouette, each keeping the other in his sights. When one opponent was despatched the victor could wheel out of the pirouette to tackle another foe. Conversely a warrior being worsted could try to whirl into flight, provided there was an opening in the mêlée's crush.

Rapid Turns

Indian chargers could turn in little more than their own length while galloping at almost full stretch. To maintain equilibrium the rider kept his weight to the outside of the turn. Unlike the movements above, which put strain on the hocks, this was done without checking the horse on to his hocks prior to turning.[27]

BATTLE TRAINING

Indian cavalry fighting was conducted in a looser order than was usual with occidental massed horse, resulting in one-to-one combats in which a high degree of skill was essential for horse and man. The Indian bloodhorse, even if used *en masse*, lacked the bulk of European destrier units. The weight of most Indian warhorses would have been in the region of 750–900 lb (340–408 kg), according to breed. Such a horse with the inherent strength and wiriness of the oriental equine is well able in battle to cope with full panoply (on long marches this was carried on pack-beasts). The average Indian cavalryman's physique differed from that of his taller, heavier, European counterpart, most being spare-framed, lightly fleshed and several inches shorter. The charger had to be agile and biddable, be able to move rapidly, work off his haunches and be so balanced he could move in any direction at touch of the rein on his neck or the rider's calf or heel on his side. The Indian cavalryman rode his mount on a loose rein using bitting that could, if misused, be severe, and in a saddle that gave closer contact with his horse's movements than the European war saddle.

At no time would the charger be out of control, but combat horses frequently suffered horrific wounds. The most famous equestrian exploit of medieval India, the battle of Haldighati, concerns the horses of Kathiawar and Marwar.

THE HORSES OF HALDIGHATI

The battle of Haldighati on 18 June 1576 on the plains between the pass of Haldighati and Khamnor village at the foot of the Kumbhalgarh hills not far from Udaipur brought together the Rajput clans of Sisodiya and Jhala against Akbar's army for whom the Kachawas fought. Under Rana Pratap Singh, his troopers mounted largely on Kathiawari and Marwari horses, Mewar, the only major independent principality of Rajasthan, fought the Moghul might. Jodhpur (Marwar) was divided, Marwaris fighting on both sides. The Hindu general, Kinwar Singh Kachawa of Amber (Jaipur), led Akbar's armies. He had a score to settle with Pratap for a wound received in an earlier engagement. Foremost among Pratap's allies was Jhala Man Singh's clan, which originated from North Sind; *c.* 1090 it had come to Kankavati in Kathiawar, settling in Jhalawar, Saurashtra. During the time of Rana Sangha (1509–28) of Mewar, the first alliance occurred between Mewar and the Jhalas who ruled Halavad, near Drangdhra. When the Maharana of Halavad died, two sons, Ajoji and Sajoji, were usurped by a stepbrother, Ranoji. They sought sanctuary, offering to serve Marwar, but were rejected; they turned to Rana Sangha who took them into his service, and thereafter the Jhala clan fought for Mewar. There was a long-standing enmity between Mewar and the Moghuls who coveted it to complete their subjugation of Rajasthan.

Kathiawari horses were in great demand, and Chetak's story begins at Halavad. The Jhalas gave two sibling stallions – Chetak and Natak – to the Danti clan's Charan bards. Using the Jhala link as a recommendation they sold both horses to Pratap, who, not trusting horse-dealers, questioned the horses' provenance and insisted on a barbarous test of courage. Natak's hooves and limbs were embedded in earth to the fetlocks and the horse was then whipped to gauge reaction. Natak lunged up and out fighting for freedom, fatally stripping flesh and horn away. Chetak was spared, his 'courage' proved by his brother. He became the rana's battle-charger.

The field of Haldighati, where the Jhalas fought bravely at great cost to their clan, was a close-run battle. Numbers on both sides have been variously given – from 3,000 to 22,000 for Mewar; from 5,000 to 80,000 for the Moghuls – but the generally accepted figure is 22,000 for Pratap and 60,000 for Man Singh Kachawa. First blood went to Mewar: Pratap's vanguard followed by his right wing forced the Imperial left wing back. Then Mewar's left wing charged under Man Singh Jhala, defeating the Imperial right. In Mewar's attack on the Imperial centre both sides committed their elephants. Opposing Rajput clans fought fiercely. Pratap riding the grey Chetak attacked Man Singh Kachawa on the Imperial elephant. Chetak launched into the oran, Pratap thrusting with his lance at Man Singh, who leaned back in the howdah to evade the blow. Thinking he had despatched him, Pratap brought Chetak down in a 180° turn, the elephant also wheeling. Chetak then sprang into a courbette and hammered his hooves on the elephant's head as Pratap despatched the mahout. The elephant turned and fled carrying Man Singh out of the battle.

Mewar was prevailing until the Moghul reserve under Mihtar Khan was sent in. The kettle-drums resounded, bringing news of Akbar's arrival, and the rout was halted. Pratap, surrounded, was about to go down when Man Singh Jhala of Badi Sadri seized Pratap's umbrella insignia, drawing the fighting to himself. Reluctantly Pratap rode Chetak off the field (both had been wounded), hotly pursued by two Moghul chieftains. In flight Chetak leaped a mountain stream to safety, but the Moghuls checked at the torrent, giving Shakti Singh, Pratap's half-brother, who had reneged from Akbar's side when he saw his brother's plight, time to despatch them. Chetak's leap was his last. His injury was so severe that it was a miracle he had got so far: his off hind pastern and hoof had been severed and it was on three legs only that he had made his dash and leap for freedom.

Chetak attacking an elephant in the typical Oran movement at the battle of Haldighati.

Pratap lived on, waging guerrilla warfare against Akbar who in 1587 finally gave up the struggle against Mewar to campaign on the north-west frontier and in the Punjab. Ten years later Pratap died. He rewarded the Jhalas' loyalty with the title of rana for all male Jhalas. Subsequently they were given a small principality in Chuda state at Minapur. Thereafter the clan head was known as Jhala Rana of Minapur.[28]

At Haldighati monuments commemorate the bravery of Chetak and Man Singh Jhala. There is now a Chetak Horse Society, and one of India's light aircraft is named after him. A painting of Chetak prior to the battle hangs in Jodhpur fort.[29]

DANTA

Another influence on India's equestrian history is the kingdom of Danta in Gujarat. Its heritage may be traced to 1206. Today HH Maharana Mahipendra Singh of Danta is the foremost breeder of Marwari horses with a nucleus of excellent mares and a superb stallion. His Highness discussed with me his homeland's medieval warfare and the Marwari horse.

Danta is tiny, only 360 square miles (932 square km), totally ringed by formidable mountains with only two passes from the south via Amba Ghata and from the north via Trisuliya giving access to fertile lowlands and the ancient capital of Chandrawati. The maharana's family reaches back through 123 generations in unbroken line to their original home, Ujain, the old Indian capital of the Sakae invaders. The Parmar clan migrated from Ujain to Sind and in 1206 settled in Danta, where they established themselves as the ruling house, maintaining this position throughout the Delhi sultanate in which there were

HH Mahipendra Singh's champion Marwari stallion. (Photo: author)

confrontations between Danta and Alauddin Khalji. Akbar conferred the status of maharana on the clan head in 1570. In 1857 the British confirmed Danta's position as a kingdom. Danta was frequently under pressure from neighbouring states, particularly Idar in Gujarat, which in the fifteenth century repeatedly challenged Danta, necessitating a constant call to arms to maintain its boundary.

Danta's military system was replicated throughout medieval India. At most the population was 100,000. From this the kingdom could raise only 7,000 or 8,000 horse and 10,000 foot, the latter an untrained mass. All males were eligible for service between 18 and 60. *Jagirs* were reserved for members of the ruling house, and among the 20 members there was a rotation system for providing troops. Each *jagirdar* owed a specified number of horse and foot according to his land-grant, and failure to provide it could result in the *jagir* being rescinded. The maharana retained 2,500 horse and as many foot in his permanent army, which was maintained by a tax in kind on the cultivators. The standing army was rotational so that no member was absent too long from his land, crops, or family. Troops were not allowed to opt out by paying scutage, as happened in medieval Europe.

Prior to a campaign at least one month's warning was given and troops were raised either by drum, whose reverberations carried far, or by mounted couriers sent to the further reaches of the kingdom. In Imperial service Danta owed 5,000 troops, mostly cavalry. The maharana equipped his permanent retainers with horses (one each), armour for horse and man, and weapons. This created employment for artisans such as saddlers, armourers, fletchers, bowyers, etc. A considerable back-up force provisioned the army in the field. Remounts were included to replace equine casualties, although it was hoped that many replacements could be made from enemy stocks. Danta's cavalry operated in units of approximately 250 horse, and in mountainous territory as individuals fighting guerrilla-type warfare, although in such terrain more foot than horse could be expected.[30]

THE HORSE'S EQUIPMENT

Functional accoutrements did not change markedly over the centuries, but were more elaborate in wealthy circles.

Saddles

Saddles were of two basic types. The *khogeer* in Jaipur Palace armoury dates from the late Akbar/early Jahangir period. It is a thick felt pad, the front portion split and raised, affording the rider's knees some protection, with loops for attaching a breastcollar. The girth is secured to a buckle 4 inches wide by 2 inches deep (100 by 50 mm), fixed by a knot and run over the saddle surcingle style. A variation was two separate felt pads attached by strong straps over the spine, the whole over a felt pad, the *aragheer*, which absorbed sweat and kept the back sound. Additions could be a shaped cantle, pommel, seat, and large circular flaps affording protection to the rider's legs against sweat, and some barrel protection against friction from the rider's armoured legs. Girths were of soft folded cloth or supple sambhar deerskin. Stirrups were triangular or arched and could have wide treads. A *charjama* (a shaped broadcloth) could be used over or under the *khogeer*. Wealthy nobles used elaborately tooled saddles with circular saddle flaps on rigid trees which bore fully armoured riders, dispersing weight efficiently over the horse's back while keeping the spine free of pressure. Duarte Barbosa comments on the high-pommelled saddles used by the King of Gujarat's troopers.[31]

Other Harness

Bits were snaffles or curbs, but differed from most European varieties. Snaffles varied: plain ring; jointed with burred cannons; unjointed with a squared mouthpiece; and unjointed with movable spikes known as the *choukra*. The burred and spiked varieties had appeared as long ago as Xenophon's day. There were varieties of curb: one was joined with a jagged-edge mouthpiece; another, shown in the *Ain-i-Akbari*, had a single mouthpiece with port, its upper edge jagged. Most bits had single reins stitched together in their last section which could be used as a quirt. The looped section was slipped over the pommel to free the rider's hands. No doubt mounted archers used the thin thong attached to one finger and linking it to the reins, which permitted a degree of control even when handling the bow (see Chapter 6). Some bits, as shown in the *Ain*, had double reins. Most Indian bits were exceptionally severe, but loose-rein riding and sound training meant contact was momentary and light.[32]

The stable equipment, saddle and bridle for an Indian warhorse, from Abul Fazl, Ain I
Akbari, *plate XIV. (Photo: Cambridge University Library, classmark 811.b.6.85.
Reproduced by permission of the Syndics of Cambridge University Library)*

Other equipment supplied to Akbar's *Khāsa* horses was as follows: an *artak*, or quilt; *yalposh*, or mane cover; saddle-cloth, leg-ropes, girth, fly whisk, headstall; *qayza*, or bit – this is Urdu for snaffle, so presumably the standard bit was a snaffle; plus items for cleaning and feeding. Today a horse is secured by ropes to either head or neck and one hind foot to pegs driven into the ground. The higher value horses received the better quality equipment.[33]

HORSE ARMOUR

Indian art shows horses barded in a variety of armour, much influenced by Persia. Indeed Persian/Iranian armourers found ready employment in India; the work of Ashok Dispani, the famous sixteenth-century armourer, is on display in Jaipur. Due mostly to the climate very little pre-sixteenth-century armour survives, but styles changed slowly. Horse armour could be of many-layered hide, a combination of mail and plate, all mail trappers, quilted materials, or metal-

The armour used for both warrior and his mount during the Mughal period in India, from Abul Fazl Ain I Akbari, *plate XVI. (Photo: Cambridge University Library, classmark 811.b.6.85. Reproduced by permission of the Syndics of Cambridge University Library)*

studded fabric. The horse armour for army commanders detailed by the *Ain* consists of *kajam*, or quilted trapper; *artak-i-kajam*, or mail caparison; *kashka*, or metal chamfron; *gardani*, or crinet.[34] Only heavy cavalry, wealthy princes, nobles and *jagirdars* could afford full panoply as Indian cavalry numbers were vast. Eyewitness proof of its use for considerable numbers in royal retinues comes from Tome Pires who described the 'many caparisoned horses' of the kingdom of Cambay.[35] Duarte Barbosa commented only on the steel 'foreparts' of Cambayan and the chamfrons of Goan horses.[36] Domingo Paes, present at a review of troops by Krishna Rao of Vijayanagar, noted the richness of horses and equipment, describing 'fully caparisoned horses, all with metal chamfrons'. The caparisons varied, some richly embroidered, some set with jewels. Some chamfrons were animal masks (many books published in India show horses with mail head armours like an elephant's head and trunk). The functional parts were of quilted fabric, sometimes reinforced with leather and metal. Paes wrote in awe of the 35,000 cavalry horses: 'you would see them so covered with metal plates that I have no words to express what I saw'. He almost fell off his horse craning his neck to view the extravaganza. Obviously a rich king could afford such panoply, even though the foot wore only padded cotton protection.[37]

Babur is considerably more sparing with comments, recording only the use of mail on horses or the occasional boost to his supplies of armour from defeated enemies, and the gifts of horses, some in mail, from tribesmen when he crossed into Sind in 1519 – tribute or a bribe to leave the donors in peace.[38]

An array of Moghul cavalry lances displayed in Jodhpur Fort, Rajasthan. (Photo: author)

TROOPERS' ARMOUR AND WEAPONS

Troopers' armour came in leather, padded fabric, mail, mail and plate, or studded fabric, and was influenced by successive invasions. The basic type was mail or mail and plates, worn over a padded tunic, the mail reaching mid-calf and split for riding. Trousers were fabric either with mail stitched all over them or with the seat and the backs of the legs up to the knee as fabric only, for comfort when riding. Vambraces went over mail-clad forearms. Greaves could cover shins. Feet were sometimes mail-clad, as were the hands in mail mittens. A *char-aina* – a cuirass of

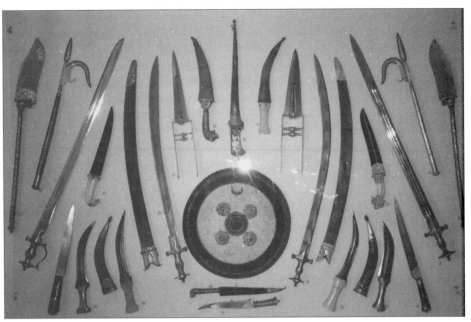

An array of Moghul weaponry displayed in Jodhpur Fort, Rajasthan. (Photo: author)

metal plates laced together – was sometimes worn over mail. Helmets, worn over a mail hood, varied; they were often of conical segmented type with ear- and nose-flaps, sometimes with a movable nasal. A mail face-cover added protection, either fabric-lined with eye-holes, or unlined with sighting through the mail links.[39] The Jaipur armoury horseman wears sixteenth-century full armour of simple mail, feet and hands uncovered, a *char-aina* with three back segments and two overlapping plates in front. His conical segmented helmet has ear- and nose-flaps.

Indian weaponry is extremely varied. Not all horsemen carried all weapons. Basic weapons of offence were lance, sword, Turkish bows with a variety of arrows and heads, dagger(s) many of which were double-bladed, maces, battleaxes and lassos.

Domingo Paes records troopers with quilted tunics made of strong leather strengthened with iron plates; some helmets with neck and face guards were similarly fashioned, others of steel. Arms included swords, battleaxes and javelins.[40] Tome Pires expands on this, commenting on the Cambayan troops' plate armour and mail coats, lances, long swords and daggers – all beautifully ornamented.[41] Duarte Barbosa gives the fullest weaponry: Cambayans had a strong round shield, two swords, dagger, Turkish bow and arrows, and steel maces; Moors of Goa had whips, long light lances with heads a cubit long (approximately 20 inches/50 cm), battleaxes, two or three Turkish bows with very long arrows, two swords, each with its own dagger. For Delhi he added the *chakra*, a steel quoit whose edges were razor-sharp with a central hole by means of which it was spun unerringly at an enemy, inflicting damage that was always severe, usually fatal.[42]

Among the collection in the Jaipur armoury other items stand out, including tiger claws, like a knuckle-duster armed with lethal curved claws. There is a great variety of swords, from straight, serrated-edge swords for cutting through mail, to the sword Man Singh Kachawa used at Haldighati and in campaigns in Bengal, Kabul and Qandahar, which weighs 11 lb (4.9 kg) and has a curved blade tapering from 4 inches (10 cm) at the hilt to its point. His helmet, a deep-crowned, flat-topped hat of a type worn only by commanders, is of brass, copper and iron inlaid with gold. Akbar's officers were required to provide full armour on pain of being fined.[43]

ARMY ORGANIZATION

Army organization changed as rulers sought to increase efficiency, stamp out irregularities, inculcate loyalty and improve training. An army had two distinct elements: the smaller standing army attached to the ruler's person; and the larger force made up of nobles' contingents, each comprised of a lord's own men and those enlisting under a leader offering good prospects. Indian military titles are numerous and over time changes occurred in 'job descriptions', major alterations being made under Akbar.

In the Delhi sultanate the most important officer was the *Adab-u'l-Mulk*. He appointed heads of government departments, including those of the *karkanahs* dealing with state and army animals: *Paigah*, the stables and breeding of horses; *Pilkhana*, elephants; *Sutar*, oxen, mules, kennels, falcons, camels, medicines; *Rikhabhana*, saddlery, harness, etc.; *Zarr Addkhanah*, armour and war *matériel*. All military requirements had to be referred to him.[44]

The *Diwan-i-Ard*, or war ministry, headed by the *Arid-i-Mumalik*, kept the descriptive roll of horses and men. The *arid* was inspector-general and he or his assistant recruited men, tested their proficiency, fixed pay levels according to skill, held reviews of troops and horses at least annually. Campaign preparations and assignments of troops were left to him, although the sultan appointed the commander-in-chief. The command structure paralleled the Mongol decimal system: a *khan* commanded 10,000 horse, a *malik* 1,000, an *amir* 100, and a *sipah salar* fewer than 100. The first three ranks came from the nobility and the privileged.[45] A *naqib* maintained charts showing each soldier's place in review and battle. The basic review order was left wing, centre, right wing. The roll describing the troops was called the *Huliyah*. Alauddin Khalji instigated the *dagh* – branding of horses. The *Huliyah* and *dagh* were attempts to prevent abuses whereby unsuitable men and sub-standard horses could be passed as fit, or even presented twice. Feroz Shah discontinued them, allowing substitutes to be sent, but Sher Shah Lodi reintroduced the systems,[46] which again fell into abeyance. It was never successful in fully regulating human or equine recruits. Akbar reintroduced branding on an annual basis. Some horses' flanks must have carried multiple brands if they survived many campaigns.

The army was distributed as necessary. A standing army was kept with the sultan at Delhi. Styled the *Hash'n-i-qalb*, it consisted of the *Khisa-i-khel*, or household brigade of royal slaves, and the *Jandars*, or elite royal bodyguard. The *Afwdj-i-qalb* troops under royal command and picked troops serving under nobles remained at the capital. Provincial garrisons were called the *Hashm-i-atraf*. The north-west frontier especially was guarded by picked troops under high-ranking princes and veteran generals.

Cavalry was the superior arm. Pay was decided by ability and how many horses a trooper had: the *murattab* rank had two horses, the *sawar* had one, and the *do-aspah*, the lowest grade, no horse of its own. Under Alauddin Khalji pay was 234, 156 and 78 *tankas* respectively; i.e. 78 for the trooper and 78 for each horse. According to Qureshi the term *do-aspah* has given rise to confusion because under the Moghuls it changed its meaning to indicating a two-horse trooper.[47]

Ibn Battuta was present at a review where prospective troopers were tested. Lancers undertook two demanding tests at the gallop: to hit a target; and to spear a ring suspended from a low wall. Mounted archers shot a ball on the ground from a gallop; the level of their pay depended on their accuracy,[48] and the test was harder than the lance exercises due to the angle of fire changing at each stride. All tests needed straight-moving horses. In Gujarat state the mounted police ride their Kathiawari horses at full gallop in tent-pegging practice. Travelling at *c.* 30 mph (48 kph) they spin their lances, level them, then lower them at a peg 4 inches by 2 (10 cm by 5) protruding from the ground. In over 20 runs I saw only two misses. In competition the target is half the size! In war usage tent-pegging could bring chaos to bivouacked armies when lancers in a surprise night swoop sent the tents crashing down as they galloped through an enemy encampment.

BATTLE CAMP AND ARRAY

Ideally cavalry was deployed near water, on ground as free as possible of stones and dust to limit sole bruising and maintain visibility. Wind and sun direction were noted and any chance of ambushing and/or surprising the enemy was used. Traditional battle order was also camp formation. Camp defences were a ditch and planking; if possible a chain fence was erected. Caltrops limited mounted enemy incursions. Behind these defences foot soldiers with shields protected archers who shot at the enemy. Armoured elephants protected the commander's position.

Moghul battle array, showing traditional Indian weaponry and 'Tufang' – firearms. This wall painting is in Jodhpur Fort, Rajasthan. (Photo: author)

The order was:

1st line – *muqadammah* (vanguard), right wing and left wing
2nd line – infantry
3rd line – main army, left, right, centre with royal camp
4th line – royal harem, kitchen, treasury, wardrobe
5th line – spare horses, camels, prisoners, sick
6th line – *saqqah* (rearguard) with back to camp.

During protracted campaigns the royal household and an extensive bazaar accompanied the army, which resembled a town in transit.

ARTILLERY

Although Feroz Shah used artillery to a limited degree it was slow to make a major impression until the Moghul era.[49] Babur made considerable use of artillery at the first battle of Panipat (1526) and the battle of Kanwa (1527), and at Ghoori in the 1529 Bengal campaign. The *Babūr Nāma* refers to matchlocks, cannon and culverins, and to the method of positioning artillery behind a line of carts roped together with rawhide after the Ottoman fashion. Between each two carts five or six mantlets were fixed behind which matchlockmen stood to fire.[50] One of the matchlocks used at Panipat is in the Jaipur armoury. It is 8 feet long (2.4 m), of which 1 foot (0.3 m) is the stock, 7 feet (2.1 m) the barrel. To operate it took three men – one to fire, two to shoulder it. In the later Moghul period some cavalry carried firearms. Babur first mentions using matchlocks at the siege of Bagaur in 1519 so by Panipat his artillery chief, Ustad Ali Quli, had obtained much useful experience.[51]

BOOTY

The sultan retained horses, elephants and treasure. Of other spoils the state kept one-fifth, the balance being shared among the army. Horsemen received a double share. Prisoners could be killed, enslaved, or freed according to the captor's decision, but were never allowed to return home.[52]

AKBAR'S CONQUESTS

Amir Khusrau called the warhorse a *Ghāzi*, a victor.[53] In Akbar's reign the warhorse held premier place, the elephant being unreliable and likely to damage his own side when panicked.

When Babur invaded, India was an empire in name only. The Lodis ruled in the kingdom of Delhi, Sultan Muzaffar in Gujarat, Nasrat Khan in Bengal, the Bahmanis in the Deccan, Maharana Sanga in Chitor, and the Raja of Vijayanagar in the south. Babur consolidated much of India, including most of Rajputana, the northern Muslim states, reaching the boundaries of Bengal. Under his successor Humayan great losses occurred, and Akbar inherited a much reduced kingdom, but he too consolidated, making his empire the greatest in Asia.[54]

Bairam Khan, a member of the Baharlu sept of the Qaraquilu Turks, Humayan's most faithful adherent, was appointed Akbar's guardian. After Humayan's death when Akbar was 13, Bairam Khan's influence as regent in 1556–60 was enormous; Akbar appointed him *Khan Khanan*, a title awarded to commanders-in-chief, and *wakil*, prime minister. During his regency much territory was regained. At the second battle of Panipat (1556) Akbar defeated Hemu, King Adali Sur's general, thus regaining Delhi and Agra; Gwalior in central India fell to him, as did Jaunpur. In 1560 Akbar took control, dismissing Bairam Khan, who was ordered to make pilgrimage to Mecca, a kind of honourable banishment, but was assassinated by an Afghan whose father he had killed at the battle of Machhiwarah when fighting for Humayan.[55] Akbar raised Bairam's son Abdurrahim, who became a successful general, governor of Gujarat and guardian of Akbar's son Prince Selim (Jahangir); he too was created *Khan Khanan* by Akbar, outliving him well into Jahangir's reign.[56]

The early years set the acquisitorial tone of Akbar's reign, most of which was spent in the saddle campaigning, for he was present at many of the battles and sieges undertaken in his name, and at one period spent 13 years away from his capital, Fathepur Sikri.

With north-west India secure Akbar turned to other conquests. In 1573 he conquered Gujarat, which soon rebelled. Travelling by camel and horse, Akbar and a small punitive taskforce left the capital on 25 August 1573 and covered 600 miles (965 km) to Ahmadabad, where the battle of Ahmadabad was fought on 2 September; Akbar's 3,000 cavalry defeated *c*. 20,000 of the enemy, and he was back in Fathepur Sikri six weeks after leaving it. Bengal and Bihar were subdued in 1576, only to rebel repeatedly until finally crushed in 1590. In 1576 the battle of Haldighati, described above (pp. 171ff), was successfully fought against Rana Pratap of Mewar, but was a pyrrhic victory as Mewar was never wholly conquered. Conquests and annexations continued: Kabul 1585; Kashmir 1586; Sind 1591; Orissa 1592; Qandahar 1595. In 1593 campaigning got under way in the Deccan and continued for eight years until in 1601 with the fall of Asigarh Akbar's writ ran over the widest tracts of India to date.[57]

CAVALRY NUMBERS AND TYPES

Akbar's total cavalry numbers cannot be easily computed, changing according to circumstances, particularly those from nobles' contingents. The standing army cavalry, according to Blochman, who based his figure on the number of horses in the charge of the Mirza Khan Khanan Abdurrahim in the Imperial stables, was 12,000.[58] However, Father Monserrate, a Jesuit at Akbar's court, and present with the army sent against Mirza Mohammed Hakin in the 1581 Kabul campaign, says: '[the] whole force of war lies in cavalry . . . for apart from the forces which follow the leader like hereditary masters and comprise cavalry, infantry and elephants paid by these same leaders from revenues of provinces handed over to them by the King, he [Akbar] pays from his treasury 45,000 horse, 5,000 elephants and many thousands of foot.'[59]

Total numbers were given as 384,758, which included all militia and zamindar levies throughout the provinces, besides the army proper.[60]

Types of cavalry trooper and army classifications in Akbar's time were numerous, as were abuses of the system. Most nobles held land in *jagir*, owing Akbar military assistance in return. There were also *khalicah* (crown) lands from which Akbar drew revenue, but according to Badaoni 'the whole country' was held in *jagirs* by amirs who, when ordered to muster, brought insufficient troops, often servants dressed as soldiers riding borrowed horses.[61] Major reforms were needed and were implemented from 1573. Branding of horses was reintroduced, and the *mansabdari* system whereby a man was paid and ranked according to the number of troops he supplied was instigated. Although the *Ain* notes 66 ranks, in practice there were only 33; the lowest *mansab* (rank) was of 10 troopers, the highest 10,000.[62] The highest grade that a non-royal commander could hold was a *mansab* of 7,000. Under Akbar few ranked above 5,000 except princes who could hold from 7,000 upwards, well exceeding the nominal 10,000 top grade. However, lower-ranking officers held important commands.[63] A *mansabdar*'s troopers were his *tabinan* (followers).[64] Lower *mansabdars* could serve under those of higher rank. Abu Fazl gives instances: e.g. a *hazari* of 1,000 men serving under a commander of 10,000.[65] *Mansabdars* were paid in *naqd* (cash) or in *jagirs*, but where possible Akbar converted *jagirs* into crown lands. Unless the *mansabdar* was a great noble or high in Imperial favour his *jagir* was distant from court, or in a province not completely subdued,[66] thereby preventing nobles getting too powerful. *Jagirs* could also be rescinded whenever Akbar chose.

Mansab organization was complicated. *Zat* was a commander's personal rank. To this was added his *suwar* rank, entitling him to extra pay for supplementary horsemen. He was graded accordingly. From 5,000 down he was first-class if his *zat* and *suwar* were equal; second-class if his *suwar* was at least half his *zat*; third-class if it was less than half or if he had no *suwars* at all; e.g. 1,000 *zat* plus 1,000 *suwar* meant first-class. *Mansabdars* of 5,000 and above were all first-class regardless of *suwars*.[67]

Dakhilis were cavalry troopers raised by the state and placed under *mansabdars* who had trouble raising sufficient men.[68]

A *dahbashi*, the lowest *mansab*, had initially to present with 10 troopers and 25 horses: two *chaharaspah* (four horses each), three *sihaspah* (three horses), three *duaspah* (two horses) and two *yakaspah* (one horse). This was lowered to three *sihaspah*, four *duaspah* and three *yakaspah* troopers – a total of 10 men, 18 horses.[69] All ranks were run similarly. A *hazari* commanding 1,000 brought 1,800 horses.[70]

Horses brought for branding were inspected; if they were found to be above standard, the officer might be upgraded, if sub-standard, demoted.[71] The standard meant quality and/or breed and numbers. Higher-ranking officers were expected to provide greater numbers of better horses and a *hazari* had to produce horses in proportion to his position: 10 Iraqi, 10 Mujannas; 21 Yabus; 21 *tazis*; 21 *janglahs*. Commanders of 100 providing 180 horses were required to produce an equal number of each type.[72]

Fines

The *Tafawat-i-asp* was a classification of horses according to breed and/or size. Officers were fined if horses did not meet standards.[73] Other fines were levied against stable *daroghas*, who in turn fined stable staff, in respect of horses in the *khasa* and other Imperial stables, such as those for *bargir* mounts. The amount depended on the horses' value. The reasons were death, theft, or injury, especially injury to the mouth.[74] This sheds light on expertise. To avoid injury with Moghul bitting delicate handling was essential, indicating that troopers were skilled horsemen.

AHADIS

Ahadis were independent gentlemen troopers and appear often in the *Ain*. Sometimes information about them is conflicting. I have extrapolated the relevant equestrian content. While referring specifically to *ahadis* the details give us an insight into equestrian management in Akbar's military as some 'common-sense rules' would apply to other Imperial cavalry, and to *mansadbars' tabinan*.

Ahadis provided their own horses and accoutrements. They were elite troopers paid direct by the treasury, and served under their own officers. They 'went through the school of learning their duties, and had their knowledge tested', i.e. their military prowess and horsemanship. Initially *ahadis* could bring eight horses, but this was later lowered to five. Most were three-, two-, or one-horse troopers. Some shared a horse. Under one head it states the *ahadi* was paid on a monthly basis, but on a reckoning of 10 months to the year, one-twentieth of his pay being retained for his horse's (or horses') keep and other expenses. A considerable saving to the state accrued when the numbers of permitted horses were reduced. If his horse died the treasury paid for a new one, but withheld maintenance till actual purchase. If an *ahadi* was accepted but had no horse a prest (*musā adat*) was advanced. Half the price was paid by the treasury, the balance deducted in four instalments, or, if the *ahadi* was in debt, in eight.[75] A dead *ahadi*'s horses were redistributed among his needy fellows, either as presents or at a price charged to their monthly salaries. There is conflicting information on this point, as on others. On joining, an *ahadi* received a *sanad* (pay chit), made out in *dams* at 38 to the rupee (later raised to 40) and 9 rupees to the mohur. The *ahadi* received one-half in rupees, one-quarter in mohurs, the balance in *dams* for stores. *Dams*, money of account, represented purchasing power.[76]

> Every year one month's pay was subtracted on account of the horse, and the horse's value raised 50 per cent above its prime cost, and for accoutrements, but as much care is shown in buying horses this increase is not productive of any loss for the soldier. Besides *ahadis* are continually employed for affairs of importance and are permitted to carry the orders of his majesty, and whatever is given to them as an acknowledgement of their services by the recipients of the orders is allowed to be kept by the *ahadis* as a present, if they bear a good character, but if not, a part of it is reckoned as monthly pay.

With the view of teaching zeal and removing laziness soldiers [are] fined for absence from guard; an *ahadi* loses 15 days' pay, other soldiers one week's [pay].

The commander of every contingent is allowed to keep for himself the twentieth part of the pay of his men, which reimburses him for various expenses.[77]

This quote shows discrepancies. It appears under a heading concerning *ahadis* and other soldiers as '*Commanders of every contingent*'. Surely it applies to all categories? Also a month's pay was a tenth, not a twelfth. It was worth while for the *ahadi* to maintain standards in order to be considered of 'good character' and to keep tips, which in many instances could be construed as bribes. The passage indicates that *ahadis* held considerable power.

On an equine level the above shows the system was flexible, if somewhat muddled. All horses benefited the state, either fighting in battle, or being reissued to an *ahadi* whose horse had died or an *ahadi* who paid half its value, or even being given away as a present, because for every mohur of its value 10 *dams* were charged to be paid in tips to stable staff, the tips being reckoned on value plus 50 per cent.[78] When claiming because of a dead horse the *ahadi* had to provide proof of death to headquarters, and if on distant duty send a piece of the horse's branded hide and its tail to headquarters.[79]

Bargirs

Bargirs were raised, horsed and paid by the state. Their horses were maintained in separate stables and issued only when a *bargir*'s services were required. When not in use the horses were returned as Akbar 'would not trust' the *bargirs* 'with the keeping of a horse'. The full title was *bargirsuwar*.[80]

Other Kinds of Troopers

Other kinds of troopers were men enlisting with their own horses and forming part of a *mansabdar*'s corps. A man providing his own mount got monthly pay and allowances according to the quality, breed and number of his horses. On presenting an Iraqi horse he received 30 rupees, a Mujanna 25, a Turki 20, a Yabu 18, a *tazi* 15 and a *janglah* 12. If he possessed two horses he was provided with a camel or an ox and an allowance to maintain it. Initially troopers could bring up to four horses, but later this was reduced to three.[81]

Apart from state *bargirs* and *dakhilis* posted to a *mansabdar*'s contingent a commander raised two types of trooper: *silahdar* cavalry, who provided their own mount(s) and equipment; and his own *bargirs*, a proportion of whose salary, as much as he pleased, was retained by him in return for equipping them.[82]

THE IMPERIAL STABLES

The Imperial stables were organized in minute detail and run on military lines as all horses, except maybe Arabian racehorses, were considered in terms of battle usage, even polo horses. Although defined as an amusement, *chaugan* (polo) was used to teach the art of hard riding and to improve a horse's agility and responsiveness to the reins. Akbar was said to be 'fond of this game . . . majesty unrivalled for skill':[83] Abul 'Fazl could hardly say less of his royal master. Polo was used by all oriental cavalry to keep horses fit.

Although we do not have comparable information for commanders' military stables, common sense dictates that large contingents under senior *mansabdars* must have had a similar set-up.

Each trooper was expected to be able to do tack repairs, and to castrate and/or bleed his horse to make it manageable. Minimal iron rations were carried for man and horse on campaign.[84]

Shoeing

In the Iimperial stables shoes were renewed twice a year at a cost of 10 *dams* per set.[85] However, allowances for army animals show discrepancies. Arabians got 7 *dams* per month for shoes; Persians 6, Mujannas 4, and other grades 2.[86] It is not clear if this was for the 12-month year or the 10-month pay cycle. No costing is shown for removal and reshoeing with the same set. The farrier's job was separately considered. Arabian and Persian horses received new shoes at approximately the same rate used *responsibly* today, and Mujannas once a quarter, which with a remove in between would be adequate, but cheaper horses had bad hoof care. As Arabian and Persian horses do not appear in the *mansabdar*'s list of mandatory animals, army stock came off badly, which must have been reflected in lameness and loss of cavalry efficiency on numerous occasions.

'Officers and Servants Attached to the Imperial Stables'[87]

Stable appointments are listed. The most senior administrative sections were held by high-ranking *mansabdars* and *ahadis* who clearly did no stable work but to whom lesser appointees were responsible:

1 The *atbegi*, Master of Horse, was one of the highest state appointments. He directed all stable staff.
2 The *darogha* was in charge of the smooth running of the whole stable.
3 The *mushrif* was the accountant.
4 The *dida-war* was an inspector who assessed and graded Imperial horses.

The next five grades got an *ahadi*'s pay and were 'hands-on' officials:

The *akhtachis* were tack superintendents.
The *chāsbuksuwar* was a trainer and assessor of horses' performance.
The *hādā's* were always Rajputs (they were considered excellent horsemen). A *hādā's* schooled a green horse to elementary standard – an army roughrider.
The *mirdana* was a senior groom set over ten subordinates. He also cared for two horses.
The *baytar* was a horse doctor.

There were more menial positions – *naqib*, a supervisor who reported to the *darogha*; *sāis*, a groom; *nadlband*, a farrier; *abkash*, a water-carrier – and others of still less importance; even one for a furniture duster. Posts which carry immense importance today, such as veterinary surgeon or farrier, did not receive their true standing in Akbar's day, but both sciences have made their great strides only in modern times.

Part III has given only a brief glimpse of the Indian warhorse and his selection, importance and care; how avidly monarchs sought to add superb animals to their stables and cavalry contingents; how warhorses were used in battle with age-old manoeuvres and split-second timing in intricate movements that won for the most agile safety and the chance to fight another day.

In the seventeenth century India's cavalry expertise reached a peak with the Mahrattas who were possibly the world's most talented horse-trainers from a warrior's point of view. They fought in a way completely different from that of the new incursives into their ancient land: the French, the Dutch and, most of all, the British. There can be no doubt that in sheer horsemanship the British learned from the Indians, even though their systematic approach to warfare gave them eventual supremacy over the disparate warring cultures of India. Under British rule, too, much that was new to Indian equestrianism was implanted. India continued to receive new waves of foreign horses, albeit still putting her own stamp upon them.

PART IV
North and South America

TEN

European Settlement in the Americas

Bernal Díaz del Castillo, one of Cortés's warriors, claimed that the conquest of the Americas was due first to God, then to their horses.

EARLY EQUINE IMPORTS: SPANISH INFLUENCE

The Andalusian had a major impact in the Americas, the Spaniards being the first to (re)introduce and breed horses long before French, English and Dutch colonists introduced their breeds. However, except in the favourable Antillean conditions horses did not reproduce until well into the sixteenth century. Nor were all Spanish horses noble Andalusians. Muster rolls and contemporary accounts indicate quality, or its lack. On one occasion at least, low-grade horses were shipped subverting official orders. The *casta distinguida* stock was too costly for some. Therefore a mix of breeds is indicated, although the Crown ensured that noble stock was regularly shipped.

The introduction of horses into the Americas cannot be treated in military isolation. After conquest came colonization, administration, abstraction of metallic wealth, and huge exports of leather and other commodities. The conquerors frequently had to defend their new and expanding territories.

The first Spanish hold was in the Greater Antilles, where Cuba, Jamaica, Puerto Rico and Hispaniola (Haiti and Santo Domingo) were colonized between 1492 and 1512. Hispaniola was Columbus's first landfall, on 12 October 1492. Eagerness to colonize is illustrated by early correspondence and royal decrees. Both Crown and conquerors had much to gain – the former tremendous wealth, the latter land-grants and position. One of the earliest decrees, held in the Archives of the Indies in Madrid, dates to 23 May 1495:

> We command that a certain fleet be prepared to send to the islands and mainland which have been newly discovered . . . and to prepare the vessels for Admiral Don Christopher Columbus . . . there shall be sent 20 lancers with horses . . . and 5 of these shall take 2 horses each, and the 2 horses which they take shall be mares.[1]

Titian's painting of Charles V at Muhlberg shows him mounted on a casta distinguida *horse of Spain. This animal is very different from the Duke of Newcastle's representation and far closer to the true type of Andalusian. (Photo: Museo del Prado, Spain)*

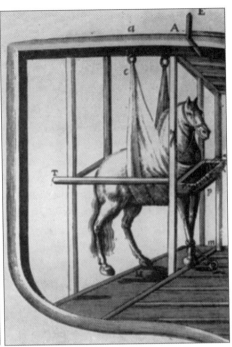

The method of loading and shipping horses overseas in the sixteenth century, depicted by Manuel Alvarez Ossorio y Vega in Manejo real en que se propone lo que deben saber los cavalleros *(Madrid, 1769). (Reproduced from R.M. Denhardt,* The Horse of the Americas, *Norman, University of Oklahoma Press, 1947)*

Clearly land was to be taken and colonized by force, and livestock bred from imports, which included sheep, heifers, etc. In the 17 vessels of the second expedition (September–November 1493) were soldiers, missionaries, artisans, field labourers, knights, young courtiers.[2]

In January 1494 Columbus complained about his cavalrymen's substitution of government issue for inferior mounts. Research indicates these mounts were Sorraias or Sorraia-cross Andalusian, which cost a tenth the price of an Andalusian purebred. Recognized by hippologists as the Iberian horse's primitive ancestor, the Sorraia came from the area of the rivers Sor and Raia. For centuries it was used by Spanish cowherders. Historians are convinced of Sorraia influence in American feral herds and in the Criolla of Argentina.[3]

In 1494 Columbus suggested that every Spanish ship should carry broodmares.[4] Immediately his patron Isabella of Castile decreed that 'henceforth every ship should carry on it 12 breeding mares of *casta distinguida* to serve the needs of the new colonies'.[5] Regular shipments followed, initially at government expense. Few detailed records survive, most stating simply '*y caballos y yeguas*' (horses and mares). A few are specific: 9 April 1495, 6 mares; 23 April 1497, 14 mares. On his third voyage (1498) Columbus carried 40 *jinetes* and their horses. By 1500 on one royal stud farm there were 60 broodmares. In 1501 the new governor, Nicolas de Ovando, imported 18 *casta distinguida* horses and six years later Ferdinand of Aragon authorized export of 106 broodmares from Seville, Sanlúcar and Huelva. Due to resource depletion, Spain then forbade future exports,[6] but exceptions were made, even after the Antillean studs were well established. Some *hidalgos* shipped their own warhorses; others contracted with the Crown for taking horses (and other stock) from Spain at their own expense in later expeditions. But most of the *conquistadores'* horses came from Antillean royal stud farms and ranches of wealthy immigrants.

In 1497 it was decreed that a public farm be established and open to cultivation by Spaniards who should be loaned '50 bushels [1800 litres] each of corn and wheat, and as many couple of cows and mares and other beasts of burden', to be paid back to the Crown by a tithe of the annual crop.[7] A detailed list authorized by Ferdinand for Columbus, dated 9 April 1495, shows cattle, horses, mules, sheep, goats and hogs.[8] Doubtless Spanish jacks were sent for mule-breeding, which became big business on a par with horse- and cattle-raising.[9]

RANCHING

War logistics meshed with ranching. Ranches provided warhorses, meat on the hoof or trotter, grain, pack-mules and manpower. The Andalusian cattle-ranching system was transplanted to the Antilles and later to the mainland. Cattle raised in Seville and Cadiz provinces were longhorned and unruly, and the only way they could be managed was from horseback.[10] To face such cattle *vaqueros* needed nimble, fast, well-reined, courageous horses. They were ridden *ginete* style, working off their haunches which enabled rapid turns and stops; riders wielded traditional *garrochas* – 14-foot (4.2 m) lances – couched underarm for impact. *Vaqueros* still work cattle from horseback, usually riding Andalusian partbred geldings. Competitions exhibit their skills, and on *estancias* where fighting bulls are raised these are tested by pairs of *vaqueros*, one rider keeping the bull moving straight, while the other, at the gallop, bowls the bull over with the *garrocha* aimed at the hip from behind. In England Peter Madison-Greenwell, of *El Caballo de Espana*, a trainer of classical Spanish horsemanship, demonstrates the techniques on his Hispano-Arab gelding Chico. Executing serpentines and flying changes the horse unerringly passes under the *garrocha*.[11] These traditions translated well to New World battlefields where highly trained, courageous horses and practised lancers had different quarry.

The greatest concentration of emigrants came from Andalusia and Las Marismas; before 1540, almost 19 per cent. From Seville and its environs alone came 15 per cent, a figure which rose to 22 per cent if the Andalusian coastal towns were added. In pre-1520 Jamaica 35 per cent of emigrants came from the provinces of Seville and Huelva. African slaves from the cattle-herding areas of the Sahelo-Sudan, brought to Spain by Moorish slave-traders, and later by Spaniards, were sent to the new colonies and by 1517 went direct to the New World from Africa. Ranching developed on Spanish/African lines with regular imports of cattle, totalling around 500 by 1512.

Equestrian skills were acclaimed in Andalusia. The provinces of Seville and Cadiz were horse-breeding centres; by 1500 the largest numbers were in

Aznalcazar and Coria. Horses and cattle prospered in the fertile savannahs; one Jamaican ranch had 1,650 cattle and 60 broodmares by 1520. Large herds of cattle from Jamaica were supplied to Mexico and Panama by 1521, plus dried meat and other animal products for the new colonies and to supply more expeditions. Hides were exported in bulk to Spain,[12] and were converted to armour for men and horses according to contemporary records.

In 1495 an Indian revolt was quashed, tribute imposed and commutation to labour on farms accepted. From this arose the *repartimiento* and *encomienda* system whereby the Crown granted land and Indians to work it.[13] In 1507 the practice of grazing crown lands without permission, adopted by early entrepreneurs to benefit their cattle- and horse-breeding enterprises, was officially sanctioned; the ownership of cattle now carried the right to grazing. Subsequently graziers petitioned for outright land-grants.[14]

Animal proliferation had several results. Fortunes were made from stock-raising, and land-grants eagerly sought and exploited. The products enabled men to launch more expeditions and to supply the new colonies they found, enriching the suppliers. The Crown, especially under Charles V (reigned 1519–55), was notoriously mean with funds while claiming a fifth of all precious metal mined. As stock multiplied some went feral; some areas became overgrazed.

THE CONQUESTS

The major expeditions spanned just over 30 years, from Cortés's expedition to Mexico in 1519 to Valdivia's Chilean enterprises in the 1540s and early 1550s, but other conquests, settlements and resettlements bridged the gap, bringing 1.15 million square miles (3 million square km) under Spanish rule – about one-fifth of the total. Later campaigns extended this. By 1680 Spanish and European control extended, imperfectly, to about half the landmass. The sheer extent of Spain's domains hindered conquest.[15] The first problem was subjugation of native populations. As conquests spread, other hazards took a heavy toll: wild climatic swings; difficult, almost impassable terrain; extreme natural conditions. Added risks were starvation, fever, disease, dehydration, etc. Expedition mortality was high, especially among the cavalry horses, which also risked being eaten when supplies failed. At first only a few horses were supplied for each expedition, but the risk of losing the horses was counterbalanced by the real fear they engendered among the Indians. The presence of a single horse could turn an engagement in favour of heavily outnumbered Spaniards.

HISPANIOLA SETTLED AND SUBJUGATED

Once back in Hispaniola with the first colonists and his 20 lancers' horses, Columbus set about establishing settlements. He had made friendly contact with Indians in 1492 and some went back with him to Spain, returning to Hispaniola on his second voyage. His log notes that Guacamari, a *cacique* (an Indian chief), was greatly impressed by the horses and other stock on board the returning fleet.[16] With Isabela, the first settlement, as his base, Columbus left for Cibao on

12 March 1494, with all fit foot and cavalry. He found 'goldfields' and established Fort St Tomas after a journey along trackways difficult for horses. Provisions being scant, mules were sent to Isabela for supplies. Subsequently Columbus returned to Isabela where fertile land encouraged agriculture. No sooner had he returned than news came that the peaceful St Tomas Indians were fleeing in fear of the *cacique* Caonabo, who threatened to burn the fort:

> but the Admiral knowing that these Indians were cowards did not make much of this rumour especially as he trusted in the horses of which the Indians were much afraid, fearing that they would eat them. In fact they were in such dread of horses that they dare not enter any building in which one of them was.

A *cacique* was captured; in reprisal his subjects ambushed five Spaniards *en route* to Isabela. When a messenger despatched from St Tomas rode through this *cacique*'s town, his Indians fled across the river in fear of the horse, two being injured. The Spaniards were rescued; when the Indians returned to the attack they halted at sight of the lone horse, fearing it might 'fly' back across the river.[17]

In early 1495 Columbus returned to Isabela from an exploratory trip to Cuba. Caonabo's Indians had revolted, and Pedro Margrit, whom he had left with 360 foot and 14 horse to patrol and reduce Hispaniola, had abandoned Isabela for nearby Vega Real and subsequently sailed for Spain. The revolt was put down rapidly and savagely. Columbus left Isabela on 24 March 1495, with a force of 200 Spaniards, 20 horses, 20 hunting dogs, and allied Indians under Guacanagari, a *cacique* at enmity with Caonabo. He divided his forces to attack from two directions:

> when the infantry squadrons of both armies had attacked the mass of Indians, and they had begun to break under the fire of muskets and crossbows, the cavalry and hunting dogs charged wildly upon them to prevent them re-forming. The Indians fled like cowards in all directions, and our men pursued them, killing so many and wreaking such havoc among them that, to be brief, by God's will victory was achieved, many Indians being killed and many others captured and executed. Caonabo, the principal king of all, was taken alive with his sons and women.[18]

Clearly, with the settlement of Hispaniola less than six months old, more horses and equids must have been landed to add to the first 25-strong batch, as some horses had been left at St Tomas and Columbus still fielded 20 in putting down the revolt. Throughout the conquests when garrisoning new settlements a few horsemen were included in the military complement.

By the third expedition of 1498–1500 livestock was doing well, shown by the fair price that Roldan, a Spaniard returning to Spain, got for his *large* herd of pigs.[19]

EARLY MAINLAND OPERATIONS

Early *conquistadores* brought a wealth of military experience to the New World; others learned their craft there. Alonso de Hojeda fought at Granada, Pedrarias Davila at Oran, Pedro de Mendoza, Diego de Amalgro and Pedro de Valdivia in Italy.[20]

The first permanent mainland settlements were undertaken by Alonso de Hojeda and Diego de Nicuesa in 1509/10 at their own expense. Hojeda sailed for North Colombia in November 1509 with 4 ships, 300 men and 12 horses, and 10 days later Nicuesa followed with 700 men and 6 horses in 7 vessels. Hojeda was granted the coast from Cape de la Vela to the Gulf of Uraba in Colombia, Nicuesa the Isthmus of Panama and the coast as far as Cape Gracias á Dios in eastern Honduras. Hunger, overwork, tropical climate and hostile Indians whittled away both expeditions.[21]

Hojeda's expedition was ill-fated. He retreated into Panamanian territory, founding an ephemeral colony at the mouth of the River Darien. Francisco Pizarro, Peru's future conqueror, was one of Hojeda's captains, left in charge when Hojeda sailed to Hispaniola for relief forces and died there. Meanwhile Pizarro left for the Colombian coast, meeting the two relief ships under Fernandez de Enciso with 150 men, several horses, arms and provisions. Enciso insisted on returning to the Darien colony; one ship was wrecked, the men saving themselves though much cargo was lost. Presumably some horses also survived by swimming. Indians had attacked the colony, destroying houses and harassing the Spanish colonists.[22]

Nicuesa's expedition also suffered losses at sea. The beleaguered Darien colony was moved to Nombre de Dios on the Panamanian Atlantic coast.[23] Vasco Nunez de Balboa, one of Nicuesa's captains, established friendly contacts with Panamanian Indians who gave him gold objects, divulging that more were to be had southwards. This spurred Balboa to send to the West Indies for reinforcements for further exploration.[24] Unlike Columbus's 'goldfields' this discovery was genuine, an early trickle that swelled to a flood of gold and silver shipped to Spain by regular treasure fleets.

In 1513, reinforced, Balboa made an epic journey through the Panamanian jungle, reaching the Pacific coast on 25 September. Four months later, treasure-laden, he returned to Darien and despatched messengers to report to Spain. In response Spain sent a fleet of 15 ships and 2,000 men to Darien with Balboa's father-in-law, Pedrarias de Avila, as governor. Balboa fell foul of Pedrarias's jealousy and was tried and beheaded on a trumped-up charge of inciting Indians to attack.[25]

In Panama, which received its horses from the Antilles, stock flourished and by 1526 the isthmus had become another vital main supplier of horses and cattle. Permission was now needed from the Council of the Indies to buy horses in Spain, export them and breed from them in the New World.[26]

EQUINE SUPPLY: SURVIVAL TO PROLIFERATION

Hernando Cortés's Mexico campaign opened in spring 1519 when he sailed from Cuba with 16 horses and 508 soldiers plus the ships' complements.[27] Cortés's progress reports to Charles V on the six-year Mexican campaign show a steady increase in demand for reinforcements. Men and horses were needed for the expanding colonies, fighting forces and garrisons for the new territories. Exact numbers of horses are impossible to calculate as at first attrition was exceptionally high. Even though many were mares, few in the hard fighting conditions could have foaled successfully. One mare which foaled on board ship did not raise the foal; she was the first killed in action (see below). However, as mares were regularly brought in from the Antilles, and in later expeditions from Spain, after Mexican resistance was broken and provinces settled, Mexico superseded the Antilles and became another major supplier of horses for Spanish cavalry.[28]

After his conquest Cortés, now the Marquis del Valle de Oaxaca, founded ranching and farming enterprises near Cuernavaca, south of Mexico City, raising cash crops, cattle, sheep and horses. At his death in 1547 horses and other livestock were prominent in his will (items 27–30). Most income and increase, derived from the town of Chinantla and neighbouring ranches, and those at Tlatizapan (Taltizapan) and Matlatzinco (Matalanga), went to his natural daughter Catalina Pizarro and her mother Leonora Pizarro, wife of Juan de Salcedo. Also left to Catalina were moneys and outstanding dues from a lively trade in broodmares on Catalina's property, which Cortés had administered.[29]

By 1531 many ranches were established, worked by Indian labour on the *encomienda* system. They raised corn, wheat and livestock, particularly horses. Twenty years after settlement the Toluca valley near Mexico City boasted over 60 *estancias* with more than 150,000 cattle and horses between them. Other ranching nuclei were at Llanas de Apan (Hidalgo State), in the basin of Huemantla, south-west of Perote, and in other smaller centres.[30]

Historians of the Indies and New Spain (Mexico) remarked the sixteenth- and seventeenth-century 'droves of work horses, oxcarts, mule packtrains, livestock, and saddle-horses all over the country', and commented on the annual drove of 50,000 cattle, over 200,000 sheep, 4,000 mules and 4,000 horses driven to and sold in Mexico.[31] Consequently cattle and horse prices dropped dramatically; Cortés had paid up to 500 gold *pesos* per horse. Exceptional horses commanded fantastic prices. In 1551 Domingo Martinez de Irala, governor of Paraguay, paid 4,000 gold crowns for one, but ordinary horses dropped in price once breeding herds were established. A broken horse could be purchased for 5 gold *pesos*, or less. However, prices fluctuated according to supply and demand. The average price jumped from 200 *pesos* in 1530 to 500 in 1538, but the general trend continued downwards; by the mid-sixteenth century ordinary horses in Mexico were so cheap that the poorest Spaniard owned one. Production rates fell dramatically in the last quarter of the century. Jeronimo Lopez owned 4,000 mares, which produced 900 colts[32] – a very poor return even though the horse is not the most prolific breeder.

The drain on Spain and on the islands was enormous; in 1520 another embargo was put on the shipment of horses from Spain, and in 1525 an embargo on horses from the islands. The latter was flouted, *conquistadores* still shipping stock out of island studs, but until Mendoza was sent out in 1536 to colonize the River Plate territories, no more horses came from Spain.[33] Several cargoes of horses and mares then accompanied a new wave of Spaniards to what are now Argentina and Paraguay. In 1536 Pedro de Mendoza, *adelantado* (governor-general) of the new territories, contracted with the Crown to take 100 horses and 100 mares; in 1541 Alvar Nunez Cabeca de Vaca brought in 26; in 1572, when Zarate was appointed governor, he guaranteed to bring 200 families, 300 soldiers, 4,000 cows, 4,000 sheep, 500 goats and 300 mares. Much of this consignment was lost at sea, but many of the animals must have survived.[34]

In 1565 a campaign in what later became Florida and South Carolina was launched by Philip II of Spain, who ordered Menendez to take 100 horses and mares with his 2,464 Spaniards.[35]

In 1580 Juan de Garay, second-in-command to Governor Zarate at Asunción (Paraguay), sailed 1,000 miles downriver to the old site of Buenos Aires. Escorting cavalry followed the Paraná's banks. By now many Indians were mounted; in 1579/80, almost parallel with Garay's expedition, Sarmiento, the official sent to find news of Francis Drake, who was plundering the Spanish treasure fleets, declared that the Indians of Santa Cruz (Argentina) were already experienced horsemen. So well equipped were some that at Garay's disembarkation he was met by the *first recorded* charge of Indian horse, led by their chief Taboba. Failing to carry the assault against disciplined Spaniards, the Indians retired, launching no further attacks. The flag of Castile was raised at New Buenos Aires on 11 June 1580.[36]

Writing to the king in 1582, Garay said of the reported pampas herds: 'when I wrote this we had not seen them . . . In truth there is a goodly number of them.' However, these herds did not stem from the seven horses and five mares Mendoza was reputed to have turned loose when he embarked for Spain in 1539, dying *en route*. In the first turbulent years of Buenos Aires Mendoza's people were ravaged by starvation and by hostiles. Some accounts say they lost 1,000 of their 1,500 complement in the first three months, but Fray Alonso Baptista, desiring greater accuracy, said:

> Where it says 1,000 men who died of hunger and of Indians, that he does not swear to there being more than 850, or slightly more or less.

Cannibalism was resorted to. A German soldier, Ulderich Schmidel, reported that three Spaniards were executed for stealing and *secretly* eating a horse when the garrison was starving; the gravamen of the charge being the secrecy. Schmidel noted: 'the horses no longer sufficed' – meaning horsemeat was exhausted. Other horses may have been shipped from Spain, but it is unlikely as no records survive, and later shipments were well documented, starting with a shipment of 26 in 1541.

The huge pampas herds established prior to Garay's arrival were descendants of horses that drifted east from Chile and Tucuman,[37] which had originally been provided by Peru. Escapees from skirmishes, holding corrals and Indian thefts provided the pampas foundation stock and nature did the rest. The excellent grazing was ideal for raising horses, whether feral or domesticated.

In the compass of 61 years from Cortés to Garay the Spanish horse – imported and bred in the Antilles, Mexico, Panama, or Peru, and then throughout Spain's South American territories – had made the conquest possible. These Spanish horses, whether *casta distinguida* or Sorraia cowpony, were as suited to war as to range-riding – the dual occupation of nearly all the Spaniards who fought their way to landownership.

ELEVEN

Cortés and the Conquest of Mexico

Before joining Cortés, Bernal Díaz was with Pedrarias in Panama from 1514 to 1517. He made early probes into Yucatan with Francisco Hernandez de Cordoba in 1517, and with Juan de Grijalva in 1518.[1]

Díaz described Cortés's horses:

Captain Cortés had a dark chestnut stallion which died when we reached San Juan de Ulua.

Pedro de Alvarado and Hernando Lopez de Avila had a very good sorrel mare turning out excellent both for tilting and for racing. When we arrived in New Spain Pedro de Alvarado took his half either by purchase or by force.

Alonzo Hernandez Puerto Carrero had a swift grey mare which Cortés bought for him with his gold [shoulder] knot.

Juan Velázquez de Leon also had a sturdy grey mare which we called La Rabona [bobtail]. She was fast and well broken.

Christobal de Olid had a dark brown horse that was quite satisfactory.

Francisco de Montejo and Alonzo de Avila had a parched sorrel, useless for war.

Francisco de Morla had a dark brown stallion which was fast and well reined.

Juan de Escalante had a light bay horse with three white stockings. She was not very good.

Diego de Ordas had a barren grey mare, a pacer which seldom galloped.

Gonzalo Dominguez, an excellent horseman, had a dark brown horse, good and a grand runner.

Pedro Gonzalez de Trujillo had a good chestnut horse, a beautiful colour and he ran very well, and he was well reined.

Baena, a settler of Trinidad, had a dark roan horse with white patches but he turned out worthless.

Lares, a fine horseman, had a very good bay horse which was an excellent runner.

Ortiz the musician and Bartolomé Garcia, who had gold mines, had a black horse called 'el Arriero' [he had probably driven a pack train] and he was one of the best horses in the fleet.

Juan de Sedeno, a settler of Havana, had a brown mare that foaled on board ship. Sedeno was the richest soldier in the fleet, having a vessel, a mare, a Negro, and many provisions.[2]

Many of Cortés's men had served in earlier expeditions and were to make their own impact. Pedro de Alvarado, his second-in-command, was noted for daring, horsemanship and excessive cruelty. He was Guatemala's first governor and later attempted his own campaign in Peru, angering Pizarro, the *adelantado*, who bought him off for 100,000 gold *pesos*.[3]

THE CORTÉS EXPEDITION

From the landing at the mouth of the Tabasco river (Grijalva) on 12 March 1519 to the capture of Tenochtitlán on 13 August 1521, Díaz graphically describes the fighting, highlighting cavalry encounters with Indians. Cavalry nearly always meant groups of three, four, or five horsemen until Cortés became better supplied with mounts. Cortés comes across as tough but fair, leading from the front. He usually treated Indians fairly, with occasional lapses into savagery as when 50 Tlaxcalan spies were returned to their chieftains with their hands severed.[4] He forbade looting, although from the outset trinkets were exchanged for gold.

On landing they parleyed with the Indians. Cortés said that the Indians agreed to provide food; Díaz that 12,000 attacked, with more in the woods covering the shore. According to Cortés he met the Indians with foot and 10 horse, but from Díaz's fuller, if later, narrative it appears that horses were not used until the battle of Cintla a few days later.[5] After the initial encounters, 33 Indians lay dead and 3 captured, and Spanish losses were 2 dead, 25 wounded; Cortés now ordered the horses ashore. Stiff at first they loosened up the next day. The best – meaning the majority – were chosen to form the cavalry; 13 horsemen had been picked to ride with Cortés. For effect bells were attached to the horses' breastplates; it is unclear if these were of armour or leather – chroniclers refer to armour of cowhide and padded cotton. A lancer's favourite tactic was to aim at the Indians' faces, an order repeated throughout Díaz's tale.

At Cintla a swamp impassable to horses divided the Spanish; their foot were assailed by arrows, lances, swords and sling-shots. Spanish guns felled many Indians; hand-to-hand fighting was desperate, the tide turning only when cavalry circled the swamp and charged the Indian rear lancing at will. Caught between foot and horse, terrified of the horses – the first they had seen – the Indians fled. An earlier skirmish in which three riders and five horses were injured had delayed Cortés. Over 800 Indian dead were matched by great numbers wounded, largely in the swathe cut by the horsemen. Only two Spaniards died. Wounded men and horses were treated with fat rendered from a dead Indian.

Realizing the shock-value of horses and artillery, Cortés used it theatrically. Juan de Sedeno's mare, which had foaled on board ship, was in oestrus; she was used to tease Ortiz's stallion El Arrirero and was then led away in one direction, the stallion in another; and the biggest cannon was loaded with ball and powder. When 40 *caciques* approached to ask pardon, they were met by an irate Cortés, an explosive cannon roar that sent the ball whistling away over the hills, and El Arriero pawing the ground, neighing and extremely hard to control. After thoroughly scaring the *caciques* Cortés ordered that El Arriero be led away and assured them he had asked him not to attack as they were friendly and desired peace.

At Eastertime ambassadors from Montezuma, the Mexican emperor, arrived at San Juan de Ulua with gifts and to sketch Cortés and company, horses and hunting dogs. Cortés ordered Alvarado, mounted on his sorrel mare, to gallop the horsemen in a double column and skirmish on the shore. Impressed, the ambassadors returned to Montezuma. At this time Cortés's chestnut stallion died. It was replaced by El Arriero, either by purchase or as a gift.[6]

Cracks appeared in the company. Disgruntled members tried to hold Cortés to his earlier promise to permit the departure of those who wished to return to Cuba. At first Cortés appeared to comply, then revoked permission. Meanwhile a delegation of Totonacs arrived from Cempoalla, 15 miles (24 km) from the newly founded Veracruz, asking for help against Mexican warriors who were ravaging around Cingapacinga 25 miles (40 km) distant, having lulled Cortés into thinking it their territory. Cortés complied with 400 foot and 14 horse to add to their 2,000, but hearing of Cortés's approach the Mexicans abandoned Cingapacinga; the Cempoallans started looting. Furious, Cortés returned to Veracruz, soon receiving his first reinforcements. Francisco de Saucedo, commanding a ship from Cuba, brought a horse and 10 soldiers, and Luis Marin a mare.[7]

Cortés was gaining an insight into Indian politics from the Cempoallans who subsequently invited him into their town. Although they falsely claimed to be independent of Mexico, they paid tribute to Montezuma. Their hatred of Mexico was genuine, as was their hatred of Tlaxcala and Huexotzinco, and the fact that the rival candidate for the throne of Texcoco was also an enemy of Montezuma. They failed to say that Tlaxcala and Huexotzinco were enemies, and that only Tlaxcala was in open opposition to Mexico. Cortés's original aim had been to make a coastal settlement; this news offered a wider vista for Spanish conquest.[8]

On 16 August 1519 Cortés started for Mexico with 13 horse and 300 foot, leaving 2 horse and 150 foot at Veracruz to build a fort. He probed Tlaxcalan territory with six horses, paying the penalty when Tlaxcalans attacked; two horses were killed, three wounded, and two Spaniards also wounded. The remaining horse, arriving before the foot, turned the fight, killing 50 to 60 Indians and suffering no further losses. Cavalry proved its worth here and in further clashes with Tlaxcalans. They were not a united people; their chief apologized and offered to pay for the horses killed, blaming Indians independent of his authority. After further battles won against unfavourable odds, but balanced by fear and damage caused by artillery, crossbow fire, and the Indians' incapacity against rapid charges and manoeuvring of cavalry, peace was made with Tlaxcala. Both Xicotencatl, Tlaxcala's chief commander, and Cortés had much to gain, the former help to stay independent of Mexico, the latter massed Indian fighters, bearers and supplies for troops and horses. Fear of horses was diminishing. Two had been killed (Díaz mentions only the killing of Sedeno's mare, which was beheaded with a razor-sharp, obsidian-set Indian sword, the *maquahuitl*; her shoes were removed and offered to the Indian idol, and her rider Moron later died of his wounds), which proved their vulnerability. Excessive work was causing havoc in the diminished cavalry; on one night sortie five horses were sent back to camp when they fell from exhaustion, and Díaz noted two who colicked and were sent back.[9] But as fighting units horses remained indispensable throughout the campaign.

At Tenochtitlán (Mexico City) on 8 November, fearing Cortés would fulfil a prophecy about his overthrow, Montezuma had the company well received, the horses fed fodder and maize, and bedded on flowers. Gaining Montezuma's trust and a series of audiences Cortés engineered his capture.[10]

News came from Veracruz that Diego Velázquez, governor of Cuba, angered at Cortés founding the colony against his orders, had sent under Narvaez a fleet with 800 men, 80 horses and 10 or 12 pieces of artillery (Díaz says 1,400 men) and orders to kill or capture Cortés.[11] Leaving Alvarado with 120 men to guard Montezuma, Cortés headed back with 80 men, all the available horses, 260 men from garrisons *en route*, and 50 from Sandoval's Veracruz garrison. Narvaez and Cortés fought at Cempoalla on the night of 28/9 May 1520. Cortés's few horses were secured away from the fight; some of his men infiltrated Cempoalla, others cut the girths of Narvaez's cavalry horses. The ensuing fight was chaotic. Narvaez was badly wounded and captured, spooked horses stampeded as riders and saddles thumped to the ground. Cortés augmented his cavalry with loose and captured horses, but returned their horses to any of Narvaez's men willing to serve under his command; 70 horsemen and 500 foot were added. Díaz tallies: over 1,300 men, 96 horses, 80 crossbowmen, 80 musketeers, 2,000 Tlaxcalan allies.[12]

Cortés re-entered Tenochtitlán on 24 June to find the Mexicans in revolt, with Alvarado under siege. Because he had made a vicious attack on Mexican nobility at a religious festival, Alvarado had been informed that he was now a target; he had struck first, was overwhelmed, lost six men and was besieged in Axayacatl Palace where Montezuma was imprisoned. Montezuma, who still had influence over his people, asked to speak to Cortés but was insultingly rebuffed, which incited a Mexican attack; Díaz hints that this attack was already planned, and Cortés's choler lit the torch. Days of desperate fighting ensued and in the subsequent *Noche Triste* flight on 10 July the cavalry was severely hampered. Even though armoured, horses were riddled with arrows and other wounds; they slipped on the flagstones, some fell in the canals, some were pierced by lances. Only 23 horses survived. Many, lame and unfit for fighting, carried wounded out of the city. Those still capable formed flanking protection for foot. On gaining the plain the remaining cavalry fought a desperate action, bursting through massed Indians. At Otumba four days later the company was whittled down to 400 soldiers, 20 horses, 12 crossbowmen and 7 musketeers.[13] Earlier the captive Montezuma had assured his people that the Castilians would depart if they ceased attacking. He was stoned, receiving severe wounds from which he later died, but not before hearing that Cuitlahuac had supplanted him (he later died of smallpox brought to the New World by the Spaniards).[14]

North America, showing principal places mentioned in the text.

Defeat hardened Cortés's resolve and a new campaign was swiftly launched. Cortés had Tlaxcalan allies and a virulent new weapon, smallpox, ravaged many Indian towns. Operations centred on Texcoco; 13 brigantines were built to transport soldiers across Lake Texcoco to Tenochtitlán. Reinforcements arrived from the coast which was now busy with Antillean shipping. Messengers alerted the Tascaltecal, Guajucingo and Churultecal provinces of impending action against Tenochtitlán. A review was held in Texcoco and troops allotted, as shown in Table 11.1.

Table 11.1 Troops at the Texcoco review[15]

	Horse	Archers/Musketeers		Foot	Indians
Pedro de Alvarado	30		18	150	25,000
Christobal de Olid	30		18	160	20,000
Gonsalvo de Sandoval	24	15	4	150	30,000 plus
plus brigantine crews					

Troops were ordered to wear quilted armour at all times, even when asleep.[16] No doubt this included the horses. They were used effectively in much skirmishing around the lake but in a new assault on the city they were hampered by the terrain, until Cortés filled in the canals and deployed his horses to advantage in successive charges, feigned retreats and return attacks. He ordered Alvarado to maintain clear exits from the city for cavalry as the horses 'in reality sustained the war'. Cortés took heavy losses – 7 horses killed, 70 Spaniards captured, Cortés and Sandoval wounded. This was the last Mexican success, the city being reduced in a 75-day siege.[17]

AFTER TENOCHTITLÁN

With increasing numbers of men and horses arriving, Cortés systematically subjugated Mexican provinces and garrisoned new towns as bases for further conquests. Christobal de Olid was ordered to Cape Hibueras in Honduras and Alvarado despatched to Guatemala, Cortés backing these ventures. He sent Olid to Cuba for horses and troops, and there Olid was suborned by Diego Velázquez and, once in Honduras, rebelled against Cortés. Alvarado he equipped with 170 horses, 120 of which were chargers, the rest relay/courier mounts, 300 foot, 130 being crossbowmen and musketeers, and 4 pieces of field artillery.

Cortés now turned to agriculture and trade. He lodged a bitter complaint to the king about the Hispaniolan governor's edict forbidding export of mares and other breeding animals to New Spain (Mexico) because Hispaniola wanted a monopoly. Cortés begged him to overturn this embargo, promised to pay liberally for mares and threatened to bar the islands from purchasing any Mexican goods.[18]

To Yucatan Cortés took 230 men – 93 horse, crossbowmen and arquebusiers, and over 30 foot. The ratio of horse to foot was the highest yet raised. Again horses frightened the Indians. The greatest dangers were natural hazards – rivers, swamps, lack of food and water, and rough, stony mountainous country where horses cast shoes and went lame. In one dangerous pass 68 horses fell down a precipice and were hamstrung, the rest so exhausted and injured that it took them over three months to recover. Their target in Yucatan was Nito (San Gil de Buena Vista) founded by Gil Gonzalez de Avila. They were assailed by Indians and found Nito's inhabitants starving, but Cortés's pigs and the sudden arrival of a supply ship brought relief.

Before returning to Mexico and ranching, Cortés equipped himself with horses, men, arms and provisions from Cuba and went to crush Olid's rebellion; he executed Olid and left a strong garrison of 35 horse and 50 foot under his cousin Hernando de Saavedra. Meanwhile people in Cuba, about to sail for Mexico, heard that a rumour of Cortés's death was false and promptly rerouted to Trujillo, Honduras, carrying 32 horses, Moorish saddles and provisions for sale, knowing Cortés paid well.

In Guatemala Alvarado had burned alive eight chieftains in revenge when rebels killed some horses. The burnings provoked a rising, which, even with over 200 horse, 500 foot and several thousand Indians, meant that Cortés's intervention was still needed to restore peace.[19] Even though Cortés was hardly a mild man, he must by now have been weary of his lieutenant's savagery. Alvarado and Pizarro were two of the worst *conquistadores* in their treatment of Indians.

Cortés's letters show how rapidly equine supply improved. In Peru and Chile horses were used in their hundreds. By 1540, when Cortés returned to Spain (he died there seven years later), Coronado had over 1,000 horses from the viceroy's Mexican stud farms.

TWELVE

Peru

The Peruvian conquests were a mix of tough exploratory treks, fighting, colonization, ranching and mining. Horses were essential, their endurance and military values tested to the maximum.

PIZARRO'S PREPARATIONS

Francisco Pizarro, born *c*. 1470 in Trujillo, Estremadura, sailed for Santo Domingo (Haiti) as a youth. In 1510 he served under Hojeda in Colombia, under Balboa in Darien and Panama. Cortés's discoveries spurred him into forming a partnership with Diego de Amalgro and Fra Hernando de Luque. They targeted Peru – Luque to be based in Panama, Pizarro and Amalgro to lead the expedition.[1]

At first horses were scarce, initially coming from Panama, Nicaragua, Mexico and Jamaica; by special licence from the Council of the Indies, a few came from Spain. Within a few decades large horse- and cattle-breeding ranches were established.[2]

In 1526 Pizarro conducted initial probes taking only four horses;[3] results were encouraging. The partners assembled 160 men, a few horses, ammunition and provisions and sailed south, reconnoitring the coast to the River Santa. Amalgro returned to Panama twice for men and to buy horses with the early gold acquired. Some Indians were hostile, others friendly, as at Tumbes. Returning to Panama in 1527 Pizarro embarked for Spain where in 1528 he canvassed royal approval, being nominated governor and captain-general for life of 200 leagues (roughly 600 miles/965 km) of land from the island of Puná southwards along the coast of New Castile (Peru). Granted his father's coat-of-arms, he added symbols from his discoveries – a rapid rise for one who was an illegitimate son. His brothers Juan and Gonzalo and his half-brothers Hernando Pizarro and Francisco Martin de Alca joined him. Amalgro was awarded *hidalgo* rank and appointed commander of Tumbes fort; Luque was created bishop of Tumbes. *Not an inch of Peru had yet been conquered!* Pizarro was to fund the venture, take 150 men from Spain and recruit a further 100 in Panama. He sailed on 19 January 1530, and in Panama equipped the expedition, buying 27 horses, largely on credit. In January 1531 he sailed for Peru and 10 years of hardship in Spain's wealthiest new territories.[4] From the outset he looked to his future equine supply. In a *cedula* dated 1529 the queen permitted him to acquire 25 broodmares and a few stallions from the royal studs in Jamaica.[5]

THE PIZARRO CONQUESTS

Pizarro landed at Puná Island where Indians attacked but were repulsed by cavalry. Here Hernando de Soto arrived with reinforcements of men and horses. At Tumbes the friendly Indians helped the three-man advance party to land horses and baggage, then turned and massacred them, attacking in force as the main party landed, but as so often on first seeing horses they fled and Pizarro found Tumbes empty.

By now he had *c*. 200 men with 60 horses. San Miguel de Piura, the first Spanish colony on Peruvian soil, became their base. De Soto frequently scouted with small detachments of horse, gathering news of much gold and a good highway inland. Not so welcome was word that the Inca Atahualpa's armies were gathering to eject the Spaniards. Waverers were left to guard San Miguel. As the expedition pressed onwards, friendly Indians provided food and, curious over horses who appeared to 'eat' their iron bits, kindly supplied gold and silver to appease the dangerous animals. Their gullibility was rewarded by horses who ate ravenously, the Spaniards secreting a considerable stash, and more avid than ever.[6]

Moving south for two months Pizarro was unopposed. Scouting ahead de Soto found villages empty and was told that Atahualpa was massing his army. Suddenly hostiles tried, but failed, to prevent the Spaniards from crossing a river on rafts, their horses swimming alongside. Puzzled by the sudden hostility, Hernando Pizarro captured and tortured an Indian eliciting news that Atahualpa's army was ahead, the Inca awaiting them in Cajamarca, 250 miles (400 km) south of Piura; conflicting information put 50,000 Indians in the mountains to the south. Francisco Pizarro now diverted, taking 40 horse and 50 foot over the mountains, and descended on deserted Cajamarca to find the Inca encamped in open country. In full panoply de Soto and 15 horse visited the Inca. De Soto, before dismounting to greet him, exhibited equestrian bravura so close to Atahualpa that his horse snorted in his face; the Inca remained unmoved. Chronicler Herrera says two Peruvian soldiers were executed for showing fear; Garcilaso de la Vega disagrees.[7]

On 16 November 1532, his cavalry in three groups of 20, his foot stationed in buildings, his crossbowmen and arquebusiers on rooftops and cannon on the fortress steps, Pizarro awaited Atahualpa. The emperor with a large bodyguard advanced to meet him. Some say he was unarmed, others that his entourage had concealed weapons. The meeting developed into an unwarranted attack on and capture of Atahualpa on the flimsy excuse that he sacrilegiously threw a proffered Bible on the ground. Armed with safe conducts Hernando with 20 horse rode 400 miles (645 km) south to Pachamac, then by forced march 175 miles (280 km) east to Jauja in the mountains to collect ransom and check on the supposed massing of Peruvian troops. He returned safely to Cajamarca with a Peruvian general as hostage and with gold. Even with the royal fifth set aside, the amount must have been a soldier of fortune's dream – each cavalryman averaged 9,000 gold *pesos* and 300 *marcs* of silver; soldiers who distinguished themselves received more; colonists got little; infantrymen had half the cavalrymen's allotment. Officers and captains received much more: to Francisco Pizarro 52,222 gold *pesos* and 2,350 *marcs* of silver besides the Inca's golden throne valued at 25,000 *pesos*; to de Soto and Hernando Pizarro the largest captain's share. Amalgro's share is not stated; Fra Luque had died in Panama.[8]

On 29 August 1533 the Inca was executed.

A puppet Inca, Toparpa, was appointed and Pizarro headed for Cuzco via Jauja. A strong mounted detachment under de Soto scouted ahead across some of the worst Andean terrain – stifling lowland heat, unbearable cold and wind on the heights. When Indians impeded him he sent for Toparpa, but the Inca was dead; it was suspected that he had been murdered by a Peruvian general, whom Pizarro burned at the stake. Manco replaced Toparpa. Reinforced by Amalgro, de Soto fought steadily to Cuzco, cavalry still feared and used to full advantage on plains country near Cuzco. On sacking the town in November the Spaniards found a further haul of gold and silver, which was melted down and shared, each man getting 4,000 gold *pesos*. Naturally prices soared, a decent horse costing 3,000–5,000 *pesos*.[9]

Shortly after this de Soto returned to Spain a rich man; he had violently disagreed with Pizarro over Atahualpa's murder, and according to Herrera he was angered by disputes between Pizarro and Amalgro, who felt he had been cheated of recognition and sufficient rewards. Pizarro had already sent his half-brother Hernando to Spain to inform Charles V of Peru's riches. Hernando returned with a marquisate for Pizarro and awards for other leaders.[10]

Both Pizarro and Amalgro were furious and alarmed to hear that Alvarado and a large cavalry force had landed at Caráquez Bay to gatecrash their enterprise. After five months' tortuous journeying Alvarado's force was severely whittled down. Many horses, 2,000 Guatemalan Indians, and 85 of his 500 Spanish soldiers had died. Amalgro raced north to Riobamba (Ecuador), intercepted Alvarado and bought him off for 100,000 gold *pesos*. Many of Alvarado's soldiers joined Amalgro whose cavalry was swelled by 120 of the remaining horses.

With 500 Spaniards and hundreds of Indian porters Amalgro struck south to Chile, crossing the Bolivian tableland 12,500 feet (3,810 m) above sea level; here many mares foaled, and the foals were carried in hammocks, as were soldiers incapacitated by the rigours. Meanwhile Manco had escaped, raised an army and besieged Pizarro's brothers Juan and Hernando in Cuzco. To alleviate starvation mounted sorties were made; in one 2,000 llamas were captured but the Pizarro brothers lost many men and horses. The Indians now coped with cavalry by using staked pits, hurling stones, throwing lassos and boleadores. Manco was seen mounted, adroitly handling his horse. Throughout Peru colonists and soldiers were being killed. In Lima Pizarro was hard pressed and urged to evacuate. He refused, sending to Panama, Nicaragua, Guatemala, Mexico and the Indies for reinforcements.

Amalgro's much reduced force returned, a three-way situation developing. Amalgro fought Hernando for Cuzco having been awarded it by Charles V, then defeated Manco who escaped to the mountains. Relieved at the Indian collapse Francisco Pizarro, with Panamanian reinforcements, headed for Cuzco, where he confronted, captured and executed Amalgro, sending his son Diego to Lima.[11]

South America, showing principal places mentioned in the text.

AFTERMATH

Pizarro enjoyed his appointments, land-grants, horses and riches only briefly. Assassinated on 26 June 1541, he left a legacy of civil war. His brothers and Diego Amalgro headed rival factions and fought bitterly for years until the Crown crushed them.

The best accounts of equestrian exploits come from participants in these wars and from the Inca Garcilaso de la Vega, son of a *conquistador* and an Inca princess. He served as a lancer in crown service in the 1560s and afterwards lived in Cordoba, Spain. His *Commentaries* record his own exploits and those of returning *conquistadores*. He was a good horseman *a la gineta* and accorded horses premier place in the conquests: '*mi terra* [Peru] *se gano a la gineta*'.[12]

Garcilaso described a soldier's armour:

> He who had not Milan steel threw off his armour as it did not protect him, and put on a quilted cotton jacket such as the Indians used, which turned an arrow better than inferior plate.

Fra Pedro Aguado writing of the conquest of New Granada (Colombia) added that quilted defences covered the rider from head to foot; similar horse armour made the duo appear gigantic but ensured safety.[13]

Garcilaso's narrative of Gonzalo Pizarro's epic but disastrous 1539 campaign to extend the 'Pizarro' conquests north of the Inca empire depicts gross deprivation for man and horse. Leaving Cuzco with 100 horse and 100 foot Gonzalo rode over 1,000 miles (1,610 km) to Quito. He expanded his force to 150 horse and 190 foot, 4,000 Indians, a multitude of pigs, a herd of llamas (some of which were used to carry baggage), a pack of ferocious Spanish dogs, and a sufficiency of arms, food, iron, hatchets, knives, ropes, etc. On Christmas Day he left Quito and travelled safely through Inca territory, but in horrendous conditions that made survival questionable. Beyond Quijos province the Indians were hostile, but fearing cavalry disappeared into the jungle. An earthquake followed by torrential rain for 40 days of forest travel prefaced a sudden change into the snowy cordilleras where many Indians perished from cold, before the company dropped to a fetid Sumaco. Here with a small party Gonzalo hacked a way through jungle until he realized that he was being misled by his Indian guides; he tortured several, burning some and setting the dogs on others, and eventually broke through to friendly, well-provisioned Cuca on the banks of a turbulent river (presumed to be the Coca). They waited two months for their comrades before pushing on downriver for 100 leagues (roughly 300 miles/490 km) to where the river narrowed enough to cross. Artillery kept Indians at bay as a bridge was built over a narrow gorge. Eventually they reached Guema (Guames, Colombia). Dense forests and swamps prevented their scouting for roads from Guema. A brigantine was built to ease travel and carry gold. Francisco Orillana and 50 soldiers detailed to man it promptly deserted. Pizarro took two months to hack his way to inhabited country via thorny scrub covering swamp where men and horses starved, succumbed to scurvy and died. Only 80 Spaniards on foot reached Quito in June 1542. A depopulated Quito did its best, sending food, a scant amount of clothing and 12 horses – all the city had after the authorities sequestered the rest for service against Diego Amalgro.[14]

Goncalo de Silvestre recounted his adventures to Garcilaso. In 1546 he fought at the battle of Quito against Gonzalo Pizarro who had revolted, marched from Cuzco and routed the army of the newly arrived viceroy of Peru, Blanco Nunez Vela. Vela was killed. Captains of Horse Silvestre and Diego de Centeno with a few hundred horse were harried for 200 leagues (roughly 600 miles/965 km) by Francesco de Carbajal, a veteran of over 80 years, who had fought in Italy and Flanders before joining the Pizarros in Peru.

Dashing for Arequipa, Centeno and Silvestre fought a rearguard action, at one point setting gunpowder to explode as Carbajal crossed the trail. The ploy failed, only their horses' speed saved them. Eventually the unit dispersed. The two comrades and others hid for months supported by friendly Indians. Later they enlisted with the new viceroy, La Gasca, fighting at the bloody battle of Huarina where Centeno commanded the Crown's forces against Pizarro. Here Silvestre's greatest equestrian feat took place. Centeno's cavalry had charged Pizarro's, and Pizarro, finding himself separated from his unit, rode for his wavering foot to encourage them. Silvestre and two others pursued him. They drew level and attacked Pizarro, one man on either side of the quarry and Silvestre so close behind that his mount rested its muzzle on the rump of Pizarro's horse. Pizarro, secure in his Milanese armour, turned in his saddle and with his mace struck Silvestre's horse three blows, two cutting its muzzle to the teeth, the third shattering the orbital bone without damaging its eye. The infantry square opened ranks and Pizarro rushed in but not before Silvestre had lanced Pizarro's horse in the hip, injuring it slightly. His own horse suffered two more facial wounds. As the horse reared a pike was thrust through the fleshy part of both forearms. He whirled away snapping the pike shaft with his teeth as he bounded to safety. Miguel Vergara's horse plunged into the infantry square where both were killed; Francisco de Ulloa swerved but received a crossbow bolt; his grey horse was hamstrung but still ran 50 paces before both dropped dead. Garcilaso had this from an eye-witness.

As the battle raged Centeno accounted for over 100 of Pizarro's troopers, but Pizarro's foot and the crossbowmen brought up by Carbajal turned the day and Silvestre fled to become mixed up with Pizarro's pursuing horse. His wounded mount seemed about to collapse and plunged hock-deep into mire, pursued by Goncalo de la Nidos on an even more exhausted horse. Silvestre, who earlier had let Nidos go, now begged for his life, but Nidos's reply, reported as 'When I catch you you are a dead man, and I will tear your heart out and throw it to the dogs', made him spur his mount. To his surprise it bounded out of the morass at a gallop. He had already broken both his swords and was left with a rusty rapier taken earlier from a Negro, so wheeling his horse he turned on Nidos, dealing him so hard a blow with the flat of the blade that his opponent reeled in the saddle. Silvestre thus won a breathing space as he fled towards the viceroy's camp. Pizarro sent Alonzo de Herrera after him but his horse was so played out it could not even raise a trot.

The Inca Garcilaso's father was with Pizarro and loaned him his best mount, Salinallas, to replace the one Silvestre had wounded (much later it was returned to its owner who had thought it lost for good). Pizarro's cavalry had lost so many horses that pursuit was impossible so Silvestre escaped, collecting his bag of horseshoes, nails, pincers and foot-parer, and joining other fugitives. At night they drew rein and a band of 50 gradually assembled, most of them wounded; one horse and rider had 23 wounds between them. After 15 days Silvestre reached the safety of an Indian village.

Three months later, at the head of a new army and joined by Pedro de Valdivia from Chile, La Gasca fought the last battle of the civil wars at Aquizaguana where the rebels' power was broken and Pizarro and Carbajal executed.[15]

THIRTEEN

Chile

Diego Amalgro had campaigned briefly in Chile in 1535, but it was Pedro de Valdivia who opened it up with Spanish troops and colonists, appreciating the agricultural possibilities. Throughout his five detailed reports to Charles V, requests for horses and men, especially the former, are reiterated. In 1545 he reminds His Majesty that horses are needed but *humbly* says:

> if Majesty wishes to place someone else in charge he will revert to being a private soldier . . . on the understanding that the person undertakes responsibility for all moneys owing

– not so much a humble plea as a threat warning Charles to exert himself on Valdivia's behalf.

Francisco Pizarro ordered him to Chile in April 1539; 75 horse and 75 foot, plus baggage horses, were raised. By the end of 1540 Valdivia reached the Mapucho valley where Indians made repeated attacks. Nevertheless Santiago and Valparaiso were founded in 1541, but hardships continued. To communicate with Peru a brigantine was built; it was guarded by 12 foot and 8 horse, but Mapuchians still destroyed it. Early on, Valdivia's lieutenant Alonzo de Monroy warned him that some of his men were plotting to kill him; in reprisal he hanged five Spaniards. Then a two-pronged Indian attack erupted; Santiago was burned, but Valdivia with 90 foot and horse repulsed the second force. Food was short – a few pigs, chickens and some seed corn which when planted had to be constantly guarded. Mounted patrols broke up hostile roving bands.

Early mining by Peruvian Anaconcilla Indians showed rapid results. In 1542 Monroy and five others were sent to Peru with 7,000 *pesos* to procure recruits and horses. Indians ambushed them, took their horses, killed four Spaniards and took two prisoners, whom they spared to teach their *cacique* to ride. The Spaniards escaped while doing so, knifing the *cacique* while one rode alongside him as teacher, the other following on foot. Meanwhile 70 horsemen were coming, paid for by Christobal de Escobar. The governor of Peru raised others. In 1543 a supply ship docked at Valparaiso, and in January 1544 Monroy returned with 60 men and horses, plus baggage horses – presumably mares. That winter was desperately hard, cold and wet. Indians wasted the land to deny the Spaniards provisions. Around Santiago 40 cavalry patrolled permanently. By 1545 when La Serena was founded there were 200 Spanish troops and horses in Chile.

After emphasizing how much he was out of pocket, Valdivia said colonization went slowly as he felt settlement more profitable for the emperor than chasing after gold. However, equine supplies deteriorated because in 1545 most horses died from fighting and overwork; he again sent Monroy to Peru for recruits, horses and settlers, but in Peru Monroy died:

> and I must buy horses to give to those who lost them in the war . . . for it is not right they should go on foot . . . and some mares so that with the 50 I have here at present there may be no need in the future of sending to bring horses from elsewhere.

Antonio de Ulloa, praised as a 'very good soldier', who had brought 'very good horses and arms to serve in the war', was sent to Peru with a letter, but proved not so good when he pocketed the horse purchase money, tore the letter up and joined Gonzalo Pizarro's rebels. Later he plotted to kill Valdivia, but was recalled by Pizarro and stole the best horses, arms and armour from 20 Spaniards who had come with him but wished to remain in Chile. He left them in the Atacama Desert with 60 unbroken broodmares brought from Charcas, Peru, by Garcia de Caceres and Diego de Maldonado. The 20 reached the Copoyano valley where Indians attacked; 12 were killed, 8 escaped on some mares, the rest – Negroes, servants, a few children – were left behind, saved only when the Indians retreated on hearing that Spaniards were coming out of La Serena. But the Indians had the abandoned mares, many of whom would have foaled.

While Valdivia was in Peru with La Gasca, Coquimbo Indians attacked La Serena and '40 men and as many horses and civilians were killed'. In 1548 Valdivia brought 80 horses from Cuzco. After reprisals against the Indians La Serena was refounded in 1549.

In January 1550 conquest and settlement reached the River Biobio where fierce Araucanians repeatedly attacked; according to Valdivia there were sometimes 20,000 attackers, at other times 40,000. Seeking a settlement site at Arauco Valdivia sent 50 horse to scout but they were alarmed at the density of hostile Indians and returned into a fraught situation. Araucanians had no fear of horses, attacking them with spears and clubs, the animals jibbing at the barrage. In one encounter 60 were wounded, one dying. The Spaniards were besieged in a palisaded camp until on 12 March Geronimo Alderete and 50 horse assaulted their attackers, breaking and routing a 10,000-strong division, killing c. 2,000, wounding and capturing others, of whom 200 had their hands and noses amputated. Temporarily the Spaniards had the upper hand. On 5 October 1550 Concepcion was founded and garrisoned with 20 horse and 30 foot; the remaining 120 horse and 50 foot, confident the Indians were cowed, progressed southwards. La Imperial was founded and *encomiendas* with Indian workers were awarded to 125 *conquistadores*, before the Spaniards returned to Concepcion for winter 1551. Reinforcements were now coming in greater numbers. In a letter dated 18 May 1551, a delighted Valdivia learned that 200 men and 400 horses were coming with Francisco de Villagran from Charcas to Santiago. One of Valdivia's edicts stipulated that a guard be appointed to look after the Santiago mares, taking them to and from their grazing grounds; another that any Indian wounding mares with arrows or stones should have his hand struck off and his master be made liable for damages to be paid to the animal's owner.

In 1552 Valdivia and Villa Rica were founded, but retribution awaited: the Araucanians of Tucapel province rose. Their leader Alonzo, an *encomienda* Indian, had been a groom and understood horses' weaknesses – fear of attack, lethargy and poor endurance in searing heat, inability to operate efficiently on adverse terrain. Riding to the relief of Tucapel fort with only 40 cavalry, Valdivia was attacked. Regrouping his men into three units he charged the Indians repeatedly with heavy losses. Forced to retreat over marshy ground to the road between Valdivia and Arauco he found the passage blocked. All were killed as they struggled in the swamp. Valdivia was 56 years old.[1]

For many years the Araucanians were to threaten that part of Chile and they were soon very competent at fighting on horseback. But the conquest continued.

FOURTEEN

North America

CORONADO AND THE AMERICAN SOUTH-WEST

In summer 1539 Friar Marcos de Niza, a member of an expedition into North America, returned with tales of fabulous riches at Cibola (Zuni, near the present-day Arizona/New Mexico border).

Mexico had flourished in the 1530s. Viceroy Antonio de Mendoza fostered agriculture bringing in cattle, sheep and horses from Spain to add to the New World ranches. Also arriving were soldiers of fortune, friends and relatives of settlers. Many were sons of Spanish noblemen sent abroad to keep them out of trouble or to atone for mischief. They arrived with royal letters and introductions, needed entertaining and outstayed their welcome. Efficient in war, they were disruptive in peace and a problem for Mendoza. Friar Marcos's exaggerations provided an answer. Within two months an expedition to be led by Coronado was forming.[1]

Pedro de Castaneda, an expedition member, left an account and Coronado's muster roll has survived. Men, animals, arms, armour and the itinerary and adventures as the expedition traversed Arizona, New Mexico, the Great Buffalo Plains of Texas, Oklahoma, Kansas and Nebraska as far as Quivira on the Kansas/Nebraska border, are detailed.[2]

Coronado's army mustered at Compostela on 22 February 1540. Pedro Almadoz Cherine, royal veedor (inspector) in New Spain, inspected horses, men and arms, saying that most went freely having newly arrived from Spain to seek a living. Servan Bejarano, a businessman, said it was to Mexico's advantage for these men to go on expedition because they had no occupation and no property, and were lazy bad characters. Christobal de Onote, veedor of New Galicia, said much the same.[3] However, Coronado was better equipped with cavalry than other expeditions. Of 225 cavalrymen, the horses mustered were: 84×1; 69×2; 34×3; 11×4; 14×5; 2×6; 4×7; 1×8; Captain Garcia Lopez de Cardenas 12; Pedro de Tobar 13; the Army Master Lope de Samaniego 17; Captain-General Coronado 23. Many were armed with native weapons and leather armour – either buckskin or tapir skin. Very few had a complete Spanish outfit but many had a cuirass, a helmet (several types were worn), a coat of mail, vambraces, etc. Coronado had three or four outfits for à la brida and à la gineta riding. Captain Tristan de Arrellano with 8 horses was exceptionally well equipped with leather and mail armour, several helmets, an arquebus, a crossbow, a two-handed sword, three other swords, and

Riding a la jineta, *from* El Libro de la Monteria *by Gonzalo Argote de Molina (Seville, 1582) and* a la brida, *from* Handbuch der Waffenkunde *by Wendelin Boeheim (Leipzig, 1890). (Reproduced from R.M. Denhardt,* The Horse of the Americas, *Norman, University of Oklahoma Press, 1947)*

other arms for his servants; 5 of the 62 infantry are shown with a total of 6 horses. Of 557 equines, 2 were mares, 1 a mule.[4]

The army left on 23 February, accompanied part of the way by the viceroy. Cattle slowed the march. Each soldier transported his own gear; some did not know how to fix their packs, and as the horses started in plump condition Castaneda says they had much labour and trouble; many men got rid of excess baggage and 'in the end they became skilful'. While out foraging Samaniego was shot through the brain, dying at Chiametla. Culiacan was reached on 28 March where generous townsfolk received them hospitably providing over 600 animal-loads of provisions.[5]

Campaign estimates vary: the viceroy said there were 250 mounted Spaniards and 300 Indians, more or less; Mota Padilla, using authenticated but now lost documents, says 260 horsemen, 70 foot, over 1,000 friendly Indians; Herrera says 150 horse, 200 foot. The muster roll gives 225 horsemen and 62 foot, but some recruits arrived later. They started with 1,000 horses, 500 cows, over 5,000 rams and ewes, baggage mules, 1,500 friendly Indians and servants.[6]

The viceroy provided many horses from his ranch, plus arms and supplies. Money was advanced from the royal chest for those needing to clear debts; six *pedreros* (light swivel guns) were supplied.[7] Castaneda gives a humorous view of the advance force under Coronado that left Culiacan on 22 April 1540, two weeks before the main force. One night they were alerted by Indian yells and in their excited haste some troopers, 'the new fellows', put their horses' saddles on 'hindside before' while the veterans rode round the camp but were unable to attack any Indians.[8]

Minor discrepancies in advance guard numbers occur in reports from expedition members present but writing later. *The Relacion del Suceso* by one, name unknown, gives additional details. Coronado took 80 horses, 25 foot and some artillery. They halted at Sonora 10 leagues (30 miles/48 km) from Corazones valley, their temporary base, and from there took 80 days' provisions; 73 days later they reached Cibola. *En route* many horses and some Indians died. The journey was mostly peaceful, except at the first village, where an outbreak of fighting drew a Spanish attack with musket and artillery fire. At Sonora where Coronado established a new town 80 horsemen with only a horse each were left under Melchior Diaz.[9] Castaneda tells of the disenchantment as Friar Marcos's tales of wealth proved false. The main army arrived and as they marched into the cold regions many Indians fell sick and had to be carried on horseback while the cavalrymen walked, arriving so at Cibola.[10]

At Corazones valley the expedition rested the horses for four days, then progressed to Chicilticale, resting them again there as they were weak and underfed. In this 'last desert we lost more horses than before' and some men died from eating poisonous herbs. After another 30 mountainous leagues (90 miles/145 km) they reached good grazing. So far only a few skirmishes had occurred. Even when the Indians were hostile a Spanish charge had little effect on them as they retired into a village. The crossbows were useless, and the musketmen too weak to fire their guns. A few Spaniards were injured with stones and arrows. Coronado was a target because of his gilded armour; three horses were killed, seven or eight others were wounded but recovered. In Zuni territory it was cold, mountainous and dangerous to the horses. The sheep suffered and had to be left to follow with four horsemen, travelling slowly, but still most died. Food was short; 10 or 12 horses died from overwork and underfeeding – from the beginning cavalry horses had been used as pack-animals. Some Indians and Negro servants died. Cibola was needed for the food it contained. Once it had been taken there was good grazing for the horses and hay was cut.[11]

From Cibola mounted detachments were sent on varying missions. Horses continued to have a physical and psychological impact on Indian tribes. In Tusayan province, home of the Moqui, 25 leagues (75 miles/120 km) from Cibola, the Indians heard of Cibola's capture by 'fierce men who travelled on animals which ate people'. Nevertheless one brave Moqui clubbed a horse on the head, drawing a 17-strong cavalry charge which rapidly subdued them.

In September Hernando Alvarado, the artillery captain, was sent with 20 horse on an 80-day mission to check on 'cows' (buffalo) at Acoma, Tiguex (near Bernalillo) and Cicuye. Coronado investigated along the Rio Grande before taking up winter quarters at Tiguex for 1540/1.

So far there had been little opposition, but relations now deteriorated fast. Alvarado imprisoned two notable Cicuye Indians accusing them of withholding gold; a Spaniard molested an Indian woman at Tiguex; in reprisal a stable guard was killed and seven mules and several horses were run off. Some horses were recaptured immediately, others found being chased and shot at in corrals. The Spaniards attacked the village, which surrendered and was granted peace, but subsequently revengeful Spaniards burned some Indian captives. Indian reprisals and Spanish retaliation, with a continuous diminution in horses and men, followed.[12]

The *Relacion del Suceso* describes the risky buffalo hunting; until the horses gained experience, many were killed and injured. In the above raid it says 40 horses and mules were killed, a huge loss in an already depleted number.[13] In the wide sweep of the Great Plains distances and directions became confused, and one horseman was lost and two tacked-up horses.[14] In the great days of Plains cattle-raising a cowboy afoot was in real danger.

In April 1541 Coronado headed for west central Texas and the Canadian River territory, then pressed on north-eastwards to Quivira with 40 horse, leaving it in mid-August and arriving at Tiguex on 2 October. In December while racing against Captain Maldonado he fell when a rotten girth broke and Maldonado's horse, galloping over him, struck him on the head. Common soldiers grumbled against preferential treatment for noblemen; Coronado found his projected return to the rich agricultural possibilities of Quivira blocked. To cap it all, Captain Carderas who had been sent to New Spain with the sick returned with news that he had fled from Sonora where Indians had risen and massacred all.

With sinking morale the army prepared to return to New Spain, but at Culiacan many men refused to accompany Coronado further leaving him with only 100 men. Mendoza received him coldly and soon afterwards Coronado resigned his governorship of New Galicia and retired to his estates.[15]

Castaneda paid tribute to the horses: 'the horse, the most necessary things in the new countries, and they frighten the enemy the most.' It is a sentiment applicable to conquests throughout the sixteenth century.

THE MIXTON WAR

While Coronado was in Cibola, Indians in New Galicia revolted, attacked frontier settlements and drove Spaniards into larger towns. Onate, the deputy governor, fled to Guadalagara. Winter gave a respite and in June 1541 Pedro de Alvarado raised reinforcements. At Nochistlan on 24 June the Indians defeated the Spanish who fled. Alvarado on foot was crushed under a falling horse and died from injuries on 4 July. Mendoza despatched a force of 450 Spaniards and over 10,000 allied Aztec warriors. In this final phase of the Mixton War, Indians were *allowed* the use of horses and Spanish weapons. It was the last and fiercest war against the Spanish conquerors.[16]

The viceroyalty of Peru expanded into South America and by 1574 comprised the Panamanian isthmus and all lands south of Venezuela to Patagonia, except Brazil. It had five *audencias* (supreme courts) at Lima, Los Charcos, Quito, New Granada and Panama, and ten governments. The Kingdom of New Spain was divided into four *audencias*: Mexico, Espanola (plus the other islands and Venezuela), New Galicia and Guatemala.[17]

In the latter part of the sixteenth century and throughout the seventeenth the Indians were gradually able to achieve horse ownership. The horse became their most valuable asset, giving mobility to the tribes fighting against the invaders of their North American homelands.

Glossary

Horse Related Words

barbed horse (also barded, covered)	horse equipped with head, neck and body armour of either mail, plate, leather, padded cloth, sometimes with a combination of these
cantle	rear part of saddle, raised on war saddles
'capital horse'	Hungarian description denoting superior mount
carectarius	medieval carthorse; not the same as the modern heavy draught horse, but of smaller frame and lighter build
cavesson	part of bridle that goes over the nose; a noseband. However, a modern cavesson is a different article in English tack and is used on the horse's head during lungeing. In American equestrian parlance a cavesson can be what the English term a drop noseband
chamfron	head armour for horse
charger	cavalryman's warhorse
cobby	medium height, stockily built horse
courser	in medieval terms a warhorse, but could also be used for hunting; in post-medieval terms a racehorse
crinet	neck armour for horse
cuir bouilli	leather boiled, shaped and hardened into armour for horse and rider
curb	swelling, which can later thicken, of the calcaneo cuboid ligament below the point of the hock and situated on the inner side of the leg
destrier	from Latin *dextrarius*, the medieval war-horse, also called the Great Horse. Usually a horse of greater value and of larger size and greater weight that the average equine of the era. Not a huge animal, as has often mistakenly been stated
flanchard(s)	flank armour for horse (and over loin area)
genet (also jenet)	Spanish horse of superior quality, notably from Castile and Andalusia
Hakney (also hakenai in documents)	medium grade, small horse, usually a trotter, of the medieval era. Not to be confused with the Hackney harness horse of the nineteenth and twentieth centuries
hand	measurement of 4 inches, used in determining height of horse
harness (1)	the tack worn by a horse; could be either tack for a saddle horse or for a carthorse (in recent times, harness meant tack worn by a carthorse or any horse used to pull a vehicle (i.e. a hackney, a vanner)
harness (2)	the full gear worn by a mounted soldier, i.e. his armour, weapons and his horse's outfit
Hobby	small breed of the medieval era; a type rather than a breed. The Hobelar was mounted on a Hobby, but whether the horse gave the name to the man or vice versa is a moot point
limoner	artillery horse; name used in Tudor times and documents
Jibbah	the pronounced forehead possessed by some Arabians, especially those with marked concave profiles

pacer	horse moving in a lateral manner, the offside legs moving forward together, and then the nearside legs. A two-beat gait (pace)
palfrey	a quality, comfortable horse of small to medium size. Usually noted as ambling, which is a four-beat gait (some writers say the amble is two-beat, but on examination of hoofbeats the sequence is four-time, with the hind foot striking the ground a split second before the fore foot on the same side, so that to the casual observer it appears two-beat)
pommel	front part of saddle, raised in war saddles
racker	a horse that 'racks', i.e. ambles in medieval terms
rouncy	horse of almost all work (except hauling carts). Of moderate size, moderate value and moderately bred. Used as a warhorse by a man-at-arms, as well as by servants, and also used as a pack animal
spavin	bony enlargement on lower, inner aspect of the hock
sumpter	baggage horse
trotter	horse moving with a diagonal gait, i.e. near fore and off hind together, then the off fore and near hind

Coinage

akces	coin of the Ottoman Empire
crown	gold coin used in many European countries
cruzado	Spanish coin
denier	Arabic/Middle Eastern coin
dinar	Arabic/Middle Eastern coin
dirham	Arabic/Middle Eastern coin
ducat	Italian coin
ecu	French coin
florin	coin originating in Florence and later used in England
lakh	not a coin, but used as a measure equating with 100,000
librate	one pound
livre tournois	French pound, of which there were four to the pound sterling
marc/mark	coin used in England, with a value of 13s 4d. Documents showing accounts use mark and pound in the same accounts
mohur	Indian high-value coin
pardao	Portuguese coin used in India
peso	small value coin used in the early Americas
rupee	small value Indian coin
tanka	small value Indian coin

General

Aguazil Mor	Portuguese tax collector in their Indian domains
caltrop	three-pronged spike used to lame cavalry horses when scattered around a fortification. They were designed so that however they fell, at least one spike remained pointing upwards
cedule	decree issued by the Spanish crown
chevauchée	swift raid conducted by an invading army, always with mounted troops
conquistador	name given to the Spaniards who conquered New World territories
coutillier	auxiliary mounted swordsman, member of a lance
dacoit	Indian bandit, robber
insight	household goods
ginete (jinete)	mounted Spanish man-at-arms riding after the *ginete* method (with short stirrups). Derived from the zenete tribe of the Mahgreb
pricker	lancer, light horseman, especially in Border warfare
Thakur	Indian village headman
vintenar	leader of twenty infantry, usually mounted

Notes

Abbreviations

Bain, *Scot.*	*Calendar of Documents relating to Scotland*, Vols II and III
Bain, *Border*	*The Border Papers*, Vols I and II
BSOAS	*Bulletin of the School of Oriental and African Studies*
CSPV	*Calendar of State Papers Venetian*
EHR	*English Historical Review*
JESHO	*Journal of Economic and Social History of the Orient*
JRAS	*Journal of the Royal Asiatic Society*
Lib.Q.	Drokensford, *Liber Quotidianus Contrarotulatoris Garderobae*
L & P	*Letters and Papers/Foreign and Domestic Henry VIII*
Persian Travels	*A Narrative of Italian Travels in Persia in the Fifteenth and Sixteenth Centuries*, Book I, ed. and tr. C. Grey, Book II, tr. W. Thomas and S.A. Roy
SPD, HVIII	State Papers (Domestic) Henry VIII
WMA	Oman, *A History of the Art of War in the Middle Ages*
W16C	Oman, *A History of the Art of War in the Sixteenth Century*

Introduction

1. Usāmah ibn Munqidh, *Memoirs of Usāmah ibn Munqidh*, tr. P.L. Hitti (Cairo, Princeton University Press at the Cairo Press, 1961), p. 126
2. British Library, Royal MSS, 12.F.xiii.F.42b (no. 100683, p. 98)
3. Y. Renouard, 'L'exportation de chevaux de la Péninsule Ibérique . . . au moyen âge' in *Maluquer de Motes Nicolaus*, ed. Homenaje J.V. Vives (Barcelona, 1965), Vol. I, pp. 571–7
4. A. Hyland, *The Medieval Warhorse* (Stroud, Sutton Publishing, 1994), pp. 3, 57; T. Blundeville, *Four Chiefest Offices belonging to Horsemanship* (pr. R. Yardley, pub. Short, edn of 1593), p. 6; G. Markham, *Cavalrice* (1617), p. 16; Marquis of Newcastle, *Méthode de Dresser les Chevaux*, 2nd edn (London, J. Brindley, 1737)
5. J.P. Hore, *History of Newmarket* (London, A.H. Baily, 1886), Vol. I, p. 75
6. *Calendar of State Papers Venetian* (henceforth *CSPV*), ed. Rawdon Brown (London, Longman Green, 1869), Vol. III, 1520–6, no. 50
7. L. da Vinci, *Notebooks of Leonardo da Vinci*, ed. I.A. Richter (Oxford, Oxford University Press, 1989 [1952])
8. J. Hook, *Lorenzo de Medici* (London, Hamish Hamilton, 1984), pp. 34, 154, 179
9. P. Martin, *Armour and Weapons*, tr. R. North (London, Herbert Jenkins, 1968), p. 210
10. E. Oakeshott, *A Knight and his Horse* (London, Lutterworth Press, 1962), p. 36 f.
11. J. Froissart, *Chronicles*, ed. and tr. G. Brereton (Harmondsworth, Penguin, 1983 [1968]), pp. 411, 414
12. W. Gaitzsch, 'Pferdegeschirr aus Pergamon', *Istmitt*, 37 (1987), 219–56, Pls. 60–9
13. I Sparkes, *Discovering Old Horseshoes*, Discovering Series no. 19 (Princes Risborough, Shire Publications, 1983 [1976]), pp. 10–16 *passim*

1. England and the Three Edwards

1. M. Prestwich, *The Three Edwards* (London, Book Club Associates edn, 1980), p. 10
2. M. Prestwich, *Edward I* (London, Methuen, 1988), Ch. 15 *passim*
3. W. Norwell, *The Wardrobe Book of Wm. de Norwell*, ed. Mary Lyon, Bryce Lyon and Henry S. Lucas with Jean de Sturler (Brussels, 1983), pp. 309–25
4. ibid., p. civ
5. ibid., pp. 386–92
6. M.W. Labarge, *A Baronial Household of the Thirteenth Century* (London, Eyre & Spottiswoode, 1965), pp. 194 ff., 133, 163 f., 151
7. M. Prestwich, 'Victualling Estimates for the English Garrisons in Scotland during the Early 14th Century', *English Historical Review* (henceforth *EHR*), 82 (1967), 536–43
8. J. Bain (henceforth Bain, *Scot.*), *Calendar of Documents relating to Scotland,* HM PRO, pub. HM Gen. Register House, Edinburgh, Vol. II, 1272–1307, p. 1884; Vol. III, 1307–1357, p. 1887; Vol. II, no. 1144, Chancery Misc. Portfolios no. $^{41}/_{92}$
9. J.L. Bolton, *The Medieval English Economy* (London, Dent, 1980), pp. 132 and 136
10. P. Tafur, *Travels and Adventures 1435–39*, ed. and tr. M. Letts (London, Routledge, 1926), pp. 192–205 *passim*
11. C. Walford, *Fairs Past and Present* (London, Elliot Stock, 1883), pp. 250–60
12. W. Childs, *Anglo-Castilian Trade in the Later Middle Ages* (Manchester, Manchester University Press, 1978), pp. 120 f.
13. Langlois, *Le Règne de Philippe III Le Hardi* (Paris, 1887), pp. 371–2
14. The year began in March. By modern dating it was 1307.
15. Bain, *Scot.*, Vol. II, no. 1882
16. Bain, *Scot.*, Vol. III, no. 190
17. K. Chivers, *The Shire Horse* (London, J.A. Allen, 1976), p. 6
18. *The Plantagenet Chronicles*, ed. E. Hallam (London, Guild Publishing, 1986), p. 264
19. C. Richardson, *The Fell Pony* (London, J.A. Allen, 1990), p. 17
20. Norwell, *Wardrobe*, pp. 386–92 *passim*
21. M. Prestwich, unpublished paper consulted by permission of the author
22. R.H.C. Davis, 'The Medieval Warhorse' in *Horses in European Economic History*, ed. F.M.L. Thompson (Reading, 1983), p. 7
23. Chivers, *Shire Horse*, p. 4
24. W.M. Ormrod, *The Reign of Edward III* (London, Guild Publishing, 1990), p. 99
25. Chivers, *Shire Horse*, pp. 4
26. Bain, *Scot.*, Vol. II, no. 577, royal letters 1140
27. ibid., Vol. II, no. 1075 and no. 1076, Chancery Misc. Portfolio nos. 11 and 41
28. Chivers, *Shire Horse*, p. 4 f.
29. Ormrod, *Edward III*, pp. 12, 75, 108, 104
30. Chivers, *Shire Horse*, p. 4
31. Norwell, *Wardrobe*, pp. 386–92 *passim*
32. Bain, *Scot.*, Vol. II, no. 1116
33. H. Harrod, 'Some Details of a Murrain of the Fourteenth Century from Court Rolls of a Norfolk Manor', *Archaeologia*, XLI (1867), 1–14
34. M.M. Reese, *The Royal Office of Master of the Horse* (London, Threshold Books, 1976), p. 54
35. H.P.R. Finberg, *The Formation of England 550–1042* (London, Hart-Davis, McGibbon, 1974), p. 77
36. Sir W. Gilbey, *The Great Horse* (London, Vinton, 1899), pp. 16 f.
37. Davis, 'Warhorse', p. 9
38. Reese, *Master of Horse*, p. 46
39. ibid., pp. 51 f.; M. Burrows, *The Family of Brocas of Beaurepaire and Roche Court* (London, Longman Grant, 1886), pp. 53, 58
40. Norwell, *Wardrobe*, Indentures, pp. 346–7; *Restauro Eq.*, p. 319; ship passage, p. 389
41. Davis, 'Warhorse', p. 9
42. Reese, *Master of Horse*, pp. 45, 42, 48
43. Locations drawn from H.J. Hewitt, *The Horse in Medieval England* (London, J.A. Allen, 1983); Davis, 'Warhorse'; H. Colvin et al., *The History of the King's Works* (London, HMSO, 1963), Vol. II; S. Lysons, 'Copy of a Roll of Expenses of King Edward I at Rhuddlan Castle in the 10th and 11th Years of his Reign', *Archaeologia*, XVI (1812), 32–79
44. Colvin et al., *King's Works*, Vol. II, p. 941; Prestwich, *Edward I*, pp. 68, 176
45. Colvin et al., *King's Works*, Vol. II, pp. 941, 919, 997
46. Hewitt, *Horse in Med. Eng.*, pp. 16 ff.
47. ibid., pp. 14 ff.
48. Reese, *Master of Horse*, p. 49
49. Hewitt, *Horse in Med. Eng.*, pp. 22 f.

50. Reese, *Master of Horse*, p. 49
51. Hewitt, *Horse in Med. Eng.*, p. 19
52. Bain, *Scot.*, Vol. II, no. 1413
53. Childs, *Anglo-Castilian Trade*, p. 120
54. Reese, *Master of Horse*, pp. 42 ff.
55. Lady Wentworth, *The Authentic Arabian Horse* (London, Allen & Unwin, 1945), p. 50
56. Reese, *Master of Horse*, pp. 46, 42 ff.
57. Davis, 'Warhorse', p. 11; ibid., p. 179, n. 25
58. Wentworth, *Authentic Arabian*, p. 50
59. Reese, *Master of Horse*, pp. 49 f.
60. Childs, *Anglo-Castilian Trade*, p. 120
61. Reese, *Master of Horse*, p. 50
62. Prestwich, *Edward I*, p. 163
63. Wentworth, *Authentic Arabian*, p. 50
64. Drokensford, *Liber Quotidianus Contrarotulatoris Garderobae*, 28 Edward I, 1299–1300 (henceforth *Lib. Q.*) (London, Society of Antiquaries, J. Nichols, 1787), pp. 165/130 and 166/130
65. Prestwich, *Edward I*, p. 163
66. Bain, *Scot.*, Vol. II, no. 1520
67. Prestwich, *Edward I*, p. 471
68. Bain, *Scot.*, Vol. II, no. 962
69. Prestwich, *Three Edwards*, p. 34
70. *Lib. Q.*, pp. 57/71, 64/83, 71/94
71. Bain, *Scot.*, Vol. II, no. 1413
72. Childs, *Anglo-Castilian Trade*, p. 121
73. C. Blair, *European Armour* (London, Batsford, 1958), pp. 184 f.
74. Davis, 'Warhorse', pp. 11, 18
75. A. Hyland, *Equus* (London, Batsford, 1990), pp. 172 ff.
76. Norwell, *Wardrobe*, p. xcii
77. Reese, *Master of Horse*, p. 53
78. Childs, *Anglo-Castilian Trade*, p. 121
79. Hewitt, *Horse in Med. Eng.*, pp. 25 f.
80. Norwell, *Wardrobe*, p. 268 f.108v(216); p. 262 f.106v(212); p. 230 f.95v(190)
81. ibid., pp. 241–66 *passim*
82. ibid., p. 230 f.95v(190)
83. ibid., p. 257 f.106v(208); p. 262 f.106v(212); p. 263 f.107(213); p. 260 f.105v(210)
84. Prestwich, *Edward I*, pp. 111, 480
85. *Lib. Q.*, p. 40/43, 42/46
86. Bain, *Scot.*, Vol. II, no. 994
87. P. Chaplais, 'Some Private Letters of Edward I', *EHR*, 77 (1962), 79–86
88. M. Prestwich, *War Politics and Finance under Edward I* (London, Faber, 1972), pp. 45 ff.
89. Bain, *Scot.*, Vol. II, no. 1011
90. *Lib. Q.*, fees, p. 188/151, 192/154; robes, p. 245/310; retinue, p. 196/157; lost horses, p. 174/135

91 Bain, *Scot.*, Vol. II, no. 946
92. ibid., Vol. II, no. 1011
93. ibid., Vol. II, no. 1057
94. ibid., Vol. II, no. 1124
95. *Lib. Q.*, p. 137/100, p. 176/136
96. Bain, *Scot.*, Vol. II, no. 1164
97. ibid., Vol. II, no. 1330
98. ibid., Vol. II, no. 1432
99. ibid., Vol. II, no. 1754
100. M.R. Powicke, 'The General Obligation to Cavalry Service under Edward I', *Speculum*, 28 (1953), 814–33
101. ibid.
102. ibid.
103. J.E. Morris, *Welsh Wars of Edward I* (Oxford, Clarendon Press, 1901), pp. 54 f., 45
104. Bain, *Scot.*, Vol. II, no. 1007
105. ibid., Vol. II, no. 1170
106. ibid., Vol. II, no. 171
107. *Lib. Q.*, p. 48/103; p. 104/151; p. 155/187; p. 130/165; p. 130/166; p. 140/183; p. 140/184
108. Prestwich, unpublished paper
109. *Lib. Q.*, p. 137/178
110. Norwell, *Wardrobe*, pp. 309–25 *passim*
111. Bain, *Scot.*, Vol. II, no. 1132, Chapter House (Scots. Docs) box 93 n. 18
112. Prestwich, *Edward I*, pp. 182, 189 f., 208–11 *passim*
113. Lysons, 'Rhuddlan Roll'
114. Morris, *Welsh Wars*, pp. 36, 44 f; *Lib. Q.*, pp. 133/170–143/187 *passim*
115. Bain, *Scot.*, Vol. II, no. 1413
116. S Lysons, 'Copy of Purchases for Tournament at Windsor Park 6 Edward I', in *Archaeologia*, XVII (1814), 297–310
117. Morris, *Welsh Wars*, pp. 81 f.
118. ibid.
119. Bain, *Scot.*, Vol. II, no. 1044
120. ibid., Vol. II, no. 1022
121. ibid., Vol. II, no. 1036
122. ibid., Vol. II, no. 1172
123. ibid., Vol. II, no. 1286
124. ibid., Vol. II, no. 1007 – horses of troopers not in household; no. 1011 – those in household
125. *Lib. Q.*, *Restauro* lists 1330/170–143/187 *passim*
126. Bain, *Scot.*, Vol. II, no. 1190
127. ibid., Vol. II, no. 1949
128. R.F. Scharff, 'The Irish Horse and its Early History' in *Proceedings of the Royal Irish Academy*, Vol. XXVII, Sec. B, 81 ff.

129. Blundeville, *Four Chiefest Offices*, p. 6; G. Cambrensis, *The First Version of the Topography of Ireland*, tr. J.H. O'Meara (Dundalk, 1951), p. 85

130. J.E. Morris, 'Mounted Infantry in Medieval Warfare', *Transactions of the Royal Historical Society*, 3rd ser., VIII (1914), 77–102

131. Bain, *Scot.*, Vol. II, no. 1084

132. ibid., Vol. II, no. 1115

133. ibid., Vol. II, no. 1127

134. ibid., Vol. II, no. 1133

135. ibid., Vol. II, no. 1128

136. J.F. Lydon, 'The Hobelar', *Irish Sword*, II (1954–6), 12–16; *Lib. Q.*, p. 195/245; p. 196/248; p. 197/249; p. 200/255

137. J.F. Lydon, 'Irish Levies in the Scottish Wars 1298–1302', *Irish Sword*, V (1961–2), 214

138. Bain, *Scot.*, Vol. II, no. 1229

139. ibid., Vol. II, no. 1295

140. Lydon, 'Irish Levies'

141. S.R. Meyrick, *A Critical Enquiry into Antient Armour*, Vol. I (London, R. Jennings, 1824), p. 175

142. Bain, *Scot.*, Vol. II, no. 1805

143. ibid., Vol. II, no. 1128

144. ibid., Vol. II, no. 1168

145. *Lib. Q.*, 99/127 and 128

146. From a study of medieval shoes in the Museum of London by kind permission of the curator, John Clark

147. Bain, *Scot.*, Vol. II, no. 1324

148. Prestwich, *Three Edwards*, p. 67

149. Morris, *Welsh Wars*, p. 87

150. Bain, *Scot.*, Vol. III, no. 668

151. ibid., Vol. III, no. 1240

152. ibid., Vol. III, no. 1238

153. ibid., Vol. III, no. 1316

154. ibid., Vol. III at Roxburgh, no. 1240 as above; at Edinburgh, no. 1382

155. Prestwich, *Edward I*, p. 180

156. Morris, *Welsh Wars*, pp. 127, 170, 153–60 *passim*

157. C. Oman, *A History of the Art of War in the Middle Ages* (henceforth *WMA*), Vols I and II, rev. edn (New York, Burt Franklin, 1924), ref. Vol. II, pp. 69 f.

158. J.G. Edwards, 'The Battle of Maes Madog and the Welsh Campaign of 1294–95', *EHR*, 39 (1924), 1–12

159. A horse working cattle may bite and/or strike them. Harrying brought out identical aggression

160. G.W.S. Barrow, *Robert Bruce and the Community of the Realm of Scotland* (London, Eyre & Spottiswoode, 1965), p. 101

161. W. Seymour, *Battles in Britain* (London, Sidgwick & Jackson, 1979), pp. 73 f.

162. Bain, *Scot.*, Vol. II, p. xxviii

163. ibid., Vol. II, no. 956

164. Seymour, *Battles in Britain*, p. 75; Barrow, *Robert Bruce*, pp. 140 ff.

165. ibid., pp. 142–5 *passim*

166. Prestwich, *Edward I*, p. 481; Bain, *Scot.*, Vol. II, no. 1011

167. ibid., Vol. II, no. 1913

168. ibid., Vol. III, no. 1308–9

169. Froissart, *Chronicles*, pp. 46 f.

170. Barrow, *Robert Bruce*, pp. 279, 281

171. Bain, *Scot.*, Vol. III, pp. 413–32 (horse valuation lists)

172. ibid., Vol. III, no. 337, Tower Misc. Rolls 459 and Foedera ii 247

173. Barrow, *Robert Bruce*, pp. 249 f.

174. J. Barbour, *The Bruce*, ed. and tr. A.A.H. Douglas (Glasgow, Wm McClellan, 1964), verse 48

175. Barrow, *Robert Bruce*, pp. 293 f.

176. Barbour, *The Bruce*, verse 35

177. Barrow, *Robert Bruce*, p. 298

178. Barbour, *The Bruce*, verse 49

179. Barrow, *Robert Bruce*, pp. 311 f.

180. Barbour, *The Bruce*, verses 52 and 51

181. Barrow, *Robert Bruce*, pp. 315–18, 323, 322

182. Barbour, *The Bruce*, verses 54, 56, 57, 58, 59

183. Bain, *Scot.*, Vol. III, no. 369

184. R. Nicholson, *Edward III and the Scots* (Oxford, Oxford University Press, 1965), p. 27

185. R. Nicholson, 'The Last Campaign of Robert Bruce', *EHR* 77 (1962), 233–46

186. Froissart, *Chronicles*, Book I, pp. 46–51 *passim*

187. Barbour, *The Bruce*, verses 93–7

188. Nicholson, 'Last Campaign'

189. Barbour, *The Bruce*, verse 98

190. Nicholson, *Edward III and the Scots*, pp. 87, 133 f., 181

191. ibid., Appendices IV–VIII

2. *The Hundred Years War: Crecy, Poitiers, Agincourt*

1. Oman, *WMA*, Vol. II, p. 124

2. Jean le Bel, for whose chronicle see *Contemporary Chronicles of the Hundred Years War*, ed. and tr. P.E. Thompson (London, Folio Society, 1966), p. 48

3. Prestwich, *Three Edwards*, pp. 192 ff.
4. Le Bel, in *Contemporary Chronicles*, pp. 54 ff., 61, 66 f.
5. Froissart, *Chronicles*, Book I, p. 69
6. Le Bel in *Contemporary Chronicles*, p. 68
7. Froissart, *Chronicles*, Book I, pp. 72, 83, 88 f.
8. Oman, *WMA*, Vol. II, p. 144
9. Le Bel, in *Contemporary Chronicles*, p. 70
10. Froissart, *Chronicles*, Book I, pp. 94 f., 95 n. 1
11. H.J. Hewitt, *The Black Prince's Expedition 1355–57* (Manchester, Manchester University Press, 1958), pp. 20 f., 33
12. Chandos Herald, *Life of the Black Prince*, ed. M.K. Pope and E.C. Lodge (Oxford, Clarendon Press, 1910), p. 140; A. Lloyd, *The Hundred Years War* (London, Book Club Associates edn, 1977), p. 70
13. Hewitt, *Black Prince's Expedition*, for dates and route see pp. 50–68
14. ibid., p. 50
15. Lloyd, *Hundred Years War*, pp. 70–7 *passim*
16. Chandos Herald, *Life of Black Prince*, p. 140
17. Hewitt, *Black Prince's Expedition*, pp. 92 f.
18. Chandos Herald, *Life of Black Prince*, p. 141; Froissart, *Chronicles*, p. 127
19. Lloyd, *Hundred Years War*, pp. 83, 87
20. ibid., pp. 90–100 *passim*; Froissart, *Chronicles*, pp. 128–39
21. Lloyd, *Hundred Years War*, p. 131
22. E. de Monstrelet, for whose work see *Contemporary Chronicles*, p. 266
23. C Hibbert, *Agincourt* (London, Pan Books edn, 1968), Ch. 2 *passim*
24. ibid., pp. 157 f.
25. ibid., map, pp. 82, 85, 89 ff; de Monstrelet, in *Contemporary Chronicles*, pp. 269–73 *passim*
26. Hibbert, *Agincourt*, p. 93
27. Lloyd, *Hundred Years War*, p. 157; de Monstrelet, in *Contemporary Chronicles*, pp. 273–80
28. Lloyd, *Hundred Years War*, pp. 166 ff.

3. *Encounters with the Orient and Africa*

1. Oman, *WMA*, Vol. I, pp. 491, 496 ff.; G. Gurney, *Kingdoms of Europe* (New York, Crown, 1982), p. 34
2. R. Muntaner, *The Chronicles of Muntaner*, 2 vols, tr. Lady Goodenough (London, Hakluyt Society, 1920 and 1921, Vol. I, pp. xli, 104
3. C.C. Bayley, *War and Society in Renaissance Florence* (Toronto, University of Toronto Press, 1961), pp. 19–31 *passim*
4. M. Mallet, *Mercenaries and Their Masters* (London, Bodley Head, 1974), pp. 16–20 *passim*
5. ibid., Ch. 1, pp. 9–19 *passim*
6. Bayley, *War and Society*, p. 267
7. Mallet, *Mercenaries and Masters*, p. 148; P. Contamine, *War in the Middle Ages*, tr. M. Jones (Oxford, Blackwell, 1984), p. 169
8. Mallet, *Mercenaries and Masters*, pp. 166-18 *passim*, 140
9. P. Commynes, *Memoirs of Philippe de Commynes*, 2 vols, ed. S. Kinser, tr. I. Caseaux (Columbia, SC, University of South Carolina Press, 1969 and 1973), Vol. II, p. 520
10. Gurney, *Kingdoms of Europe*, p. 596; Mallet, *Mercenaries and Masters*, pp. 152 f.; M.E. Mallet and J.R. Hale, *Military Organization in a Renaissance State: Venice 1400–1617* (Cambridge, Cambridge University Press, 1984), pp. 376 f.; G.J. Millar, 'The Albanian Stradiot', *History Today*, 16 (1976), 468–72
11. Hyland, *Equus*, pp. 11–15; Hyland, *The Medieval Warhorse*, pp. 55 ff., and 40–7 *passim* for Moors/Arabs
12. Lady Wentworth, *Thoroughbred Racing Stock* (London, Allen & Unwin, 1938), pp. 247 f.
13. Mallet, *Mercenaries and Masters*, p. 141
14. J. Barbaro, 'Travels to Tana and Persia' in *A Narrative of Italian Travels in Persia in the Fifteenth and Sixteenth Centuries* (henceforth *Persian Travels*), Book II, tr. W. Thomas and S.A. Roy (London, Hakluyt Society, 1873), pp. 37–65
15. A Contarini, in *Persian Travels*, Book II, pp. 113–26
16. ibid., pp. 143–73
17. C. Zeno, in *Persian Travels*, Book I, ed. and tr. C. Gray (London, Hakluyt Society, 1873), pp. 18–27 *passim*; G.M. Angiolello, in ibid., pp. 77–90 *passim*
18. D'Alessandri, ibid., pp. xi–xvi, 227
19. Hyland, *Equus*, p. 15
20. M. Jankovich, *They Rode into Europe*, tr. A. Dent (London, Harrap, 1971), p. 106
21. Mallet and Hale, *Military Organization in Venice*, pp. 138 f.

22. B. de la Brocquière, 'Travels of Bertrandon de la Brocquière' in *Early Travels in Palestine*, ed. T. Wright (London, Henry G. Bohn, 1848), pp. 371 ff.
23. Tafur, *Travels*, pp. 191–205 *passim*
24. Muntaner, *Chronicles*, Vol. I, p. 208
25. ibid., Vol. I, pp. 107–39 *passim*
26. ibid., Vol. I, pp. 152, 155 ff.
27. ibid., Vol. I., pp. 252 ff.
28. ibid., Vol. II, pp. 378 f.
29. ibid., Vol. II, pp. 393 f.
30. ibid., Vol. II, pp. 296–309 *passim*
31. ibid., Vol. II, pp. 311 f.
32. ibid., Vol. II, pp. 337–43 *passim*
33. ibid., Vol. II, pp. 593–615 *passim*
34. ibid., Vol. II, pp. 515–25, 680 ff.
35. ibid., Vol. II, pp. lxxiv ff.
36. De Commynes, *Memoirs*, Vol. I, p. 137
37. ibid., Vol. I, Book 6, Ch. 3
38. ibid., Vol. I, Book 1 *passim*
39. ibid., Vol. I, pp. 231 ff.
40. ibid., Vol. I, p. 252
41. ibid., Vol. I, p. 253
42. ibid., Vol. I, p. 262
43. *Edward IV's French Expedition 1475*, ed. F.P. Barnard (Oxford, Clarendon Press, 1925), p. 141, no. 69
44. De Commynes, *Memoirs*, Vol. I, pp. 266–86 *passim*
45. E.R. Chamberlain, *The World of the Italian Renaissance* (London, Book Club Associates, 1982), p. 271
46. De Commynes, *Memoirs*, Vol. II, pp. 455, 477 f., 483
47. C. Oman, *A History of the Art of War in the Sixteenth Century* (henceforth *W16C*) (London, Methuen, 1937), p. 109 f.
48. De Commynes, *Memoirs*, Vol. II, pp. 526–35, 539, 542

4. Eastern Europe and Russia

1. J.L.H. Keep, *Soldiers of the Tsar* (Oxford, Clarendon Press, 1985), p. 15
2. G. Vernadsky, *History of Russia*, 5 vols, Vols II–V (New Haven, Yale University Press, 1948–69), Vol. V, Part I, pp. 91, 120, 130 ff., 133–5, 140
3. L.J.D. Collins, 'Military Organization and Tactics of the Crimean Tatars' in *War Technology and Society in the Middle East*, ed. V.J. Parry and M.E. Yapp (Oxford, Oxford University Press, 1986), pp. 257–76
4. Keep, *Soldiers of Tsar*, p. 87
5. Vernadsky, *Russia*, Vol. IV, pp. 176, 223, 233
6. Orbis, *Polish Armed Forces* (Orbis Polish Travel Office, 1944)
7. E. Rosetti, 'Stephen the Great of Moldavia', *Slavonic Review*, 6 (1927–8), 86–103
8. Collins, 'Crimean Tatars'
9. ibid.
10. A. Seaton, *The Horsemen of the Steppes* (London, Bodley Head, 1985), p. 173
11. V. Kalinin, 'Horse-Breeding in the Soviet Union', tr. H. Fox in *Book of the Horse*, ed. B. Vesey-Fitzgerald (London and Brussels, Ivor Nicholson & Watson, 1947), pp. 610 f. for Kabardin, pp. 608 f. for Karabair
12. Hyland, *The Medieval Warhorse*, p. 127
13. R.H.A. Merlen, 'Horses in Old Russia', *Horse World*, 7 (July 1972), 13–15
14. Vernadsky, *Russia*, Vol. II, pp. 105, 110 f., 119, 162 f.
15. C. Porphyrogenitus, *De Administrando Imperio*, ed. Gy. Moravcsik, tr. R.J.H. Jenkins (from Greek text) (Budapest, 1949), pp. 51, no. 4, p. 55, nos. 7 and 8, p. 64, no. 11
16. C.A. Macartney, *The Magyars in the Ninth Century* (Oxford, Oxford University Press, 1968 [1930]), pp. 189–200 *passim*
17. Jankovich, *They Rode into Europe*, p. 94
18. J. Held, 'Military Reform in Early Fifteenth-Century Hungary', *East European Quarterly*, XL, 2 (1977), 129–39
19. Hyland, *The Medieval Warhorse*, p. 50 f.
20. E. Schiele, *The Arab Horse in Europe* (London, Harrap, 1970), p. 179
21. Jankovich, *They Rode into Europe*, pp. 96, 158, notes 19, 21, 17
22. Personal comment, Alojsa Dragas
23. Schiele, *The Arab Horse in Europe*, pp. 139 f.; Jankovich, *They Rode into Europe*, pp. 96 f.
24. Animex, *The Purebred Arab Horse in Poland* (Warsaw, Foreign Trade Office, *c*. 1958)
25. E. Christiansen, *The Northern Crusades* (London, Macmillan, 1960), maps 1 and 6, pp. 9 f., 41
26. ibid., pp. 93 f.; Henry of Livonia, *Chronicle of Henry of Livonia*, tr. J.A. Brundage (Madison, Wi, University of Wisconsin Press, 1961), pp. 32–40 *passim*
27. ibid., under years 1203–6
28. ibid., under years 1207 and 1208
29. ibid., p. 83
30. ibid., under years 1211–18

31. ibid., under years 1220, 1222, 1225; Christiansen, *Northern Crusades*, pp. 97 f., 108

32. ibid., pp. 75, 79; O. Halecki, *Poland* (London, Routledge & Kegan Paul, 1983), pp. 34 f.

33. Christiansen, *Northern Crusades*, pp. 206 f.

34. M. Toeppen, 'Topographisch-statistische Mittheilungen über de Domanen-vorwerke des Deutschen Ordens in Preussen', *Altpreussische Monatsschrift*, 7 (1870), 433 ff.

35. Jankovich, *They Rode into Europe*, pp. 111 f.

36. M. Burleigh, *Prussian Society and the German Order* (Cambridge, Cambridge University Press, 1984), p. 28

37. Henry of Livonia, *Chronicle*, p. 76

38. Christiansen, *Northern Crusades*, p. 136

39. M. Burleigh, *Prussian Society and the German Order*, pp. 39, 41.

40. P.M. Tumler, *Der Deutsche Orden im Werden, Wachsen und Wirken* (Vienna, Panorama, 1955), p. 376

41. M. Perlbach, *Die Statuten der Deutsche Orden* (Halle, 1890), p. 155

42. *Das Grosse Anterbuch des Deutschen Ordens*, ed. W. Ziesemer (Wiesbaden, 1968 [1921]), pp. 87, 89

43. Burleigh, *Prussian Society and the German Order*, p. 77

44. *Das Grosse Anterbuch*, pp. 103 f.

45. Burleigh, *Prussian Society and the German Order*, p. 77

46. Christiansen, *Northern Crusades*, pp. 80, 149 ff.

47. Derby, Earl of (accounts of); *Expeditions to Prussia and the Holy Land*, ed. L. Toulmin-Smith (London, Camden Society, Vol. XXX, 1894), pp. 262 f.

48. Burleigh, *Prussian Society and the German Order*, map/plan p. 45

49. P.G. Thielen, *Die Verwaltung des Ordenstaates Preussen vornehmlich im 13th Jahrhundert* (Cologne and Graz, Bohlau Verlag, 1965), p. 108

50. Burleigh, *Prussian Society and the German Order*, pp. 27, 35 f.

51. Christiansen, *Northern Crusades*, pp. 145 f.

52. ibid., pp. 132 ff.

53. ibid., pp. 161–7 *passim*

54. ibid., pp. 219 f.; Halecki, *Poland*, Chs 7 and 8 *passim*; D. Seward, *The Monks of War* (London, Eyre Methuen, Paladin edn, 1972), p. 121

55. ibid., pp. 131 ff.; Halecki, *Poland*, Ch. 9 *passim*; Burleigh, *Prussian Society and the German Order*, p. 8

56. Hyland, *The Medieval Warhorse*, pp. 131, 136 f.

57. Vernadsky, *Russia*, Vol. III, pp. 163–74 *passim*

58. ibid., pp. 111, 145

59. ibid., pp. 163–88 *passim*

60. ibid., p. 208

61. ibid., pp. 245–9

62. ibid., pp. 228, 201 f.

63. ibid., pp. 252–66

64. Arabshah Ahmed ibn Arabshah, *Tamerlane or Timur the Great*, tr. J.H. Sanders (London, Luzac, 1936), Ch. VIII; H. Lamb, *Tamerlane* (N.Y., Thornton Butterworth, 1929), pp. 103 ff., 111, 119 ff., 126 ff.; Vernadsky, *Russia*, Vol. III, pp. 269–77 *passim*, 332

65. Keep, *Soldiers of the Tsar*, pp. 30–50 *passim*

66. ibid., p. 87

67. G. Fletcher, *In Russia at the Close of the Sixteenth Century. Of the Russe Commonwealth, and the travels of Sir Jerome Horsey, Kt*, ed. Edward A. Bond (London, Hakluyt Society, 1856), pp. x, 14

68. Vernadsky, *Russia*, Vol. III, p. 145

69. A.M. Kurbsky, *History of Ivan IV*, ed. and tr. J.L.I. Fennel (Cambridge, Cambridge University Press, 1965), Ch. 2 *passim*

70. ibid., p. 75

71. ibid., pp. 91 f.

72. ibid., Ch. 4 *passim*, p. 120, n. 1

73. A. Kurbsky, *Correspondence between Prince A.M. Kurbsky and Tsar Ivan IV of Russia*, ed. and tr. J.L.I. Fennell (Cambridge, Cambridge University Press, 1955), pp. 115 ff., 139, 181 ff.

74. F. Carr, *Ivan the Terrible* (Newton Abbot, David & Charles, 1981), pp. 140 f.; Vernadsky, *Russia*, Vol. V, Part 1, pp. 110 ff.

75. H. von Staden, *The Land and Government of Muscovy*, ed. and tr. T. Esper (Stamford, Stamford University Press, 1967), pp. 115, 119

76. Horsey in Fletcher, *Russe Commonwealth*, pp. 182 f.

5. The Tudors

1. Oman, *W16C*, pp. 40 ff., 51 ff., 63 f., 69 ff.

2. Chivers, *Shire Horse*, p. 6.

3. Raphael Holinshed, *Chronicles*, 6 vols (London, 1808), Vol. I, p. 311

4. P. Edwards, *The Horse Trade of Tudor and Stuart England* (Cambridge, Cambridge University Press, 1988), pp. 46 f.

5. J. Bain, *The Border Papers*, 2 vols, Vol. I., 1560–94, Vol. II, 1595–1603 (henceforth Bain, *Border*) (Gen. Register House, Edinburgh, 1894 and 1896), Vol. I, nos. 42, 43, 74, 75

6. ibid., Vol. II, no. 652 and 796

7. ibid., Vol. II, no. 1368

8. ibid., Vol. II, no. 323

9. ibid., Vol. II, no. 433

10. ibid., Vol. II, no. 921

11. Edwards, *Horse Trade*, pp. 21–4

12. Chivers, *Shire Horse*, p. 19

13. State Papers (Domestic) Henry VIII (henceforth SPD, HVIII), Vol. VII, ro. 1674, in Montgomeryshire Collections, Vol. 22 (1888), 17–34 (London); SPD HVIII, 923, Vol. VII, p. 351, no. 1673

14. G. Fleming, *Horseshoes and Horseshoeing* (London, Chapman & Hall, 1869), p. 435

15. Chivers, *Shire Horse*, p. 19

16. Edwards, *Horse Trade*, p. 56

17. Chivers, *Shire Horse*, p. 22

18. J. Ridley, *The Tudor Age* (London, Constable, 1988), p. 303

19. C. Falls, *Elizabeth's Irish Wars* (London, Methuen, 1950), pp. 53, 56 f.

20. J.M. Gilbert, *Hunting and Hunting Preserves in Medieval Scotland* (Edinburgh, John Donald, 1979), pp. 66 f.

21. Holinshed, *Chronicles*, Vol. V, p. 424

22. ibid., Vol. V., p. 468

23. James IV (King of Scotland), *Letters of James IV, 1505–1513*, calendared R.K. Hannay, ed. R.L. Mackie and A. Spilman (Edinburgh, 1953), nos. 68, 124, 163, 219, 231, 233, 234, 235, 248, 398; also 230, 338

24. Holinshed, *Chronicles*, Vol. V, p. 424

25. Bain, *Scot*, Vol. III, no. 1505, Patent 21 E.III.p.2.m.3

26. Bain, *Border*, Vol. I, no. 597, 15 May 1582

27. Hore, *History of Newmarket*, Vol. I, pp. 28–32 *passim*

28. Edwards, draft paper on Henry VIII's stables, p. 8 (used by kind permission of the author)

29. Hore, *History of Newmarket*, pp. 71–5 *passim*

30. *CSPV*, Vol. III, 1520–6, nos. 682, 1255, 1437

31. *Letters and Papers Foreign and Domestic Henry VIII* (henceforth *L & P*) ed. Brewer, J. Gairdner and R.H. Brodie, 21 vols (London, HMSO, 1862–1910), Vol. I, no. 127; J. Thirsk, *Horses in Early Modern England for Service, for Pleasure, for Power*

32. Hore, *History of Newmarket*, pp. 71–5 *passim*

33. C.M. Prior, *The Royal Studs of the Sixteenth and Seventeenth Centuries* (London, Horse & Hound, 1935), p. 5

34. Loch, S., *The Royal Horse of Europe* (London, J.A. Allen, 1986), p. 80

35. ibid., pp. 33 f.

36. P. d'Osma, report quoted in Prior, *Royal Studs*, pp. 10–38

37. ibid.

38. H.C.B. Rogers, *The Mounted Troops of the British Army* (London, Seeley Service, 1959), pp. 33–5

39. Thirsk, *Horses in Early Modern England*, pp. 13 ff.

40. C.G. Cruikshank, *Army Royal* (Oxford, Clarendon Press, 1969), p. 189

41. Thirsk, *Horses in Early Modern England*, pp. 13 ff.

42. Reese, *Master of Horse*, p. 159

43. Bain, *Border*, Vol. II, no. 1053

44. J.J. Scarisbrick, *Henry VIII* (London, Methuen, 1990 [1968]), pp. 453 ff.

45. ibid., p. 33

46. Oman, *W16C*, pp. 291 ff.

47. Cruikshank, *Army Royal*, pp. 28–31 *passim*

48. Thirsk, *Horses in Early Modern England*, p. 8

49. Cruikshank, *Army Royal*, pp. 69–78 *passim*

50. *L & P*, Vol. XIX, pt i, 272, no. 12

51. ibid., Vol. XIX, pt i, 763

52. ibid., Vol. XIX, pt i, 318, 323

53. ibid., Vol. XIX, pt i, 381

54. ibid., Vol. XIX, pt i, 318

55. ibid., Vol. XIX, pt i, 877

56. Edwards, *Horse Trade*, p. 10

57. *L & P*, Vol. XIX, pt i, 792

58. ibid., Vol. XIX, pt i, 832

59. ibid., Vol. XIX, pt ii, 403

60. ibid., Vol. XIX, pt ii, 450

61. Cruikshank, *Army Royal*, p. 71

62. ibid., p. 58

63 Oman, *W16C*, p. 292

64. ibid., pp. 294 ff.; Cruikshank, *Army Royal*, pp. 114 f.

65. Oman, *W16C*, pp. 324 ff.

66. Elis, G., 'The Grufydd Elis Chronicle', tr. M. Bryn Davies, in *Bulletin of the Faculty of Arts* (Cairo, Fouad I University Press), Vols VI–VIII (1942–6), 33–43, Vol. XI, pt i (1949), 37–95, Vol. XII, pt i (1950), 1–90, Vols VI–VIII, 33–43 *passim*

67. Oman, *W16C*, p. 336 ff.

68. *L & P*, Vol. XIX, pt i, 312, 328, 713, 728, 729, 767, 770
69. ibid., Vol. XIX, pt i, 752
70. ibid., Vol. XIX, pt i, 788, 789, 793
71. ibid., Vol. XIX, pt i, 96
72. ibid., Vol. XIX, pt ii, 28
73. ibid., Vol. XIX, pt ii, 401
74. ibid., Vol. XIX, pt ii, 28
75. G.J. Millar, *Tudor Mercenaries and Auxiliaries 1485–1547* (Charlottesville, University Press of Virginia, 1980), p. 182
76. *L & P*, Vol. XIX, pt i, 247
77. ibid., Vol. XIX, pt i, 784, 849
78. ibid., Vol. XIX, pt ii, 259
79. ibid., Vol. XIX, pt ii, 230
80. Elis, 'Chronicle', in Vol. XI, 37–95
81. James IV, *Letters*, no. 427
82. ibid., no. 472
83. ibid., no. 475
84. ibid., no. 498
85. ibid., no. 506
86. ibid., no. 552
87. ibid., no. 560
88. ibid.
89. G.M. Fraser, *Steel Bonnets* (London, Barrie & Jenkins, 1971; rep. London, Collins, Harvill edn, 1986), pp. 213 ff.
90. James IV, *Letters*, no. 566
91. Fraser, *Steel Bonnets*, pp. 213 ff.
92. Bain, *Scot.*, Vol. II, no. 183
93. Fraser, *Steel Bonnets*, p. 85
94. Bain, *Border*, Vol. II, nos. 169, 52, 59
95. Fraser, *Steel Bonnets*, p. 48
96. ibid., p. 5
97. ibid., pp. 213 ff.
98. ibid., p. 222
99. *L & P*, Vol. XVII, no. 862
100. ibid.; Millar, *Tudor Mercenaries*, pp. 59 f.; Fraser, *Steel Bonnets*, pp. 245–54 *passim*; Scarisbrick, *Henry VIII*, pp. 427 ff., 435 f., 439, 442
101. *L & P*, Vol. XIX, pt i, 51
102. ibid., Vol. XIX, pt i, 59, no. 1
103. ibid., Vol. XIX, pt i, 71, 83
104. ibid., Vol. XIX, pt i, 193, 388, 83, 387
105. ibid., Vol. XIX, pt i, 314, 98, 223, 248, 596
106. ibid., Vol. XIX, pt i, 484, 596, 684
107. ibid., Vol. XIX, pt ii, 625
108. ibid., Vol. XIX, pt i, 483, 762, pt ii, 284
109. Fraser, *Steel Bonnets*, p. 260
110. Millar, 'Mercenaries under Henry VIII', *History Today*, 27, 3 (1977), 173–82
111. ibid.; Seymour, *Battles in Britain*, Ch. 14 *passim*; Oman, *W16C*, Book IV, Ch. 6
112. Fraser, *Steel Bonnets*, p. 272

113. C. Corte, *The Art of Riding*, tr. H. Bedingfield (London, H. Denham, 1584), Chs 1–9, 29, 32, 33, 28
114. J. Astley, *The Art of Riding*, tr. H. Bedingfield, in Corte, *Art of Riding*, pp. 74 ff., chap. 2
115. Sir J. Smythe, *Certain Discourses Military*, ed. J.R. Hale (Ithaca, Cornell University Press, 1964 [1590]), pp. xxxl f., 19 f., 64 f., 74 ff., 112 ff.
116. Bain, *Border*, Vol. II, no. 841
117. ibid., Vol. I, nos. 175, 180
118. ibid., Vol. I, nos. 234, 185, 6
119. ibid., Vol. I, nos. 330, 331, 343, 359
120. ibid., Vol. I, no. 41
121. ibid., Vol. I, no. 50
122. ibid., Vol. I, no. 159
123. ibid., Vol. II, nos. 168, 169, 170
124. ibid., Vol. II, no. 957
125. ibid., Vol. II, no. 711
126. ibid., Vol. II, nos. 869, 870
127. ibid., Vol. II, nos. 138, 140, 145, 164, 187, 186
128. ibid., Vol. II, nos. 209, 211, 222, 227, 232
129. ibid., Vol. II, nos. 234, 636
130. ibid., Vol. II, no. 230
131. ibid., Vol. II, nos. 255, 265
132. ibid., Vol. II, nos. 279, 508
133. ibid., Vol. II, no. 485
134. R. Carey, *Memoirs of Robert Carey*, ed. F.H. Mares (Oxford, Clarendon Press, 1972), pp. xii, 7
135. ibid., pp. 45 ff.
136. ibid., p. 57

6. *The Mongols and the Mamlūks*

1. J.B. Glubb, *Soldiers of Fortune* (London, Hodder & Stoughton, 1973), p. 45
2. Vernadsky, *Russia*, Vol. III, pp. 69, 73
3. J. Masson Smith, 'Ayn Jalūt. Mamlūk Success or Mongol Failure?', *Harvard Journal of the Asiatic Society*, 44 (1984), 307–45
4. Glubb, *Soldiers of Fortune*, pp. 62 f.; E.D. Phillips, *The Mongols* (London, Thames & Hudson, 1969), pp. 115 f.
5. Masson Smith, 'Ayn Jalūt', p. 327
6. Glubb, *Soldiers of Fortune*, p. 67
7. ibid., pp. 37 f.
8. H. Rabie, 'The Training of the Mamlūk Fāris' in *War, Technology and Society in the Middle East*, ed. V.J. Parry and M.E. Yapp (Oxford, Oxford University Press, 1986)

9. Masson Smith, 'Ayn Jalūt', p. 312
10. Glubb, *Soldiers of Fortune*, pp. 37, 79
11. A.N. Polliak, 'The Influence of Chingis Khan's Yasa upon the General Organization of the Mamlūk State', *Bulletin of the School of Oriental and African Studies* (henceforth *BSOAS*), 10 (1942), 862–76
12. Glubb, *Soldiers of Fortune*, pp. 135 f., 37, 79, 138 f.
13. D. Ayalon, 'The System of Payment in Mamlūk Military Society', *Journal of Economic and Social History of the Orient* (henceforth *JESHO*) (Leiden), I (1958), 37–65, 257–96
14. Abou Bekr ibn Bedr, *Le Naceri*, tr. M. Perron, 3 vols (Paris, Ministry of Agriculture of France, 1860), Vol. II, *Third Exposition*, Ch. 7, iii, pp. 388 f.
15. Ayalon, 'Payment'
16. Hyland, *Equus*, pp. 78, 179
17. Wentworth, *The Authentic Arabian Horse*, p. 35; letter on Barb from HH El Sherif Sidi Hassan Raissuli of Algeria (no date)
18. Abou Bekr, *Naceri*, Vol. II, Ch. 4, x, p. 378
19. ibid., Vol. II, Ch. 7, iii, pp. 388 f.
20. ibid., Vol. II, p. 164
21. ibid., Vol. I, pp. 68 ff., quoting Maqrizi
22. ibid., Vol. I, sec. IV, Ch. III, ii, p. 112
23. ibid., Vol. I, sec. V, Ch. I, p. 71
24. Ayalon, 'Payment'
25. Abou Bekr, *Naceri*, Vol. I, sec. V, Ch. I, p. 66
26. ibid., p. 71
27. ibid., p. 70; and Ayalon, 'Payment'
28. Abou Bekr, *Naceri*, Vol. I, sec. IV, Ch. I, p. 48
29. Ayalon, 'Payment'
30. Abou Bekr, *Naceri*, Vol. I, sec. V, Ch. I, p. 69
31. ibid., Vol. I, sec. V, Ch. III, ii, p. 114
32. Ayalon, 'Payment'
33. Abou Bekr, *Naceri*, Vol. I, sec. V, p. 66
34. Ayalon, 'Payment'
35. D. Ayalon, 'Furusiyya Exercises and Games in the Mamlūk Sultanate' in *Scripta Hierosolymitana*, Vol. IX (Jerusalem, Magnus Press and the Hebrew University, 1961), pp. 31–62
36. Rabie, 'Training of Mamlūk Fāris', p. 162
37. Ayalon, 'Furusiyya'
38. Umar ibn Ibrahim al-Awsi al Ansari, *A Muslim Manual of War*, ed. and tr. G.T. Scanlon (Cairo, American University Press, 1961), Book VI, Ch. 2, p. 72
39. Ayalon, 'Furusiyya'
40. Rabie, 'Training of Mamlūk Fāris', pp. 154 f.
41. Ibn Hodeil (Aly ben Abderrahman ben Hodeil el Andalusy), *La Parure de cavaliers et l'insigne de preux*, tr. L. Mercier (Paris, Librairie Orientaliste, Paul Geuthner, 1924), pp. 141–57 *passim*
42. Abou Bekr, *Naceri*, Vol. II, p. 145
43. Ibn Hodeil, *Parure*, pp. 141–57
44. Ayalon, 'Furusiyya'; Abou Bekr, *Naceri*, Vol. II, Ch. XVI, iii, pp. 250 f.
45. Ayalon, 'Furusiyya'
46. Rabie, 'Training of Mamlūk Fāris', p. 157
47. Ibn Hodeil, *Parure*, p. 245
48. Rabie, 'Training of Mamlūk Fāris', p. 156
49. Taybugha al Baklamishi al-Yunani, *Saracen Archery*, tr. J.D. Latham and W.F. Paterson (London, Holland Press, 1970), pp. 75 f., iv, v, vi
50. H. Inalcik, *The Ottoman Empire* (London, Weidenfeld & Nicolson, 1973), pp. 31 and 33; Glubb, *Soldiers of Fortune*, p. 280; Ayalon, 'Payment', p. 274
51. Ayalon, *Gunpowder and Firearms in the Mamlūk Kingdom* (London, Vallentine Mitchell, 1950), pp. 57 f.
52. Ibn Hodeil, *Parure*, p. 139
53. Al Ansari, *Muslim Manual of War*, Book 15, Ch. 1, p. 97
54. ibid., Book VIII, Ch. 1, p. 80
55. ibid., Book VIII, Ch. 2, pp. 81 f.
56. ibid., Book IX, Ch. 2, p. 85
57. ibid., Book X, Ch. 2, pp. 87 f.
58. ibid., Book XII, Chs 1–2, pp. 91 f.
59. ibid., Book XVI, Ch. 2, pp. 100 ff.
60. ibid., Book XVII, Ch. 1, pp. 104 ff.; Book XVIII, Ch. 1, pp. 112 f.
61. ibid., Book XVII, Ch. 2, p. 107, and Ch. 3, p. 109
62. ibid., Book XVII, Ch. 3, p. 109

7. *The Ottoman Empire*

1. Oman, *WMA*, Vol. II, pp. 337 f.
2. V.J. Parry *et al.*, *A History of the Ottoman Empire to 1730* (Cambridge, Cambridge University Press, 1976), pp. 15–24 *passim*
3. Arabshah, *Tamerlane*, p. xxv
4. Oman, *WMA*, p. 342
5. Parry, *History of Ottoman Empire*, pp. 103 f., 32 f.
6. Inalcik, *The Ottoman Empire*, pp. 107–15 *passim*
7. De la Broquière, 'Travels', pp. 348 f., 363–7 *passim*
8. Tafur, *Travels*, pp. 125 ff., 133 f.

9. Parry *et al.*, *History of Ottoman Empire*, pp. 24 f.
10. Oman, *WMA*, Vol. II, pp. 349–53 *passim*; H. Savage, 'Enguerrand de Coucy VII and the Campaign of Nicopolis', *Speculum*, XIV, 4 (October 1939); J. Schiltberger, *The Bondage and Travels of Johann Schiltberger*, tr. J. Buchan Telfer, notes P. Brunn (London, Hakluyt Society, 1879), p. 3
11. Arabshah, *Tamerlane*, Preface, p. 3, Ch. V; Lamb, *Tamerlane*, pp. 30–43 *passim*, 114
12. ibid., pp. 188–91, 196; Arabshah, *Tamerlane*, pp. lxviii, lxix
13. ibid., p. lxiii; Lamb, *Tamerlane*, pp. 192 f.
14. Abu l'Mahasin ibn Taghri Birdi, *History of Egypt*, tr. W. Popper (Berkeley and Los Angeles, University of California Press, 1954, in series on Semitic Philology, Vols 14–16, Part I, 1382–1469, Part II, 1399–1411), Part III, pp. 34–49
15. ibid., pp. 197 f., 218
16. Arabshah, *Tamerlane*, p. xviii (Arabshah was in favour of Bayezid and loathed Timur)
17. R.G. de Clavijo, *Narrative of the Embassy of Ruy Gonzalez de Clavijo to the Court of Timour at Samarcand 1403–6*, tr. C.H. Markham (New York, B. Franklin; orig. pub. London, Hakluyt Society, first series, XXVI, 1859), pp. xx, 90, 105 f., 111, 135, 150
18. Taghri Birdi, *History of Egypt*, Vol. XV, pp. 45–54
19. Lamb, *Tamerlane*, pp. 207 ff.; D. Nicolle, *The Mongol Warlords* (Firebird Books, 1990), pp. 182 f.
20. Zeno, in *Persian Travels*, Book I, p. 18
21. Angiolello, in ibid., p. 77
22. Jalal al din Muhammad ben As'ad Davani, 'A Civil and Military Review in Fārs in 881/1476', tr. V. Minorsky, *BSOAS*, 10 (1942), 141–69
23. Parry *et al.*, *History of Ottoman Empire*, p. 4
24. Zeno, in *Persian Travels*, Book I, pp. 27 f.
25. Barbaro, in *Persian Travels*, Book II, pp. 65 ff.
26. Davani, 'Civil and Military Review'
27. ibid.
28. ibid.

8. The Warhorse in India: Military Background

1. *Encyclopaedia of Ancient Civilizations*, ed. A. Cotterell (London, Windward, 1980), p. 180
2. HH Darbar Satyajit Khacha of Jasdon (henceforth Jasdan), personal communication
3. *Encyclopaedia of Ancient Civilizations*, pp. 182–8
4. R. Thapar, *A History of India*, Vol. I (Harmondsworth, Penguin, 1981), pp. 76 ff., 82 f.
5. A. Hyland, 'Alexander's Cavalry', unpublished paper for the Roman Army course, University of Durham (1995)
6. Abou Bekr, *Le Naceri*, Vol. II, p. 164; Jahiz of Basra, 'Exploits of the Turks and the Army of the Khalifate in General', tr. C.T. Harley-Walker, *Journal of the Royal Asiatic Society* (henceforth *JRAS*) (1915), 631–97
7. M. Polo, *The Travels of Marco Polo*, tr. W. Marsden (from the Italian edn by Remusio) (London, Cox & Bayliss, 1818), pp. 456, 632, 674, 693, 725, 728, 735
8. A. Nikitin, 'Travels of A. Nikitin of Tver', in *India in the Fifteenth Century*, ed., tr. and intro. R.H. Major (London, Hakluyt Society, 1857), p. 10
9. E. Rangin, *The Faras Nama*, tr. D.C. Phillot (from Urdu) (London, Bernard Quaritch, 1911), Vol. III
10. Hēmasūri, *Asva Sastra*, tr. V. Vijayaraghavacharya (from Sanskrit) (Tirupati, PN Press, 1928), *passim*
11. Polo, *Travels*, tr. Marsden, p. 632
12. R. Sewell, *A Forgotten Empire* (Vijayanagar) (London, Swan Sonnenschein, 1900), p. 4
13. Thapar, *India*, pp. 266–77 *passim*
14. H.D. Martin, 'The Mongol Army', *JRAS* (April 1943), 46–85
15. Thapar, *India*, p. 280
16. Sewell, *Forgotten Empire*, pp. 5, 7, 30–77 *passim*, 113, 132, 202 ff.
17. B.S. Shastry, *The Portuguese in South India* (Bangalore, Ibn Prakashana Gandhinagar, 1981), pp. 47–56
18. Thapar, *India*, p. 280
19. *Bābur Nāma*, tr. A.S. Beveridge (London, Luzac, 1969 [1922]), pp. 187 ff., 438–75 *passim*
20. S. Digby, *Warhorse and Elephant in the Delhi Sultanate* (Oxford, Oxford University Press, 1971), pp. 21, 26 ff.
21. M. Polo, *Travels of Marco Polo*, tr. T. Waugh (from the Italian edn by M. Bellonci) (London, Book Club Associates edn, 1984), pp. 23, 25, 30, 32, 42, 103, 105, 111

22. Sir H.M. Elliot and J. Dawson, *The History of India as told by its own historians* (London, Trubner, 1871), Vol. III, pp. 168 (Barani), 357 and 309 ('Afif), 578 (Abbas Ahmed)

23. Abou Bekr, *Le Naceri*, Vol. I

24. Elliot and Dawson, *History*, pp. 417, 470 (Abu Talib Husaini)

25. Shastry, *Portuguese in South India*, pp. 49, 93–114 *passim*

26. Sewell, *Forgotten Empire*, pp. 127, 186

27. Ibn Battuta, *The Travels of Ibn Battuta, AD 1325–1354*, tr. H.A.R. Gibb, Vol. I (London, Hakluyt Society [second series, no. CX], 1956; and Cambridge, Cambridge University Press, 1958); Vol. II (1962), pp. 478 f.; Vol. III (1971), pp. 546, 604 f., 595 f.; Vol. IV (1994), pp. 773 ff.

28. Hyland, *Medieval Warhorse*, pp. 42–7 *passim*

29. Ibn Battuta, *Travels*, Vol. IV, p. 879

30. K.D. Swaminathan, 'The Horsetraders of Malai-Mandalam', *Journal of Indian History*, 32–3 (1954–5), 139–43

31. Rangin, *Faras Nama*, p. ix

32. Ibn Battuta, *Travels*, Vol. III, p. 746

33. Digby, *Warhorse and Elephant*, pp. 37 ff.

34. ibid., p. 40

35. Amir Khusrau, *Khaizan-ul-Futuh*, tr. W. Mirza (Lahore, 1975), *passim*

36. ibid., pp. 5, 8, 31

37. ibid., pp. 20–36 *passim*

38. ibid., pp. 39–55 *passim*

39. Digby, *Warhorse and Elephant*, pp. 45 ff.

40. Abul 'Fazl, *Ain-i-Akbari*, tr. H. Blochmann (Calcutta, Madrasah, 1873), Vol. I (i), p. 49

41. Amir Khusrau, *Khaizan*, pp. 77, 88 ff., 60 f.

42. Nikitin, *Travels*, pp. 10–15 *passim*, 26 f.

43. L. Varthema, *Travels of Ludovico Varthema, 1503–1508*, tr. J.W. Jones (London, Hakluyt Society, 1863), pp. 126, 123, 179

44. D. Barbosa, *The Book of Duarte Barbosa*, tr. M.L. Dames, Vol. I (London, Hakluyt Society [second series, no. XLIV], 1918), pp. 178, 64, 232

45. P. Domingo, 'Chronicle' in Sewell, *Forgotten Empire*, p. 237

46. F. Nuniz, 'Chronicle' in Sewell, *Forgotten Empire*, pp. 381, 361

47. T. Pires, *The Suma Oriental of Tome Pires*, tr. A. Coresao (from Portuguese) (London, Hakluyt Society, 1944), Vol. I, pp. 14 ff. and 43

48. Hyland, *Medieval Warhorse*, p. 115

49. Pires, *Suma Oriental*, pp. 21, 44 f., 36, 57

50. ibid., pp. 111–17 *passim*, 167–74 *passim*, 201, 227

9. *Cavalry and the Moghul Empire*

1. *Bābur Nāma*, p. 518

2. E. Bretschneider, *Medieval Researches from Eastern Asiatic Sources*, Vol. I (London, Trubner, 1882), p. 140

3. *Bābur Nāma*, p. 55; Hyland, *Medieval Warhorse*, pp. 19, 126

4. ibid., pp. 108 ff., 114 ff.

5. ibid., pp. 187 f.

6. ibid., pp. 202 ff., 215, 221 ff. (for fuller information on geographical grazing areas)

7. Abul 'Fazl, *Ain-i-Akbari*, Vol. I, Bk (i), no. 49

8. ibid., no. 50

9. ibid., no. 51

10. ibid., Vol. I (ii), no. 2

11. Elliot and Dawson, *History*, p. 32 ('Afif)

12. *Bābur Nāma*, pp. 30 f.

13. H.M. Hayes, *Veterinary Hints for Horseowners* (London, Stanley Paul, 1976 edn), Ch. 15 *passim*

14. Hyland, *Medieval Warhorse*, pp. 40–3

15. Abul 'Fazl, *Ain-i-Akbari*, Vol. I, Bk (i), no. 49

16. Arrian, *The Campaigns of Alexander*, tr. A. de Selincourt (Harmondsworth, Mx, Penguin, 1986 edn), pp. 286–90

17. Raghuraj Sinh Jhala (henceforth Jhala), personal comment

18. Jasdan, personal comment

19. *Cambridge Encyclopaedia of India*, ed. F. Robinson (Cambridge, Cambridge University Press, 1989)

20. Thakur Hanwat Singh of Khandeza (henceforth Khandeza), personal comment

21. Amir Khusrau, *Khaizan*, pp. 45, 85, 36, 41, 71

22. Raja Bhupat Singh (henceforth Bhupat), personal comment

23. Jhala, personal comment

24. Bhupat, personal comment

25. Jhala, personal comment

26. W. Reuter, *The Lipizzaners and the Spanish Riding School* (Frankfurt am Main, Umschau, 1969), p. 3

27. S.A.H.A.A. Iman, personal discussion

28. Jhala, personal comment

29. S. Goyal, *The Invincible Maharana Pratap* (Surajpole, Udaipur, Goyal Brothers, 1983), *passim*; S.A.H.A.A. Iman, *Chetak* (Hazaribagh, Bihar, Indian Heritage, 1984), *passim*
30. HH Mahipendra Singh, Maharana of Danta (henceforth Danta), personal discussion
31. Barbosa, *Book*, pp. 117 ff.
32. S.A.H.A.A. Iman, *The Centaur* (Hazaribagh, Bihar, Indian Heritage, 1987), pp. 139–45 *passim*; Abul 'Fazl, *Ain-i-Akbari*, Vol. I, Bk (i), no. 52 and Pl. XVI
33. ibid., no. 52
34. R. Robinson, *Oriental Armour* (London, Herbert Jenkins, 1967), pp. 116 f.
35. Pires, *Suma Oriental*, p. 34
36. Barbosa, *Book*, pp. 117 ff., 180 f.
37. Paes, 'Chronicle' in Sewell, *Forgotten Empire*, pp. 275–9 *passim*
38. *Bābur Nāma*, pp. 108 ff., 139, 160, 187 ff., and the year AD 1519/AH 925
39. Robinson, *Oriental Armour*, Ch. 15 *passim*
40. Paes in Sewell, *Forgotten Empire*, pp. 275 f.
41. Pires, *Suma Oriental*, p. 33
42. Barbosa, *Book*, pp. 117 ff., 180 f., 232
43. W. Irvine, *The Army of the Indian Moghuls* (London, Luzac, 1903), p. 63
44. I.H. Qureshi, *The Administration of the Sultanate of Delhi*, 4th edn (Karachi, Pakistan Historical Society [pub. no. 10], 1958 [1942]), pp. 69, 80
45. M.A. Makhdoomee, 'Art of War in Medieval India', *Islamic Culture*, II (1937), 460–86
46. Qureshi, *Sultanate of Delhi*, pp. 37 f.
47. ibid., pp. 139 ff., 250 f.
48. Ibn Battuta, *Travels*, Vol. III, p. 605
49. Qureshi, *Sultanate of Delhi*, p. 149; Makhdoomee, 'Art of War'
50. *Bābur Nāma*, pp. 468(t), 563(c), 667 ff.
51. ibid., year 925
52. Makhdoomee, 'Art of War'
53. ibid.
54. S.T. Das, *The Indian Military – Its History and Development* (New Delhi, Sage, 1969), pp. 42 ff.
55. Abul 'Fazl, *Ain-i-Akbari*, Vol. I, p. 315; V. Smith, *Akbar the Great Mogul* (Oxford, Clarendon Press, 1919), pp. 35–41 *passim*
56. Abul 'Fazl, *Ain-i-Akbari*, Vol. I(i), p. 334
57. N. Prawdin, *Builders of the Mogul Empire* (London, Allen & Unwin, 1963), list of dates; Smith, *Akbar*, Chs IV, V, VI and IX *passim*
58. Abul 'Fazl, *Ain-i-Akbari*, Vol. I, p. 246
59. W.H. Moreland, 'Monserrate on Akbar's Army', *Journal of Indian History*, 15 (1936), 50–3
60. Irvine, *Army*, p. 61
61. Abul 'Fazl, *Ain-i-Akbari*, Vol. I, Bk (ii), p. 246
62. ibid., Vol. I(i), pp. 248 f.
63. Irvine, *Army*, p. 4
64. Abul 'Fazl, *Ain-i-Akbari*, Vol. I, p. 242
65. ibid., Vol. I(ii), p. i
66. Irvine, *Army*, pp. 14 f.; Smith, *Akbar*, p. 365
67. ibid., p. 364
68. Abul 'Fazl, *Ain-i-Akbari*, Vol. I (ii), p. 1
69. ibid., Vol. I (i), no. 5
70. ibid., Vol. I (ii), p. 247
71. ibid., Vol. I, Bk. (ii), p. 242
72. ibid., Vol. I, Bk (ii) table pp. 248 f.
73. Irvine, *Army*, p. 22
74. Abul 'Fazl, *Ain-i-Akbari*, Vol. I (i), no. 57
75. ibid., Vol. I (ii), p. 4
76. ibid., Vol. I (i), p. 76
77. ibid., Vol. I (ii), p. 14
78. ibid., Vol. I, Bk (i), no. 60
79. Irvine, *Army*, p. 25
80. Abul 'Fazl, *Ain-i-Akbari*, Vol. I (i), no. 54
81. ibid., Vol. I(ii), p. 5
82. Irvine, *Army*, p. 46
83. Abul 'Fazl, *Ain-i-Akbari*, Vol. I (ii), no. 29
84. Makhdoomee, 'Art of War'
85. Abul 'Fazl, *Ain-i-Akbari*, Vol. I (i), no. 52
86. ibid., Vol. I (ii), no. 2
87. ibid., Vol. I (i), no. 53

10. European Settlement in the Americas

1. Loch, *Royal Horse*, p. 208
2. E.G. Bourne, *Spain in America 1450–1580* (New York and London, Harper, 1904), pp. 34 f.
3. Loch, *Royal Horse*, pp. 21 f., 208, 218
4. R.M. Denhardt, *The Horse of the Americas* (Norman, University of Oklahoma Press, 1947), p. 30
5. Bourne, *Spain in America*, p. 38
6. Denhardt, *Horse of the Americas*, pp. 30 ff.
7. Bourne, *Spain in America*, p. 215
8. Denhardt, *Horse of the Americas*, p. 32
9. T.G. Jordan, *North American Cattle Ranching Frontiers* (Albuquerque, NM, University of New Mexico Press, 1993), p. 137
10. ibid., pp. 23 f.

11. Personal discussion with Peter Madison-Greenwell and demonstration by him
12. Jordan, *Cattle Ranching Frontiers*, pp. 35, 23, 67, 72 f.
13. Bourne, *Spain in America*, p. 206
14. Jordan, *Cattle Ranching Frontiers*, pp. 74 f.
15. F. Braudel, *The Perspective of the World*, tr. S. Reynolds (from French), Vol. III (London, Collins, 1984), p. 388
16. C. Columbus, *The Four Voyages* (Harmondsworth, Penguin, 1969), p. 129
17. ibid., pp. 150–67 *passim*
18. ibid., pp. 187 ff.
19. ibid., p. 249
20. J.M. White, *Cortes* (London, Hamish Hamilton, 1970), p. 36
21. Bourne, *Spain in America*, p. 106
22. A.F. Tschiffely, *Coricancha* (London, Hodder & Stoughton, 1943), pp. 11 ff.
23. Bourne, *Spain in America*, p. 107
24. Tschiffely, *Coricancha*, pp. 14 ff.
25. ibid., pp. 16–22 *passim*
26. Denhardt, *Horse of the Americas*, pp. 151 f.
27. B. Diaz, *Conquest of New Spain* (Harmondsworth, Penguin, 1988 [1963]), pp. 58 f.
28. Bourne, *Spain in America*, pp. 196 f.
29. H. Cortés, *Letters of Cortes*, Vol. I (New York and London, Putnam, 1908), pp. 87–9 *passim*
30. Jordan, *Cattle Ranching Frontiers*, pp. 97 ff.
31. Denhardt, *Horse of the Americas*, p. 41
32. H.B. Barclay, *The Role of the Horse in Man's Culture* (London, J.A. Allen, 1980), pp. 203 f.
33. Denhardt, *Horse of the Americas*, p. 40
34. R.B. Cunninghame-Graham, *Conquest of the River Plate* (London, Heinemann, 1924), Chs 2 and 6 *passim*
35. T. Chard, 'Did the First Spanish Horses Landed in Florida and Carolina Leave Progeny?', *American Anthropologist*, 42 (1940), 90–106
36. Cunninghame-Graham, *River Plate*, Ch. 17 *passim*
37. M.W. Nichols, 'The Spanish Horse of the Pampas', *American Anthropologist*, 41 (1939), 119–29

11. Cortés and the Conquest of Mexico

1. Diaz, *Conquest of New Spain*, pp. 15 f., 27; Denhardt, *Horse of the Americas*, p. 152
2. Quoted in Denhardt, pp. 50 f.
3. Tschiffely, *Coricancha*, pp. 53, 127–34
4. Cortés, *Letters*, Vol. I., p. 204
5. ibid., pp. 150 f.; Diaz, *Conquest of New Spain*, pp. 68, 74–9 *passim*
6. ibid., pp. 80, 91
7. ibid., pp. 117 f., 136
8. H. Thomas, *Conquest of Mexico* (London, Hutchinson, 1943), p. 207
9. Cortés, *Letters*, Vol. I, pp. 188–205; Diaz, *Conquest of New Spain*, pp. 140–55 *passim*
10. ibid., pp. 218–21; Thomas, *Conquest of Mexico*, pp. 181 ff.
11. Cortés, *Letters*, Vol. II, p. 270; Diaz, *Conquest of New Spain*, pp. 280 ff.
12. ibid., p. 284; Cortés, *Letters*, Vol. II, p. 285; Thomas, *Conquest of Mexico*, pp. 377–81 *passim*
13. Diaz, *Conquest of New Spain*, pp. 283–306 *passim*
14. Cortés, *Letters*, Vol. I, p. 319
15. ibid., Vol. II, third letter, *passim*
16. Diaz, *Conquest of New Spain*, p. 254
17. Cortés, *Letters*, Vol. II, third letter, *passim*
18. ibid., Vol. II, fourth letter, *passim*
19. ibid., Vol. II, fifth letter

12. Peru

1. Tschiffely, *Coricancha*, pp. 10–25 *passim*
2. Denhardt, *Horse of the Americas*, p. 152
3. ibid., p. 82; Tschiffely, *Coricancha*, p. 25
4. ibid., pp. 32–58 *passim*
5. Denhardt, *Horse of the Americas*, p. 152
6. Tschiffely, *Coricancha*, pp. 61–72 *passim*
7. ibid., pp. 75–87 *passim*; Denhardt, *Horse of the Americas*, p. 74
8. Tschiffely, *Coricancha*, pp. 88–115 *passim*
9. ibid., pp. 118–25 *passim*
10. R.B. Cunninghame-Graham, *Hernando de Soto* (London, Heinemann, 1912), pp. 43, 47, 36 f.
11. Tschiffely, *Coricancha*, Chs 10–13 *passim*
12. Cunninghame-Graham, *Hernando de Soto*, p. 218
13. R.B. Cunninghame-Graham, *Horses of the Conquest* (London, Heinemann, 1930), pp. 89 ff.
14. Garcilaso de la Vega, quoted in 'Expedition of Goncalo Pizarro' in *Expeditions into the Valley of the Amazons* (London, Hakluyt Society [first series no. XXIV], 1859), pp. 3–20 *passim*
15. G. Silvestre, quoted in Cunninghame-Graham, *Hernando de Soto*, Ch. III, *passim*

13. Chile

1. P. Valdivia, letters to Charles V, quoted in R.B. Cunninghame-Graham, *Pedro de Valdivia* (London, Heinemann, 1926), letters 1–5, pp. 113 ff.; Denhardt, *Horse of the Americas*, pp. 156 f.

14. North America

1. G.P. Winship, 'Coronado's Expedition', *14th Annual Report of the Smithsonian Museum* (1892–6) (Washington, DC, 1896), pp. 364 and 375 f.
2. Castaneda, quoted in Winship, *14th Annual Report*, map and Pl. XXXVIII; A.S. Aiton, 'Coronado's Muster Roll', *American Historical Review*, XLIV (1939), 556–70
3. Winship, 'Coronado's Expedition', pp. 596 ff.
4. Aiton, 'Coronado's Muster Roll'
5. Castaneda, in Winship, *Report*, pp. 479, 481
6. ibid., p. 542; Winship, 'Coronado's Expedition', p. 377; Aiton, 'Coronado's Muster Roll'
7. Winship, 'Coronado's Expedition', pp. 377 ff.
8. Castaneda, in Winship, *Report*, p. 483
9. ibid., pp. 572–9
10. ibid., Ch. 10
11. F.V. Coronado, letter to Mendoza, in Winship, 'Coronado's Expedition', pp. 552–63
12. Castaneda, in Winship, *Report*, pp. 487–97 *passim*
13. *Relacion del Suceso*, in Winship, *Report*, pp. 572–9
14. J.G. Icazbalceta, in ibid., pp. 568 ff.
15. Castaneda, in ibid., pp. 531–8 *passim*
16. Winship, in *Report*, pp. 408 ff.
17. Bourne, *Spain in America*, p. 229

Bibliography

PRIMARY SOURCES

Abou Bekr ibn Bedr, *Le Naceri*, tr. M. Perron, 3 vols, Paris, Ministry of Agriculture of France, 1860

Abul 'Fazl 'Allami, *Ain-i-Akbari*, tr. H. Blochmann, Vol. I, Calcutta, Madrasah, 1873

Aiton, A.S., 'Coronado's Muster Roll' in *American Historical Review*, XLIV (1939), 556–70

Al-Ansari, 'Umar ibn Ibrahim al-Awsi, *A Muslim Manual of War*, ed. and tr. George T. Scanlon, Cairo, American University Press, 1961

Amir Khusrau, *Khaizan-ul-Futuh*, tr. Wahid Mirza, Lahore, 1975

Angiolello, Giovan Maria, quoted in *A Narrative of Italian Travels in Persia in the Fifteenth and Sixteenth Centuries*, Book I, ed. and tr. C. Grey, London, Hakluyt Society, 1873

Animex, *The Purebred Arab Horse in Poland*, Warsaw, Foreign Trade Office, *c.* 1958

Arabshah, Ahmed ibn, *Tamerlane or Timur the Great*, tr. J.H. Sanders, London, Luzac, 1936

Arrian, *The Campaigns of Alexander*, tr. A. de Selincourt, Harmondsworth, Penguin, 1986 edn

Astley, J., *The Art of Riding*, tr. H. Bedingfield, in C. Corte, *The Art of Riding*, London, H. Denham, 1584

Bābur Nāma, tr. A.S. Beveridge, London, Luzac, 1969 (1922)

Bain, J., *Calendar of Documents relating to Scotland, preserved in HM PRO*, pub. Gen. Register House, Edinburgh: Vol. II, 1272–1307, 1884; Vol. III, 1307–57, 1887

—— *The Border Papers*, pub. Gen. Register House, Edinburgh: Vol. I, 1560–94, 1894; Vol. II, 1595–1603, 1896

Barbaro, J., 'Travels to Tana and Persia', quoted in *A Narrative of Italian Travels in Persia in the Fifteenth and Sixteenth Centuries*, Book II, tr. W. Thomas and S.A. Roy, London, Hakluyt Society, 1873

Barbosa, D., *The Book of Duarte Barbosa*, tr. M. Longworth Dames, Vol. I, London, Hakluyt Society (second series, no. XLIV), 1918

Barbour, J., *The Bruce* (*c.* 1375), ed. and tr. A.A.H. Douglas, Glasgow, Wm McClellan, 1964

Bejarano, S., quoted in G.P. Winship, 'Coronado's Expedition', *14th Annual Report of the Smithsonian Museum* (1892–6), Washington, DC, 1896

Blundeville, T., *The Four Chiefest Offices belonging to Horsemanship*, printed R. Yardley, published Short, 1593 edn

Calendar of State Papers Venetian, Vol. III, 1520–6, ed. Rawdon Brown, London, Longman Green, 1869

Cambrensis, Giraldus, *The First Version of the Topography of Ireland*, tr. John H. O'Meara, Dundalk, 1951

Carey, Robert, *Memoirs of Robert Carey*, ed. F.H. Mares, Oxford, Clarendon Press, 1972

Castaneda, quoted in G.P. Winship, *14th Annual Report of the Smithsonian Museum* (1892–6), Washington, DC, 1896

Chandos Herald, *Life of the Black Prince*, ed. M.K. Pope and E.C. Lodge, Oxford, Clarendon Press, 1910

Cherine, P.A., quoted in G.P. Winship, 'Coronado's Expedition', *14th Annual Report of the Smithsonian Museum* (1892–6), Washington, DC, 1896

Clavijo, R.G. de, *Narrative of the Embassy of Ruy Gonzalez de Clavijo to the Court of Timour at Samarcand 1403–6*, tr. C.R. Markham, New York, B. Franklin, orig. pub. Hakluyt Society, first series, no. XXVI, 1859

Columbus, C., *The Four Voyages*, ed. and tr. J.M. Cohen, Harmondsworth, Penguin, 1969

Contarini, A., quoted in *A Narrative of Italian Travels in Persia in the Fifteenth and Sixteenth Centuries*, Book II, tr. W. Thomas and S.A. Roy, London, Hakluyt Society, 1873

Coronado, F.V., quoted in G.P. Winship, 'Coronado's Expedition', *14th Annual Report of the Smithsonian Museum* (1892–6), Washington, DC, 1896

Corte, C., *The Art of Riding*, tr. H. Bedingfield, London, H. Denham, 1584

Cortés, H., *Letters of Cortes*, ed. and tr. F.A. MacNutt, New York and London, Putnam, 1908

D'Allesandri, Vincentio, quoted in *A Narrative of Italian Travels in Persia in the Fifteenth and Sixteenth Centuries*, Book I, ed. and tr. C. Grey, Book II, tr. W. Thomas and S.A. Roy, London, Hakluyt Society, 1873

Das Grosse Anterbuch des Deutschen Ordens, ed. W. Zeisemer, Wiesbaden, 1968 (1921)

Davani, Jalal al din Muhammad ben As'ad, 'A Civil and Military Review in Fārs in 881/1476', tr. V. Minorsky, *Bulletin of the School of Oriental and African Studies*, 10 (1942), 141–69

Da Vinci, L., *Notebooks of Leonardo da Vinci*, ed. I.A. Richter, Oxford, Oxford University Press, 1989 (1952)

De Commynes, P., *Memoirs of Philippe de Commynes*, 2 vols, ed. S. Kinser, tr. I. Caseaux, Columbia, University of South Carolina Press, 1969 and 1973

De la Brocquière, Bertrandon, 'Travels of Bertrandon de la Brocquière' in *Early Travels in Palestine*, ed. T. Wright, London, Henry G. Bohn, 1848

De la Vega, Garcilaso, quoted in 'Expedition of Gonzalo Pizarro' in *Expeditions into the Valley of the Amazons*, ed. and tr. C. Markham, London, Hakluyt Society (first series no. XXIV), 1859

De Monstrelet, Enguerrand, for his chronicle see *Contemporary Chronicles of the Hundred Years War*, ed. and tr. P.E. Thompson, London, Folio Society, 1966

Derby, Earl of, accounts of, quoted in *Expeditions to Prussia and the Holy Land*, ed. L. Toulmin-Smith, London, Camden Society, Vol. XXX, 1894

Díaz, B., *Conquest of New Spain*, tr. J.M. Cohen, Harmondsworth, Penguin, 1988 (1963)

Domingo, P., 'Chronicle' in R. Sewell, *A Forgotten Empire*, London, Swan Sonnenschein, 1900

D'Osma, Prospero, report quoted in C.M. Prior, *The Royal Studs of the Sixteenth and Seventeenth Centuries*, London, Horse & Hound, 1935, pp. 10–38.

Drokensford, *Liber Quotidianus Contrarotulatoris Garderobae*, 28 Edward I, 1299–1300, London, Society of Antiquaries, J. Nichols, 1787

Edward IV's French Expedition 1475, ed. F.P. Barnard, Oxford, Clarendon Press, 1925

Elis, G., 'The Grufydd Elis Chronicle', tr. M. Bryn Davies, in *Bulletin of the Faculty of Arts*, Cairo, Fouad I University Press, Vols VI–VIII, 1942–6, pp. 33–43, Vol. XI, Part 1, 1949, pp. 37–95, Vol. XII, Part 1, 1950, pp. 1–90

Elliot, Sir H.M. and Dawson, J., *The History of India as told by its own historians*, Vol. III, London, Trubner, 1871

Fletcher, G., in *Russia at the Close of the Sixteenth Century. Of the Russe Commonwealth, and the Travels of Sir Jerome Horsey, kt.*, ed. Edward A. Bond, London, Hakluyt Society, 1856

Froissart, J., *Chronicles*, ed. and tr. G. Brereton, Harmondsworth, Penguin, 1983 (1968)

Hall, Edward, *Chronicle*, quoted in Holinshed, London, 1808

Hēmasūri, *Asva Sastra*, 'Science of Horses', tr. V. Vijayaraghavacharya (from Sanskrit), Tirupati, PN Press, 1928

Henry of Livonia, *Chronicle of Henry of Livonia*, tr. J.A. Brundage, Madison, University of Wisconsin Press, 1961

Herberstein, Sigismund von, *Description of Moscow*, London, J.M. Dent, 1969

Holinshed, Raphael, *Chronicles*, 6 vols, London, 1808

Horsey, Sir Jerome, *see* Fletcher

Ibn Battuta, *The Travels of Ibn Battuta 1325–1354*, tr. H.A.A. Gibb, Vol. I, London, Hakluyt Society (2nd series CX), 1956 and Cambridge, Cambridge University Press, 1958; Vol. II, 1962; Vol. III, 1971; Vol. IV, 1994

Ibn Hodeil (Aly ben Abderrahman ben Hodeil el Andalusy), *La Parure des cavaliers et l'insigne des preux*, tr. L. Mercier, Paris, Librairie Orientaliste, Paul Geuthner, 1924

Icazbalceta, J.G., quoted in G.P. Winship, 'Coronado's Expedition', *14th Annual Report of the Smithsonian Museum* (1892–6), Washington, DC, 1896

Jahiz of Basra (Amr. b. Bahr b. Mahbub Abu Othman al Jahiz), 'Exploits of the Turks and the Army of the Khalifate in General', tr. C.T. Harley-Walker, *Journal of the Royal Asiatic Society* (1915), 631–97

James IV (King of Scotland), *Letters of James IV, 1505–1513*, calendared R.K. Hannay, ed. R.L. Mackie and A. Spilman, Edinburgh, 1953

Kalinin, Victor, 'Horse-Breeding in the Soviet Union', tr. H.P. Fox in *Book of the Horse*, ed. B. Vesey-Fitzgerald, London and Brussels, Ivor Nicholson & Watson, 1947

Kurbsky, Prince A.M., *Correspondence between Prince A.M. Kurbsky and Tsar Ivan IV of Russia*, ed. and tr. J.L.I. Fennell, Cambridge, Cambridge University Press, 1955

—— *History of Ivan IV*, ed. and tr. J.L.I. Fennell, Cambridge, Cambridge University Press, 1965

Le Bel, Jean, for his chronicle see *Contemporary Chronicles of the Hundred Years War*, ed. and tr. P.E. Thompson, London, Folio Society, 1966

Leicester, Countess of, expense roll of, quoted in *A Baronial Household of the Thirteenth Century*, ed. M.W. Labarge, London, Eyre & Spottiswoode, 1965

Letters and Papers Foreign and Domestic Henry VIII, ed. Brewer, J. Gairdner and R.H. Brodie, 21 vols, London, HMSO, 1862–1910, Vols I, II, III and XIX Parts I and II (1544)

Lysons, S., 'Copy of a Roll of Expenses of King Edward I at Rhuddlan Castle in the 10th and 11th Years of his Reign', *Archaeologia*, XVI (1812), 32–89

—— 'Copy of Purchases for Tournament at Windsor Park 6 Edward I', *Archaeologia*, XVII (1814), 297–310

Markham, G., *Cavalrice*, 1617

Muntaner, R., *The Chronicles of Muntaner*, 2 vols, tr. Lady Goodenough, London, Hakluyt Society, 1920 and 1921

Narrative of Italian Travels in Persia in the Fifteenth and Sixteenth Centuries, Book I, ed. and tr. C. Grey, Book II, tr. W. Thomas and S.A. Roy, London, Hakluyt Society, 1873

Newcastle, Duke of, *Méthode de Dresser les Chevaux*, 2nd edn, London, printed J. Brindley, 1737

Nikitin, A., 'The Travels of A. Nikitin of Tver', in *India in the Fifteenth Century*, ed., tr. and intro. R.H. Major, London, Hakluyt Society, 1857

Norwell, W., *The Wardrobe Book of Wm. de Norwell*, 12 July 1338–27 May 1340, ed. Mary Lyon, Bruce Lyon and Henry S. Lucas with Jean de Sturler, Brussels, 1983

Nuniz, F., 'Chronicle', quoted in R. Sewell, *A Forgotten Empire*, London, Swan Sonnenschein, 1900

Onote, C., quoted in G.P. Winship, 'Coronado's Expedition', *14th Annual Report of the Smithsonian Museum* (1892–6), Washington, DC, 1896

Paes, D., 'Chronicle' in R. Sewell, *A Forgotten Empire*, London, Swan Sonnenschein, 1900

Perlbach, M., *Die Statuten der Deutsche Ordern*, Halle, 1890

Pires, T., *The Suma Oriental of Tome Pires*, tr. Armando Coresao (from Portuguese), Vol. I, London, Hakluyt Society, 1944

Plantagenet Chronicles, The, ed. E. Hallam, London, Guild Publishing, 1986

Polo, M., *The Travels of Marco Polo*, tr. W. Marsden (from the Italian edn by Remusio), London, Cox & Bayliss, 1818

—— *The Travels of Marco Polo*, tr. T. Waugh (from the Italian edn by M. Bellonci), London, Book Club Associates, 1984

Porphyrogenitus, C., *De Administrando Imperio*, ed. Gy. Moravcsik, tr. R.J.H. Jenkins (from Greek text), Budapest, 1949

Rangin, E., *The Faras Nama*, tr. D.C. Phillot (from Urdu), London, Bernard Quaritch, 1911

Relacion del Suceso, quoted in G.P. Winship, 'Coronado's Expedition', *14th Annual Report of the Smithsonian Museum* (1892–6), Washington, DC, 1896

Rhuddlan Roll, *see* Lysons.

Royal MSS, 12 F.xiii.F.42b (no. 100683, p. 98, bk 113), British Library

Schiltberger, J., *The Bondage and Travels of Johann Schiltberger*, tr. J. Buchan Telfer, notes P. Brunn, London, Hakluyt Society, 1879

Silvestre, G., quoted in R.B. Cunninghame-Graham, *Hernando de Soto*, London, Heinemann, 1912

Smythe, Sir J., *Certain Discourses Military*, ed. J.R. Hale, N.Y., Cornell University Press, 1964 (1590)

Staden, Heinrich von, *The Land and Government of Muscovy*, ed. and tr. T. Esper, Stamford, Stamford University Press, 1967

State Papers (Domestic) Henry VIII, Vol. VII, ro. 1674, in *Montgomeryshire Collections*, Vol. 22, London, 1888, pp. 17–34

Tafur, P., *Travels and Adventures 1435–39*, ed. and tr. M. Letts, London, Routledge, 1926

Tahgri Birdi, Abu l-Mahasin ibn, *History of Egypt*, tr. W. Popper, Berkeley and Los Angeles, University of California Press, 1954, in series on Semitic Philology, Vols 14–16, Part I, 1382–1469, Part II, 1399–1411

Taybugha al Baklamishi al-Yunani, *Saracen Archery*, tr. J.D. Latham and W.F. Paterson, London, Holland Press, 1970

Traslado de las Nuevas, quoted in G.P. Winship, 'Coronado's Expedition', *14th Annual Report of the Smithsonian Museum* (1892–6), Washington, DC, 1896

Usāmah ibn Munqidh, *Memoirs of Usāmah ibn Munqidh*, tr. P.L. Hitti, Cairo, Princeton University at the Cairo Press, 1961

Valdivia, P., letters to Charles V, quoted in R.B. Cunninghame-Graham, *Pedro de Valdivia*, London, Heinemann, 1926

Varthema, Ludovico, *Travels of Ludovico Varthema, 1503–1508*, tr. J.W. Jones, London, Hakluyt Society, 1863

Windsor Tournament Roll, *see* Lysons

Zeno, C., quoted in *A Narrative of Italian Travels in Persia in the Fifteenth and Sixteenth Centuries*, Book I, ed. and tr. C. Grey, London, Hakluyt Society, 1873

SECONDARY SOURCES

Ayalon, David, 'Furusiyya Exercises and Games in the Mamlūk Sultanate' in *Scripta Hierosolymitana*, Vol. IX, Jerusalem, Magnus Press and the Hebrew University, 1961, pp. 31–62

—— *Gunpowder and Firearms in the Mamlūk Kingdom*, London, Vallentine Mitchell, 1950

—— 'The System of Payment in Mamlūk Military Society', *Journal of Economic and Social History of the Orient* (Leiden), I (1958), 37–65, 257–96

Barclay, H.B., *The Role of the Horse in Man's Culture*, London, J.A. Allen, 1980

Barrow, G.W.S., *Robert Bruce and the Community of the Realm of Scotland*, London, Eyre & Spottiswoode, 1965

Bayley, C.C., *War and Society in Renaissance Florence*, Toronto, University of Toronto Press, 1961

Blair, C., *European Armour*, London, Batsford, 1958

Bolton, J.L., *The Medieval English Economy 1150–1500*, London, Dent, 1980

Bourne, E.G., *Spain in America 1450–1580*, New York and London, Harper, 1904

Braudel, F., *The Perspective of the World*, tr. S. Reynolds (from French), London, Collins, 1984

Bretschneider, E., *Medieval Researches from Eastern Asiatic Sources*, Vol. I, London, Trubner, 1882

Burleigh, M., *Prussian Society and the German Order*, Cambridge, Cambridge University Press, 1984

Burrow, T., *see Encyclopedia of Ancient Civilizations*, ed. A. Cotterell, Windward, 1980

Burrows, M., *The Family of Brocas of Beaurepaire and Roche Court*, London, Longman Grant, 1886

Cambridge Encyclopaedia of India, ed. F. Robinson, Cambridge, Cambridge University Press, 1989

Carr, F., *Ivan the Terrible*, Newton Abbot, David & Charles, 1981

Chamberlain, E.R., *The World of the Italian Renaissance*, London, Book Club Associates, 1982

Chaplais, P., 'Some Private Letters of Edward I', *English Historical Review*, 77 (1962), 79–86

Chard, T., 'Did the First Spanish Horses Landed in Florida and Carolina Leave Progeny?', *American Anthropologist*, 42 (1940), 90–106

Childs, W., *Anglo-Castilian Trade in the Later Middle Ages*, Manchester, Manchester University Press, 1978

Chivers, K., *The Shire Horse*, London, J.A. Allen, 1976

Christiansen, E., *The Northern Crusades*, London & Macmillan, 1980

Collins, L.J.D., 'Military Organization and Tactics of the Crimean Tatars' in *War Technology and Society in the Middle East*, eds V.J. Parry and M.E. Yapp, Oxford, Oxford University Press, 1986

Colvin, H., Brown, R. and Taylor, A.J., *The History of the King's Works*, Vol. II, London, HMSO, 1963

Contamine, P., *War in the Middle Ages*, tr. M. Jones, Oxford, Blackwell, 1984

Cruikshank, C.G., *Elizabeth's Army*, Oxford, Clarendon Press, 1966

—— *Army Royal*, Oxford, Clarendon Press, 1969

Cunninghame-Graham, R.B., *Hernando de Soto*, London, Heinemann, 1912

—— *Conquest of the River Plate*, London, Heinemann, 1924

—— *Pedro de Valdivia*, London, Heinemann, 1926

—— *Horses of the Conquest*, London, Heinemann, 1930

Das, S.T., *The Indian Military – Its History and Development*, New Delhi, Saga Publications, 1969

Davis, R.H.C., 'The Medieval Warhorse' in *Horses in European Economic History*, ed. F.M.L. Thompson, Reading, 1983

Denhardt, R.M. *The Horse of the Americas*, Norman, University of Oklahoma Press, 1947

Digby, S., *Warhorse and Elephant in the Delhi Sultanate*, Oxford, Oxford University Press, 1971

Edwards, J.G., 'The Battle of Maes Madog and the Welsh Campaign of 1294–5', *EHR*, 39 (1924), 1–12

Edwards, P., *The Horse Trade of Tudor and Stuart England*, Cambridge, Cambridge University Press, 1988

—— draft paper on Henry VIII's stables, used by kind permission of the author

Encyclopaedia of Ancient Civilizations, ed. A. Cotterell, London, Windward, 1980

Esper, T., 'Military Self Sufficiency in Muscovite Russia', *Slavic Review*, 28 (1969), 186–208

Falls, C., *Elizabeth's Irish Wars*, London, Methuen, 1950

Finberg, H.P.R., *The Formation of England 550–1042*, London, Hart-Davis, McGibbon, 1974

Fleming, G., *Horseshoes and Horseshoeing*, London, Chapman & Hall, 1869

Fraser, G.M., *Steel Bonnets*, London, Barrie & Jenkins, 1971; rep. London, Collins, Harvill edn, 1986

Gaitzsch, W., 'Pferdegeschirr aus Pergamon', *Istmitt*, 37 (1987), 219–56, Plates 60–9

Gilbert, J.M., *Hunting and Hunting Preserves in Medieval Scotland*, Edinburgh, John Donald, 1979

Gilbey, Sir W., *The Great Horse*, London, Vinton, 1899

Glubb, J.B., *Soldiers of Fortune*, London, Hodder & Stoughton, 1973

Goyal, Suresh, *The Invincible Maharana Pratap*, Surajpole, Udaipur, Goyal Brothers, 1983

Gurney, G., *Kingdoms of Europe*, New York, Crown, 1982

Halecki, O., *Poland*, London, Routledge & Kegan Paul, 1983

Harrod, H., 'Some Details of a Murrain of the Fourteenth Century from Court Rolls of a Norfolk Manor', *Archaeologia*, XLI (1867), 1–14

Hayes, H.M., *Veterinary Notes for Horseowners*, London, Stanley Paul, 1976 edn

Held, J., 'Military Reform in Early Fifteenth-Century Hungary', *East European Quarterly*, XI, 2 (1977), 129–39

Hewitt, H.J., *The Horse in Medieval England*, London, J.A. Allen, 1983

—— *The Black Prince's Expedition 1355–57*, Manchester, Manchester University Press, 1958

Hibbert, C., *Agincourt*, London, Pan Books, 1968 edn

Hook, J., *Lorenzo de Medici*, London, Hamish Hamilton, 1984

Hore, J.P., *The History of Newmarket*, Vol. I, London, A.H. Baily, 1886

Hyland, A., *The Medieval Warhorse*, Stroud, Glos, Sutton Publishing, 1994

—— *Equus*, London, Batsford, 1990

—— 'Alexander's Cavalry', for Roman Army course, University of Durham, 1995

Iman, S.A.H.A.A., *The Centaur*, Hazaribagh, Bihar, Indian Heritage, 1987

—— *Chetak*, Hazaribagh, Bihar, Indian Heritage, 1994

Inalcik, H., *The Ottoman Empire*, London, Weidenfeld & Nicolson, 1973

Irvine, W., *The Army of the Indian Moghuls*, London, Luzac, 1903

Jankovich, M., *They Rode into Europe*, tr. A. Dent, London, Harrap, 1971

Jordan, T.G., *North American Cattle Ranching Frontiers*, Albuquerque, University of New Mexico Press, 1993

Keep, J.L.H., *Soldiers of the Tsar*, Oxford, Clarendon Press, 1985

Labarge, M.E., *A Baronial Household of the Thirteenth Century*, London, Eyre & Spottiswoode, 1965

Lamb, H., *Tamerlane*, New York, Thornton Butterworth, 1929

Langlois, *Le Règne de Philippe III Le Hardi*, Paris, 1887

Lloyd, A., *The 100 Years War*, London, Book Club Associates, 1977

Loch, S., *The Royal Horse of Europe*, London, J.A. Allen, 1986

Lydon, James F., 'Irish Levies in the Scottish Wars 1298–1302', *Irish Sword*, 5 (1961–2), 207–17

—— 'The Hobelar', *Irish Sword*, II (1954–6), 12–16

Macarthey, C.A., *The Magyars in the Ninth Century*, Oxford, Oxford University Press, 1968 (1930)

Makhdoomee, M. Akram, 'Art of War in Medieval India', *Islamic Culture* II (1937), 460–86

Mallet, M., *Mercenaries and Their Masters*, London, Bodley Head, 1974

Mallet, M.E. and Hale, J.R., *Military Organization in a Renaissance State: Venice 1400–1617*, Cambridge, Cambridge University Press, 1984

Martin, H.D., 'The Mongol Army', *JRAS* (April 1943), 46–85

Martin, P., *Armour and Weapons*, tr. R. North, London, Herbert Jenkins, 1968

Masson Smith, J., 'Ayn Jalut. Mamlūk Success or Mongol Failure?', *Harvard Journal of the Asiatic Society*, 44 (1984), 307–45

Merlen, R.H.A., 'Horses in Old Russia', *Horse World*, 7 (July 1972), 13–15

Meyrick, S.R., *A Critical Enquiry into Antient Armour*, Vol. I, London, Robert Jennings, 1824

Millar, G.J., 'The Albanian Stradiot', *History Today*, 16 (1976), 468–72

—— 'Mercenaries under Henry VIII', *History Today*, 27, 3 (1977), 173–82

—— *Tudor Mercenaries and Auxiliaries 1485–1547*, Charlottesville, University Press of Virginia, 1980

Moreland, W.H., 'Monserrate on Akbar's Army', *Journal of Indian History*, 15 (1936), 50–3

Morris, J.E., *The Welsh Wars of Edward I*, Oxford, Clarendon Press, 1901

—— 'Mounted Infantry in Medieval Warfare', *Transactions of the Royal Historical Society*, 3rd series, VIII (1914), 77–102

Museum of London Catalogues, no. 7, Medieval, London, HMSO, 1940

Nichols, M.W., 'The Spanish Horse of the Pampas', *American Anthropologist*, 41 (1939), 119–29

Nicholson, R., 'The Last Campaign of Robert Bruce', *EHR*, 77 (1962), 233–46

—— *Edward III and the Scots*, Oxford, Oxford University Press, 1965

Nicolle, D., *The Mongol Warlords*, Firebird Books, 1990

Oakeshott, E., *A Knight and His Horse*, London, Lutterworth Press, 1962

Oman, C., *A History of the Art of War in the Middle Ages*, Vol. I and Vol. II, rev. edn New York, Burt Franklin, 1924

—— *A History of the Art of War in the Sixteenth Century*, London, Methuen, 1937

Orbis, *Polish Armed Forces*, Orbis Polish Travel Office, 1944

Ormrod, W.M., *The Reign of Edward III*, London, Guild Publishing, 1990

Parry, V.J. et al., *A History of the Ottoman Empire to 1730*, Cambridge, Cambridge University Press, 1976

Phillips, E.D., *The Mongols*, London, Thames & Hudson, 1969

Polliak, A.N., 'The Influence of Chingis Khan's Yasa upon the General Organization of the Mameluk State', *Bulletin of the School of Oriental and African Studies*, 10 (1942), 862–76

Powicke, M.R., 'The General Obligation to Cavalry Service under Edward I', *Speculum*, 27 (1953), 814–33

Prawdin, N., *Builders of the Mogul Empire*, London, Allen & Unwin, 1963

Prestwich, M., 'Victualling Estimates for the English Garrisons in Scotland during the Early 14th Century', *EHR*, 82 (1967), 536–43

—— *War, Politics and Finance under Edward I*, London, Faber, 1972

—— *The Three Edwards*, London, Book Club Associates, 1980

—— *Edward I*, pbk edn, London, Methuen, 1990 (1988)

Prior, C.M., *The Royal Studs of the Sixteenth and Seventeenth Centuries*, London, Horse & Hound, 1935

Qureshi, I.H., *The Administration of the Sultanate of Delhi*, 4th edn, Karachi, Pakistan Historical Society (pub. no. 10), 1958 (1942)

Rabie, H., 'The Training of the Mamlūk Fāris', in *War Technology and Society in the Middle East*, eds V.J. Parry and M.E. Yapp, Oxford, Oxford University Press, 1986

Reese, M.M., *The Royal Office of Master of the Horse*, London, Threshold Books, 1976

Renouard, Y., 'L'exportation de chevaux de la Péninsule Ibérique en France et en Angleterre au moyen âge' in *Maluquer de Motes Nicolaus*, ed. Homenaje J.V. Vives, Barcelona, 1965, Vol. I, pp. 571–7

Reuter, W., *The Lipizzaners and the Spanish Riding School*, 2nd edn, Innsbruck, Pinguin and Frankfurt am Main, Umschau, 1969

Richardson, C., *The Fell Pony*, London, J.A. Allen, 1990

Ridley, J., *The Tudor Age*, London, Constable, 1988

Robinson, Russell, *Oriental Armour*, London, Herbert Jenkins, 1967

Rogers, H.C.B., *The Mounted Troops of the British Army*, London, Seeley Service, 1959

Rosetti, E., 'Stephen the Great of Moldavia', *Slavonic Review*, 6 (1927–8), 86–103

Sarkar, J.N., *The Art of War in Medieval India*, Munshiram Mancharlal Ltd, 1984

Savage, H., 'Enguerrand de Coucy VII and the Campaign of Nicopolis', *Speculum*, XIV, 4 (October 1939)

Scarisbrick, J.J., *Henry VIII*, London, Methuen, 1990 (1968)

Scharff, R.F., 'The Irish Horse and its Early History', *Proceedings of the Royal Irish Academy*, 27, B, pp. 81 ff.

Schiele, E., *The Arab Horse in Europe*, London, Harrap, 1970

Seaton, A., *The Horsemen of the Steppes*, London, Bodley Head, 1985

Seward, D., *The Monks of War*, London, Eyre Methuen, Paladin edn, 1972

Sewell, R., *A Forgotten Empire*, London, Swan Sonnenschein, 1900

Seymour, W., *Battles in Britain*, London, Sidgwick & Jackson, 1979 edn

Shastry, B.S., *The Portuguese in South India*, Bangalore, Ibn Prakashana Gandhinagar, 1981

Smith, V., *Akbar the Great Mogul*, Oxford, Clarendon Press, 1919

Sparkes, I.G., *Discovering Old Horseshoes*, Discovering Series no. 19, Princes Risborough, Shire Publications, 1983 (1976)

Swaminathan, K.D., 'The Horsetraders of Malai-Mandalam, *Journal of Indian History*, 32–3 (1954–5), 139–43

Thapar, R., *A History of India*, Vol. I, Harmondsworth, Penguin, 1981

Thielen, P.G., *Die Verwaltung des Ordenstaates Preussen vornehmlich im 13th Jahrhundert*, Cologne and Graz, Bohlau Verlag, 1965

Thirsk, J., *Horses in Early Modern England for Service, for Pleasure, for Power*, Reading, University of Reading, 1977

Thomas, H., *Conquest of Mexico*, London, Hutchinson, 1993

Toeppen, M., 'Topographisch-statistische Mittheilungen über de Domanen-vorwerke des Deutschen Ordens in Preussen', *Altpreussische Monatsschrift* (1870), 433 ff.

Tschiffely, A.F., *Coricancha*, London, Hodder & Stoughton, 1943

Tumler, P.M., *Der Deutsche Orden im Werden, Wachsen und Wirken*, Vienna, Panorama, 1955

Vernadsky, G., *History of Russia*, 5 vols, New Haven, Yale University Press: Vol. II, *Kievan Russia*, 1948; Vol. III, *The Mongols and Russia*, 1953; Vol. IV, *Russia at the Dawn of the Modern Age*, 1959; Vol. V, Part 1, *Tsardom of Moscow* 1547–1682, 1969

Walford, C., *Fairs Past and Present*, London, Elliot Stock, 1883

Wentworth, Lady, *The Authentic Arabian Horse*, London, Allen & Unwin, 1945

—— *Thoroughbred Racing Stock*, London, Allen & Unwin, 1938

White, J.M., *Cortes*, London, Hamish Hamilton, 1970

Wilberforce-Bell, H., *The History of Kathiawad*, New Delhi, Ajay Book Service, no date

Winship, G.P., 'Coronado's Expedition', *14th Annual Report of the Smithsonian Museum* (1892–6), Washington, DC, 1896

Index of Horse-Related Subjects

General Index